Improving Information Security Practices through Computational Intelligence

Wasan Shaker Awad
Ahlia University, Bahrain

El Sayed M. El-Alfy
King Fahd University of Petroleum and Minerals, Saudi Arabia

Yousif Al-Bastaki
University of Bahrain, Bahrain

A volume in the Advances in Information Security,
Privacy, and Ethics (AISPE) Book Series

Information Science
REFERENCE
An Imprint of IGI Global

Managing Director:	Lindsay Johnston
Managing Editor:	Keith Greenberg
Director of Intellectual Property & Contracts:	Jan Travers
Acquisitions Editor:	Kayla Wolfe
Production Editor:	Christina Henning
Development Editor:	Austin DeMarco
Cover Design:	Jason Mull

Published in the United States of America by
Information Science Reference (an imprint of IGI Global)
701 E. Chocolate Avenue
Hershey PA, USA 17033
Tel: 717-533-8845
Fax: 717-533-8661
E-mail: cust@igi-global.com
Web site: http://www.igi-global.com

Library of Congress Cataloging-in-Publication Data

Improving information security practices through computational intelligence / Wasan Shaker Awad, El Sayed M. El-Alfy, and Yousif Al-Bastaki, editors.
    pages cm
 Includes bibliographical references and index.
 ISBN 978-1-4666-9426-2 (hardcover) -- ISBN 978-1-4666-9427-9 (ebook) 1. Computational intelligence. 2. Computer security. 3. Data protection. I. Awad, Wasan Shaker, 1969- editor. II. El-Alfy, El Sayed M., 1968- editor. III. Al-Bastaki, Yousif A. Latif, editor.
 Q342.I46 2015
 005.8--dc23
                              2015028208

This book is published in the IGI Global book series Advances in Information Security, Privacy, and Ethics (AISPE) (ISSN: 1948-9730; eISSN: 1948-9749)

British Cataloguing in Publication Data
A Cataloguing in Publication record for this book is available from the British Library.

For electronic access to this publication, please contact: eresources@igi-global.com.

Advances in Information Security, Privacy, and Ethics (AISPE) Book Series

ISSN: 1948-9730
EISSN: 1948-9749

MISSION

As digital technologies become more pervasive in everyday life and the Internet is utilized in ever increasing ways by both private and public entities, concern over digital threats becomes more prevalent.

The **Advances in Information Security, Privacy, & Ethics (AISPE) Book Series** provides cutting-edge research on the protection and misuse of information and technology across various industries and settings. Comprised of scholarly research on topics such as identity management, cryptography, system security, authentication, and data protection, this book series is ideal for reference by IT professionals, academicians, and upper-level students.

COVERAGE

- Privacy Issues of Social Networking
- Information Security Standards
- Global Privacy Concerns
- Device Fingerprinting
- Tracking Cookies
- Electronic Mail Security
- Privacy-Enhancing Technologies
- Risk Management
- Cyberethics
- CIA Triad of Information Security

IGI Global is currently accepting manuscripts for publication within this series. To submit a proposal for a volume in this series, please contact our Acquisition Editors at Acquisitions@igi-global.com or visit: http://www.igi-global.com/publish/.

Titles in this Series

For a list of additional titles in this series, please visit: www.igi-global.com

Handbook of Research on Security Considerations in Cloud Computing
Kashif Munir (King Fahd University of Petroleum & Minerals, Saudi Arabia) Mubarak S. Al-Mutairi (King Fahd University of Petroleum & Minerals, Saudi Arabia) and Lawan A. Mohammed (King Fahd University of Petroleum & Minerals, Saudi Arabia)
Information Science Reference • copyright 2015 • 409pp • H/C (ISBN: 9781466683877) • US $325.00 (our price)

Emerging Security Solutions Using Public and Private Key Cryptography Mathematical Concepts
Addepalli VN Krishna (Stanley College of Engineering and Technology for Women, India)
Information Science Reference • copyright 2015 • 302pp • H/C (ISBN: 9781466684843) • US $225.00 (our price)

Handbook of Research on Emerging Developments in Data Privacy
Manish Gupta (State University of New York at Buffalo, USA)
Information Science Reference • copyright 2015 • 507pp • H/C (ISBN: 9781466673816) • US $325.00 (our price)

Handbook of Research on Securing Cloud-Based Databases with Biometric Applications
Ganesh Chandra Deka (Ministry of Labour and Employment, India) and Sambit Bakshi (National Institute of Technology Rourkela, India)
Information Science Reference • copyright 2015 • 434pp • H/C (ISBN: 9781466665590) • US $335.00 (our price)

Handbook of Research on Threat Detection and Countermeasures in Network Security
Alaa Hussein Al-Hamami (Amman Arab University, Jordan) and Ghossoon M. Waleed al-Saadoon (Applied Sciences University, Bahrain)
Information Science Reference • copyright 2015 • 450pp • H/C (ISBN: 9781466665835) • US $325.00 (our price)

Information Security in Diverse Computing Environments
Anne Kayem (Department of Computer Science, University of Cape Town, South Africa) and Christoph Meinel (Hasso-Plattner-Institute for IT Systems Engineering, University of Potsdam, Potsdam, Germany)
Information Science Reference • copyright 2014 • 354pp • H/C (ISBN: 9781466661585) • US $245.00 (our price)

Network Topology in Command and Control Organization, Operation, and Evolution
T. J. Grant (R-BAR, The Netherlands) R. H. P. Janssen (Netherlands Defence Academy, The Netherlands) and H. Monsuur (Netherlands Defence Academy, The Netherlands)
Information Science Reference • copyright 2014 • 320pp • H/C (ISBN: 9781466660588) • US $215.00 (our price)

DISSEMINATOR OF KNOWLEDGE

www.igi-global.com

701 E. Chocolate Ave., Hershey, PA 17033
Order online at www.igi-global.com or call 717-533-8845 x100
To place a standing order for titles released in this series, contact: cust@igi-global.com
Mon-Fri 8:00 am - 5:00 pm (est) or fax 24 hours a day 717-533-8661

Editorial Advisory Board

Table of Contents

Section 1
Introduction

Section 2
Applications of Evolutionary Computation in Cryptology

Section 3
Intelligent Intrusion Detection

Detailed Table of Contents

Section 1
Introduction

This section provides an overview of existing computational intelligence paradigms, and reviews the literature and potential applications in cryptology.

Chapter 1

    El-Sayed M. El-Alfy, King Fahd University of Petroleum and Minerals, Saudi Arabia
    Wasan Shaker Awad, Ahlia University, Bahrain

The evolution of communication networks and information systems, to support wireless access, cloud and grid computing, and big data, provides great business opportunities. However, it also generates a new trend of sophisticated network threats and offers several challenges in securing information and systems confidentiality, integrity and availability. The traditional techniques used by security experts are mostly static and lack the much needed characteristics of adaptation and self-organization, computational efficiency and error resilience to deal with evolving attacks. The inherent characteristics of computational intelligence (CI) paradigms provide a promising alternative that has gained popularity resulting in significant applications in information security. There is a plethora of CI paradigms commonly used in this domain including artificial neural networks, evolutionary computing, fuzzy systems, and swarm intelligence. This chapter provides an overview of the widely-recognized CI paradigms and shades the light on some of their potential applications in information security.

Chapter 2

    Wasan Shaker Awad, Ahlia University, Bahrain
    El-Sayed M. El-Alfy, King Fahd University of Petroleum and Minerals, Saudi Arabia

Computational intelligence (CI) has attracted the attention of many researchers for its effectiveness in solving different kinds of problems. It has been applied to solve problems in a wide area of applications. The aim of this chapter is to present an overview of existing literature about the applications of CI in cryptology. It demonstrates and studies the applicability of CI in cryptology. The problems examined in this chapter are the automated design of cipher systems, and the automated cryptanalysis of cipher systems. It has been shown that CI methods, such as genetic algorithms, genetic programming, Tabu search, and memetic computing are effective tools to solve most of cryptology problems.

Section 2
Applications of Evolutionary Computation in Cryptology

This section presents two applications of evolutionary computation in cryptology, namely design of stream ciphers and chaotic-based cryptosystems for securing images.

The main objective of this chapter is to propose a new effective algorithm to design stream cipher systems automatically using simulated annealing algorithm and genetic programming with a different method for representing the genetic programming population individuals. Usually the individual programs represented as LISP expressions; in the proposed method the programs are represented as strings of integers representing the individual program syntactic rule numbers. Genetic programming with this representation method is called genetic algorithm for developing software (GADS). The performance of the proposed algorithm will be studied by applying different genetic methods and parameters. Furthermore, it will be compared with other representation methods such as LISP expression.

Protecting confidentiality of sensitive data is growing in importance in many personal, commercial, governmental, medical and military applications. Data encryption remains the most prevalent mechanism for this goal in cybersecurity to store and communicate data in unintelligible form. However, images are known to have intrinsic characteristics different from text, which limit the applicability of conventional cryptographic algorithms. This chapter provides a review of the work related to image cryptosystems based on chaos theory and biologically-inspired algorithms. Then, a case study is presented using ideas from genetic crossover and mutation to confuse and diffuse images to generate secure cipher images with very low correlation between pixels.

Section 3
Intelligent Intrusion Detection

This section illustrates the approaches utilized to build optimal, adaptive and comprehensive intrusion detection systems.

Chapter 5

Mradul Dhakar, ITM University Gwalior, M.P., India
Akhilesh Tiwari, Madhav Institute of Technology and Science, Gwalior, India

The tremendous work in the field of security has made enormous efforts towards the ascertainment of innovative ideas along with their practical applicability. These motivated the security agencies to adopt them practically. But adequate remedies are not accomplished yet due to the enhanced technological aspects even in the unlawful communities. These communities have become a major concern for the security agencies and can be considered as unaddressed issue. This concern led to the introduction of Intrusion Detection Systems (IDSs). The IDS is a means for detecting the intrusive events concealed among the activities of normal users. Additionally, such systems also provide necessary assistance in preventing future intrusions. The present chapter focuses on improving the performance of the IDS in order to meet the contemporary progression by proposing a system that is able to achieve a system that is effective, adaptive and intelligent in nature and is able to remarkably detect intrusions. In order to accomplish the desired system, the chapter involves development of intelligent IDS.

Chapter 6

Leila Mechtri, Badji Mokhtar University, Algeria
Fatiha Djemili Tolba, Badji Mokhtar University, Algeria
Salim Ghanemi, Badji Mokhtar University, Algeria

Mobile Ad-hoc NETworks (MANETs) are believed to be highly vulnerable to security threats due to the numerous constraints they present such as: the absence of a fixed infrastructure, the dynamic topology change, their dependence on cooperative communication, the unreliability of wireless links and most importantly the absence of a clear line of defense. Since intrusion detection and agent technology proved to offer several potential advantages, there has been a great tendency for using agents to build optimal, adaptive and comprehensive intrusion detection systems to fit MANET security requirements. This chapter presents a survey and analysis of the work that has been recently done for the deployment of agent technology in the area of MANET intrusion detection. In particular, recent advances in that field in terms of existing frameworks, architectures and implementations as well as a discussion of the obtained advantages in addition to the potentially introduced vulnerabilities are presented.

Section 4
Authentication

This section discusses entity and message authentication utilizing cryptography. It covers digital signature certificates and biometric authentication.

Chapter 7

    Mohammad Tariq Banday, University of Kashmir, India

Information security has been the focus of research since decades; however, with the advent of Internet and its vast growth, online information security research has become recurrent. Novel methods, techniques, protocols, and procedures are continuously developed to secure information from growing threats. Digital signature certificates, currently offers one of the most trusted solutions to achieve CIA-trio for online information. This chapter discusses online information security through cryptography. It explains digital signature certificates; their benefits, the underlying standards, involved techniques, procedures, algorithms, processes, structure, management, formats, and illustration of their working. It highlights the potential of digital signatures and certificates in information security across different devices, services, and applications. It introduces a few useful tools to learn, train, and implement digital signature certificates.

Chapter 8

    Martin Drahanský, Brno University of Technology, Czech Republic
    Petr Hanáček, Brno University of Technology, Czech Republic
    František Zbořil, Brno University of Technology, Czech Republic
    Martin Henzl, Brno University of Technology, Czech Republic
    František V. Zbořil, Brno University of Technology, Czech Republic
    Jaegeol Yim, Dongguk University at Gyeongju Gyeongbuk, South Korea
    Kyubark Shim, Dongguk University at Gyeongju Gyeongbuk, South Korea

This chapter shows how cryptomodules can increase security of wireless sensor network and possibilities of biometric authentication against a node or the whole network. For secure operation of a wireless sensor network, security objectives such as confidentiality, integrity, and authentication must be implemented. These security objectives typically employ cryptography, therefore sensor nodes should be able to compute cryptographic algorithms and provide secure tamper-resistant storage for cryptographic keys. Use of dedicated secure hardware for this purpose and security threats are discussed. Two scenarios where the biometric authentication would be appreciated are introduced – smart home and storehouse with medicaments. Biometric generation of cryptographic keys, biometric authentication in wireless network and possible attacks on biometrics are presented. When designing and verifying communication protocols using informal techniques, some security errors may remain undetected. Formal verification methods that provide a systematic way of finding protocol flaws are discussed.

Section 5
Multimedia Security

This section deals with methods for improving information security of multimedia and implementation on graphical processing unit.

Chapter 9

    V. Santhi, VIT University, India
    D. P. Acharjya, VIT University, India

In recent days, due to the advancement in technology there are increasing numbers of threats to multimedia data which are floating around in the Internet especially in the form of image data. Many methods exist to provide security for digital images but transform domain based digital watermarking could be considered as a promising method. Many transformation techniques are used to insert watermark in cover data, but this chapter deals with watermarking approaches in Hadamard transform domain. In traditional watermarking approaches the scaling parameter is empirically considered for inserting watermark but to maintain the quality of underlying cover images it needs to be calculated based on the content of the cover images. In order to make the watermarking algorithm completely automated the embedding and scaling parameters are calculated using the content of cover images. Many methods are existing for calculating scaling parameter adaptively but this chapter discusses various approaches using computational intelligence to arrive at optimum value of scaling and embedding parameters.

Chapter 10

    Sedat Akleylek, Ondokuz Mayis University, Turkey
    Zaliha Yuce Tok, Middle East Technical University, Turkey

In this chapter, the aim is to discuss computational aspects of lattice-based cryptographic schemes focused on NTRU in view of the time complexity on a graphical processing unit (GPU). Polynomial multiplication algorithms, having a very important role in lattice-based cryptographic schemes, are implemented on the GPU using the compute unified device architecture (CUDA) platform. They are implemented in both serial and parallel way. Compact and efficient implementation architectures of polynomial multiplication for lattice-based cryptographic schemes are presented for the quotient ring both $Z_p[x]/(x^n-1)$ and $Z_p[x]/(x^n+1)$, where p is a prime number. Then, by using these implementations the NTRUEncrypt and signature scheme working over $Z_p[x]/(x^n+1)$ are implemented on the GPU using CUDA platform. Implementation details are also discussed.

Preface

The explosive growth in computer systems and their interconnections via networks has increased the dependence of organizations on the information stored and communicated using these systems. With the increasing degree of sophistication and evolution of threats, it becomes crucial to propose and explore novel methodologies to protect data and systems confidentiality, integrity and availability. Several innovative ideas have been proposed including computational intelligence (CI) paradigms due to their very attractive inherent characteristics including adaptation, self-organization, parallelizability, computational efficiency, fault tolerance and error resilience. These paradigms are widely recognized as a significant source of competitive advantage by many authors.

Information security is the process of protecting information from unauthorized access, use, disclosure, destruction, modification, or disruption. It is the protection of information and its elements, including the systems and hardware that use, store, and transmit that information.

To protect stored, processed, and transmitted information, there are different mechanisms. Security mechanisms are the means for implementing security services. They can be divided into three broad categories: Prevention, Detection, and Recovery.

One of these mechanism is encryption. Any cryptographic system (cryptosystem, or cipher system) has five elements: plaintext (clear text), ciphertext (encrypted text), encryption algorithm which is a procedure used to encipher (encrypt) the plaintext and transform it to ciphertext. Decryption algorithm which is the inverse of the encryption algorithm, and the key which is a parameter used to prevent the plaintext from being easily revealed by an authorized person. A number of cryptosystems for encrypting the private information have been proposed which are of different levels of security; these cryptosystems can be classified into modern and classical systems. The basic building blocks of all cryptosystems are substitution and transposition.

Cryptology is the study of encryption techniques for protecting information, and also the techniques used to attack encryption techniques. Thus it is combination of two areas: cryptanalysis and cryptography.

We have other security mechanisms, such as entity authentication, digital signature, and information hiding. Steganography is an art and science of hiding information within other information. Entity authentication is a technique designed to let one party prove the identity of another party. By using the digital signature, the sender uses a signing algorithm to sign the message, then the message and the signature are sent to the receiver. The receiver receives the message and the signature and applies the verifying algorithm to the combination. If the result is true, the message is accepted; otherwise, it is rejected.

On the other hand, there are a number of CI techniques can be used in information security. Genetic algorithm (GA) is a search algorithm based on the mechanics of natural selection and natural genetic. GA attempts to identify optimal solution by applying the techniques of natural selection to a population of solutions, the solutions are evaluated, the bad solutions are killed, and the remaining solution are recombined (mate) to form a new generation of solution.

Genetic programming (GP) is an application of GA, in which the structure under adaption is a set of computer programs. It is capable of evolving computer program that solve, or approximately solve, a variety of problem. Thus, GP individual is designed to store computer programs in such a way that they can be optimized using an evolutionary approach.

Cryptology problems, such as designing good cryptographic systems and analyzing them, attract many researchers, and hence we can find in the literatures different techniques and methods that have been proposed to solve these problems. In recent years, many algorithms that take advantage of approaches based on computational intelligence techniques (such as genetic algorithms, genetic programming, etc.) have been proposed.

In this proposed edited book, the most important achievements in solving security problems using CI techniques such as GA and GP are presented. The main objective is to show the applicability of these techniques in solving these problems, in addition to give interested researchers an overview of the new methodologies and new directions in information security.

The proposed book is to create an integrated and coherent book of the applications of CI and other advanced techniques in information security which will add value to the current research, and which will contribute to a better understanding of the factors that influence successful security systems design in security industry.

Moreover, it will encourage the security industry to take a proactive attitude toward CI techniques; thus resulting in a better design of security systems. Hence, publishing this book will be of interest to researchers, academics, students and practitioners of information security.

Very few studies have been conducted into the applications of CI techniques in information security. The proposed book will therefore contribute and add to the current research in information technology; furthermore, this book will instigate several opportunities for future research.

The book will have implications for information security in general, and specifically for practitioners. Firstly, this study will expand on the current understanding of CI techniques by exploring and investigating various factors and how they relate to the success of security systems design. A number of methods will be applied, in order to overcome the elements that are missing in the current research, and particular focus will be placed on testing the effectiveness of CI techniques.

There is little research that examines the effectiveness of CI on security industry; this book will therefore examine its impact, furthermore, it will determine the most effective way of designing and attacking security systems.

The prospective audience for this book will be researchers, academics and practitioners from the following fields of research: computational intelligence, information security, security engineering.

This book will increase information security awareness in organizations by providing a clear direction for the effective implementation of information security and CI, which could improve organizational learning and performance excellence. The book covers the most important concepts and key issues which relate CI to information security, and also cover emerging practices in information security. This book also aims to increase CI awareness in information security by providing a clear direction for the effective implementation of CI techniques which would improve information security industry. In this sense, the intended audience will include all researchers who are trying to find effective methods for designing and attacking security systems.

On the other hand, computational intelligence (CI) and information security has become an agenda issue in various academic and professional journals. It has become recognized as a significant source of competitive advantage by many authors.

Although the applications of CI (and other advanced techniques) in information security has been widely discussed by many academicians and practitioners, there is no specific book to discuss and provide information on how we can apply the CI techniques to solve the problems of information security.

The book is organized into ten chapters. A brief description of each of the chapters follows:

Chapter 1 provides a detailed introduction to major CI paradigms. It includes a discussion of Neural Networks (NN) which is an important area of CI mainly inspired by the biological system of neurons in human brain, and Evolutionary Computation (EC) which is inspired by the evolution of biological objects. Furthermore, it presents Swarm Intelligence (SI), Fuzzy Systems (FS), and Hybrid Systems (HS). It also shades the light on some of potential applications in information security and cryptography.

Chapter 2 demonstrates how CI has attracted the attention of many researchers for its effectiveness in solving different kinds of problems in cryptology. The chapter aims at demonstrating the applicability of CI in cryptology and presenting an overview of existing applications of CI in cryptology. The problems examined in this chapter are the automated design of cipher systems, and the automated cryptanalysis of cipher systems. It has been shown that CI methods, such as genetic algorithm and genetic programming, can be effective tools to solve many cryptology problems.

Chapter 3 proposes a new effective algorithm to deign stream cipher systems automatically using simulated annealing and genetic programming with a different representation method for the population individuals. In the proposed method, the candidate programs (population individuals) are represented as strings of integers representing the individual program syntactic rule numbers. Genetic programming with this representation method is called genetic algorithm for developing software (GADS). The performance of the proposed algorithm is evaluated by applying different genetic methods and parameters. Finally, the proposed method is compared with other representation methods such as LISP expressions.

Chapter 4 shows how important it is to protect sensitive data in many personal, commercial, governmental, medical and military applications. The chapter provides an approach for data encryption in cyber security by storing and communicating data in unintelligible form. It provides a review of the work related to image cryptosystems based on chaos theory and biologically-inspired algorithms. Then, a case study is presented using ideas from genetic crossover and mutation to confuse and diffuse images to generate secure cipher images with very low correlation between pixels.

Chapter 5 illustrates the work in the field of security and its impact on ascertainment of innovative ideas along with their practical applicability. It explains that adequate remedies are not accomplished yet due to the enhanced technological aspects even in the unlawful communities and how they become a major concern for the security agencies and can be considered as unaddressed issue. The chapter provides an introduction to Intrusion Detection Systems (IDSs) and explains how IDS is a means for detecting the intrusive events concealed among the activities of normal users. Additionally, such systems also provide necessary assistance in preventing future intrusions. The present chapter focuses on improving the performance of the IDS in order to meet the contemporary progression by proposing a system which is effective, adaptive and intelligent in nature and is able to remarkably detect intrusions. In order to accomplish the desired system, the chapter involves development of intelligent IDS.

Chapter 6 starts by explaining how Mobile Ad-hoc NETworks (MANETs) are believed to be highly vulnerable to security threats due to the numerous constraints they present such as: the absence of a fixed infrastructure, the dynamic topology change, their dependence on cooperative communication, the unreliability of wireless links, and most importantly the absence of a clear line of defense. The chapter illustrates the approaches to utilize agent technology to build optimal, adaptive and comprehensive intrusion detection systems to fit MANET security requirements. It presents a survey and analyzes the work that has been recently done for the deployment of agent technology in the area of MANET intrusion detection. In particular, recent advances in that field in terms of existing frameworks, architectures and implementations as well as a discussion of the obtained advantages in addition to the potentially introduced vulnerabilities are presented.

Chapter 7 aims to describe the applications of Digital Signature Certificates for Online Information Security. The chapter discusses online information security through cryptography. It explains and illustrates digital signature certificates; their benefits, underlying standards, involved techniques, procedures, algorithms, processes, structure, management, and formats. It highlights the potential of digital signatures and certificates in information security across different devices, services, and applications. It introduces a few useful tools to learn, train, and implement digital signature certificates. Further, it illustrates systematic procedures for securing documents and e-mail messages through digital signature certificates.

Chapter 8 shows how cryptomodules can increase security of wireless sensor network and possibilities of biometric authentication against a node or the whole network. It describes an approach for secure operation of wireless sensor networks with implemented security objectives such as confidentiality, integrity, and authentication. Then the chapter illustrates these security objectives typically employ cryptography, therefore sensor nodes should be able to compute cryptographic algorithms and provide secure tamper-resistant storage for cryptographic keys. Use of dedicated secure hardware for this purpose and security threats are discussed. Two scenarios where the biometric authentication would be appreciated are introduced – smart home and storehouse with medicaments. Biometric generation of cryptographic keys, biometric authentication in wireless network and possible attacks on biometrics are presented. When designing and verifying communication protocols using informal techniques, some security errors may remain undetected. Finally the chapter concludes by describing the formal verification methods that provide a systematic way of finding protocol flaws.

Chapter 9 describes the threats to multimedia data which are floating around in the Internet especially in the form of image data. It also shows different methods to provide security for digital images and techniques which are used to insert watermark in cover data. The chapter focuses on watermarking approaches in Hadamard transform domain. The chapter describes the approaches to make the watermarking algorithm completely automated by calculating the embedding and scaling parameters using the content of cover images. Many methods exist for calculating scaling parameter adaptively but this chapter discusses various approaches using computational intelligence to determine the optimal values of scaling and embedding parameters.

Chapter 10 aims to discuss computational aspects of lattice-based cryptographic schemes with focus on NTRU in view of the time complexity on a graphical processing unit (GPU). Polynomial multiplication algorithms, having a very important role in lattice-based cryptographic schemes, are implemented on the GPU using the compute unified device architecture (CUDA) platform in both serial and parallel ways. Compact and efficient implementation architectures of polynomial multiplication for lattice-based cryptographic schemes are presented.

There has been increased attention toward information technology and information security degrees at universities and public administration institutes around the world. The number of students studying these disciplines/degrees is also increasing; hence, this book will be very useful as an academic source for students completing these areas of study.

Security system designers and developers would benefit from reading such a book as they would gain an understanding of CI elements that are needed for developing effective and efficient security systems.

The book will also be of value to a wider range of readers who are interested in understanding CI and information security.

The Editors

Acknowledgment

The editors would like to acknowledge the help of all the people involved in this project and, more specifically, to the authors and reviewers that took part in the review process. Without their support, this book would not have become a reality.

First, the editors would like to thank each one of the authors for their contributions. Our sincere gratitude goes to the chapter's authors who contributed their time and expertise to this book.

Second, the editors wish to acknowledge the valuable contributions of the reviewers regarding the improvement of quality, coherence, and content presentation of chapters. Most of the authors also served as referees; we highly appreciate their double task.

Wasan Shaker Awad
Ahlia University, Bahrain

El-Sayed M. El-Alfy
King Fahd University of Petroleum and Minerals, Saudi Arabia

Section 1
Introduction

This section provides an overview of existing computational intelligence paradigms, and reviews the literature and potential applications in cryptology.

Chapter 1
Computational Intelligence Paradigms:
An Overview

El-Sayed M. El-Alfy
King Fahd University of Petroleum and Minerals, Saudi Arabia

Wasan Shaker Awad
Ahlia University, Bahrain

ABSTRACT

The evolution of communication networks and information systems, to support wireless access, cloud and grid computing, and big data, provides great business opportunities. However, it also generates a new trend of sophisticated network threats and offers several challenges in securing information and systems confidentiality, integrity and availability. The traditional techniques used by security experts are mostly static and lack the much needed characteristics of adaptation and self-organization, computational efficiency and error resilience to deal with evolving attacks. The inherent characteristics of computational intelligence (CI) paradigms provide a promising alternative that has gained popularity resulting in significant applications in information security. There is a plethora of CI paradigms commonly used in this domain including artificial neural networks, evolutionary computing, fuzzy systems, and swarm intelligence. This chapter provides an overview of the widely-recognized CI paradigms and shades the light on some of their potential applications in information security.

INTRODUCTION

There are several problems encountered in the field of information security and cryptography that can be handled using computational intelligence paradigms, e.g. (Laskari et al., 2005, Wu & Banzhaf, 2013). These problems require optimization, adaptation, self-organization, parallelizability, fault tolerance, error resilience, and computational efficiency. According to Papadimitriou and Steiglitz (1982), a combinatorial optimization (CO) problem $P = (S, f)$ is an optimization problem in which we are given a finite set of objects S (search space) and an objective function $f: S \to \Re$ that assigns a positive cost value to each

DOI: 10.4018/978-1-4666-9426-2.ch001

of the objects $s \in S$. The goal is to find an object that has the minimal cost value. CO problems can be modeled as discrete optimization problems in which the search space is defined over a set of decision variables with discrete domains. Therefore, the terms combinatorial optimization and discrete optimization can be used interchangeably.

Due to the practical importance of CO problems, many algorithms to solve them have been proposed. These algorithms can be classified as either complete or approximate algorithms. Complete algorithms are guaranteed to find, for every CO problem instance, an optimal solution in polynomial time, but for CO problems that are *NP*-hard (Garey & Johnson, 1979), no polynomial time algorithms exist. Therefore, complete methods might need exponential computation time in the worst case. Thus, the development of approximate methods including CI techniques has received a growing attention where finding optimal solutions cannot be guaranteed but getting good solutions in a significantly reduced amount of time is desirable.

Computational intelligence is used to solve problems that only humans and animals can solve, i.e., problems requiring intelligence (Chen et al., 2001). Artificial Intelligence (AI) has been already established since the mid 1950s, addressing problems that require intelligence in order to be solved. Thus, one may ask, what is the difference between AI and CI? Zadeh (1994, 1998) distinguishes hard computing techniques based on AI from soft computing techniques based on CI. In hard computing, imprecision and uncertainty are undesirable features of a system whereas these are the foremost features in soft computing. Figure 1 shows the difference between AI and CI along with their relationship to hard computing (HC) and soft computing (SC). Zadeh defines soft computing as "a consortium of methodologies that provide a foundation for designing intelligent systems".

Many attempts have been made by different authors and researchers to define CI. Bezdek (1994) first proposed and defined the term CI as follows: "a system is called computationally intelligent if it deals with low-level data such as numerical data, has a pattern-recognition component and does not use knowledge in the AI sense; and additionally when it begins to exhibit computational adaptivity, fault tolerance, speed approaching human-like turnaround and error rates that approximate human performance" (Bezdek, 1994). He argues that CI is a subset of AI. Since then there has been much explanation published on the term CI. The IEEE Computational Intelligence Society (formerly the IEEE Neural Networks Council) defines its subject of interest as Neural Networks (NN), Fuzzy Systems (FS)

Figure 1. Artificial intelligence (AI) versus computational intelligence (CI)

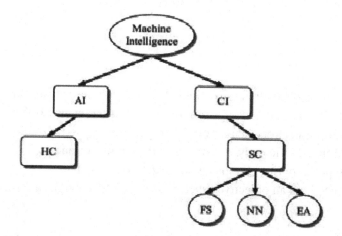

and Evolutionary Algorithms (EA) (Dote & Ovaska, 2001). In Wikipedia, the free encyclopedia, CI is a set of nature-inspired computational methodologies and approaches to address complex real-world problems to which traditional approaches, i.e., first principles modeling or explicit statistical modeling, are ineffective or infeasible. According to Konar (2005), CI is the construction of a process or system model, which is not amenable to mathematical or traditional modeling because:

1. The process is too complex to represent mathematically,
2. The process models are difficult and expensive to evaluate,
3. There are uncertainties in the process operation, and
4. The process is nonlinear, distributed, incomplete and stochastic in nature.

In this chapter, we will present a detailed account of major CI paradigms. The chapter will include a discussion of widely used CI models inspired by nature including:

1. **Neural Networks (NN):** This is being the major area of CI that has been mainly inspired by the system of neurons present in human brain which is fault tolerant, compact, flexible and adaptive.
2. **Evolutionary Computations (EC):** Mainly inspired by the evolution of biological objects in nature this is a second major area in CI. The basic principles and terminology of evolutionary computation will be introduced along with some major classes of evolutionary computation. These include variants of genetic algorithms, and genetic programming.
3. **Swarm Intelligence (SI):** Optimization algorithms based on the behavior of swarms of organisms will be presented with focus on particle swarm optimization and ant colony optimization.
4. **Fuzzy Systems (FS):** The mechanism of approximate reasoning using the idea of fuzzy membership functions instead of crisp membership will be introduced and the operators of fuzzy set theory will be reviewed along with various state-of-the-art inference operators.
5. **Hybrid Systems (HS):** There are several variants of such systems that combine two or more of the above paradigms in different manners. For example, neural networks and fuzzy systems are combined into what is known as neuro-fuzzy inference systems, of which ANFIS (Adaptive Neuro-Fuzzy Inference System) (Jang, 1993) is a widely recognized approach.

NEURAL NETWORKS

Inspired by the biological neural system, researchers have proposed several computational models to mimic its behavior. These models consist of simple processing elements (units or neurons) connected together to form a network (Mehrotra et al., 1997). The network receives signals or inputs from outside and processes them as they pass from neuron to neuron to generate an output. The connections between neurons have adaptive weights or strengths that affect the signals while they transfer through the network. As a branch of machine leaning, the network has the capability to adjust the strengths of the connections during the training phase to approximate some unknown nonlinear function. This gives the network popularity for its predictive power and universal function approximation (Hornik et al., 1989). Consequently, a wide spectrum of successful applications has emerged over the years in many engineering and scientific disciplines. Examples of these applications include pattern classification and clustering, system identification and control, regression analysis, time-series forecasting, robotics and computer vision, medical diagnosis, troubleshooting, information security, cryptography and cryptanalysis. A variety of neural networks exist depending on the network topology or structure of neurons, and the learning paradigm (Haykin, 2009; Specht, 1990; Grossberg, 1988). Among these types are feedforward multilayer perceptrons (MLPs), recurrent neural networks (RNNs), radial-basis function (RBF) networks, learning vector quantization (LVQ) networks, probabilistic neural networks (PNN), abductive networks of polynomial units, and self-organizing maps (SOM). Neural networks have also been combined with other computational intelligence paradigms such as fuzzy logic and evolutionary methods to form hybrid computational models. Among these models are the neuro-fuzzy systems (Jang & Sun, 1995; Nauck et al., 1997; Fortuna et al., 2001) and evolutionary neural networks (Yao, 1999). More recent advances and breakthroughs in neural networks are driven by spiking neural networks (Maass, 1997; Paugam-Moisy & Bohte, 2012; Grüning & Bohte, 2014) and deep learning (Bengio, 2009; Deng & Yu, 2014). For a recent review of the advances in neural networks, we refer the reader to (Woźniak et al., 2015).

Examples of Neural Network Models

A. General Neuron Model

The simplest neural network model consists of a single neuron that processes its inputs to mimic the operation of a biological neuron or nerve cell. A biological neuron is composed of a soma (cell body), a set of dendrites, and a long axon. The end of the axon is divided into a set of fine branches terminating with little bulbs (synapses). The information transfers through the axon and its branches going out from one neuron to other neurons at the synapses. Each axon has a connection strength and modifies the signal passing through accordingly. Figure 2 shows a schematic diagram for the structure of a biological neuron and Figure 2 shows the corresponding abstract computational model. In this model, the activation or transfer function can be a linear or nonlinear function that can take various shapes, e.g. sigmoid, step, tanh, signum and linear functions. The simplest and early computational model, known as McCulloch-Pitts Model, was introduced in 1940s by Warren McCulloch and Walter Pitts who represented the neuron as a linear threshold gate. It is very similar to Figure 3 but the output is binary generated by a step transfer function (Haykin, 2009).

Figure 2. Schematic diagram of a biological neuron

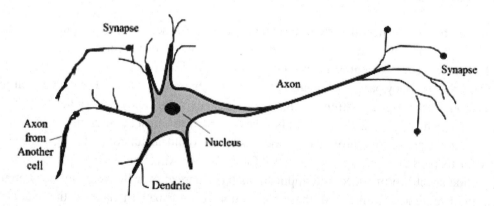

Figure 3. A computational neuron model for its biological counterpart

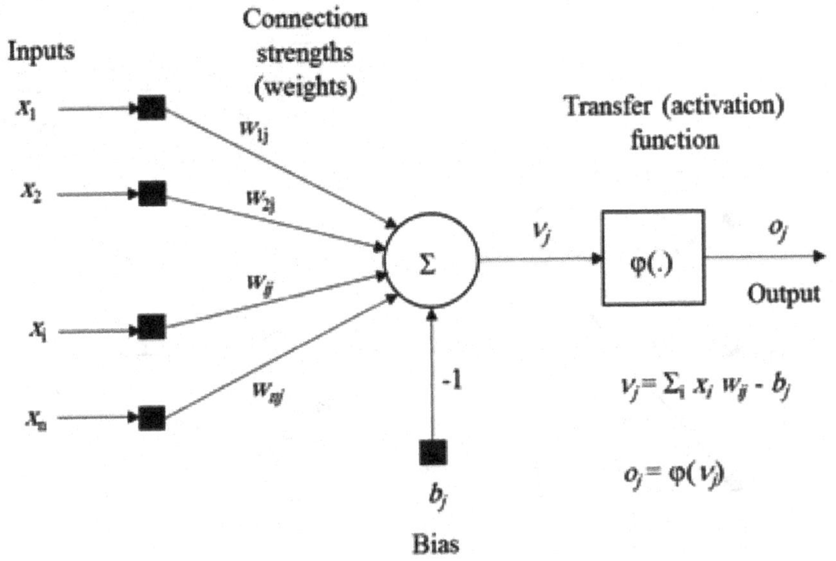

B. Feedforward Multilayer Perceptron

Feedforward multilayer perceptrons (MLPs) are known for their attractive capability as universal function approximators. A typical example of an MLP is shown in Figure 4. It has a set of layers each consists of a set of processing units (neurons). The output from each layer is fed into the subsequent layer. The first layer is known as input layer and is composed of a number of neurons equal to the number of input variables. The last layer is known as output layer and it generates an approximate value for each dependent variable. The other layers are optional and are known as hidden layers. The links connecting neurons have weights and each neuron has a bias and an activation function. For n-h-1 MLP, there are n inputs at the input layer, h neurons in the hidden layer, and one neuron in the output layer. Referring to Figure 4, the output is calculated as a nonlinear function of the inputs as follows:

$$y = \sum_{j=0}^{h} \varphi\left(w_j^{(2)} z_j - b\right) \tag{1}$$

$$z_j = \sum_{i=0}^{n} \varphi\left(w_{ij}^{(1)} x_i - b_j\right) \tag{2}$$

where $x_0 = 1$, $z_0 = 1$, b and b_j are biases, and $\varphi(.)$ is an activation function. The network parameters, aka weights and biases, are determined using a learning algorithm such as back propagation or conjugate gradient learning algorithm.

Figure 4. A typical example of a feedforward multilayer perceptron

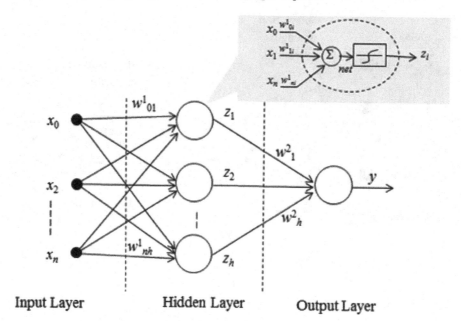

C. Radial-Basis Function Networks

A Radial-Basis Function Network (RBFN) is a special type of artificial feedforward neural networks (Haykin, 2009). Radial-Basis Functions (RBFs) were introduced for solving multivariate problems numerically (Powell, 1987). Figure 5 shows the structure of a typical example of an RBFN. It is normally composed of an input layer, a single hidden layer and an output layer. The input layer acts as a fan-out for the input variables and does not perform any processing. The number of neurons in the input layer equals the number of real-valued predictors (independent variables). Neurons in the hidden layer use nonlinear RBF kernel activation functions. Although various types of radial-basis functions can be used, Gaussian bell-shaped functions are the most common at this layer. The output of each neuron in the hidden layer is inversely proportional to the Euclidean distance from the center of the neuron. The purpose of the hidden layer is to nonlinearly map the patterns from a low-dimension space to a high-dimension space where the patterns become more linearly separable. Neurons in the output layer normally use linear activation functions. The output layer has one or more units based on the number of dependent variables. RBFN calculates a function as a linear weighted summation of the outputs of the units in the hidden layer. It has many applications in universal function approximation, pattern recognition and classification, prediction and control in dynamical systems, signal processing, chaotic time-series prediction, and weather and power load forecasting.

For the RBFN shown in Figure 5, there are n inputs, m outputs, and h units in the hidden layer with Gaussian kernel transfer functions. The output of i-th unit in the hidden layer is given by:

$$g_i(\vec{x}) = \exp\left(-\frac{\|\vec{x} - \vec{\mu}_i\|^2}{2\sigma_i^2}\right), i = 1, 2, ..., h \qquad (3)$$

Figure 5. Structure of a radial-basis function neural network

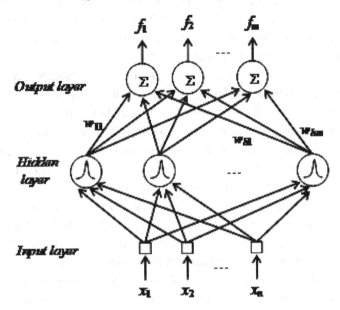

where $\vec{\mu}_i$ and σ_i denote the center and width (or spread) parameters of the radial-basis function of the i-th unit, and $\left\| \vec{x} - \vec{\mu}_i \right\|^2$ denotes the square of the Euclidean distance between the input vector $\vec{x}$ and the unit center $\vec{\mu}_i$. The width parameter determines the radius of the area around the center at which the activation function is significant. The smaller the radius, the more selective the function is. These two parameters have major impact on the performance of the RBF networks and they can be fixed for the whole network and vary for each unit. The j-th component of the output is given by the weighted sum of the outputs of the units in the hidden layer as follows:

$$f_j(\vec{x}) = \sum_{i=1}^{h} w_{ij} g_j(\vec{x}), j = 1, 2, ..., m .$$

(4)

The design of an RBF network model means determining the number of basis function (i.e. units in the hidden layer), connection weights between the hidden layer and the output layer, and centers and widths of the hidden layer units. These parameters are determined by training the network for a given dataset using one of the available training algorithms.

Neural Networks in Cryptography

This branch is also known as neural cryptography (Kinzel & Kanter, 2002; Godhavari et al., 2005; Ruttor et al., 2007) which is dedicated for applications of neural networks in encryption and cryptanalysis. Recently, Mu and Liao, (2013) analyzed the factor impacting the security of neural cryptography and proposed a generalized architecture for designing novel neural cryptography.

The generation of random-numbers plays important role in cryptography. One of the areas that has attracted considerable attention is exchanging secret key between two neural networks on a public channel. Kanter et al. (2002) described an ephemeral key exchange protocol for secure transport of confidential messages based on the synchronization of neural network weights by Hebbian learning. The authors also analyzed the protocol's complexity and resistance to attacks. Mislovaty et al. (2003) combined two different kinds of synchronization to build a hybrid network for secure generation of secret encryption keys. In this approach, two dynamical systems are synchronized by a common external signal using chaotic maps and neural networks to increase its protection against attacks. Ruttor et al. (2004) showed that adding a feedback mechanism to a neural cryptography system can increase its security for the generated pseudorandom bit sequence, and as a result increase the security of the encrypted message. Godhavari et al. (2005) discussed the concept of synchronization of two neural networks by mutual learning for secure key exchange over a public unsecure channel. This generated key is then used for data encryption and decryption. Based on the analysis presented in (Ruttor et al., 2006), it has been shown that key-exchange protocols that use neural networks are secure against known attacks. Yayik and Kutlu (2013) used a multilayer perceptron to strengthen a traditional random number generator.

Another class of neural networks that has found application in cryptography is known as random neural networks (Gelenbe, 1989; 1990). Aguilar and Molina (2013) described an extended model of random neural networks using multilayer architecture and applied it to data encryption.

Arvandi et al. (2006) attempted to apply the parallel processing capability of neural networks for the design of a robust symmetric cipher that is resisting to different cryptanalysis attacks. The analysis of this method against chosen-plaintext attacks is studied in (Arvandi & Sadeghian, 2007). Liu et al. (2011) proposed a method for securing message in mobile ad hoc networks (MANETs). In this method, a real-time recurrent neural network-based (RRNN) cipher is combined with a trust-based multipath routing scheme to deal with confidentiality, integrity, and access control issues.

Papadimitriou et al. (1999) designed a nonlinear adaptive chaotic system using a radial basis function network for effective information encryption and robust communication security. This approach is based on the existence of a large number of parameters offered by RBF while it can learn to implement the dynamics of a chaotic system.

EVOLUTIONARY COMPUTATION

One of the prominent methodologies of computational intelligence is evolutionary computation (EC). Evolution is an optimization process, where the aim is to improve the ability of a system to survive in a dynamically changing environment.

There are a number of evolutionary computation techniques, such as Genetic Algorithms (GA) and Genetic Programming (GP). Regardless of the technique used, evolutionary computation applications follow a similar procedure (Eberhar & Shi, 2008):

1. Initialize a population.
2. Evaluate each individual in the population.
3. Select individuals.
4. Produce a new population by applying a number of operations on selected individuals.
5. Loop to step 2 until some condition is met.

Evolutionary computation has been used with great success for the solution of hard optimization problems, e.g., multi-modal, noisy, NP-hard or dynamic optimization problems.

EC algorithms can be analyzed theoretically and/or empirically. The theoretical analysis is required for understanding the underlying phenomena and characteristics of evolutionary search. On the other hand, empirical analysis can be used to assess the EC algorithms in solving problems. However, it is necessary to consider the following (Sendhoff et al., 2006):

1. The choice of the empirical test function has to be well founded. It should represent either the characteristics of a certain practically relevant problem class or of a theoretical problem property.
2. The empirical analysis must be sound, i.e., the right statistical tools must be employed.
3. The analysis must be transparent and reproducible.

If these are considered, then we will be able to decide which evolutionary algorithm, or parts of an algorithm, like representation method or genetic operators, is most suitable for a particular problem.

Genetic Algorithms

Genetic Algorithm (GA) is a search algorithm based on the mechanics of natural selection and evolution. GA theoretical foundation was developed by John Holland (1975) in the 1970's. The main idea of GA has been derived from the evolutional process in natural biological life: the natural population develops according to the natural selection principle "survival of the fittest". Before explaining GA, the following key terms need to be defined (Goldberg, 1989; Beasley & Chu, 1996; Holland, 1975):

1. **Search Space:** All possible solutions to the problem.
2. **Chromosome or Individual:** Any candidate solution in the search space of a problem, and it is an element in GA population.
3. **Population:** A set of chromosomes or individuals, and population size is the number of the chromosomes in the population.

GA attempts to identify an optimal solution by progressively applying certain operations to a population of solutions: the solutions are evaluated, the bad solutions are eliminated, and other solutions are recombined (mate) to form a new generation of solutions. Over a number of generations, the individuals in a population will have fewer bad traits, resulting in an overall increase in the quality of the best solution in the population. Thus, GA is an iterative procedure, which maintains a constant size population of candidate solutions. During each iteration step (generation), the structures in the current population are evaluated, and, on the basis of those evaluations, a new population of candidate solutions is formed. Side-by-side GAs use probabilistic rules to guide search, not deterministic rules (Goldberg, 1989; Sivanandam & Deepa, 2008).

There are various forms of GAs but they all share a basic structure and have adjustable parameters including:

1. **The Solution Representation:** Refers to how a particular solution to the problem is encoded as a chromosome.
2. **The Fitness Function:** A figure of merit computed using any domain knowledge that applies.

3. Population size.
4. The maximum number of generations.
5. Maximum and minimum chromosome length.
6. Rates of genetic operations (e.g. mutation and crossover)
7. Other parameters that are specific to the problem.

The advantages of GA can be summarized as follows (Beasley & Chu, 1996; Holland, 1975):

1. Powerful methods can create high quality solutions to a problem.
2. GA can work well in complex, poorly understood and large search spaces.
3. GA can be a useful tool if there is no mathematical analysis available.
4. GA can work effectively when traditional search methods fail.

However, GA has also its own disadvantages: it can take a long time to run and provide the best solution; therefore, it's not always feasible for real-time use. Although GA has gained wide acceptance in many applications, it is reported that the simple GA suffers from many troubles such as parameters dependence and potential trap in local optima (Eiben et al., 1999). Therefore, there are many improvements and extensions have been proposed to improve its performance, such as adaptive GA (Srinivas et al., 1994).

Genetic Operations

This section will expose a number of genetic operations that can be used to update the current population of GA and generate a new population. All genetic operations are applied in specific rates (Goldberg, 1989; Syswerda, 1989; Spears & De Jong, 1990; Kellegoz et al., 2008; Kellegoz et al., 2008).

In the crossover operation, more than one chromosome are selected from the old population to produce new chromosomes that will be added to the new population. This can be done by creating a crossover point in each chromosome, and all the genes behind that point are swapped with the other chromosomes to produce the new chromosomes. There are different types of crossover operations that can be applied in GA, such as single-point crossover, multi-point crossover, and uniform crossover.

In contrast, mutation operation creates a new chromosome from each selected chromosome of the old population by changing some parts of that chromosome randomly.

The process of elitism consists of selecting certain chromosomes from the old population and copying them into the new one without any change. The selection depends on the fitness measurement. The purpose of using this operator is to reuse the individuals that have proven themselves capable of solving the problem so that they will not be lost. However, if the operator is overused, it can damage the goal of the GA; therefore, the operator has to be used wisely.

The selection strategy in GA consists of choosing a chromosome in the existing population and using it to generate the new population, so the fitness of the new population will be better. That can be done by giving the chromosome with higher fitness high probability to move to the next population. There are different methods of selection with different strategies, but all of them are built on the principle of survival of the fittest, such as tournament selection, roulette wheel selection, and rank selection.

Qualitative analysis of the selection strategies must be done to adopt the best strategy since the selection performance is highly dependent on the different criteria at the time of selection of chromosomes. These criteria could be anything like type of population, type of representation method used, or population size (Noraini & John, 2011).

Genetic Programming

Genetic programming (GP) (Koza, 1992) is a closely related field to genetic algorithms, in which the structure under adaption is a set of computer programs typically represented in the form of expression trees. It is capable of evolving computer programs to solve, or approximately solve, a variety of problems. Thus, each GP individual is designed to store a computer program in such a way that it can be optimized using an evolutionary approach. The operators like mutation and crossover depend on the representation of the attributes of an individual and also the calculation of the fitness of an individual. The fitness of an individual can be evaluated by executing the program under varying conditions and its behavior or output can be used to estimate the fitness. Such programs could also be simplified to represent mathematical functions.

The GP crossover is performed by selecting two sub-trees by chance from the parents and exchanging them to create the descendants. The GP mutation is performed by selecting a sub-tree of the descendant by chance and replacing it with an arbitrary generated new sub-tree. Due to the very rugged search space of possible program configurations, very big populations (> 1000 individuals) but only a small number of generations (<50) are usually used for GP. GP approaches can be classified into three categories: traditional GP, strongly typed GP (Haynes et al., 1995), and hierarchical GP (automatically defined functions ADF) (Koza, 1994).

The major steps needed in preparing GP to solve a problem include:

1. Determining function and terminal sets, from which an individual program constructed.
2. Determining the representation scheme of the individuals.
3. Determining the fitness function.

The population of GP is a set of candidate solutions which are programs. Each program is composed of a number of primitive functions and terminals. To apply GP, it is necessary to define the terminal set which includes constants and variables of the population individuals (programs). The primitive functions are chosen based on the problem at hand. The function set may include arithmetic functions such as subtraction, addition, division and multiplication. It can also be a set of logical functions (OR, AND, XOR, ..., etc.) and so on. Terminal and function sets together define the alphabetic of the program that will be evolved by GP.

Koza (Koza, 1992; Koza & Rice, 1994) used LISP programming language to represent the candidate programs in the GP populations. The LISP program consists of two types of entities: atoms and lists. An atom can be a constant such as 4, or a variable like "Counter". The list in LISP is represented by a collection of items placed between parentheses, such as (+ 6 8). The syntactic form in LISP is called S-expression (symbolic expression). In an S-expression, the item in the outermost left parenthesis is a function that is applied to the other items of the list. For example, consider the LISP S-expression: (* 3 10 (- (+ 1 7 2) 5)). In this example, the first function in the list is "*" applied on three arguments: 3, 10 and the sub S-Expression (- (+ 1 7 2) 5)). In this sub S-expression, the function is "-" which has two arguments: the sub expression (+ 1 7 2) and constant 5. The sub expression (+ 1 7 2) has "+" as a function that will add the 3 arguments 1, 7 and 2. The result of the last sub expression will be 10, the result of (- (+ 1 7 2) 5) will be 5, and the result of the overall expression will be 150.

Another representation method used in GP is GADS (Genetic Algorithm for Developing Software) that was first introduced by Paterson and Livesey (1996). The chromosomes of GADS are not represented using the tree structure, but a list of integers. GADS makes use of BNF (Backus–Naur Form), which is a method used for representing context-free grammar that is used to characterize the formal language syntax in computer science.

SWARM INTELLIGENCE

Swarm intelligence (Kennedy & Eberhart, 1995; Eberhart et al., 2001) is a powerful suite of tools that effectively model the social behavior and interaction of individuals in self-organized groups, such as ant colonies, bird flocks, animal herds, fish schools, and bacterial growth. The goal of swarm intelligence is to design intelligent multi-agent systems with similar characteristics. Swarm intelligence shares many similarities with evolutionary computation in the sense that both are stochastic optimization methodologies based on a population of random solutions that are updated to explore the search space for the global optimum. However, there are no evolution operators in swarm intelligence. Several applications of swarm intelligence have been witnessed in various domains including information security and cryptography. An example of the recent work is the cryptanalytic analysis of knapsack cryptosystems with binary particle swarm optimization (Jain & Chaudhari, 2014). In (Qureshi et al., 2011), swarm intelligence is used to detect malicious beacon nodes in hostile environments of wireless sensor networks. Another application is presented in (Castiglione et al., 2014). In this application, a botnet-based command and control architecture is presented based on swarm intelligence to ensure spontaneous, implicit coordination and collaboration among independent bot agents.

An intriguing book to read in this area is the one by Eberhart et al. (2001) which develops concrete insights of the principal concepts and foundations of the swarm intelligence methodology including social psychology, cognitive science, artificial life, and artificial intelligence, statistics and evolutionary computation. A recent review of swarm intelligence is presented in (Yang, 2015) with emphasis on particle swarm optimization, bat algorithm, discrete cuckoo search, firefly algorithm, harmony search, and convergent hybridization. Another timely edited volume (Dehuri, et al. 2015) covers the theoretical and practical advances of multi-objective swarm intelligence paradigms including Multi-objective Particle Swarm Optimization (MOPSO), Bacteria Foraging Optimization (BFO), and Ant Colony Optimization (ACO). In the following subsections, we provide the details of two approaches: PSO and ACO.

Particle Swarm Optimization (PSO)

PSO is a population-based metaheuristic search technique. The early work on PSO is attributed to Kennedy and Eberhart (1995). Among its widely proposed applications, PSO has some applications in information security and cryptography. For instance, Srinoy (2007) proposed a method for intrusion detection using PSO and support vector machine. Chung and Wahid (2012) proposed a hybrid approach for network intrusion detection using intelligent dynamic swarm based rough set (IDS-RS) for feature selection and simplified swarm optimization with weighted local search for intrusion data classification.

Li and Wang (2007) applied PSO for data hiding in JPEG images. For cryptanalysis of the 16 round Data Encryption Standard, a known-plaintext attack is designed based on PSO in (Abd-Elmonim et al., 2011).

The idea of PSO is inspired by the behavior of bird flocks and fish schools. Assume a group of birds is searching randomly for a food location (global optimum) that is unknown to any of the birds, but only the distance to the location is known. Since none of the birds knows where the food is, they repeatedly follow the bird that is closer to the food. In reality, the distance to the food may not be known; hence the algorithm keeps track of the location that seems to be globally the best. To mimic this behavior, PSO starts with a population (swarm) of randomly initialized candidate solutions (particles). Each particle is described with two variables representing its position, x_p, and velocity, v_p, respectively. Each particle also memorizes its best local position, $p_{best,p}$, and tracks the global best position, g_{best}. According to (Eberhart et al., 2001), the positions and velocities of particles are iteratively updated as follows:

$$v_p(t) = v_p(t-1) + \varphi_1 \times \left(p_{best,p} - x_p\left(t-1\right)\right) + \varphi_2 \times \left(g_{best} - x_p\left(t-1\right)\right) \tag{5}$$

$$x_p(t) = x_p(t-1) + v_p(t) \tag{6}$$

where $v_p(t)$ and $x_p(t)$ are the velocity and position of particle p at time instance t, $v_p(t\text{-}1)$ and $x_p(t\text{-}1)$ are the velocity and position of particle p at time instance $t\text{-}1$, and φ_1 and φ_2 are random values. Putting all together, the main steps of the algorithm can be outlined as follows:

- Initialize the swarm with random positions and velocities.
- Evaluate the fitness function for each particle.
- Change the best local position of a particle if its position has higher fitness than the current best local.
- Determine the best global for particles in the neighborhood.
- Update the velocity and position for each particle.
- Repeat from the second step until some termination criteria are met.

Ant Colony Optimization

Ant colony optimization (ACO) is one of the most successful strands of swarm intelligence (Bonabeau et al., 1999; Dorigo & Stützle, 2010). ACO provides elegant metaheuristic techniques for approximate optimization of hard combinatorial problems. ACO is inspired by the complex foraging behavior of real ants searching for shortest paths from their nest to food sources. Observations of this have been utilized for the development of a large number of ant-based computational algorithms to solve combinatorial optimization problems. A dedicated website with several details and pointers to the literature can be found at http://www.aco-metaheuristic.org/.

Several algorithms of ACO have been proposed in the literature. The first algorithm, known as Ant System, was developed in early 1990s by Marco Dorigo in his Ph.D. dissertation (Dorigo, 1992; Dorigo et al., 1996; Dorigo & Stützle, 2004; Dorigo et al., 2006). A couple of years later, two other variants have been proposed, namely the Max-Min Ant System (MMAS) (Stützle & Hoos, 1996; Stützle &

Hoos, 2000) and the Ant Colony System (ACS) (Gambardella & Dorigo, 1996). Since then, a number of ant-based algorithms were proposed for different applications. The ant system is composed of two main parts: tour construction, and pheromone trail update. By observing the behavior of ants, ants can pass along the path of previous ants since they leave chemical substances, called pheromones, on their way. Following pheromones, ants can find the optimal routes. Several improvements of ACO have been devised as illustrated by Andries (2006).

ACO algorithms are typically used to solve minimum cost problems. Assume there are N nodes and A undirected arcs or path segments. Although there are several variants of ACO, the general behavior can be summarized as follows (Dorigo & Stützle, 2004):

1. The ant's memory allows it to retrace the path it has followed while searching for the destination node.
2. While moving, ants leave pheromones on the arcs they traverse.
3. The ants evaluate the cost of the paths they have traversed.
4. The shorter paths will receive a greater deposit of pheromones. An evaporation rule will be tied with the pheromones, which will reduce the chance for poor quality solutions.

At the beginning of the search process, a constant amount of pheromone is assigned to all arcs. When located at a node i, an ant k uses the pheromone trail to compute the probability of choosing j as the next node:

$$
p_{ij}^{k} = \begin{cases} \dfrac{\tau_{ij}^{\alpha}}{\sum_{l \in N_i^k} \tau_{il}^{\alpha}} & \text{if } j \in N_i^k \\[2mm] 0 & \text{if } j \notin N_i^k \end{cases}
\tag{7}
$$

where N_i^k is the neighborhood of ant k when it is in node i, τ_{ij} is the amount of pheromone deposited on arc (i, j), and α is a constant controlling the influence of τ_{ij}.

6. When the arc (i, j) is traversed, the pheromone value changes as follows:

$$
\tau_{ij} \leftarrow \tau_{ij} + \Delta \tau^k
\tag{8}
$$

By using this rule, the probability increases that forthcoming ants will use this arc.

7. After each ant k moves to the next node, the pheromones evaporation with rate ρ is modeled by the following equation to all the arcs:

$$
\tau_{ij} \leftarrow (1 - \rho)\tau_{ij}, \forall (i, j) \in A
\tag{9}
$$

FUZZY LOGIC

Fuzzy Logic (FL) was first introduced by Lotfi Zadeh in 1960s at the University of California, Berkeley (Zadeh, 1965). His seminal paper has opened a very dynamic area of modern mathematical thinking that laid the foundation of possibility theory. Fuzzy logic deals with the phenomenon of vagueness and uncertainty, and the decision that is related to the process of human being judgments.

In real-world applications, information is often imperfect, uncertain and several concepts are better defined by words than by mathematics. Therefore, a fuzzy logic and its expression in fuzzy sets provide a discipline that can construct better models of reality, or in another definition fuzzy set theory is simply a generalization of the classical set theory and provides a means for the illustration of imprecision and vagueness. Fuzzy logic, fuzzy sets, fuzzy inference, and fuzzy reasoning have found a wide spectrum of applications in knowledge based systems (Ross, 2009). Relatively recent, several fuzzy based solutions have been proposed in information security, such as security risk assessment, intrusion detection, and trust evaluation and management (Li et al., 2011; Lee and Chang, 2014; Yao et al., 2005; Schmidt et al., 2007).

One of the characteristics of fuzzy logic is its ability to be both linguistically tractable and mathematically sound. It looks like human decision-making with its ability to work from approximate information and find precise results. The most interesting fact about fuzzy logic is that fuzzy inferences make it possible to assume a proposition similar to the consequence from some proposition that is similar to the antecedent. Hence, fuzzy logic allows expressing knowledge with subjective beliefs and expert judgments. For example, this project is good or that risk management plan is poor. It is a judgmental situation that needs human decision rather than computer software.

One of Zadeh's main ideas was that mathematics can be used to associate language and human intelligence. Since Zadeh developed the fuzzy logic and the fuzzy set theory, a massive amount of papers and publications around the world has appeared exploring his basic ideas of vagueness and its industrial applications. Fuzzy sets can be thought of as an extension of classical sets. In a classical set (or crisp set), the objects in the set are called elements or members of the set. An element x belonging to a set A is defined as $x \in A$, whereas an element that is not a member in A is noted as $x \notin A$. A characteristic function or membership function $\mu_A(x)$ is defined for each element in the universe U to have a crisp value of 1 or 0:

$$\mu_A\left(x\right) = \begin{cases} 1 \; for \; x \in A \\ 0 \; for \; x \notin A \end{cases} \tag{10}$$

For fuzzy sets, the membership function takes values in the interval [0, 1] defining the grade or degree of membership. There are different types of membership functions that have been proposed can be classified into two groups: those made up of straight lines being "linear" ones, and to the contrary, the Gaussian forms, or "curved" ones.

Fuzzy set theory has operations analogous to those in crisp set theory. The extension principle, introduced by Zadeh (1975), allows for the generalization of Boolean logic of classical mathematical crisp sets to fuzzy sets. Operations are extended to fuzzy sets in this manner using the membership function. Given the fuzzy sets A and B with membership functions $\mu_A(x)$ and $\mu_B(x)$ $\forall x$, respectively, the fuzzy set operations can be defined as shown in Table 1.

Table 1. Fuzzy set operations

Operation	Description
Equality	$A = B \Leftrightarrow \mu_A(x) = \mu_B(x) \ \forall x$
Containment	$B \supseteq A \Leftrightarrow \mu_B(x) \geq \mu_A(x) \ \forall x$
Complement	$B = \neg A \Leftrightarrow \mu_B(x) = 1 - \mu_A(x) \ \forall x$
Union	$C = A \cup B \Leftrightarrow \mu_C(x) = \max(\mu_A(x), \mu_B(x)) \ \forall x$
Intersection	$C = A \cap B \Leftrightarrow \mu_C(x) = \min(\mu_A(x), \mu_B(x)) \ \forall x$

HYBRID SYSTEMS

Hybridization tends to provide some improvements by combining multiple paradigms to gain the advantages and strengths of each (Jang, 1993; Nauck et al., 1997; Fortuna et al., 2001; Shi & Eberhart, 2001; Tsakonas & Dounias, 2002; Chadha & Jain, 2015); as illustrated in Figure 6. Typical integrations are Neuro-Genetic hybrid, Neuro-Fuzzy hybrid, Fuzzy-Genetic hybrid, Fuzzy-Swarm hybrid. Several other variations have appeared and continue to appear in the literature. The hybridization can be achieved in one of three categories:

1. Sequential hybrid system, in which different techniques are used in a pipelining fashion where the output from one approach becomes as input to the other approach. For instance, GA can be used to determine the output parameters which are then sent to NN or FS for further processing.
2. Auxiliary hybrid system, in which one technique calls another to perform some task, e.g. a neural network can use a genetic algorithm to determine the optimal structure or parameters.
3. Embedded hybrid system, in which different techniques are fused and become hard to separate, e.g. Adaptive Neuro-Fuzzy Inference System (ANFIS).

Figure 6. Hybridization of computational intelligence paradigms

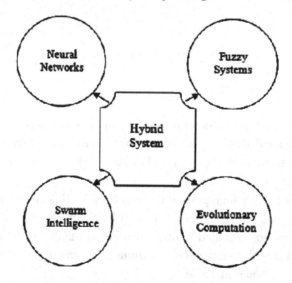

The following subsection provides more details of a typical example of hybrid systems, the ANFIS.

Neuro-Fuzzy Networks

Since its introduction by Lotfi Zadeh, fuzzy logic and fuzzy inference systems have been applied to many fields (Zadeh, 1965; Ross, 2009). One example is using fuzzy logic with neural networks to construct hybrid systems. Neuro-fuzzy network combines the capabilities of neural networks with that of fuzzy logic based systems (Jang et al., 1997). In 1993, Jang proposed an adaptive neuro-fuzzy inference system known as ANFIS that combines the capability of neural network to learn with the capability of fuzzy systems to incorporate linguistic variables and domain-expert knowledge (Jang, 1993). ANFIS has been widely used to solve several problems in different domains (Abraham, 2001; Kar, 2014). LeeJeong-Gi et al. (2013) proposed a smart home security system based on adaptive network fuzzy inference system. The proposed system uses information collected by sensors to make decisions dynamically.

An example of a Sugeno-type ANFIS network with two linguistic input variables and one output variable is shown in Figure 7. Each input variable is assumed to have two terms (e.g. small and large). This system consists of five layers; where the output from each node within a layer is represented by O_i^l where l denotes the layer number and i denotes the node number in the layer. The purpose of the first layer is to fuzzify the crisp input values using a set of linguistic terms (e.g., small, medium, and large). Membership functions of these linguistic terms determine the output of this layer as given by:

$$O_{A_i}^1 = \mu_{A_i}(x), O_{B_i}^1 = \mu_{B_i}(x) \tag{11}$$

where $\mu_{A_i}(x)$ and $\mu_{B_i}(y)$ represent the membership functions that establish the degree to which the given input values x and y satisfy the quantifiers A_i and B_i. A variety of membership functions exists such as bell-shaped, trapezoidal, triangular, Gaussian, and sigmoidal functions.

Figure 7. Two inputs and single output ANFIS architecture

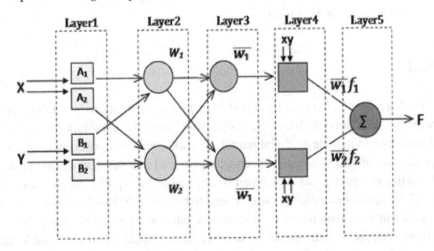

The firing strength for each rule quantifies the extent that any input data belongs to that rule, and is computed in the second layer as the multiplication of all the incoming signals at each node as follows:

$$O_i^2 = w_i = \mu_{A_i}(x) * \mu_{B_i}(x) \tag{12}$$

The nodes in the third layer perform normalization operation by calculating the ratio of the i-th rule's firing strength to the sum of all rule's firing strengths as follows:

$$O_i^3 = \bar{w}_i = \frac{w_i}{w_1 + w_2} \tag{13}$$

In Sugeno-type ANFIS system, the consequent part of each rule is expressed as a linear combination of the inputs. The fourth layer has square-shaped nodes with node functions given as:

$$O_i^4 = \bar{w}_i f_i = \bar{w}_i (p_i x + q_i y + r_i) \tag{14}$$

Finally, the last layer node conducts summation of all incoming signals to generate the output as weighted sum:

$$O_1^5 = \bar{w}_1 f_1 + \bar{w}_2 f_2 \tag{15}$$

The objective of a learning algorithm is to update the consequent and premise parameters in order to achieve the least error between the predicted and the desired target output. A hybrid training algorithm is normally applied to tune the parameters of an ANFIS network. Such a learning technique is composed of least square estimates and a gradient descend (back-propagation) algorithm. The first stage updates the consequent parameters through least-square estimates by passing of function signals forward until layer 4. In the second stage, the error rates are propagated backward which help in updating the premise parameters by a gradient descent algorithm.

CONCLUSION

Computational intelligence refers to a family of nature-inspired computational models that can be applied to solve highly complex problems which lack exact algorithmic or analytical solutions. The most commonly used models in this domain include artificial neural networks, evolutionary computing, fuzzy systems, swarm intelligence, and hybrid systems. This chapter provided an overview of the widely-recognized computational intelligence paradigms which can be applied to hard problems in information security and cryptology. There are some challenges which need to be carefully handled, such as, data collection, preprocessing, problem formulation and representation, parameters settings, and proper definition of objective functions. Yet, these methods and innovative ideas appear to provide viable and promising alternative and complementary solutions.

REFERENCES

Abd-Elmonim, W. G., Ghali, N. I., & Abraham, A. (2011, October). Known-plaintext attack of DES-16 using particle swarm optimization. In *Proceedings of Third World Congress on Nature and Biologically Inspired Computing* (NaBIC), (pp. 12-16). doi:10.1109/NaBIC.2011.6089410

Abraham, A. (2001). Neuro fuzzy systems: State-of-the-art modeling techniques. In Connectionist Models of Neurons, Learning Processes, and Artificial Intelligence (pp. 269-276). Springer Berlin Heidelberg.

Aguilar, J., & Molina, C. (2013). The multilayer random neural network. *Neural Processing Letters*, *37*(2), 111–133. doi:10.1007/s11063-012-9237-x

Andries, P. E. (2006). *Fundamentals of Computational Swarm Intelligence*. John Willey & Sons.

Arvandi, M., & Sadeghian, A. (2007, August). Chosen plaintext attack against neural network-based symmetric cipher. In *Proceedings of the International Joint Conference on Neural Networks*. IJCNN. doi:10.1109/IJCNN.2007.4371068

Arvandi, M., Wu, S., Sadeghian, A., Melek, W. W., & Woungang, I. (2006). Symmetric cipher design using recurrent neural networks. In *Proceedings of the International Joint Conference on Neural Networks*. IJCNN.

Beasley, J. E., & Chu, P. C. (1996). A genetic algorithm for the set covering problem. *European Journal of Operational Research*, *94*(2), 392–404. doi:10.1016/0377-2217(95)00159-X

Bengio, Y. (2009). Learning deep architectures for AI. *Foundations and Trends in Machine Learning*, *2*(1), 1–127. doi:10.1561/2200000006

Bezdek, J. C. (1994). Chapter. In J. Zurada, B. Marks, & C. Robinson (Eds.), What is computational intelligence? Computational Intelligence Imitating Life (pp. 1–12). Piscataway, NJ: IEEE Press.

Blum, C. (2005). Ant colony optimization: Introduction and recent trends. *Physics of Life Reviews*, *2*(4), 353–373. doi:10.1016/j.plrev.2005.10.001

Bonabeau, E., Dorigo, M., & Theraulaz, G. (1999). *Swarm Intelligence: From Natural to Artificial Systems*. New York: Oxford University Press.

Castiglione, A., De Prisco, R., De Santis, A., Fiore, U., & Palmieri, F. (2014). A botnet-based command and control approach relying on swarm intelligence. *Journal of Network and Computer Applications*, *38*, 22–33. doi:10.1016/j.jnca.2013.05.002

Chadha, K., & Jain, S. (2015). Hybrid genetic fuzzy rule based inference engine to detect intrusion in networks. *Advances in Intelligent Systems and Computing*, *321*, 185–198. doi:10.1007/978-3-319-11227-5_17

Chen, Z., Fanelli, A. M., Castellano, G., & Jain, L. C. (2001). Introduction to computational intelligence paradigms. In *Computational Intelligence in Games* (pp. 1–38). Physica-Verlag HD. doi:10.1007/978-3-7908-1833-8_1

Chung, Y. Y., & Wahid, N. (2012). A hybrid network intrusion detection system using simplified swarm optimization (SSO). *Applied Soft Computing, 12*(9), 3014–3022. doi:10.1016/j.asoc.2012.04.020

Dehuri, S., Jagadev, A. K., & Panda, M. (Eds.). (2015). *Multi-objective Swarm Intelligence: Theoretical Advances and Applications* (Vol. 592). Springer. doi:10.1007/978-3-662-46309-3

Deng, L., & Yu, D. (2014). Deep learning: Methods and applications. *Foundations and Trends in Signal Processing, 7*(3–4), 197–387. doi:10.1561/2000000039

Dorigo, M. (1992). *Optimization, Learning and Natural Algorithms* (Doctoral Dissertation in Italian). Dipartimento di Elettronica, Politecnico di Milano, Milan, Italy.

Dorigo, M., Birattari, M., & Stützle, T. (2006). Ant colony optimization. *IEEE Computational Intelligence Magazine, 1*(4), 28–39. doi:10.1109/CI-M.2006.248054

Dorigo, M., Maniezzo, V., & Colorni, A. (1996). Ant system: Optimization by a colony of cooperating agents. *IEEE Trans. Systems, Man, and Cybernetics -- Part B, 26*(1), 29–41. doi:10.1109/3477.484436

Dorigo, M., & Stützle, T. (2004). *Ant Colony Optimization*. MIT Press. doi:10.1007/b99492

Dorigo, M., & Stützle, T. (2010). Ant colony optimization: overview and recent advances. In Handbook of Metaheuristics (pp. 227-263). Springer US. doi:10.1007/978-1-4419-1665-5_8

Dote, Y., & Ovaska, S. J. (2001). Industrial applications of soft computing: A review. *Proceedings of the IEEE, 89*(9), 1243–1265. doi:10.1109/5.949483

Eberhart, R., & Shi, Y. (2008). *Computational Intelligence: Concepts to Implementation*. Morgan Kaufmann.

Eberhart, R. C., Shi, Y., & Kennedy, J. (2001). *Swarm intelligence*. Elsevier.

Eiben, A. E., Hinterding, R., & Michalewic, Z. (1999). Parameters control in evolutionary algorithms. *IEEE Transactions on Systems, Man, and Cybernetics, 16*(1), 122–128.

Fortuna, L., Rizzotto, D. G., Lavorgna, D. M., Nunnari, G., Xibilia, M. G., & Caponetto, D. R. (2001). Neuro-fuzzy networks. In *Soft Computing* (pp. 169–178). Springer London. doi:10.1007/978-1-4471-0357-8_9

Gambardella, L. M., & Dorigo, M. (1996, May). Solving symmetric and asymmetric TSPs by ant colonies. In *Proceedings of International Conference on Evolutionary Computation* (pp. 622-627). Academic Press. doi:10.1109/ICEC.1996.542672

Garey, M. R., & Johnson, D. S. (1979). *Computers and Intractability; A guide to the theory of NP Completeness*. New York: WH Freeman.

Gelenbe, E. (1989). Random neural networks with negative and positive signals and product form solution. *Neural Computation, 1*(4), 502–510. doi:10.1162/neco.1989.1.4.502

Gelenbe, E. (1990). *Theory of the random neural network*. Technical Report. University of Maryland at College Park College Park.

Godhavari, T., Alamelu, N. R., & Soundararajan, R. (2005, December). Cryptography using neural network. In Proceedings of IEEE Annual INDICON (pp. 258-261). IEEE. doi:10.1109/INDCON.2005.1590168

Goldberg, D. E. (1989). *Genetic Algorithms in Search, Optimization, and Machine Learning*. Addison-Wesley.

Grossberg, S. (1988). Nonlinear neural networks: Principles, mechanisms, and architectures. *Neural Networks*, *1*(1), 17–61. doi:10.1016/0893-6080(88)90021-4

Grüning, A., & Bohte, S. M. (2014). Spiking neural networks: Principles and challenges. In *Proceedings of European Symposium on Artificial Neural Networks, Computational Intelligence and Machine Learning*. Bruges, Belgium: Academic Press.

Haykin, S. (2009). *Neural Networks and Learning Machines* (3rd ed.). Upper Saddle River, NJ: Pearson Education.

Haynes, T., Wainwright, R., Sen, S., Sen, I., & Schoenefeld, D. (1995). Strongly typed GP in evolving cooperation strategies. In *Proceedings of the Sixth International Conference on Genetic Algorithms*. Morgan Kaufmann.

Holland, J. H. (1975). *Adaptive in Natural and Artificial Systems*. University of Michigan.

Hornik, K., Stinchcombe, M., & White, H. (1989). Multilayer feedforward networks are universal approximators. *Neural Networks*, *2*(5), 359–366. doi:10.1016/0893-6080(89)90020-8

Jain, A., & Chaudhari, N. S. (2014, January). Cryptanalytic results on knapsack cryptosystem using binary particle swarm optimization. In *Proceedings of International Joint Conference SOCO'14-CISIS'14-ICEUTE'14* (pp. 375-384). Springer International Publishing.

Jang, J. S. (1993). ANFIS: Adaptive-network-based fuzzy inference system. *IEEE Transactions on Systems, Man, and Cybernetics*, *23*(3), 665–685. doi:10.1109/21.256541

Jang, J. S., & Sun, C. T. (1995). Neuro-fuzzy modeling and control. *Proceedings of the IEEE*, *83*(3), 378–406. doi:10.1109/5.364486

Jang, J. S. R., Sun, C. T., & Mizutani, E. (1997). *Neuro-Fuzzy and Soft Computing: A Computational Approach to Learning and Machine Intelligence*. Prentice-Hall, Inc.

Kanter, I., Kinzel, W., & Kanter, E. (2002). Secure exchange of information by synchronization of neural networks. *Europhysics Letters*, *57*(1), 141–147. doi:10.1209/epl/i2002-00552-9

Kar, S., Das, S., & Ghosh, P. K. (2014). Applications of neuro fuzzy systems: A brief review and future outline. *Applied Soft Computing*, *15*, 243–259. doi:10.1016/j.asoc.2013.10.014

Kellegoz, T., Toklu, B., & Wilson, J. (2008). Comparing efficiencies of genetic crossover operators for one machine total weighted tardiness problem. *Applied Mathematics and Computation*, *199*(2), 590–598. doi:10.1016/j.amc.2007.10.013

Kenndy, J., & Eberhart, R. C. (1995). Particle swarm optimization. In *Proceedings of IEEE International Conference on Neural Networks* (Vol. 4, pp. 1942-1948). IEEE. doi:10.1109/ICNN.1995.488968

Kinzel, W., & Kanter, I. (2002). Neural cryptography. In *Proc. of the 9th International Conference on Neural Information Processing*. Academic Press. doi:10.1109/ICONIP.2002.1202841

Konar, A. (2005). *Computational Intelligence: Principles, Techniques and Applications*. Springer. doi:10.1007/b138935

Koza, J. R. (1992). *Genetic Programming: On the Programming of Computers by Means of Natural Selection*. MIT Press.

Koza, J. R., & Rice, J. P. (1994). *Genetic Programming II: Automatic Discovery of Reusable Programs*. Cambridge, MA: MIT Press.

Laskari, E. C., Meletiou, G. C., & Vrahatis, M. N. (2005). Problems of cryptography as discrete optimization tasks. *Nonlinear Analysis: Theory, Methods & Applications*, 63(5), e831–e837.

Lee, Z. J., & Chang, L. Y. (2014). Apply fuzzy decision tree to information security risk assessment. *International Journal of Fuzzy Systems*, 16(2), 265–269.

Lee, J.-G., Sang-Hyun, L. & Kyung-Il, M. (2013). Smart Home Security System Based on ANFIS. In *Proceedings of the 7th International Conference on Information Security and Assurance*. Academic Press.

Li, X., & Wang, J. (2007). A steganographic method based upon JPEG and particle swarm optimization algorithm. *Information Sciences*, 177(15), 3099–3109. doi:10.1016/j.ins.2007.02.008

Li, Y., Yin, J., & Wu, G. (2011). An approach to evaluating the computer network security with intuitionistic fuzzy information. *AISS: Advances in Information Sciences and Service Sciences*, 3(7), 195–200. doi:10.4156/aiss.vol3.issue7.23

Liu, C. Y., Woungang, I., Chao, H. C., Dhurandher, S. K., Chi, T. Y., & Obaidat, M. S. (2011, December). Message security in multi-path ad hoc networks using a neural network-based cipher. In *Proceedings of Global Telecommunications Conference* (GLOBECOM 2011). Academic Press.

Maass, W. (1997). Networks of spiking neurons: The third generation of neural network models. *Neural Networks*, 10(9), 1659–1671. doi:10.1016/S0893-6080(97)00011-7

Mehrotra, K., Mohan, C. K., & Ranka, S. (1997). *Elements of Artificial Neural Networks*. MIT Press.

Mislovaty, R., Klein, E., Kanter, I., & Kinzel, W. (2003). Public channel cryptography by synchronization of neural networks and chaotic maps. *Physical Review Letters*, 91(11), 118701. doi:10.1103/PhysRevLett.91.118701 PMID:14525461

Mu, N., & Liao, X. (2013). An approach for designing neural cryptography. In Advances in Neural Networks (pp. 99-108). Springer Berlin Heidelberg. doi:10.1007/978-3-642-39065-4_13

Nauck, D., Klawonn, F., & Kruse, R. (1997). *Foundations of Neuro-Fuzzy Systems*. John Wiley & Sons, Inc.

Noraini, M. R., & John, G. (2011, July). Genetic algorithm performance with different selection strategies in solving TSP. In *Proceedings of the World Congress on Engineering*. Academic Press.

Obaidat, M. S., & Macchairolo, D. T. (1994). A multilayer neural network system for computer access security. *IEEE Transactions on Systems, Man, and Cybernetics*, 24(5), 806–813. doi:10.1109/21.293498

Papadimitriou, C. H., & Steiglitz, K. (1982). *Combinatorial Optimization—Algorithms and Complexity*. New York: Dover.

Papadimitriou, S., Bezerianos, A., & Bountis, T. (1999). Radial basis function networks as chaotic generators for secure communication systems. *International Journal of Bifurcation and Chaos in Applied Sciences and Engineering, 9*(01), 221–232. doi:10.1142/S0218127499000109

Paterson, N. R., & Livesey, M. (1996). Distinguishing genotype and phenotype in genetic programming. In *Proceedings of Late Breaking Papers at the Genetic Programming Conference*. Stanford University.

Paugam-Moisy, H., & Bohte, S. (2012). Computing with spiking neuron networks. In *Handbook of Natural Computing* (pp. 335–376). Springer Berlin Heidelberg. doi:10.1007/978-3-540-92910-9_10

Powell, M. J. (1987, January). Radial basis functions for multivariable interpolation: A review. In *Algorithms for Approximation* (pp. 143–167). Clarendon Press.

Qureshi, S., Asar, A., Rehman, A., & Baseer, A. (2011). Swarm intelligence based detection of malicious beacon node for secure localization in wireless sensor networks. *Journal of Emerging Trends in Engineering and Applied Sciences, 2*(4), 664–672.

Ross, T. J. (2009). *Fuzzy Logic with Engineering Applications*. John Wiley & Sons.

Ruttor, A., Kinzel, W., & Kanter, I. (2007). Dynamics of neural cryptography. *Physical Review E: Statistical, Nonlinear, and Soft Matter Physics, 75*(5), 056104. doi:10.1103/PhysRevE.75.056104 PMID:17677130

Ruttor, A., Kinzel, W., Naeh, R., & Kanter, I. (2006). Genetic attack on neural cryptography. *Physical Review E: Statistical, Nonlinear, and Soft Matter Physics, 73*(3), 036121. doi:10.1103/PhysRevE.73.036121 PMID:16605612

Ruttor, A., Kinzel, W., Shacham, L., & Kanter, I. (2004). Neural cryptography with feedback. *Physical Review E: Statistical, Nonlinear, and Soft Matter Physics, 69*(4), 046110. doi:10.1103/PhysRevE.69.046110 PMID:15169072

Schmidt, S., Steele, R., Dillon, T. S., & Chang, E. (2007). Fuzzy trust evaluation and credibility development in multi-agent systems. *Applied Soft Computing, 7*(2), 492–505. doi:10.1016/j.asoc.2006.11.002

Sendhoff, B., Roberts, M., & Yao, X. (2006). Evolutionary computation benchmarking repository. *IEEE Computational Intelligence Magazine*, 50–60.

Shi, Y., & Eberhart, R. C. (2001). Fuzzy adaptive particle swarm optimization. In *Proceedings of the 2001 Congress on Evolutionary Computation*, (Vol. 1, pp. 101-106). doi:10.1109/CEC.2001.934377

Sivanandam, S. N., & Deepa, S. N. (2008). *Introduction to Genetic Algorithms*. New York: Springer.

Spears, W., & De Jong, K. A. (1990). *An Analysis of Multi-Point Crossover*. Morgan Kaufmann.

Specht, D. F. (1990). Probabilistic neural networks. *Neural Networks, 3*(1), 109–118. doi:10.1016/0893-6080(90)90049-Q PMID:18282828

Srinivas, M., & Patnaik, L. M. (1994). Adaptive probabilities of crossover and mutation in genetic algorithms. *IEEE Transactions on Systems, Man, and Cybernetics, 24*(4), 656–667. doi:10.1109/21.286385

Srinoy, S. (2007, April). Intrusion detection model based on particle swarm optimization and support vector machine. In *Proceedings of IEEE Symposium on Computational Intelligence in Security and Defense Applications, CISDA 2007* (pp. 186-192). IEEE. doi:10.1109/CISDA.2007.368152

Stützle, T., & Hoos, H. (1996). *Improving the Ant System: A detailed report on the max-min ant system. Technical Report*. Technical University of Darmstadt.

Stützle, T., & Hoos, H. H. (2000). Max–min ant system. *Future Generation Computer Systems, 16*(8), 889–914. doi:10.1016/S0167-739X(00)00043-1

Syswerda, G. (1989). Uniform crossover in genetic algorithms. In *Proceedings of the 3rd International Conference on Genetic Algorithms*. San Francisco, CA: Academic Press.

Tsakonas, A., & Dounias, G. (2002, April). Hybrid computational intelligence schemes in complex domains: An extended review. In *Proceedings of the Second Hellenic Conference on AI: Methods and Applications of Artificial Intelligence* (pp. 494-512). Springer-Verlag.

Woźniak, S., Almási, A. D., Cristea, V., Leblebici, Y., & Engbersen, T. (2015). Review of advances in neural networks: Neural design technology stack. In *Proceedings of ELM-2014* (vol. 1, pp. 367-376). Springer International Publishing. doi:10.1007/978-3-319-14063-6_31

Wu, S. X., & Banzhaf, W. (2013). The use of computational intelligence in intrusion detection systems: A review. *Applied Soft Computing, 10*(1), 1–35. doi:10.1016/j.asoc.2009.06.019

Yang, X. S. (2015). *Recent Advances in Swarm Intelligence and Evolutionary Computation*. Springer. doi:10.1007/978-3-319-13826-8

Yao, J. T., Zhao, S. L., & Saxton, L. V. (2005, March). A study on fuzzy intrusion detection. In *Defense and Security* (pp. 23–30). International Society for Optics and Photonics.

Yao, X. (1999). Evolving artificial neural networks. *Proceedings of the IEEE, 87*(9), 1423–1447. doi:10.1109/5.784219

Yayik, A., & Kutlu, Y. (2013, April). Improving Pseudo random number generator using artificial neural networks. In *Proceedings of Signal Processing and Communications Applications Conference* (SIU). doi:10.1109/SIU.2013.6531494

Zadeh, L. A. (1965). Fuzzy sets. *Information and Control, 8*(3), 338–353. doi:10.1016/S0019-9958(65)90241-X

Zadeh, L. A. (1975). The concept of a linguistic variable and its application to approximate reasoning—I, II, III. *Information Sciences, 8*(4), 301–357. doi:10.1016/0020-0255(75)90046-8

Zadeh, L. A. (1994). Fuzzy logic, neural networks, and soft computing. *Communications of the ACM, 37*(3), 77–84. doi:10.1145/175247.175255

Zadeh, L. A. (1998). Some reflections on soft computing, granular computing and their roles in the conception, design and utilization of information/intelligent systems. *Soft Computing, 2*(1), 23–25. doi:10.1007/s005000050030

ADDITIONAL READING

Al-Qaheri, H., Mustafi, A., & Banerjee, S. (2010). Digital watermarking using ant colony optimization in fractional Fourier domain. *Journal of Information Hiding and Multimedia Signal Processing, 1*(3), 179–189.

Barni, M., Orlandi, C., & Piva, A. (2006, September). A privacy-preserving protocol for neural-network-based computation. In *Proceedings of the 8th Workshop on Multimedia and Security* (pp. 146-151).

Blum, C. (2005). Ant colony optimization: Introduction and recent trends. *Physics of Life Reviews, 2*(4), 353–373. doi:10.1016/j.plrev.2005.10.001

Chen, T., & Zhong, S. (2009). Privacy-preserving backpropagation neural network learning. *IEEE Transactions on Neural Networks, 20*(10), 1554–1564. doi:10.1109/TNN.2009.2026902 PMID:19709975

Dorigo, M., & Blum, C. (2005). Ant colony optimization theory: A survey. *Theoretical Computer Science, 344*(2), 243–278. doi:10.1016/j.tcs.2005.05.020

Gao, T., Gu, Q., & Emmanuel, S. (2009). A novel image authentication scheme based on hyper-chaotic cell neural network. *Chaos, Solitons, and Fractals, 42*(1), 548–553. doi:10.1016/j.chaos.2009.01.017

Hsu, C. S., & Tu, S. F. (2010, February). Finding optimal LSB substitution using ant colony optimization algorithm. In *Second International Conference on Communication Software and Networks* (pp. 293-297). doi:10.1109/ICCSN.2010.61

Ibrahim, S., & Maarof, M. A. (2005). A review on biological inspired computation in cryptology. *Jurnal Teknologi Maklumat, 17*(1), 90–98.

Isasi, P., & Hernandez, J. C. (2004). Introduction to the applications of evolutionary computation in computer security and cryptography. *Computational Intelligence, 20*(3), 445–449. doi:10.1111/j.0824-7935.2004.00244.x

Kinzel, W., & Kanter, I. (2002). Interacting neural networks and cryptography. In *Advances in Solid State Physics* (pp. 383–391). Springer Berlin Heidelberg. doi:10.1007/3-540-45618-X_30

Lian, S. (2009). A block cipher based on chaotic neural networks. *Neurocomputing, 72*(4), 1296–1301. doi:10.1016/j.neucom.2008.11.005

Lian, S., Liu, Z., Ren, Z., & Wang, H. (2006, May). Hash function based on chaotic neural networks. In *Proceedings of IEEE International Symposium on Circuits and Systems, ISCAS*.

Lippmann, R. P., & Cunningham, R. K. (2000). Improving intrusion detection performance using keyword selection and neural networks. *Computer Networks, 34*(4), 597–603. doi:10.1016/S1389-1286(00)00140-7

Obaidat, M. S., & Macchairolo, D. T. (1994). A multilayer neural network system for computer access security. *IEEE Transactions on Systems, Man, and Cybernetics, 24*(5), 806–813. doi:10.1109/21.293498

Pan, Z. S., Chen, S. C., Hu, G. B., & Zhang, D. Q. (2003, November). Hybrid neural network and C4.5 for misuse detection. In *International Conference on Machine Learning and Cybernetics*.

Peng, J., Zhang, D., & Liao, X. (2009). A digital image encryption algorithm based on hyper-chaotic cellular neural network. *Fundamenta Informaticae*, *90*(3), 269–282.

Ruan, D. (Ed.). (2010). *Computational Intelligence in Complex Decision Systems* (Vol. 2). Springer Science & Business Media. doi:10.2991/978-94-91216-29-9

Shihab, K. (2006). A backpropagation neural network for computer network security. *Journal of Computer Science*, *2*(9), 710–715. doi:10.3844/jcssp.2006.710.715

Volná, E. (2000). Using neural network in cryptography. In *The State of the Art in Computational Intelligence* (pp. 262–267). Physica-Verlag HD. doi:10.1007/978-3-7908-1844-4_42

Volna, E., Kotyrba, M., Kocian, V., & Janosek, M. (2012, May). *Cryptography based on neural network* (pp. 386–391). ECMS.

Wang, X. Y., Yang, L., Liu, R., & Kadir, A. (2010). A chaotic image encryption algorithm based on perceptron model. *Nonlinear Dynamics*, *62*(3), 615–621. doi:10.1007/s11071-010-9749-8

Wright, J. L., & Manic, M. (2010, July). Neural network architecture selection analysis with application to cryptography location. In *International Joint Conference on Neural Networks* (IJCNN), (pp. 1-6). doi:10.1109/IJCNN.2010.5596315

Xiao, D., & Liao, X. (2004). A combined hash and encryption scheme by chaotic neural network. In Advances in Neural Networks (ISNN 2004) (pp. 633-638). Springer Berlin Heidelberg. doi:10.1007/978-3-540-28648-6_101

Xiao, D., Liao, X., & Wang, Y. (2009). Parallel keyed hash function construction based on chaotic neural network. *Neurocomputing*, *72*(10), 2288–2296. doi:10.1016/j.neucom.2008.12.031

Yu, W., & Cao, J. (2006). Cryptography based on delayed chaotic neural networks. *Physics Letters. [Part A]*, *356*(4), 333–338. doi:10.1016/j.physleta.2006.03.069

Zhang, H., Feng, X., Qin, Z. P., & Liu, Y. Z. (2002). Evolutionary cryptosystems and evolutionary design for DES. *Journal-China Institute of Communications*, *23*(5), 57–64.

KEY TERMS AND DEFINITIONS

Computational Intelligence: It is a set of computational methodologies used to solve problems requiring intelligence.

Evolutionary Computation: It is a subfield of computational intelligence that includes a number of global optimization methods.

Fuzzy Logic: It is a form of many-valued logic that deals with partial truth, where the truth value ranges between completely true and completely false.

Genetic Algorithm: It is one of the evolutionary computation algorithms, which is a population-based iterative improvement search algorithm used to solve optimization problems using techniques inspired by natural evolution.

Genetic Programming: It is an application of genetic algorithm, in which the structure under adaption is a population of programs. Thus, the solution of a problem is given as a computer program.

Neural Networks: As the term implies, neural networks have a biologically inspired modeling capability (representing a brain) for information processing. A neural network is a set of processing elements connected using weighted links.

Practical Swarm Intelligence: It is a population-based computational method used for multi-parameter optimization. A population (swarm) of candidate solutions (particles) moves in the search space, and the movement of the particles is influenced both by their own best known position and the swarm's global best known position.

Chapter 2
Computational Intelligence in Cryptology

Wasan Shaker Awad
Ahlia University, Bahrain

El-Sayed M. El-Alfy
King Fahd University of Petroleum and Minerals, Saudi Arabia

ABSTRACT

Computational intelligence (CI) has attracted the attention of many researchers for its effectiveness in solving different kinds of problems. It has been applied to solve problems in a wide area of applications. The aim of this chapter is to present an overview of existing literature about the applications of CI in cryptology. It demonstrates and studies the applicability of CI in cryptology. The problems examined in this chapter are the automated design of cipher systems, and the automated cryptanalysis of cipher systems. It has been shown that CI methods, such as genetic algorithms, genetic programming, Tabu search, and memetic computing are effective tools to solve most of cryptology problems.

INTRODUCTION

Cryptology problems, such as designing good cryptographic systems and analyzing them, attracted many researchers, and hence we can find in the literature different techniques and methods that have been proposed to solve these problems. In recent years, many algorithms that take advantage of approaches based on computational intelligence (CI) techniques have been proposed, and there is a growing interest toward CI techniques because of these recent successes. However, there still are a number of open problems in the field that should be addressed.

In this chapter, the most important achievements in solving information security related problems using CI are presented. The main objective is to investigate the application of various CI techniques in the fields of automated cryptanalysis and automated cryptographic function generation (cipher systems design), to demonstrate the applicability of CI in solving these problems, and to give interested researchers an overview of emerging methodologies and new directions in cryptosystems as the heart of information security.

DOI: 10.4018/978-1-4666-9426-2.ch002

According to our research, several works have been found that considered the applications of CI to cryptographic problems; these techniques include Genetic Algorithms (GA), Simulated Annealing (SA), Tabu search, Ant Colony Optimization (ACO), Artificial Neural Networks (ANN), and DNA. Moreover, a number of authors gave surveys of cryptographic applications, such as designing different types of cipher systems (RSA hardware, S-Boxes, and key-stream generators) in addition to attacking cipher systems, that can be developed by using CI methods (Clark, 1998; Volná, 2000; Isasi and Julio, 2004; Isasi, 2005; Xiao et al., 2006; Laskari, et al. 2007; Anam et al., 2010; Picek and Golub, 2011; Danziger and Henriques, 2011; Zhang and Fu, 2012; Cherian et al. 2013). It has been concluded that CI techniques show potential for use in the field of automated cryptology, some promise when used to optimize existing methods for attacking certain ciphers, and CI is very effective for problems which require searching a large solution space for solutions with good characteristics. In addition, CI techniques can help to create ciphers that are more robust. However, the problem formulation and representation, and the proper definition of the fitness function have a great effect on the performance of CI methods in cryptography. In this chapter, a more comprehensive survey is presented.

In the next section, the core concepts of cryptology are first reviewed briefly. Then, the third and fourth sections discuss the CI-based methods for designing and attacking different classes of cryptographic systems.

OVERVIEW OF CRYPTOLOGY

The growth in computer systems, and computer communication and networking has increased the dependence of organizations on the information stored, processed, and communicated using these systems. This, in turn, has led to a heightened awareness of the need to security. Security is the quality or state of being secure, to be free from danger and to be protected from adversaries. Information security is the process of protecting information from unauthorized access, use, disclosure, destruction, or modification. One of information security goals is confidentiality, which is probably the most common aspect of information security. It is about protection of confidential information. An organization needs to guard against malicious actions that endanger the confidentiality of its information. Attacks threatening confidentiality are snooping and traffic analysis. The confidentiality goal can be achieved by applying encryption mechanism (Stalling, 2006).

A lot of work has been done in cryptology. Cryptology is the study of the encryption techniques to protect data and the techniques to attack the encryption techniques. Thus, it is combination of two areas: cryptanalysis and cryptography, where cryptanalysis is the study of the techniques used for breaking cryptographic (cipher) systems, and cryptography is the science of protecting private information against unauthorized access by encrypting it.

Any cryptographic system (cryptosystem, or cipher system) has five elements: plaintext (clear text), ciphertext (encrypted text), encryption algorithm which is a procedure used to encipher (encrypt) the plaintext and transform it to ciphertext, decryption algorithm which is the inverse of the encryption algorithm, and the key which is a parameter used to prevent the plaintext from being easily revealed by an authorized person (Schneier, 1996; Stalling, 2006).

Nowadays, you can find different kinds of cipher systems (cryptosystems), used for encrypting the private information. A number of cipher systems have been proposed with different levels of security. Choosing among cryptographic alternatives a critical and sensitive decision. In these situations, there is a way to evaluate alternatives and compare them in order to reach the optimized solution to the relevant security issue. The evaluation criteria for the cryptographic methods are (Schneier, 1996):

1. **Level of Security:** The number of operations required to break the cryptographic method.
2. **Functionality:** Or effectiveness.
3. **Performance:** The efficiency of a cryptographic method.
4. **Ease of Implementation:** The difficulty of realizing the cryptographic method in a practical instantiation.

The cryptosystems can be classified into modern and classical systems, as shown in Figure 1. Modern cipher systems are subdivided into block ciphers and stream ciphers. Block ciphers divide the plaintext into blocks and encipher each block independently, such as Data Encryption Standard (DES) and Advanced Encryption Standards (AES) systems (Schneier, 1996). Most symmetric block ciphers are based on a Feistel cipher structure (Feistel, 1973), which are iterated product systems combining substitution and transposition that implement the Shanon theory of information security (Shanon, 1949). The security of block ciphers depends on a number of factors, such as, block size, key size, number of rounds, subkey generation, and the complexity of round function.

Figure 1. Cipher systems classification

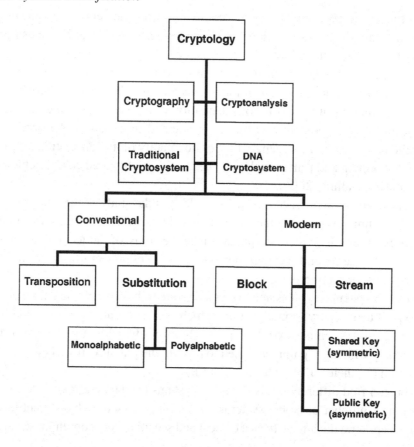

Substitution ciphers encrypt plaintexts by replacing one symbol with another. In polyalphabetic substitution, each occurrence of a character may have a different substitute. Thus, the relationship between a character in the plaintext to a character in the ciphertext is one-to-many. While, in monoalphabetic substitution, the relationship between a symbol in the plaintext to a symbol in the ciphertext is always one-to-one. Transposition ciphers encrypt plaintexts by changing the location of the symbols (Schneier, 1996; Stalling, 2006).

Stream ciphers are extremely fast and easy to implement, in addition, they usually have very minimal hardware resource requirements. Therefore stream ciphers are of great importance in applications where encryption speed is paramount and where area-constrained or memory constrained devices make it impractical to use block ciphers. Stream ciphers can operate one data unit as small as a bit or a character. Each stream cipher composed of keystream generator to generate keystream to be mixed using a mixer with plaintext to produce ciphertext. A number of stream cipher systems have been proposed which are of variety degrees of security, such as Geffe, and Stop-and-Go generators (Beker and Piper, 1982; Rueppel, 1986; Schneier, 1996). Furthermore, a number of different kinds of stream ciphers which are based on different techniques other than linear feedback shift registers (LFSRs), such as Cellular Automata (CA) (Szaban, Seredynski, and Bouvry, 2006), and Algebraic Shift Register (Goresky, and Klapper, 2006) have been proposed. The stream cipher system's security depends entirely on the inside of keystram generator. The security of this generator can be analyzed in terms of randomness, linear complexity, and correlation immunity (Massey, 1976; Zeng, 1991; Gustafson, 1994; Caballero-Gil, 2000; Garcia, and Fuster-Sabater, 2000). Thus, good keystrem generators have the following features:

1. They generate long period keystreams.
2. The generated keystreams are random.
3. The generated keystreams are of large linear complexity.
4. They have high degrees of correlation immunity.

On the other hand, classical ciphers composed of simpler encryption functions comparable with modern ciphers, and its security depends entirely on the secret keys.

AUTOMATED DESIGN OF CIPHER SYSTEMS

This section is for presenting the applications of CI in the automated design of different classes of cipher systems. The design of a good system is a hard process, that is because of the confliction in the design requirements, such as high level of security, efficiency, ease of implementation, and functionality. Therefore, this problem has attracted a number of researchers as described in this section.

Stream Ciphers

The first application of CI presented here is the design of stream cipher systems automatically. This type of cipher systems can be easily analyzed and formulated, and this makes the automated design of stream cipher is feasible.

Awad (2011a, 2011b, 2013) proposed an automated design method to design the LFSR-based keystream generators of stream ciphers, which is a new promising direction for automated stream cipher design. This method uses GP in which the structure under adaptation is a set of programs representing the candidate keystream generators (linear or nonlinear). The evaluation method used to evaluate the candidate keystream generators is based on the keystream desired properties. The keystream generators considered here are LFSR-based generators. Thus, the important basic function which is the shift register should be included. There are a number of metrics used to analyze keystream generators, which are keystream randomness, linear complexity and correlation immunity. Therefore, these metrics had to be taken in account in designing keystream generators, and they are in general hard to be achieved. It has been shown the capability of GP in designing the desired stream ciphers. Stream cipher design methods presented can be used for evolving any generator that satisfies the given requirements, such as period length, and randomness. These requirements are expressed mathematically in the fitness function. Three algorithms have been designed and applied: simple GP (SGP), simulated annealing programming (SAP), and adaptive GP (AGP). The numerical results have showed that the application of GP in stream cipher design is useful. Also, SAP and AGP methods are more effective than SGP that is because; the performance of SGP algorithm has been improved by the dynamic setting of the algorithm parameters and by using SA with GP.

Also, Abdulsalam (2011) presented a simulated annealing algorithm for generating random keystreams with large complexity. He considered randomness, and linear complexity in the evaluation. Results are presented demonstrating the effectiveness of the method.

LFSR is the building block of the keystream generators, recently CA has been used instead of LFSR. GAs have been applied to solve the problem of generation by CA of high quality pseudorandom sequences (PNS) useful in cryptography. CA is in the simplest case a collection of two-state cells arranged in a lattice, and locally interacting in a discrete time t. The transition function, called rule, defines the rule of updating the cells. Not all rules are suitable for cryptography. Goresky and Klapper (2006) used GA to find a set of rules suitable for cryptographic purposes. In this method, an individual of a population is a set of rules. Rules of an individual are assigned randomly to cells of CA, and CA runs some predefined number of time steps producing PNSs. Next, a fitness of each rule is calculated according to the quality of corresponding PNSs, and the genetic operators are applied. GA runs a predefined number of generations. The results showed that GA is an effective technique for solving this complex problem, i.e., the design of CA-based keystream generators.

Another CI tool used is NN. Karras, and Zorkadis (2003), presented novel techniques, which rely on ANN architectures, to generate pseudorandom Binary sequences. It proposed a non-linear test method for the quality assessment of the required non-predictability property, which relies on feedforward neural networks. ANN based pseudorandom keystream generators have been evaluated using different factors. The results showed that the proposed generators behave significantly better than the traditional ones, in particular, in terms of non-predictability.

Thus, so far, four CI techniques have been used to design stream cipher automatically, which are NN, GP, GA, and SA. These techniques have been applied successfully to design good keystream generators of two types, LFSR and CA generators.

Block Ciphers

The automated design of block cipher has been implemented using a number of CI techniques. The following are examples of the work done in this field.

Xiangyang (2010) presented an optimization method of S-box based on genetic Tabu algorithm. The proposed method made use of niche technology to maintain the population diversity and prevent premature convergence. The authors used different performance characteristics of S-box as the evaluative target. Experimental results showed that the improved genetic Tabu algorithm in this paper is a feasible and effective method to construct S-box, at the same time, a number of high non-linearity and low differential uniformity S-box can be found.

Another application of GA is the construction of Boolean functions for cipher systems, such as block ciphers and stream ciphers. In symmetric cryptology the resistance of attack depends on the nonlinearity properties of the Boolean functions describing cipher components such as S-boxes of block ciphers, and the nonlinear combination functions of nonlinear stream ciphers. The design of Boolean functions with properties of cryptographic significance is a hard task. Thus, this problem has been considered by a number of researchers such as Clark and Jacob (2004), and Millan, Clark, and Dawson (1997) who have proposed a GA-based method for finding Boolean functions which are nearly always have high degree of nonlinearity. The population individuals are the candidate highly nonlinear Boolean functions. The fitness function used is to measure the nonlinearity degree of the Boolean functions.

GP has been also examined to solve the problem of nonlinear function design. Hernández, Isasi, and Arco-Calderón (2003), proposed the use of GP for finding nonlinear functions using only very efficient operations, so that the resulting functions are extremely efficient both in hardware and in software.

Furthermore, some other researchers used GA as encryption functions. Agarwal (2012) proposed a GA based secret key image encryption method. After the examinations of the proposed method, the authors found that this encryption method satisfies the requirements of any encryption method needed to encrypt images. Also, Rajendra and Kaur (2011) proposed a new approach to data security using the concept of GA and brain mu waves with pseudorandom binary sequence to encrypt and decrypt the plaintexts. It has been shown that this approach is of high security level, and high feasibility for practical implementation.

Various paradigms of ANNs have also been investigated in this area. For example, multilayer perceptron has been used to design symmetric block ciphers (Yee and De Silva, 2002). Another approach for S-box design based on ANN is presented in (Kotlarz and Kotulski, 2005). A combination of ANN and chaos, known as chaotic neural network, have been proposed to design a block ciphers (Yu and Cao, 2006; Lian, 2009). Recurrent neural networks for designing symmetric block ciphers have also been addressed by Arvandi and Sadeghian (2008).

Based on the above demonstration, the only CI methods used are GA, Tabu search, and ANN, which have been used to design nonlinear Boolean functions and block ciphers automatically. Nonlinear Boolean functions and S-boxes are components that have great influence on the security level of block ciphers. Furthermore, GP has been used for evolving efficient nonlinear functions.

Other Cryptography Applications

One of the problems related to public-key cryptography that has been addressed using CI methods is the solution of Diophantine equation (Mordell, 1969). The Diophantine equation is a polynomial equation of the form $f(a_1, a_2, ..., a_n, x_1, x2, ..., x_n) = N$, where a_i and N are integer constants and x_i are variables.

Regardless of its importance in elliptic curve cryptography, it has no general solution method. Hence, it can be of great interest as an application area for CI techniques. For instance, Abraham and his colleagues have developed several CI methods to find numerical solutions for equations with reasonable number of variables and large values of N, e.g. using GA (Abraham & Sanglikar, 2001), using simulated annealing (Abraham & Sanglikar, 2008), using swarm optimization (Abraham et al., 2010), and using ant colony optimization (Abraham et al., 2013). Recently, Perez et al. (2013) applied a discrete particle swarm optimization technique to find numerical solutions for some exponential and nonlinear Diophantine systems of equations. Another recent attempt is the application of fuzzy adaptive simulated annealing for global optimization of Diophantine equations (Aguiar Jr, 2014).

Unlike traditional cryptography, DNA cryptographic systems have emerged as a promising alternative (Leier et al., 2000; Xiao et al., 2006; Popovici, 2010; Anam et al., 2010; Vijayakumar et al., 2011; Zhang and Fu, 2012; Mantha, 2012; Jacob et al. 2013; Liu and Yin, 2013). A number of prominent algorithms based on biological processes and DNA computing have been developed, e.g. Polymerase Chain Reaction (PCR) and DNA chip. DNA-based cryptography have been applied to data encryption and decryption. For instance, Tanaka et al. (2005) proposed a public-key cryptography system with one-way function using DNA. Another asymmetric cryptosystem based on DNA and biological processes is presented in (Lai et al. 2010). Other examples can be found in (Cui et al. 2008; Tornea and Borda, 2009; Yang et al., 2014). DNA technology has also found applications in symmetric-key cryptosystems (Lu et al. 2007; Roy et al. 2011). For a recent survey on DNA cryptographic methods, we refer the reader to (Cherian et al. 2013). A hardware implementation of DNA based cryptography is presented in (Naveen et al. 2013).

AUTOMATED CRYPTANALYSIS OF CIPHER SYSTEMS

Many automated attacks have been proposed in the literature for attacking different kinds of cipher systems utilizing different CI techniques such as GA, GP, SA, and the Tabu search. This section is to demonstrate these attacking methods to break the following cipher systems.

Block Ciphers

Garg (2009a) presented a memetic algorithm and GA approach for the cryptanalysis of Simplified Data Encryption Standard (SDES) algorithm. Though SDES is a simple cipher, its building blocks are also used in other ciphers. A memetic algorithm is an extension of the traditional GA which is used to keep high population diversity and reduce the likelihood premature convergence. The performance of memetic algorithm has been compared with GA in the cryptanalysis of SDES. The experimental result showed that memetic algorithm is better for finding the number of keys accurately in comparison with GA. The second comparison was made upon the computation time for recovering the keys from the search space. From the experiments, it was found that GA is most efficient algorithm as almost same keys is achieved in shorter time but in contrast for a large amount of cipher text the memetic algorithm can be seen outperform GA. Results indicated that memetic algorithm is extremely powerful technique for the cryptanalysis of SDES.

In the study of Garg (2009b), the author studied the applicability and effectiveness of EC techniques in solving the NP-Hard combinatorial problem. Thus, the author tested several EC techniques such as memetic algorithm, GA and SA for the cryptanalysis of SDES. Also, the authors compared between memetic algorithm, GA and SA to investigate the performance of these algorithms in attacking SDES. The computational results showed that memetic algorithm performs better than GA and SA.

Nalini and Raghavendra (2007) have demonstrated that optimization heuristics such as GA and its extension of adaptive GA, Tabu search, SA, and PSO, are ideally suited for the cryptanalysis of SDES and a modified version of DES. Experimental results demonstrated good performance for Tabu search to break SDES, and for PSO to break the modified DES.

Nalini and Raghavendra (2007) presented a systematic study of efficient heuristics in the attack of SDES. One of these optimization heuristic algorithms used in this study is GA. In this method, the population of individuals consists of different keys considered for cryptanalysis and the fitness function is based on the pair of letters frequency. The genetic operations used are selection, crossover, and mutation. The keys are represented as strings of bits. The experiments showed that GA did not perform better than other brute force methods.

ANNs have also been used as a cryptanalysis tool for a Fiestel-type block cipher (Albassal and Wahdan, 2004; Rao et al., 2009). Another example is presented in (Alani, 2012a,b) where an ANN is trained to attack DES and Triple-DES.

As a result, the only cipher system considered in the automated cryptanalysis is SDES. Different CI methods have been examined, which are GA and its extension of adaptive GA, Tabu search, SA, memetic algorithm and PSO. It has been shown that memetic algorithm and Tabu search is better than GA in breaking SDES and GA did not perform better than brute force search. In addition, ANN has been used to attack DES.

Stream Ciphers

Stream ciphers have also been attacked using CI as presented in this section. For example, Awad (2008) proposed a GA-based method to find the linear equivalence of a Binary keystream given a keystream of sufficient length. The output of the proposed method is a shortest LFSR that can generate a given keystream. It has been shown by the computational results that GA is very effective in solving this problem.

Also, in the study of Al-Bastaki and Awad (2004), an attacking method has been proposed to attack stream ciphers using GA. The aim of GA was to find the feedback polynomial and the initial state in addition to the length of LFSR, knowing part of plaintext. In the known–plaintext attack, the known plaintext is XORed with the corresponding ciphertext to find the corresponding keystream which is the output of the keystream generator. This method provides successful results in determining the feedback polynomials and the initial states. Variant lengths of shift registers have been examined. Increasing the size of population can reduce the number of generations required to find the correct setting, but it needs more storage space. In general, the number of generations required in determining the correct initial setting and the correct feedback polynomial of a keystream generator depends on the key space size.

Another attacking method has been proposed by Abbas (1998), he proposed a GA-based correlation attack to break stream ciphers. In this method, GA has been used successfully to reduce the number of trails of the correlation attack.

Bhateja and Din (2013) presented an artificial neural network approach to distinguish RC4 key stream with respect to random key stream.

Public-Key Ciphers

Ramani and Balasubramanian (2011) proposed a GA-based method to break knapsack cipher with a knapsack sequence of size 16. They studied the performance of GA with different control parameters. The authors also presented the previous related works, and as they claimed all previous attempts to attack knapsack ciphers with sequence of size 8 (which supports ASCII encoding of characters).

Simple Transposition Ciphers

To attack transposition ciphers two CI methods have been used, which are GA and PSO. But, we couldn't find any comparison between these two methods.

Al-khalid et al. (2013) investigated the use of GA in attacking transposition ciphers. It has been shown that such algorithm could be used to discover the key for transposition cipher. The fitness evaluation used was based on bi- and tri-gram frequency.

Hammood et al. (2010) presented a PSO-based method for breaking transposition cipher. PSO is utilized for the automated discovery of the key, and hence the plaintext, knowing ciphertext only. The algorithm has been shown to be effective in finding good solutions. Experimental results showed the ability of PSO in finding the correct secret key which is used to recover the plaintext, and the PSO is efficient in determining the optimal choice of key to break ciphertexts. The number of possible visited keys required for finding the secret key is less than the number of possible visited keys required in the brute force attack.

Monoalphabetic Substitution Ciphers

Li et al. (2014) proposed a niche GA to break substitution ciphers based on the code analysis method. This algorithm can keep the population diversity and prevent premature convergence. The experiments results showed that the niche GA is successful attacker, thus the application of niche GA as a crypt-analysis method is feasible.

Verma (2007) presented a cryptanalysis method based on GA and Tabu search to break a monoalphabetic substitution ciphers. The performance of these algorithms in automated attack on monoalphabetic substitution ciphers has been compared and analyzed. It was found that the tabu search required less time to find the correct solution. Results indicated that Tabu search is extremely powerful technique for attacking monoalphabetic substitution cipher.

Gründlingh and Vuuren (2007) proposed a GA to break simple substitution cipher system. The search space of this method is a set of keys which is a set of all text language characters permutations. The fitness evaluation is based on the language statistical features such as letter frequency.

In Awad (1998) thesis, a GP based attacking method has been proposed. GP with Automatically defined function (ADF) (Koza, 1994) and strongly typed GP (Haynes, 1995) has been used. This method can be used for deducing the symbolic representation of a cipher system for a given ciphertext. The structure under adaption (population individuals) is a set of candidate decryption functions. The language features are used as a measurement of program (decryption function) fitness. The stopping criteria used in this method is based also on the language features, or the GP run stops after a predefined number of generations. The experimental work showed that this method is able to evolve a decryption function (with the key) for a given ciphertext only in a few number of generations.

Spillman et al. (1993) proposed a new approach to cryptanalysis based on GA. It has been shown that such algorithm could be used to discover the key for a simple substitution cipher by searching the key space. The evaluation function used in this work is based on single character and diagram frequency analysis. The experimental results showed that the proposed method can reduce the number of trails required by exhaustive search.

From the above survey, we can conclude that GA and Tabu search are effective techniques for attacking monoalphabetic substitution cipher by searching the key space, and Tabu search is more efficient than GA. Moreover, GP can be used to find the encryption function with the key for a given ciphertext, and this GP-based method can be generalized to break an intercepted ciphertext produced using different cipher systems.

Simple Polyalphabetic Ciphers

Garg (2010) presented a parallel memetic algorithm to break polyalphabetic ciphers after determining the period length. It has been proved that the proposed method is more efficient that parallel GA.

Toemeh and Arumugam (2008) proposed a cryptanalysis of polyalphabetic method by applying GA, and the applicability of GA in searching the key space of the cipher system has been studied. The frequency analysis was used as an essential factor in the fitness function. The results showed the effect of ciphertext size on recovered plaintext letters. In general, the time needed to break Vigenere cipher is less by using GA compared with other attacking methods.

Clark and Dawson (1997) proposed a parallel GA for breaking polyalphabetic ciphers; that is; after determining the period length d using Kasiski method (Beker and Piper, 1982), the given ciphertext is partitioned into d subtexts, and each one is given to a processor and breaking it using the proposed method.

Lin and Kao (1995) proposed a cryptanalysis method based on GA to break the Vernam cipher. The proposed approach is a ciphertext-only attack in which the only thing known is the plaintext which is an English document. The proposed method can find the keystream from an intercepted ciphertext and use it to break the Vernam cipher.

All attacking methods are based on GA (and parallel GA) and memetic algorithm which have been used to search the key space of polyalphabetic ciphers, and made use of language features in the objective functions.

CONCLUSION

In this survey, an overview of CI-based methods used to solve different problems in cryptology have been given, such as attacking classical, block, and stream cipher systems, designing different classes of stream cipher systems, and constructing Boolean functions necessary in cryptography. Table 1 summarizes the applications of CI in solving different cryptology problems. It has been shown that CI methods are effective tools to solve all problems considered in this survey. However, there are some difficulties in applying CI methods in cryptology, such as problem formulation and representation, and the proper definition of the objective function. Therefore, more CI techniques and Hybrid CI methods can be explored further, in addition to improve the used CI methods in different ways, such as, dynamic setting of algorithm parameters, and examining different representation methods.

Table 1. Example applications of CI techniques in cryptology

CI Cryptology	GA	GP	SA	ANN	ACO	Tabu	Memetic	PSO	DNA
Cryptanalysis of Stream Ciphers	✓			✓					
Cryptanalysis of Block Ciphers	✓		✓	✓	✓	✓	✓	✓	
Cryptanalysis of Monoalphabetic Ciphers	✓	✓				✓			
Cryptanalysis of Transposition Ciphers	✓							✓	
Cryptanalysis of Polyalphabetic Ciphers	✓						✓		
Cryptanalysis of Public-key Ciphers	✓								
Stream Ciphers Design	✓	✓	✓	✓					
Block Ciphers Design	✓	✓	✓	✓		✓			✓
Diophantine equations	✓		✓		✓			✓	

From this survey, we conclude the following:

1. GA has been used to solve all problems considered in this survey.
2. In cryptanalysis, it has been shown that Tabu search and memetic algorithm are more effective than GA.
3. Most CI applications are in cryptanalysis, and many works showed good results compared to classical methods.
4. Most of automated cryptanalysis methods are based on searching the key space of cipher systems.
5. Few works have been done in designing cipher systems automatically. We believe that CI techniques can be used to design strong cipher systems.
6. Results obtained for classical cipher systems are better than modern cipher systems.
7. CI methods can be used to improve the classical attacking methods, such as, correlation attack.
8. We found a few number of studies that discussed the problems of public key cipher systems and solving it by CI methods.
9. In the literature, we found a few number of studies to compare between CI methods applied to cryptology.
10. Finally, we advise people in the security industry to pay more attention to the capabilities of CI in breaking cipher systems, and hence, they have to consider it in the evaluation of cipher system security levels.

REFERENCES

Abbas, S. A. (1998). *Use of GA in the cryptanalysis of a class of stream cipher systems*. (Ph.D. thesis). University of Technology, Baghdad, Iraq.

Abdulsalam, A. A. (2011). Keystream generator based on simulated annealing. *Journal of Applied Computer Science & Mathematics, 10*(5).

Abraham, S., & Sanglikar, M. (2001). *A Diophantine equation solver-a genetic algorithm application* (Vol. 15). Mathematical Colloquium Journal.

Abraham, S., & Sanglikar, M. (2008). Finding numerical solution to a Diophantine Equation: simulated annealing as a viable search strategy. In *Proceedings of the International Conference on Mathematical Sciences* (*Vol. 2*, pp. 703-712). Academic Press.

Abraham, S., Sanyal, S., & Sanglikar, M. (2010). Particle swarm optimization based Diophantine equation solver. *International Journal of Bio-inspired Computation, 2*(2), 100–114. doi:10.1504/IJBIC.2010.032126

Abraham, S., Sanyal, S., & Sanglikar, M. (2013). Finding numerical solutions of Diophantine equations using ant colony optimization. *Applied Mathematics and Computation, 219*(24), 11376–11387. doi:10.1016/j.amc.2013.05.051

Agarwal, A. (2012). Secret key encryption algorithm using genetic algorithm. *International Journal of Advanced Research in Computer Science and Software Engineering, 2*(4), 216–218.

Aguiar, H. Jr. (2014). *Diophantine Equations and Fuzzy Adaptive Simulated Annealing* (Vol. 13). WSEAS Transactions on Mathematics.

Al-Bastaki, Y., & Awad, W. S. (2004, March). Attacking stream ciphers using genetic algorithm. *Asian Journal of Information Technology*, 206-211.

Al-khalid, A. S., Omran, D. S. S., & Hammood, A. (2013). Using genetic algorithms to break a simple transposition cipher. In *Proceedings of the 6th International Conference on Information Technology (ICIT)*. Academic Press.

Alani, M. M. (2012a). Neuro-cryptanalysis of DES. In *Proceedings of World Congress on Internet Security (WorldCIS)*. Academic Press.

Alani, M. M. (2012b). *Neuro-Cryptanalysis of DES and Triple-DES. In Neural Information Processing* (pp. 637–646). Springer Berlin Heidelberg. doi:10.1007/978-3-642-34500-5_75

Albassal, E. M. B., & Wahdan, A. (2004). Neural network based cryptanalysis of a feistel type block cipher. In *Proceedings of International Conference on Electrical, Electronic and Computer Engineering, ICEEC'04.* (pp. 231-237). Academic Press. doi:10.1109/ICEEC.2004.1374430

Anam, B., Sakib, K., Hossain, M., & Dahal, K. (2010). Review on the Advancements of DNA Cryptography. *arXiv preprint arXiv:1010.0186.*

Arvandi, M., Wu, S., & Sadeghian, A. (2008). On the use of recurrent neural networks to design symmetric ciphers. *IEEE Computational Intelligence Magazine, 3*(2), 42–53. doi:10.1109/MCI.2008.919075

Awad, W. S. (1998). *Ciphertext-only attack using genetic programming.* (Ph.D. thesis). University of Technology, Baghdad, Iraq.

Awad, W. S., (2008). Finding the linear equivalence of keystream generators using genetic simulated annealing. *Information Technology Journal, 7*(3), 541-544.

Awad, W. S. (2011a). On the application of evolutionary computation techniques in designing stream cipher systems. *International Journal of Computational Intelligence Systems, 4*(5), 921–928. doi:10.1080/18756891.2011.9727842

Awad, W. S. (2011b). Designing stream cipher systems using genetic programming. In Learning and optimization (LNCS), (vol. 6683, pp. 308-320). Berlin: Springer.

Awad, W. S. (2013). The effect of mutation operation on GP-based stream ciphers design algorithm. In *Proceedings of 5th International Conference on Agents and Artificial Intelligence* (pp. 455-450). Academic Press.

Beker, H., & Piper, F. (1982). *Cipher systems: The protection of communications*. Northwood Publications.

Bhateja, A. K., & Din, M. (2013). ANN Based Distinguishing Attack on RC4 Stream Cipher. In *Proceedings of Seventh International Conference on Bio-Inspired Computing: Theories and Applications (BIC-TA 2012)* (pp. 101-109). Academic Press. doi:10.1007/978-81-322-1041-2_9

Caballero-Gil, P. (2000). New upper bounds on the linear complexity. *Computers & Mathematics with Applications (Oxford, England), 39*(3-4), 31–38. doi:10.1016/S0898-1221(99)00331-4

Cherian, A., Raj, S. R., & Abraham, A. (2013). A Survey on Different DNA Cryptographic Methods. *International Journal of Science and Research*.

Clark, A., & Dawson, E. (1997). A parallel genetic algorithm for cryptanalysis of polyalphabetic substitution cipher. *Cryptologia, 21*(2), 129–138. doi:10.1080/0161-119791885850

Clark, A., Jacob, L., Maitra, S., & Stanica, P. (2004). Almost Boolean functions: The design of Boolean functions by spectral inversion. *Computational Intelligence, 20*(3), 450–462. doi:10.1111/j.0824-7935.2004.00245.x

Clark, A. J. (1998). *Optimisation Heuristics for Cryptology*. (Ph.D. thesis). Queensland University of Technology.

Cui, G., Qin, L., Wang, Y., & Zhang, X. (2008). An encryption scheme using DNA technology. In *Proceedings of 3rd International Conference on Bio-Inspired Computing: Theories and Applications, BICTA*. Academic Press.

Danziger, M., & Henriques, M. A. A. (2011). Computational intelligence applied on cryptology: A Brief Review. Paper presented at CIBSI 2011, Bucaramanga, Colombia.

Feistel, H. (1973). *Cryptography and computer privacy*. Scientific American.

Garcia, L. J., & Fuster-Sabater, A. (2000). On the linear complexity of the sequences generated by non-linear filtering. *Information Processing Letters, 76*(1-2), 67–73. doi:10.1016/S0020-0190(00)00117-4

Garg, P. (2009a). Cryptanalysis of SDES via evolutionary computation techniques. *International Journal of Computer Science and Information Security, 1*(1).

Garg, P. (2009b). A Comparison between Memetic algorithm and Genetic algorithm for the cryptanalysis of Simplified Data Encryption Standard algorithm. *International Journal of Network Security & Its Applications, 1*(1), 34–42.

Garg, P. (2010). Cryptanalysis of polyalphabetic substitution cipher using parallel memetic algorithm. *International Journal of Computational Intelligence and Information Security, 1*(4), 31–41.

Goresky, M., & Klapper, A. (2006). Pseudonoise sequence based on algebraic feedback shift registers. *IEEE Transactions on Information Theory, 52*(4), 1649–1662. doi:10.1109/TIT.2006.871045

Gründlingh, W. R., & Vuuren, J. (2007). *Using genetic algorithms to break a simple cryptographic cipher.* Retrieved from http://dip.sun.ac.za/~vuuren/papers/genetic.ps

Gustafson, H., Dawson, E., Nielsen, L., & Caelli, W. (1994). A computer package for measuring the strength of encryption algorithm. *Computers & Security, 14*(8), 687–697. doi:10.1016/0167-4048(94)90051-5

Hammood, D. N. (2010). Particles swarm optimization for the cryptanalysis of transposition cipher. *Journal of Al-Nahrain University, 13*(4), 211–215.

Haynes, T. (1995). Strongly typed GP in evolving cooperation strategies. In *Proceeding of 6th International Conference on GA* (pp. 271-278). Academic Press.

Hernández, J. C., Isasi, P., & Arco-Calderón, C. L. (2003). Finding efficient nonlinear functions by means of genetic programming. In Knowledge-Based Intelligent Information and Engineering Systems (LCNS), (vol. 2773, pp. 1192-1198). Berlin: Springer.

Isasi, P. (2005). Evolutionary Computation in Computer Security and Cryptography. *Generation Computing, 23*(3), 193–199. doi:10.1007/BF03037654

Isasi, P., & Julio, C. H. (2004). Introduction to the applications of evolutionary computation in computer security and cryptography. *Computational Intelligence, 20*(3), 445–449. doi:10.1111/j.0824-7935.2004.00244.x

Jacob, G., & Murugan, A. (2013). DNA Based Cryptography: An Overview and Analysis. *International Journal of Emerging Sciences, 3*(1), 36–27.

Karras, D. A., & Zorkadis, V. (2003). On neural network techniques in the secure management of communication systems through improving and quality assessing pseudorandom stream generators. *Neural Networks, 16*(5-6), 899–905. doi:10.1016/S0893-6080(03)00124-2 PMID:12850049

Koza, J. R. (1994). *Automatic discovery of reusable programs.* MIT Press.

Lai, X., Lu, M., Qin, L., Han, J., & Fang, X. (2010). Asymmetric encryption and signature method with DNA technology. *Science China Information Sciences, 53*(3), 506–514. doi:10.1007/s11432-010-0063-3

Laskari, E. C., Meletiou, G. C., Stamatiou, Y. C., & Vrahatis, M. N. (2007). Cryptography and Cryptanalysis through Computational Intelligence. In *Computational Intelligence in Information Assurance and Security* (pp. 1–49). Springer Berlin Heidelberg. doi:10.1007/978-3-540-71078-3_1

Leier, A., Richter, C., Banzhaf, W., & Rauhe, H. (2000). Cryptography with DNA binary strands. *Bio Systems, 57*(1), 13–22. doi:10.1016/S0303-2647(00)00083-6 PMID:10963862

Li, T., Li, J., & Zhang, J. (2014). A Cryptanalysis Method based on Niche Genetic Algorithm. *Appl. Math. Inf. Sci., 8*(1), 279–285. doi:10.12785/amis/080134

Lian, S. (2009). A block cipher based on chaotic neural networks. *Neurocomputing, 72*(4), 1296–1301. doi:10.1016/j.neucom.2008.11.005

Lin, F., & Kao, C. (1995). A Genetic Algorithm for Ciphertext-Only Attack in Cryptanalysis. In *Proceedings of the 1995 IEEE International Conference on Systems, Man and Cybernetics*. Vancouver: IEEE.

Liu, J., & Yin, Z. (2013). Based on DNA Self-Assembled Computing to Solve MH Knapsack Public Key Cryptosystems of the Knapsack Problem. In *Proceedings of The Eighth International Conference on Bio-Inspired Computing: Theories and Applications (BIC-TA)* (pp. 975-983). Springer Berlin Heidelberg. doi:10.1007/978-3-642-37502-6_114

Lu, M., Lai, X., Xiao, G., & Qin, L. (2007). Symmetric-key cryptosystem with DNA technology. *Science in China Series F: Information Sciences, 50*(3), 324–333. doi:10.1007/s11432-007-0025-6

Mantha, A. (2012). *Improving Reliability in DNA based Computations with Applications to Cryptography.* (Doctoral dissertation). University of Cincinnati, Cincinnati, OH.

Massey, J. L. (1976). Shift register sequences and BCH decoding. *IEEE Transactions on Information Theory, 15*(1), 122–127. doi:10.1109/TIT.1969.1054260

Millan, W., Clark, A., & Dawson, E. (1997). An effective genetic algorithm for finding highly nonlinear Boolean functions. In *The First International Conference on Information and Communications Security* (LNCS), (vol. 1334, pp. 149-158). Berlin: Springer.

Mordell, L. J. (Ed.). (1969). *Diophantine equations* (Vol. 30). Academic Press.

Nalini, N., & Raghavendra, R. G. (2007). Attacks of simple block ciphers via efficient heuristics. *Information Sciences, 177*(12), 2553–2569. doi:10.1016/j.ins.2007.01.007

Nalini, N., & Raghavendra, R. G. (2007). Attack of simple block ciphers via efficient heuristics. *Information Sciences, 177*(12), 2553–2569. doi:10.1016/j.ins.2007.01.007

Naveen, J. K., Karthigaikumar, P., Sivamangai, N. M., Sandhya, R., & Asok, S. B. (2013). Hardware implementation of DNA based cryptography. In *Proceedings of IEEE Conference on Information & Communication Technologies (ICT)*. IEEE. doi:10.1109/CICT.2013.6558184

Picek, S., & Golub, M. (2011). On evolutionary computation methods in cryptography. In *MIPRO, 2011 Proceedings of the 34th International Convention*. Academic Press.

Popovici, C. (2010). Aspects of DNA cryptography. *Annals of the University of Craiova-Mathematics and Computer Science Series, 37*(3), 147–151.

Rajendra, G. N., & Kaur, B. R. (2011). A New Approach for Data Encryption Using Genetic Algorithms and Brain Mu Waves. *International Journal of Scientific and Engineering Research, 5*(5), 1–4.

Ramani, R. G., & Balasubramanian, L. (2011). Genetic algorithm solution for cryptanalysis of knapsack cipher with knapsack sequence of size 16. *International Journal of Computer Applications, 35*(11).

Rao, K. S., Krishna, M. R., & Babu, D. (2009). Cryptanalysis of a Feistel Type Block Cipher by Feed Forword Neural Network Using Right Sigmoidal Signals. *International Journal of Soft Computing, 4*(3), 131–135.

Roy, B., Rakshit, G., Singha, P., Majumder, A., & Datta, D. (2011). An improved Symmetric key cryptography with DNA Based strong cipher. In *Proceedings of International Conference on Devices and Communications (ICDeCom)* (pp. 1-5). Academic Press. doi:10.1109/ICDECOM.2011.5738553

Rueppel, R. A. (1986). *Aanalysis and design of stream ciphers*. Berlin: Springer-Verlag. doi:10.1007/978-3-642-82865-2

Schneier, B. (1996). *Applied cryptography*. John Wiley and Sons.

Shanon, C. (1949). Communication theory of secrecy systems. *The Bell System Technical Journal, 28*(4), 656–715. doi:10.1002/j.1538-7305.1949.tb00928.x

Spillman, R., Janssan, M., Nelson, B., & Kepner, M. (1993). Use of genetic algorithms in the cryptanalysis of simple substitution ciphers. *Cryptologia, 17*(1), 31–44. doi:10.1080/0161-119391867746

Stalling, W. (2006). *Cryptography and network security: Principles and practices* (4th ed.). Prentice Hall.

Szaban, M., Seredynski, F., & Bouvry, P. (2006). Collective behavior of rules for cellular automata-based stream ciphers. In *Proceedings of IEEE Congress on Evolutionary Computation* (pp. 179-183). IEEE. doi:10.1109/CEC.2006.1688306

Tanaka, K., Okamoto, A., & Saito, I. (2005). Public-key system using DNA as a one-way function for key distribution. *Bio Systems, 81*(1), 25–29. doi:10.1016/j.biosystems.2005.01.004 PMID:15917125

Toemeh, R., & Arumugam, S. (2008). Applying Genetic Algorithms for Searching Key-Space of Polyalphabetic Substitution Ciphers. *The International Arab Journal of Information Technology, 5*(1), 87–91.

Tornea, O., & Borda, M. E. (2009). DNA cryptographic algorithms. In *Proceedings of International Conference on Advancements of Medicine and Health Care through Technology* (pp. 223-226). Springer Berlin Heidelberg. doi:10.1007/978-3-642-04292-8_49

Verma, A. K., Dave, M., & Joshi, R. C. (2007). Genetic Algorithm and Tabu Search Attack on the Mono-Alphabetic Subsitution Cipher in Adhoc Networks. *Journal of Computer Science, 3*(3), 134–137. doi:10.3844/jcssp.2007.134.137

Vijayakumar, P., Vijayalakshmi, V., & Zayaraz, G. (2011). DNA Computing based Elliptic Curve Cryptography. *International Journal of Computers and Applications, 36*.

Volná, E. (2000). Using Neural network in cryptography. In *The State of the Art in Computational Intelligence* (pp. 262–267). Physica-Verlag HD. doi:10.1007/978-3-7908-1844-4_42

Xiangyang, X. (2010). A New Genetic Algorithm and Tabu Search for S-Box Optimization. In *Proceedings of International Conference on Computer Design and Applications (ICCDA 2010)* (vol. 4, pp. 492-495). Academic Press.

Xiao, G., Lu, M., Qin, L., & Lai, X. (2006). New field of cryptography: DNA cryptography. *Chinese Science Bulletin, 51*(12), 1413–1420. doi:10.1007/s11434-006-2012-5

Yang, J., Ma, J., Liu, S., & Zhang, C. (2014). A molecular cryptography model based on structures of DNA self-assembly. *Chinese Science Bulletin, 59*(11), 1192–1198. doi:10.1007/s11434-014-0170-4

Yee, L. P., & De Silva, L. C. (2002). Application of multilayer perceptron networks in symmetric block ciphers. In *Proceedings of the 2002 International Joint Conference on Neural Networks, IJCNN'02. (Vol. 2*, pp. 1455-1458). Academic Press.

Yu, W., & Cao, J. (2006). Cryptography based on delayed chaotic neural networks. *Physics Letters. [Part A], 356*(4), 333–338. doi:10.1016/j.physleta.2006.03.069

Zeng, K., Yang, C., & Rao, T. R. N. (1991). Pseudorandom bit generator in stream cipher cryptography. *Computer, 24*(2), 8–17. doi:10.1109/2.67207

Zhang, Y., & Fu, L. H. B. (2012). *Research on DNA Cryptography* (pp. 357–376). Rijeka, Croatia: Applied Cryptography and Network Security, InTech Press.

KEY TERMS AND DEFINITIONS

Computational Intelligence: It is a set of computational methodologies used to solve problems that requiring intelligence.

Cryptanalysis: It is the science of breaking cipher systems.

Cryptography: It is the science of encrypting data.

Encryption: It is a process of converting plaintext to ciphertext.

Evolutionary Computation: It is a subfield of computational intelligence, that includes a number of global optimization methods.

Genetic Algorithm: It is one of evolutionary computation algorithms, which is a population-based iterative improvement search algorithm used to solve optimization problems using techniques inspired by natural evolution.

Genetic Programming: It is an application of genetic algorithm, in which the structure under adaption is a population of programs. Thus, the solution of a problem is a given as computer program.

Memetic Algorithm: It is also called hybrid genetic algorithm, its idea comes from memes, that can adapt themselves.

Particle Swarm Optimization: It is a population-based computational method used for multi-parameter optimization. A population (swarm) of candidate solutions (particles) moves in the search space, and the movement of the particles is influenced both by their own best known position and swarm's global best known position.

Simulated Annealing: It is a global optimization technique inspired by the annealing process in metallurgy. This technique can help to avoid the problem of getting stuck in a local minimum and to lead towards the globally optimum solution.

Section 2
Applications of Evolutionary Computation in Cryptology

This section presents two applications of evolutionary computation in cryptology, namely design of stream ciphers and chaotic-based cryptosystems for securing images.

Chapter 3
Automated Design of Stream Ciphers Using GADS

Wasan Shaker Awad
Ahlia University, Bahrain

Amal M. Al Hiddi
University of Bahrain, Bahrain

ABSTRACT

The main objective of this chapter is to propose a new effective algorithm to design stream cipher systems automatically using simulated annealing algorithm and genetic programming with a different method for representing the genetic programming population individuals. Usually the individual programs represented as LISP expressions; in the proposed method the programs are represented as strings of integers representing the individual program syntactic rule numbers. Genetic programming with this representation method is called genetic algorithm for developing software (GADS). The performance of the proposed algorithm will be studied by applying different genetic methods and parameters. Furthermore, it will be compared with other representation methods such as LISP expression.

INTRODUCTION

Nowadays, in the organizations, there is a great dependence on information, computer systems, and computer communication and networking. Consequently, awareness of the need to security has been also increased. Information security is the process of protecting information from unauthorized access, use, disclosure, destruction, or modification. The organizations need to protect information from malicious actions that endanger the confidentiality of its information, such as snooping and traffic analysis. There are a number of information security goals, one of them is confidentiality. It is about protection of confidential information.

Encryption is an important mechanism used to protect information. Therefore, we can see many encryption techniques proposed with different levels of security, and different structures. One of encryption systems is stream cipher which is an important class for many reasons, such as security degree, easy to implement, efficient, and with no error propagation.

DOI: 10.4018/978-1-4666-9426-2.ch003

Designing cipher systems of good characteristics, such as security level, efficiency, and ease of implementation, is hard task. Therefore, this problem has attracted a number of researchers, and some of them proposed automated methods for designing cipher systems. In this chapter, we are trying to find an efficient and effective automated method for designing cipher systems, to help the security researchers and industry to find strong cipher systems. The proposed method for designing cipher systems is based on genetic programming (GP), which is an application of genetic algorithm (GA). GP has been used to solve different kinds of problems, and attracted many researchers. Thus, we can find so many studies about applying GP to solve complex problems, and most of studies proved its effectiveness. Thus, this work is to study the effectiveness of GP in designing stream ciphers automatically. In the literature, we can find different studies about the automated design of cipher systems using computational intelligence techniques (CI). Awad (2011a, 2011b, 2013) proposed a different variations of GP-based stream cipher design algorithm, such as adaptive GP and simulated annealing programming. This chapter is to present a modified SAP algorithm using GADS.

Although GA (and GP) has gained many applications, simple GA suffers from many troubles such as getting stuck in a local minimum and parameters dependence (Eiben, Hinterding, & Michalewic, 1999). There are many improvements have been proposed to enhance the performance of the GA. Therefore, in this work, to avoid the problem of getting stuck in a local minimum and to preserve good individuals into the next generation, simulated annealing algorithm (SA) is integrated with GP, the resulted algorithm is called simulated annealing programming (SAP).

The main objectives of this chapter are:

1. Study the effectiveness of GP in the automated design of stream cipher systems of high level of security.
2. Analyze the application of GP with GA engine, i.e., genetic algorithm for developing software (GADS).
3. To study the effect of different GA techniques and parameters on the performance of GP-based design method.

In the next three sections, the concepts of stream ciphers, GP, and SA are given. The sections after are for describing the proposed method, architecture, algorithms, and experimental results.

STREAM CIPHER

Cryptology is the study of the encryption techniques to protect data and the techniques to attack the encryption techniques. Thus it is combination of two areas: cryptanalysis and cryptography, where cryptanalysis is the study of the techniques used for breaking cryptographic (cipher) systems, and cryptography is the science of encrypting information. There are different kinds of cipher systems (cryptosystems), used for encrypting the private information. The cryptosystems can be classified into modern and classical systems. Modern cipher systems are subdivided into block ciphers and stream ciphers (Paar, and Pelzl, 2010).

Stream ciphers are extremely fast and easy to implement, in addition, they usually have very minimal hardware resource requirements. Therefore stream ciphers are of great importance in applications where encryption speed is paramount and where area-constrained or memory constrained devices make it impractical to use block ciphers. Stream ciphers can operate one data unit as small as a bit or a character. Each stream cipher composed of keystream generator to generate keystream to be mixed using a mixer with plaintext to produce ciphertext (Stalling, 2006; Forouzan, 2008).

A number of stream cipher systems have been proposed which are of variety degrees of security, such as Geffe, and Stop-and-Go generators (Beker and Piper, 1982; Rueppel, 1986; Schneier, 1996). Furthermore, a number of different kinds of stream ciphers which are based on different techniques other than linear feedback shift registers (LFSRs), such as Cellular Automata (CA) (Szaban, Seredynski, and Bouvry, 2006), and Algebraic Shift Register (Goresky, and Klapper, 2006) have been proposed. The stream cipher system's security depends entirely on the inside of keystram generator. The security of this generator can be analyzed in terms of randomness, linear complexity, and correlation immunity (Massey, 1976; Zeng, 1991; Gustafson, 1994; Caballero-Gil, 2000; Garcia, and Fuster-Sabater, 2000; Qi, 2008). Thus, good keystrem generators have the following features:

1. They generate long period keystreams.
2. The generated keystreams are random.
3. The generated keystreams are of large linear complexity.
4. They have high degrees of correlation immunity.

A binary sequence is said to be random if there is no obvious relationship between the individual Bits of the sequence. The most important requirement imposed on random number generators is their capability to produce random numbers uniformly distributed in [0,1]. A number of statistical tests are applied to examine whether the pseudorandom number sequences are random or not, which are frequency test, serial test, poker test, autocorrelation test and runs test (Zeng, 1991; Gustafson, 1994; L'ecuyer, and Simard, 2007).

1. **Frequency Test:** It calculates the number of ones and zeroes of a binary sequence and checks if there is no large difference.
2. **Serial Test:** The numbers 00, 01, 10 and 11 should be uniformly distributed within the sequence.
3. **Poker Test:** A N length sequence is segmented into blocks of M bits and the total number of segments is N/M. The objective of this test is to count the frequency of occurrence of each M length segment. Ideally, all the frequency of occurrences should be equal.
4. **Runs Test:** A sequence is divided into contiguous stream of 1's that is referred as blocks and contiguous stream of 0's that is referred as gaps. If r_0^i is the number of gaps of length i, then half of the gaps will have length 1 bit, a quarter with length 2 bits, and an eighth with length 3 bits. If r_1^i is the number of blocks of length i, then the distribution of blocks is similar to the number of gaps.

Linear complexity is a well-known complexity measure in the theory of stream ciphers. Linear complexity of a keystream s is the length of the shortest LFSR which will produce the stream s, which is denoted by L(s). If the value of L(s) is L, then 2L consecutive bits can be used to reconstruct the whole sequence. Hence, to avoid the keystream reconstruction, the value of L should be large (Massey, 1976).

In order to obtain high linear complexity, several sequences can be combined in some nonlinear manner. The danger here is that one or more of the internal output sequences can be correlated with the combined keystream and attacked using linear algebra. A keysream generator has a higher degree of correlation immunity if there is no correlation between any internal output sequence and the combined keytream.

GENETIC PROGRAMMING

GP is an application of GA. GA is an intelligent search technique that can be applied to solve a set of optimization problems (Goldberg, 1989; Mitchell, 1996; Zalzala, and Fleming,1997). Holland (1975) is the one who developed the GA theoretical foundation. The main idea of GA has been developed from the evolutional process in the natural biological life, and the principle of "survival of fittest". Before explaining GA, we need to define some key terms as follows:

1. **Chromosome or Population Individual:** Any candidate solution in the search space of a problem, and it is an element in GA population.
2. **Population:** Set of chromosomes (individuals), and population size is the number of chromosomes in the population.
3. **Search Space:** All possible solutions to the problem.

GA works by creating an initial population with group of chromosomes randomly, evaluating the fitness of each chromosome. After that, chromosomes will be selected according to their fitness scores. The chromosomes with higher fitness will have more chance to be selected according to a selection method. Each two selected chromosomes (parents) will be recombined to create new chromosomes (children) that will be added to the new population. These steps will be repeated until proper solution is found or an stopping certain is met. GA is powerful method that can create high quality solutions to problems:

1. Of complex, poorly understood and large search spaces,
2. When no available mathematical analysis,
3. When traditional search methods fail.

The disadvantages of GA is that it is not always feasible for real time use.

As defined by Koza (Koza, 1992; Koza, 1994), who introduced the concept of GP, GP is an extension of GA; it deals with computer programming by finding a solution to a particular problem as computer program rather than the solution itself. GP deals with one of the important questions in computer science, which is, how the computer can perform tasks without being told exactly how to do it. Thus, the search space of GP is the space of all possible computer programs composed of functions and terminals appropriate to the problem domain.

In order to apply a GP algorithm to solve any problem, the following steps must be considered:

1. Determine the set of terminals.
2. Select the set of primitive functions.
3. Define the fitness function.
4. Decide on the parameters for controlling the run of GP.

5. Choose the method for designating a result of the run, usually, the single best-so-far individual of the last generation is designated as the result of the run.
6. Choose the representation method to represent the population individuals.

The solution of a problem evolved by GP is a computer program. Therefore, the population of GP is the set of candidate solutions which are programs. Each program is composed of a number primitive functions and terminals.

To apply GP, we have to define the terminal set. The terminals include the constants and variables of the population individuals (programs). The primitive functions are chosen based on the problem at hand. Function set may include arithmetic functions such as subtraction, addition, division and multiplication. It can be a set of logical functions (OR, AND, OXR, etc.) and so on. Terminal and function sets together define the alphabetic of the program that will be evolved by GP.

Fitness function will evaluate each population program by measuring its performance in the problem environment. Thus, we have to define how fitness measure will work, based in the type and natural of the problem. It's important and most difficult step in GP, because it determines how good are the programs in solving the problem. If the fitness measure is weak then the program that will be evolved by GP at the end will be weak too.

The control parameters of GP also must be identified. There are a number of control parameters in GP:

1. **Population Size:** The number of candidate solutions (programs/chromosomes) in each population of GP.
2. The maximum number of generations of GP run.
3. Maximum and minimum chromosome (program) length.
4. Genetic operation rates.
5. Other parameters specific to the problem.

Representation Scheme

This section is to present two representation methods used to represent the population chromosomes of GP.

Koza (1992) and others used LISP programming language (McCarthy, 1979; Siebel, and Peter, 2005) to represent the candidate programs in the GP populations. LISP program consists of two types of entities (list and atoms). An atom can be constant such as 4, or variable like (Counter). The List in LISP is represented by a collection of items placed between parentheses. For example, (+ 6 8). The syntactic form in the LISP is called S-Expressions (symbolic expressions). In S-expression, the item in the outermost left parenthesis is a function that is applied to the other items of the list. For example, the LISP S-Expression: (* 3 10 (- (+ 1 7 2) 5)) . In this example, the first function in the list is"*", and it has three arguments: 3, 10 and the sub S-Expression (- (+ 1 7 2) 5)). In this sub S-Expression, the function is " –"and it has two arguments: the sub expression (+ 1 7 2) and constant 5. The sub expression (+ 1 7 2) has "+" as a function that will add the 3 arguments 1, 7 and 2. The result of the last sub expression will be 10, and the result of (- (+ 1 7 2) 5) will be 5. The final result will be 150.This S-expression can be represented by expression tree as shown in Figure 1.

Another representation method is GADS which was first introduced by Paterson and Liveseyin (1996). The chromosomes of GADS are not represented using tree structure, but list of integers. GADS makes use of BNF (Backus–Naur Form) (Naur, 1963). BNF is a method used for representing context-

Figure 1. An expression tree

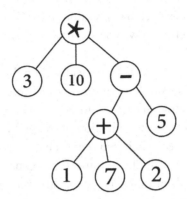

free grammars, that is used to characterize the formal language syntax in computer science. In 1950s, context-free grammars was developed by Chomsky. He developed BNF when he was working in IBM as programming language designer to represent the syntax of the new programming language. The rules of CFG for defining the syntax of a formal language has the form: S → X, where S is a nonterminal. It must be a single and in the left side. The X symbol can be terminal or nonterminal values, or mix of both of them. Here the values can be string, single or even empty (Lari, and Young, 1990).

In GADS, a genotype (chromosome or genetic search space element) is represented as a list of integers (rather than tree in normal GP). These integers will be the input for appropriate generator which is used to produce the phenotype (program or solution space element). This process of mapping genotype to phenotype is called ontogenic mapping. To modify agenotype, the same operations of GA such as crossover, mutation.. etc. are used. To evaluate the fitness of a genotype, GADS tests the phenotype in the environment in which it operates. The result of the testing gives the fitness of the phenotype, and by implication, of its genotype (Paterson, and Liveseyin,1996; Ryan, Collins, and Neill, 1998; Ferreira, 2002; O'Neill, and Conor, 2003).

The advantages of using GADS is, it uses the traditional GA engine, which is more efficient that GP, that can be used to produce a solution of a problem as program. While the problems (all are solvable) of this approach are:

1. If we have large grammar, the probability of choosing specific rule in that grammar is decreased. Thus, to solve this problem and to improve the chance of selecting particular rule, we can duplicate the rule in the grammar.
2. Sometimes, at the end of a chromosome, when it is created randomly, the non-terminals do not have any terminal chosen for them. The solution of this problem is by using a default value which is inserted into the chromosome. The default value must be tailored for each production rule.

Genetic Operations

This section is to present a number of genetic operations that can be used to update the current population and generate new population. All genetic operations are applied in specific rates.

Crossover is a genetic operation, in which more than one chromosome are selected from the old population to produce new chromosomes that will be added to the new population. This can be done by creating crossover point in each chromosome, and all genes behind that's point will be swapped with other chromosome to produce the new chromosomes.

Before we discuss different types of crossover, we will discuss the crossover of LISP-based GP (Koza, 1992). The crossover is applied to the selected expression trees. Crossover point will be selected in two trees. Then the subtree after crossover point will be swapped with the other parent subtree to create two new trees (children).

There are different types of crossover operations that can be applied in GA (Goldberg, 1989; Mitchell, 1996; Zalzala, and Fleming, 1997). In single point crossover, we choose single point randomly in the parent chromosomes. From this position until the end, the two chromosomes will exchange their values. In multi-point crossover, which is a generalization of the previous one (single point crossover, we choose several points randomly. Between each two point the chromosomes will exchange their values. While uniform Crossover works by sharing the chromosomes gene values to create new chromosomes by letting the crossover operator to determine that with some probability known as mixing ratio. For example if we set the mixing ratio to 0.5, that's mean the new chromosomes have almost half of genes from the first parent chromosome and half from the second parent chromosome. The crossover points will be chosen randomly. The advantage of this method is that, it allows the chromosomes to be mixed at the gene level rather than the segment level. But the disadvantage of using uniform crossover is it can destroy building blocks.

Another genetic operation used to update the current population of GA is mutation. Mutation operation will create a new chromosome from the selected parent of the old population by changing some part of that chromosome randomly.

Selection

The strategy of selection in GP (and GA) is to choose a chromosomes in the existing population and use it to generate new chromosomes for the new population, so the fitness of the new population will be better. That can be done by giving the chromosome with higher fitness value high probability to move to the next population. There are different methods of selection with different strategies but all of them are built on the principle of survival of the fittest. In this section we will discuss some of these methods.

Tournament selection the most popular method for selection, because of simple implementation and efficiency. Tournament selection works by doing a tournament for the chromosomes in the population as competitors. The winner in this tournament will be the chromosome with highest fitness among the other competitors. The selected chromosome will be used to create new chromosomes to be inserted into the new population. The number of chromosomes competing in each tournament is referred to as tournament size. Tournament selection gives a chance to all individuals to be selected and thus it preserves diversity, although keeping diversity it may degrade the convergence speed. In tournament selection, larger values of tournament size lead to higher expected loss of diversity. The larger tournament size means that a smaller portion of the population actually contributes to genetic diversity, making the search increasingly greedy in nature.

As Rakesh and Jyotishree (2012) stated, roulette wheel is the simplest selection methods. In this approach, the chromosomes will be placed in the roulette wheel according to their fitness value. The probability of the chromosome i "P(choice = i)" can be calculated in roulette wheel as the following:

$$P\big(choice = i\big) = def \frac{fitness\big(i\big)}{\sum_{j=1}^{n} fitness\big(j\big)} \tag{1}$$

The disadvantage of roulette wheel selection method is that the chromosomes with higher fitness have more chance to be selected to move to the new population. That's probability can lead to miss the best chromosomes in the old population, therefore there is no guarantee for the good chromosomes to find a way to reach to the new population. On the other hand, the advantage of this method, as we mentioned early, is the simplest selection methods so it's easy to implement and simulate nature more truly. It also has the propensity of setting the threshold to value of zero, at the same time it's likely converges to unlimited expansion. For those reasons it is much more appealing than the other methods.

Another selection method is rank selection method that works by first sorting the population according their values of fitness and then ranking them. According to their rank, the chromosomes will be given selection probability. The chromosome at the top of the list has more chance to be selected to transform it to the new population. The advantage of rank selection method is it can block very fit chromosomes from winning and control the new population so early and ignore the chromosomes with less fitness value. That will help not reduce the population's genetic variety and maybe block the effort of finding reasonable solution. The disadvantage of this method to implement it, it requires sorting the whole population and rank it. It may cost exhaustion time procedure.

In the literature, there are a number of studies to analyze the selection strategies, and genetic operations (Syswerda, 1989; Spears, and Jong, 1990; Alander, 1992; Miller, and Goldberg, 1995; Tobias, and Lothar, 1995; Eiben, Hinterding, and Michalewic,1999; Ochoa, Harvey, and Buxton, 1999; Al Jadaan, Lakishmi, and Rao, 2005; Kellegoz, Toklu, and Wilson, 2008; Noraini, and John, 2011; Rakesh, and Jyotishree, 2012). Most of their results proved that choosing genetic operations and parameters to be applied in a GA depends on the nature of problems.

GP Complete Algorithm

The steps of GP algorithm are the following (Koza, 1992):

1. Generate the initial population randomly;
2. Repeat
    a. Execute each program in the population and measure its fitness using the fitness function;
    b. Apply a selection and genetic operations to produce new population;
    c. Until the termination criterion is satisfied;
3. After the termination criterion is satisfied, the single best program in the last population produced during the run (the best-so-far individual) is harvested and designated as the result of the run. If the run is successful, the result may be a solution (or approximate solution) to the problem.

SIMULATED ANNEALING

SA has been introduced by Kirkpatrik, et al. (1983). It is an iterative improvement technique used to solve optimization problems, to find good solutions. SA can help to avoid the problem of getting stuck in a local minimum. The idea of how SA is working comes from the annealing process in mineralogy; when the temperature is high, the molecules of liquid move freely, and when slowly the liquids is cooled, thermal mobility is lost. In SA algorithm, if the move to next problem state improves the situation, it is always executed. Otherwise, the algorithm makes the move with some probability less than 1. The probability decreases exponentially with the "badness" of the move. The algorithm parameter **T** (temperature) is used to determine the probability. At higher values of *T*, *"bad"* moves are more likely to be allowed. As T tends to zero, they become more and more unlikely. The *schedule* determines the rate at which the temperature is lowered (Kirkpatrik, et. al., 1983; Bertsimas, and Tsitsiklis, 1993).

Many problems of different types have been solved using SA. The good thing in SA is can be integrated with GA. That will help to maintain good individuals into the next generations. The main steps of SA algorithm are the following:

1.   Evaluate the initial state;
2.   Initialize the temperature (T) according to the annealing schedule;
3.   Loop until a solution is found, or until there are no new operators left to be applied in the current state;
     3.1 Apply an operator to the current state, to produce a new state;
     3.2 Evaluate the new state, if the new state is the goal then return it, otherwise: If value of current state < value of new state, then make the new state as current state, and set best-so-far to the new state; If value of current state> value of new state, then E = value of current state- value of new state, PR = $e^{-E/T}$. Make the new state as current state with probability PR;
     3.3 Reduce Temp;
4.   Return best-so-far as the answer;

PROBLEM DEFINITION

Designing cipher system of good characteristics, such as security level, efficiency, and ease of implementation, is not an easy task. This explains why this area has been an appealing field of research and attracted the interest of many researchers, some of whom proposed automated methods for designing cipher systems. However, so far, while there are many studies about using GA and GP in block cipher design, there is just one research paper for stream cipher automated design that discusses how to use GP in its design. In this chapter, an automated design method of stream cipher is proposed which is based on GP and SA using different representation method. Accordingly, the problem under study is formulated as follows:

The Problem: Automated design of stream ciphers that fulfill desired properties.
Input: The desired properties of stream cipher, such as keystream length.
Search Space: Set of all possible programs (keystream generators).
States: Candidate solutions (programs).
Output: A program that represents LFSR-based keystream generator to generate random Binary sequence.

FUNCTION AND TERMINAL SET

In GP, the structure under adaptation is a population of programs representing the nominee LFSR-based keystream generators. The main function in the proposed function set that will be used in this method is LFSR. It is obligatory to use LFSR because the keystream generators implemented in this work are

Table 1. Functions library

Symbol	Format	Description
#	# x	LFSR and x is a feedback function.
&	& x y	AND logic operation, x and y are sequences Binary numbers.
			x y	OR logic operation, x and y are sequences Binary numbers.
^	^ x y	XOR logic operation, x and y are sequences Binary numbers.

based on LFSRs. The problem of LFSR that its linear by its inherently. This will make the security of keystream generator is weak, and the amenability to be attacked is high. To avoid that, we have to remove the linearity of LFSR by combining more than one LFSR using a nonlinear combining functions. Therefore, it is necessary to include more functions in the function set. Thus, AND (bitwise and), OR (bitwise or) and XOR (addition mod 2) are chosen to be included in the function set, as presented in Table 1.

REPRESENTATION SCHEMA

Usually in GP, LISP expressions are used to represent the population individual programs (chromosomes); in this work, the chromosomes are represented as sequences of integers. These integers represent the individual program syntactic (CFG) rule numbers. In GADS, the set of CFG rules used affects its performance. Thus, in order to find the best set of CFG rules, three sets have been examined, as shown in Tables (2, 3, 4, and 5).

According to these three sets, GADS can be classified into three classes, as follows:

1. **GADS Class1:** It uses rules set 1, in which 0 and 1 are used to represent the terminals in CFG.
2. **GADS Class2:** It uses rules set 2. It is similar to class1 except that rules 4 and 5 are duplicated to be of higher probability, and hence, there is possessed longer LFSR in the chromosomes.

Table 3. CFG rules set 2

Number	CFG Rule
0	S → & S S
1	S →	S S
2	S → ^ S S
3	S → # X
4	X → 0 X
5	X → X 0
6	X → 1 X
7	X → X 1
8	X → 0
9	X → 1

Table 2. CFG rules set 1

Number	CFG Rule
0	S → & S S
1	S →	S S
2	S → ^ S S
3	S → # X
4	X → 0 X
5	X → 1 X
6	X → 0
7	X → 1

Table 4. CFG rules set 3

Number	CFG Rule
0	S →& S S
1	S → ǀ S S
2	S → ^ S S
3	S → # X
4	X →a X
5	X →b X
6	X →c X
7	X →d X
8	X → e X
9	X → f X
10	X → g X
11	X → h X
12	X → a
13	X → b
14	X → c
15	X → d
16	X → e
17	X → f
18	X → g
19	X → h

Table 5. Terminal nodes and its equivalent Binary numbers

Terminal Latter	Equivalent Binary Number
a	000
b	001
c	010
d	011
e	100
f	101
g	110
h	111

Table 6. Example of program generation

Step	Program (Phenotype) Generation	Rule Applied
1	^SS	2
2	^#XS	3
3	^#X#X	3
4	^#bX#X	5
5	^#bdX#X	7
6	^#bdc#X	14
7	^#bdc#eX	8
8	^#bdc#ea	12
9	^#001011010#100000	

3. **GADS Class3:** It uses rules set 3. Instead of using 0 and 1 as terminals, the letters "a" to "h" are used in this class. Each of the letters will represent a sequence of three bits as shown in the Table 5. This representation will be more compact comparable with Binary representation. For example, consider the chromosome: 2, 3, 3, 5, 7, 14, 8, 12, then, the corresponding program will be generated as shown in Table 6.

To find the best class suitable for the proposed designing method in terms of effectiveness and efficiency, these classes have been implemented to study their performance. Each class has been analyzed in order to choose a class that gives good results. See Table 7.

Regarding the chromosomes structure and format, we proposed three chromosome structures, and the CFG rules of Table 4 are divided into three categories, which are:

1. The first category includes rules 0 to 3, which represent the rules for generating functions. This category is called Function Rules (FR).
2. The second category includes the terminals rules (TR) which includes the rules from 4 to 11.
3. The third category is represented by the leaves rules (LR) that have all rules from 12.

Table 7. GADS classes evaluation

GADS Class	Problems	Improvement	Enhanced Class Number
Class 1	The problem of this class faced here is the probability of choosing rules of the CFG is equal. Some rules need to be of higher probability to choose, such as rules 4 and 5 of Table 2, otherwise, the LFSR will be very short and it can contain only one bit. That will lead to generate weak keystream generator and of low fitness values	To avoid this problem, these rules are duplicated in the grammar to raise their use	Class 2
Class 2	The length of LFSR may still be insufficient. It is still small and the fitness value for it will be unsatisfactory. That is because, by using 0 and 1 as terminals which represent LFSR feedback functions, there is a need to generate long Binary sequences which is inefficient	Instead of using 0 and 1 as terminals, letters are used to get more compact representation of feedback functions. Each of the letters represents a Binary sequence of length three Bits	Class 3

Figure 2. Examples of Chromosome structures

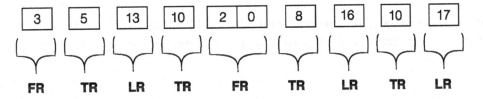

a.Chromosome Structure 1

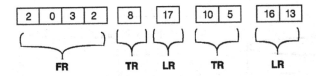

b.Chromosome Structure 2

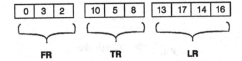

c.Chromosome Structure 3

FR → Function Rules 0-3

TR → Terminal Rules 4-11

LR → Leave Rules 12-19

Figure 3. System input and output

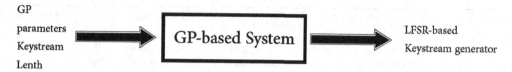

The three chromosome structures, as shown in Figure 2, are:

1. **Chromosome Structure 1:** A chromosome include any rule number without any restriction, Figure 2a.
2. **Chromosome Structure 2:** A chromosome is composed of two parts. The first block is for FR numbers, and second is for TR numbers, Figure 2b.
3. **Chromosome Structure 3:** A chromosome has three parts. The first is for FR, the second is for TR and the last block is for LR, Figure 2c.

PROPOSED SYSTEM ARCHITECTURE

The proposed system is a GP-based system used to find best keystream generator that can generate a random Binary sequence of a given length, see Figure 3. Figure 4 presents the overall architecture of the proposed system.

Figure 4. The overall architecture of the proposed system

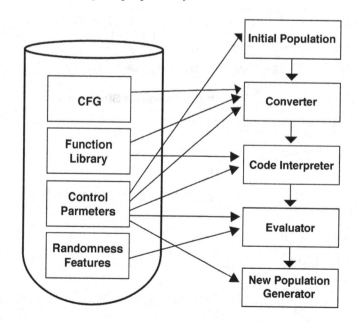

Initial Population Generation

The first step in GP is to generate the initial population. The initial population is generated randomly, that represents a set of candidate solutions. Algorithm 1 is used to generate the initial population for the proposed method.

For example, consider Table 8. It presents an example of algorithm parameters and its output.

Convertor

It is used to convert the genotype to phenotype. It is a program works as follows: read the chromosome, then search for the FR (from 0 to 3). It converts any rule number found to what it represents in CFG rules. For example, if the number found is 3 in the chromosome, it will be converted to "# X". Then it will search for the TR (from 4 to 11) and replaces the nonterminal letter "X" with the number that represents it. Therefore, if it finds rule number 5 in the chromosome, it will search for first nonterminal letter "X" and replaces it with "b X". After that, it will replace the rest of nonterminal letter "X" with a number from 12 to 19. Finally, the phenotype (candidate keystream generator) will be generated to contain the functions and terminals only.

The problem in the above conversion method is: What if the chromosome does not contain rule number 3 that represents the LFSR function? This function is the core of the CFG we use, and without it, the keystreams cannot be generated. Thus, we need to modify the above conversion method. The converter will search for any nonterminal letter "S" and replaces it with LFSR function "# X". Also, in case it does not find any number from FR (0 to 3), it will add LFSR function.

Algorithm 1. (Initial Population Generation).

```
Input: Population size (popsize), chromosome length (chromlength).
Output: Initial population.
Begin
for i =1 to popsize do
 for j = 1 to chromlength do
Cromosome_ij = random number from 0 to 19;
End;
```

Table 8. Example of parameters and output of Initial population generation algorithm

Chromosome Length	8
Population Size	5
Chromosome Structure	1
Function Operation	Generating 8 random numbers from 0 – 19 for each chromosome
Function Output (a Population)	4, 6, 7, 11, 3, 10, 6, 5 11, 2, 12, 15, 1, 19, 5, 5 7, 17, 15, 12, 1, 19, 5, 0 3, 2, 8, 11, 4, 19, 13, 9 5, 11, 12, 18, 6, 17, 7, 5

Even with this method, still there is a problem, because the converter searches for the first nonterminal letter "X" that appeared in the chromosome and it is replaced by TR. Therefore, the first LFSR function will be very long and all other LFSR functions will be short since they contain only one or two letters as feedback functions. This will affect the performance of the proposed method. To solve this problem, there is an opted need for the modification of the program so that it contains a counter that counts the number of terminals for each LFSR function, and ensures that it will not extend four letters. Algorithm 2 is the converter algorithm.

Code Interpreter

After converting genotype to phenotype, the generated phenotype (keystream generator) need to be executed in order to evaluate the generated keystream. The code interpreter is used to execute each key stream generator in GP populations. Code interpreter is the program that executes the instructions written in a programming language. It is used to analyze each statement in the program each time it is executed and then perform the desired action. Algorithm 3 is the algorithm of the code interpreter used in the proposed method.

Evaluator

This component is for evaluating the chromosomes, and computing the fitness value for each chromosome. The fitness value evaluates how good the keystream generator is, and it important in GP to create the new population. After executing each candidate keystream generator, the resulted Binary keystream

Algorithm 2. Convertor

```
Input:  Chromosome (genotype) of length chromlength
Output: Phenotype, i.e., keystream generator (KS)
Begin
for i = 1 to chromlength do
     Search in the chromosome for FR (from 0 to 3);
     Add corresponding CFG rule to KS;
End for;
If KS is empty then
     Add LFSR function;
Search for any nonterminal letter "S" left and replace it with LFSR function;
  for i = 1 to KS length do
     Search in KS for TR and LR (from 4 to 19);
          Replace it with corresponding CFG rule;
If the number of terminals of a LFSR function  = MAX then
          Replace nonterminal letter "X" with LR (from 12 to 19);
  End for;
End;
```

Algorithm 3. Code Interpreter, GACI for short

```
Input:  Individual program, keystream length in Bits, i=0;
Output: Binary keystream
Begin
if  program = 'a'..'h' then convert it to Binary;
         i
if  program = '&' then return GACI and GACI;
         i
if  program = '|' then return GACI or GACI;
         i
if  program = '^' then return GACI xor GACI;
         i
if  program = '#' then  generate keystream of a given length;
         i
i= i+1;
End;
```

is examined. There are a number of metrics used to analyze keystream generators such as correlation immunity, linear complexity and keystream randomness. Randomness and keystream period length have been considered in this study. Thus, the fitness function emanates from the fact that in a random sequence:

1. $n_0 = n_1$
2. $n_{01} = n_{11} = n_{10} = n_{00}$, where, n_w is the frequency of w in the Binary sequence.
3. $1/2^i \times n_r$ runs in the Binary sequence are of length i, where n_r is the number of runs in the sequence, i.e.,

$$\left(\frac{1}{2^i} \times n_r\right) = n_i \text{ for all } i = 1 \text{ to } M \tag{2}$$

In Equation 2, n_i is the desired number of runs of length i, and M is maximum run length. Three factors are considered in the fitness evaluation of the chromosomes which are:

1.   Randomness of the generated keystream.
2.   Keystream period length.
3.   Program size.

Therefore, the fitness function *fit(x)* (Awad, 2011a, 2011b, 2013) used to evaluate each chromosome *x* can be defined as follows, where *size* is the period length, *wt* is a constant, and *length* is the program size:

$$f_1 = \left| n_0 - n_1 \right| \tag{3}$$

$$f_2 = \left| n_{00} - \frac{size}{4} \right| + \left| n_{01} - \frac{size}{4} \right| + \left| n_{10} - \frac{size}{4} \right| + \left| n_{11} - \frac{size}{4} \right| \tag{4}$$

$$f_3 = \sum_{i=1}^{M} \left| \left(\frac{1}{2^i} \times n_r \right) - n_i \right| \tag{5}$$

$$fit(x) = \frac{size}{1 + f_1 + f_2 + f_3} + \frac{wt}{length(x)} \tag{6}$$

New Population Generator

To generate a new population, a number of genetic operations are used, which are selection, crossover, mutation, and replacement. Two selection algorithms have been examined, tournament and roulette wheel. Also, single-point and multi-point crossovers have been studied with different rates. In the replacement, the whole population is replaced by newly generated population. Algorithm 4 describes the process of generating a new population.

STREAM CIPHER DESIGN ALGORITHM

GP and SA are integrated to avoid the problem of getting stuck in a local minimum and to preserve good individuals into the next generation. Algorithm 5 presents the main steps of designing stream cipher.

Algorithm 4. (New Population Generation)

```
Input: population, population size (popsize), crossover rate (cr), and muta-
tion rate (mr)
Output: New population
Begin
        for i = 1 to popsize/2 do
                Select two chromosomes;
                Generate a random number r;
                if r ≤ cr then
                        Perform crossover;
                for each child chromosome do
                        Generate a random number r;
                        if r ≤ mr then
                                Perform mutation;
                end for;
        end for;
End;
```

Algorithm 5. (Cipher Design)

```
Input: Keystream period length (size)
Output: LFSR-based keystream generator
Begin
        Generate the initial population (pop) randomly;
        Convert genotypes to phenotypes;
        Evaluate pop,
        T = 250:
        While not Max Number of generations do
                Generate a new population (pop1) by applying crossover and mu-
tation;
                Convert genotypes to phenotypes;
                Evaluate the fitness of the new generated chromosomes of pop1;
                Calculate the averages of fitness values for pop and pop1, av
and av1 respectively;
                If (av1 > av) then replace the old population by the new one,
i.e., pop = pop1
                Else
                    Begin
                            e = av - av1;
                            Pr =  -e/T;
                            Generate a random number (rnd);
                            If (exp(pr) > rnd) then pop = pop1;
                    End Else
                EndIf
                Reduce T;
        End While
                Return the best chromosome of the last generation;
End.
```

RESULTS

The objectives of this chapter are to design efficient and effective method for designing keystream generators of stream cipher automatically. The second objective is to study the effectiveness of GADS to solve this problem. This section shows the results and findings of applying the proposed method, and its effectiveness to solve the problem of this study. The proposed method has been implemented using C++ programming language.

To study the performance of using GADS in designing keystream generators of stream cipher, a number of experiments have been carried out to compare between different genetic operations and parameters as shown in Table 9. The results of each experiment have obtained by running the program 20 times, and finding the average of best fitness values of the 20 runs. The proposed designing algorithm control parameters are the following, where, in all runs, crossover rate is 1.0, and the keystream length is 200 Bits.

Table 9. Experiments of studying the performance of the proposed method

	Exp. No.1	Exp. No.2	Exp. No.3	Exp. No.4	Exp. No.5	Exp. No.6	Exp. No.7	Exp. No.8	Exp. No.9
Chromosome structure	1	2	3	1	2	3	1	2	3
Crossover type	Single-point crossover				Multi-point crossover		Multi-point crossover		
Selection method	Tournament selection						Roulette Wheel Selection		

1. Keystream length in Bits.
2. Population size.
3. Chromosome length.
4. Maximum number of generations.
5. Crossover and mutation rates.
6. FR, LR, and TR block sizes.

The results presented in Table 10 are the results of using different population size values. From Table 10, it is clear that by increasing the population size, better fitness values can be obtained, for all chromosome structures, selection methods, and crossover methods. The results shown in Table 11 indicate that the optimal chromosome length is 30. Increasing chromosome length, above 50, does not improve the fitness values. Table 12 presents the results as the average of best fitness values in different runs for different number of generations. Based on these results, the maximum number of generations has no great effect on the performance of the proposed method. However, the maximum number of generations should be more than 20 and not more than 30. Finally, from the results of Table 13, it is apparent that the best mutation rate is 0.05.

In addition to above results, FR block size of chromosomes of structure 2 has been studied. Because, in the experiments with chromosome structure 2, there is a need to identify the length of FR block each time we run the program. The results of Table 14 shows that the best FR block size is 10.

Table 10. Results of experiments with different population sizes

Population Size	Fitness Average								
	Exp.1	Exp.2	Exp.3	Exp.4	Exp.5	Exp.6	Exp.7	Exp.8	Exp.9
15	12.65	4.32	2.74	15.97	17.47	6.32	18.66	12.54	6.45
20	12.82	9.56	4.55	16.23	15.42	10.03	16.68	10.99	9.07
30	17.55	12.85	8.56	17.65	12.23	10.27	24.28	12.99	9.57
50	22.57	14.62	10.22	25.73	11.72	15.97	22.84	15.98	13.83
100	27.72	16.16	12.05	28.74	15.28	21.28	29.94	20.94	16.81
150	29.42	16.31	13.99	30.67	19.69	22.52	30.26	23.52	19.37
200	30.71	20.23	17.05	33.55	23.58	21.08	31.87	23.23	17.91
250	32.38	22.93	17.35	34.65	23.19	21.69	31.99	24.07	22.36
300	33.19	22.89	18.71	34.35	24.34	24.62	33.81	27.03	21.66
350	33.65	23.43	22.03	35.06	24.76	22.44	34.31	28.04	23.71

Table 11. Results of experiments with different chromosome lengths

Chromosome Length	Fitness Average								
	Exp.1	Exp.2	Exp.3	Exp.4	Exp.5	Exp.6	Exp.7	Exp.8	Exp.9
10	5.4	0.4	0.4	5.4	0.4	0.4	5.4	0.4	0.4
15	25.22	10.39	6.18	32.35	7.51	9.45	32.27	12.35	8.14
20	30.56	10.82	8.26	34.27	11.85	22.07	34.1	13.16	16.44
30	33.65	23.43	22.03	35.06	24.76	24.62	34.31	28.04	23.71
40	33.49	19.89	17.62	33.68	21.82	22.32	33.47	23.35	22.68
50	33.07	16.85	16.74	36.32	21.15	20.77	30.81	25.62	21.75
60	28.45	15.43	17.82	35.62	20.67	19.99	31.47	20.93	20.54

Table 12. Results of experiments with different number of generations

Max Number of Generations	Fitness Average								
	Exp.1	Exp.2	Exp.3	Exp.4	Exp.5	Exp.6	Exp.7	Exp.8	Exp.9
5	31.04	26.29	17.05	30.32	27.13	19.15	38.13	27.15	24.11
10	32.95	27.17	20.59	31.87	28.21	27.04	36.06	23.65	22.15
20	32.97	23.47	19.33	33.75	26.74	21.64	33.25	24.06	22.52
30	33.65	23.43	22.03	35.06	24.76	24.62	34.31	28.04	23.71
40	32.88	20.41	18.98	34.13	21.26	20.17	34.38	23.57	22.78
50	32.87	19.64	18.74	34.1	21.24	19.39	32.07	25.71	21.37
60	32.36	21.53	15.85	34.53	22.02	21.58	32.97	24.56	23.19
70	31.38	21.44	18.44	32.32	24.36	23.17	32.79	24.21	23.33
80	33.74	20.89	17.89	31.88	24.84	20.74	34.7	25.25	22.69

Table 13. Results of experiments with different mutation rates

Mutation Rate	Fitness Average								
	Exp.1	Exp.2	Exp.3	Exp.4	Exp.5	Exp.6	Exp.7	Exp.8	Exp.9
0.02	32.96	21.55	16.09	35.61	23.82	22.39	32.74	25.73	23.19
0.03	33.45	20.95	17.09	34.07	23.19	21.28	33.36	23.66	23.16
0.04	34.21	22.34	19.83	34.9	23.77	21.67	31.65	24.93	21.73
0.05	33.65	23.43	22.03	35.06	24.76	24.62	34.31	28.04	23.71
0.06	31.39	21.04	14.89	33.2	23.52	20.42	33.52	26.69	22.58
0.07	32.12	20.09	15.29	34.37	19.79	21.38	32.18	25.82	22.03
0.08	31.03	20.23	19.14	32.62	23.68	19.17	33.26	24.93	22.40
0.09	30.79	21.19	18.62	32.96	21.49	20.98	30.69	24.79	22.95
0.1	30.92	22.38	16.78	32.44	21.91	19.61	32.70	23.88	18.55

Table 14. Results of experiments with different FR block lengths

FR Block Size	Exp.2	Exp.5	Exp.8
2	22.48	21.81	28.24
3	23.5	22.41	26.89
5	24.04	23.8	25.99
6	20.22	21.51	24.99
7	19.93	22.1	25.91
8	22.82	20.31	24.78
9	21.68	21.75	25.34
10	23.43	24.76	28.04
15	6.82	13.75	14.69

Furthermore, FR and TR block sizes have been studied in the experiments, in which chromosome structure 3 is used. Table 15 presents the results of experiment 3 with different values of FR and TR block sizes. The worst fitness value average is 10.99 when FR and TR block lengths are 15 because there is no space for leave rules (LR) in the chromosomes. The best fitness value is 25.12 when FR block length is 3 and TR block length is 6.

Table 16 shows that the worst fitness average value is 11.96 when FR and TR block lengths are 15. The best fitness average value is 30.72 when FR block length is 15 and TR block length is 6.

Table 17 displays the results for different lengths of FR block and TR block. The worst fitness average value is 15.94 when FR and TR block lengths are 15. The best fitness values are 28.50 and 28.52 for FR block length 15 and TR block length 5, and when FR block length is equal to TR block length and is equal to 6, respectively.

Finally, we need to compare between the proposed GADS method of this chapter and previous SAP algorithm proposed by Awad (2011a, 2011b), in which LISP expression is used as representation method, for designing stream ciphers. Table 18 presents the best fitness values obtained in the two methods, for different number of generations.

Table 15. Results of experiment 3 with different lengths of FR and TR

2	20.22	19.98	20.87	19.61	19.19	22.14	18.81	17.88	21.14
3	21.02	20.57	21.52	25.12	24.49	18.47	23.75	20.68	20.55
5	20.13	23.65	21.42	20.88	22.59	21.31	20.26	20.85	18.71
6	22.24	20.78	22.06	21.99	20.89	20.91	19.11	17.42	16.33
7	20.54	22.33	20.62	21.52	19.70	16.46	19.69	20.75	19.49
8	16.69	23.03	22.04	22.91	21.78	20.73	21.08	14.49	21.03
9	17.50	21.07	21.65	23.15	20.71	18.85	23.19	17.55	22.34
10	23.11	20.12	22.04	21.48	23.18	19.08	18.24	22.03	24.05
15	18.09	20.93	19.36	21.47	18.95	20.71	15.97	16.24	10.99
FR TR	2	3	5	6	7	8	9	10	15

Table 16. Results of experiment 6 with different lengths of FR block and TR block

2	20.45	17.89	19.75	21.2	19.41	18.97	19.57	18.21	19.54
3	20.03	25.38	23.83	25.52	20.03	22.85	23.01	24.04	22.15
5	20.14	25.79	17.89	24.67	21.63	23.47	21.41	24.62	19.24
6	21.56	23.92	21.51	19.38	23.41	19.84	25.07	20.93	21.61
7	21.72	23.81	27.14	25.13	22.58	22.72	18.17	21.66	20.45
8	21.64	23.24	23.78	22.04	22.91	19.56	24.35	19.38	21.81
9	21.32	21.82	24.41	24.45	27.47	21.99	23.08	19.68	25.54
10	24.42	25.24	26.34	26.84	22.99	21.11	23.42	21.49	23.97
15	19.04	25.79	24.55	30.72	24.81	15.63	22.21	20.21	11.96
FR **TR**	**2**	**3**	**5**	**6**	**7**	**8**	**9**	**10**	**15**

Table 17. Experiment 9 results with different lengths of FR block and TR block

2	22.64	27.91	24.70	24.53	26.64	24.77	24.51	24.34	23.06
3	26.20	25.59	24.47	25.52	27.81	25.65	24.44	23.85	22.97
5	23.25	23.39	25.74	26.62	27.16	23.75	24.49	23.12	21.26
6	24.27	27.10	25.51	28.52	25.51	26.04	28.40	23.86	22.47
7	24.96	24.91	23.98	27.66	27.13	21.28	22.79	23.11	19.13
8	24.27	26.26	25.34	28.25	25.41	25.25	23.78	21.66	24.01
9	21.93	24.99	27.70	27.19	25.86	23.82	22.86	19.84	26.03
10	26.82	26.20	26.33	26.85	25.13	25.31	24.19	23.71	27.09
15	22.09	28.09	28.50	28.02	26.40	21.50	21.93	19.84	15.94
TR **TR**	**2**	**3**	**5**	**6**	**7**	**8**	**9**	**10**	**15**

Table 18. A comparison between GADS and Awad's previous method

MAX Number of Generations	GADS	Previous SAP
30	35.06	34.6199
50	34.1	35.7214
70	32.32	36.3741
90	35.65	35.3944

Figures 5, 6, 7, 8, 9, and 10 present a number of keystream generators evolved by the proposed auto-mated design method. Genotypes, phenotypes, their fitness values, and the Binary keystream generated by each generator (phenotype) are also presented. As we can see, the keystreams have long period lengths ($\geq$ 200 Bits) and are random (pass randomness tests). Thus, it is hard to recover the cipher's key from the keystream for its unpredictability.

Figure 5. Example 1 of keystream generator evolved by the proposed method

The genotype: 9,14,9,6,11,2,19,15,14,4,2,4,6,19,13,4,17,9,4,10,11,8,9,18,14,5,14,6,3,8,19,
The phenotype: ^^^#b#hch#b#afa
　The fitness value: 41.9672
The keystream :
0111001100010001001101111100111000000111111111000111001000110100101000001011011001111001010
1001100110101100001010010000100000000100101100101110111100001111011010100010111111101010101
11101000111101100011

Figure 6. Example 2 of keystream generator evolved by the proposed method

The genotype: 8,6,617,10,15,19,14,13,12,4,11,18,8,17,2,15,19,18,9,6,3,6,4,12,4,8,6,11,12,12,
The phenotype: ^#ahg#efh
　The fitness value: 36.4571
The Keystream :
0011011000110011000000010000111101010101100001001011101011110011010000010110110101101001010
1000000110001000111111101000110111001111000101011100011101101111011110111111110000010100110
01000001100101100101

Figure 7. Example 3 of keystream generator evolved by the proposed method

The genotype: 16,18,14,17,10,11,3,17,5,18,6,10,15,10,5,16,3,6,11,2,9,16,11,11,6,12,6,15,19,12,18,
The phenotype: ^&#hdh#f#ffedg
　The fitness value: 41.1245
The keystream :
0100011001110111011001000001100011111000000000110001101110010110101111010010011000011010101
0110011001010011110101101111110111111110110110100110100010000111100010010101110100000010101
0100001011100001001110

Figure 8. Example 4 of keystream generator evolved by the proposed method

The genotype: 3,18,7,11,7,10,2,0,8,16,12,5,11,12,13,6,9,2,0,3,10,17,9,4,15,16,16,16,8,14,3,
The phenotype:^&&#a#bha#b#cfgg#e#a
　The fitness value: 35.4571
The keystream :
1011011001001110011001111110111000010101001111011010001010000110010111010010010100
1011010101011111001110111000001011100100011000011101010001110001001000010001000000
1111101011001101111000110100

Figure 9. Example 5 of keystream generator evolved by the proposed method

The genotype: 19,4,12,16,11,5,9,18,0,19,7,5,8,19,14,9,10,10,9,2,12,2,3,12,15,17,18,
The phenotype: ^^#b#ach#dd#
 The fitness value: 37.5092
The keystream :
101111101011110000001100001010100101001100101100100010011101001000011100100101000010 01001
101011011011001110001111011110100000111110010101111110110011111110001000000000101101 01010
11000110011000010111

Figure 10. Example 6 of keystream generator evolved by the proposed method

The genotype: 6,14,2,5,10,11,14,2,15,3,11,11,15,16,9,15,9,17,18,13,12,14,14,13,6,6,9,19,14,3,8,
The phenotype: ^^#hhd#e#fdh
 The fitness value: 38.9058
The keystream :
10110100111011000111000000001111100011000001001101110111001100010100010010011111001 110010
00011101000010101010000010111010100100011110000100001011001011011011111110111110110 1011110
010100110011010101100

From the results of all exterminates, we conclude the following:

1. Increasing the population size yields better results. This result has been found in many researches that approved that GP works better with high number of population size. But Further increase of the population size does not always improve the solution. Moreover, the computational time is increased significantly

2. The mutation rate (probability) should be set low because if it is high the search will turn into random search, and the solution may be different entirely from the previous solution. That will let us to loss the benefit of using GP. The best mutation rate found is 0.05.

3. The maximum number of generations has no effect on the proposed method performance. In general, it should not less than 20 and not greater than 30.

4. The best chromosome length is 30 integers.

5. According the results of all experiments, the best chromosome structure is chromosome structure 1, in which, the rule numbers are mixed in the chromosomes.

6. The results showed that using multi-point crossover gives better results comparable with single-point crossover. That is because, the disruptive nature of multi-point crossover appears to encourage the exploration of the search space, rather than favoring the convergence to highly fit individuals early in the search, thus making the search more robust.

7. Regarding the selection method, the above results showed that there is struggling between the two selection methods in the comparisons. Tournament selection performs better when the population size is small. But when the population size or the chromosome length is increased, the roulette wheel selection yields better results. As Noraini and John (2011) proved, qualitative analysis of the selection strategies must be done to adopt the best strategy, because the selection performance is very much dependent on the different criteria at the time of selection of chromosomes, these criteria could be anything like type of population, type of representation method used, and population size.

8. In term of fitness values, the proposed method of this chapter did not improve the results of Awad's previous method used for the automated design of stream ciphers.

CONCLUSION

This chapter presented an effective automated stream ciphers design using GP. The proposed method is a modified version of Awad (2011a, 2011b) SAP algorithm, which has been modified in this work by using GADS. In GADS, the population chromosomes (genotypes) are represented as sequences of integers rather than LISP expressions. Thus, GA operations, such as crossover and mutation, can be applied easily and efficiently. Three chromosome structures have been proposed and analyzed. Different GA operations and parameters have been examined, which are, chromosome structure, chromosome length, selection strategy, population size, crossover type, maximum number of generations, and mutation rate. It has been found that the best results are obtained when using chromosome structure 1, tournament selection, 30 integers as chromosome length, 0.05 as mutation rate, 30 as maximum number of generations, above 50 individuals as population size, and multi-point crossover.

REFERENCES

Al Jadaan, O., Lakishmi, R., & Rao, C. R. (2005). Improved selection operator for genetic algorithm. *Journal of Theoretical and Applied Information Technology*, 4(4), 269–277.

Alander, J. T. (1992). On optimal population size of genetic algorithms. In *Proceedings of the IEEE Computer Systems and Software Engineering* (pp. 65–69). IEEE. doi:10.1109/CMPEUR.1992.218485

Awad, W. S. (2011a). On the application of evolutionary computation techniques in designing stream cipher systems. *International Journal of Computational Intelligence Systems*, 4(5), 921–928. doi:10.1080/18756891.2011.9727842

Awad, W. S. (2011b). Designing stream cipher systems using genetic programming. In Learning and optimization (LION5) (LNCS), (vol. 6683, pp. 308-320). Berlin: Springer.

Awad, W. S. (2013). The effect of mutation operation on GP- based stream ciphers design algorithm. In *Proceedings of 5th International Conference on Agents and Artificial Intelligence*. Academic Press.

Beasley, J. E., & Chu, P. C. (1996). A genetic Algorithm for the set covering problem. *European Journal of Operational Research*, 94(2), 392–404. doi:10.1016/0377-2217(95)00159-X

Beker, H., & Piper, F. (1982). *Cipher systems: The protection of communications*. Northwood Publications.

Bertsimas, D., & Tsitsiklis, J. (1993). Simulated Annealing. *Statistical Science*, 8(1), 10–15. doi:10.1214/ss/1177011077

Caballero-Gil, P. (2000). New upper bounds on the linear complexity. *Computers and Mathematics with Applications*, 39(3), 31-38.

Eiben, A. E., Hinterding, R., & Michalewic, Z. (1999). Parameters control in evolutionary algorithms. *IEEE Transactions on Systems, Man, and Cybernetics*, 16(1), 122–128.

Ferreira, C. (2002). Gene Expression Programming: Mathematical Modeling by an Artificial Intelligence. Portugal: Angra do Heroismo.

Forouzan, B. A. (2008). *Cryptography and network security*. McGraw-Hill.

Garcia, L. J., & Fuster-Sabater, A. (2000). On the linear complexity of the sequences generated by non-linear filtering. *Information Processing Letters, 76*(1-2), 67–73. doi:10.1016/S0020-0190(00)00117-4

Goldberg, D. E. (1989). *Genetic algorithms in search, optimization, and machine learning*. Addison-Wesley.

Goresky, M., & Klapper, A. (2006). Pseudonoise sequence based on algebraic feedback shift registers. *IEEE Transactions on Information Theory, 52*(4), 1649–1662. doi:10.1109/TIT.2006.871045

Gustafson, H., Dawson, E., Nielsen, L., & Caelli, W. (1994). A computer package for measuring the strength of encryption algorithm. *Computers & Security, 14*(8), 687–697. doi:10.1016/0167-4048(94)90051-5

Holland, J. H. (1975). *Adaptive in natural and artificial systems*. University of Michigan.

Kellegoz, T., Toklu, B., & Wilson, J. (2008). Comparing efficiencies of genetic crossover operators for one machine total weighted tardiness problem. *Applied Mathematics and Computation, 199*(2), 590–598. doi:10.1016/j.amc.2007.10.013

Kirkpatrick, S., Gelatt, C. D., & Vecchi, M. P. (1983). Optimization by Simulated Annealing. *Science New Series, 220*(4598), 671–680. PMID:17813860

Koza, J. R. (1992). *Genetic programming*. Cambridge, MA: MIT Press.

Koza, J. R. (1994). *GP II: Automatic discovery of reusable programs*. Cambridge, MA: MIT press.

L'ecuyer, P., & Simard, R. (2007). TestU01: A C library for empirical testing of random number generators. *ACM Transactions on Mathematical Software, 33*(4), 22–40, es. doi:10.1145/1268776.1268777

Lari, K., & Young, S. J. (1990). The estimation of stochastic context-free grammars using the Inside-Outside algorithm. *Computer Speech & Language, 4*(1), 34–56. doi:10.1016/0885-2308(90)90022-X

Massey, J. L. (1976). Shift register sequences and BCH decoding. *IEEE Transactions on Information Theory, 15*(1), 122–127. doi:10.1109/TIT.1969.1054260

McCarthy, J. (1979). *The implementation of Lisp, History of Lisp*. Stanford University.

Miller, B. L., & Goldberg, D. E. (1995). Genetic Algorithms. Tournament Selection and the Effects of Noise. *Complex Systems, 9*(3), 193–212.

Mitchell, M. (1996). *An Introduction to Genetic Algorithm*. Cambridge, MA: MIT Press.

Naur, P. (1963). Revised report on the algorithmic language ALGOL 60. *Communications of the ACM, 6*(1), 1–17. doi:10.1145/366193.366201

Noraini, M. R., & John, G. (2011). Genetic Algorithm Performance with Different Selection Strategies in Solving TSP. In *Proceedings of the World Congress on Engineering*. London, UK: Academic Press.

O'Neill, M., & Conor, R. (2003). *Grammatical Evolution: Evolutionary Automatic Programming in an Arbitrary Language*. Springer. doi:10.1007/978-1-4615-0447-4

Ochoa, G., Harvey, I., & Buxton, H. (1999). On recombination and optimal mutation rates. In *Proceedings of the Genetic and Evolutionary Computation Conference* (vol. 1, pp. 488-495). San Francisco, CA: Academic Press.

Paar, C., & Pelzl, J. (2010). *Understanding Cryptography*. Springer. doi:10.1007/978-3-642-04101-3

Paterson, N. R., & Livesey, M. (1996). Distinguishing Genotype and Phenotype in Genetic Programming. In *Proceedings of Genetic Programming Conference*. Stanford University.

Qi, H. (2008). *Stream Ciphers and Linear Complexity*. (Thesis of Master degree in Science), Available from National University of Singapore NUS Dissertations and Theses database.

Rakesh, K., & Jyotishree. (2012). Blending Roulette Wheel Selection & Rank Selection in Genetic Algorithms. *International Journal of Machine Learning and Computing*, 2(4), 365–370.

Rueppel, R. A. (1986). *Aanalysis and design of stream ciphers*. Berlin: Springer-Verlag. doi:10.1007/978-3-642-82865-2

Ryan, C., Collins, J., & Neill, M. O. (1998). Grammatical evolution: Evolving programs for an arbitrary language. *LNCS*, *1391*, 83–96.

Schneier, B. (1996). *Applied cryptography*. John Wiley and Sons.

Siebel & Peter (2005). *Practical Common Lisp*. Author.

Spears, W., & Jong, D. C. K. A. (1990). An analysis of multi-point crossover. Morgan Kaufmann Publishers.

Stalling, W. (2006). *Cryptography and network security: Principles and practices* (4th ed.). Prentice Hall.

Syswerda, G. (1989). *Uniform crossover in genetic algorithms*. Paper presented at the 3rd International Conference on Genetic Algorithms, San Francisco, CA.

Szaban, M., Seredynski, F., & Bouvry, P. (2006). Collective behavior of rules for cellular automata-based stream ciphers. In *Proceedings of IEEE Congress on Evolutionary Computation*. Vancouver, Canada: IEEE. doi:10.1109/CEC.2006.1688306

Tobias, B., & Lothar, T. (1995). *A comparison of selection schemes used in Genetics Algorithms*. TIK Report.

Zalzala, A. M., & Fleming, P. J. (1997). *Genetic Algorithms in Engineering Systems*. IET. doi:10.1049/PBCE055E

Zeng, K., Yang, C., & Rao, T. R. N. (1991). Pseudorandom bit generator in stream cipher cryptography. *Computer*, 24(2), 8–17. doi:10.1109/2.67207

KEY TERMS AND DEFINITIONS

Cryptanalysis: It is the science of breaking cipher systems.

Cryptography: It is the science of encrypting data.

Encryption: It is a process of converting plaintext to ciphertext.

Evolutionary Computation: It is a subfield of computational intelligence, that includes a number of global optimization methods.

GADS: It is genetic algorithm used to provide solutions to problems as computer programs.

Genetic Algorithm: It is one of evolutionary computation algorithms, which is a population-based iterative improvement search algorithm used to solve optimization problems using techniques inspired by natural evolution.

Genetic Programming: It is an application of genetic algorithm, in which the structure under adaption is a population of programs. Thus, the solution of a problem is a given as computer program.

LFSR: It is a shift register with linear feedback function.

Random Sequence: It is a sequence of characters that pass a number of randomness tests, such as Frequency and Run tests.

Simulated Annealing: It is a global optimization technique inspired by the annealing process in metallurgy. This technique can help to avoid the problem of getting stuck in a local minimum and to lead towards the globally optimum solution.

Stream Cipher: It is a cipher system used to encrypt a plaintext one bit at a time.

Chapter 4
Chaotic–Based and Biologically Inspired Cryptosystems for Secure Image Communication and Storage

El-Sayed M. El-Alfy
King Fahd University of Petroleum and Minerals, Saudi Arabia

ABSTRACT

Protecting confidentiality of sensitive data is growing in importance in many personal, commercial, governmental, medical and military applications. Data encryption remains the most prevalent mechanism for this goal in cybersecurity to store and communicate data in unintelligible form. However, images are known to have intrinsic characteristics different from text, which limit the applicability of conventional cryptographic algorithms. This chapter provides a review of the work related to image cryptosystems based on chaos theory and biologically-inspired algorithms. Then, a case study is presented using ideas from genetic crossover and mutation to confuse and diffuse images to generate secure cipher images with very low correlation between pixels.

INTRODUCTION

Nowadays, digital images are prevalent in many areas such as remote sensing, satellite imagery, astrophysics, seismology, agriculture, radiology, telemedicine, ecosystems, industrial processes, military communications, medical imagery, and image archiving systems. A stringent requirement for the successful deployment of these systems is secure storage and transmission of image data. This field is gaining growing importance in recent years due to the proliferation of multimedia network applications and services.

Cryptographic algorithms have been the heart of the security techniques for protecting confidentiality, checking integrity, and authenticating the origin of the data (Forouzan, 2007; Menezes et al., 2010). Encrypted images are stored or transmitted over public transmission lines but only intended recipients can decrypt and view them in comprehensible form. Although several conventional techniques and stan-

DOI: 10.4018/978-1-4666-9426-2.ch004

dards (such as DES, AES and RSA) have been developed, they are mainly for text and short messages. Applying such techniques to images has been found to be inefficient due to the bulk size of image data. Additionally, image pixels often have higher redundancy and correlation which can enable reasonable pixel value prediction from neighboring pixels (Mao and Chen, 2005; Younes and Jantan; 2008). Therefore, new image encryption schemes have been introduced in the literature to take into consideration these special requirements (Patel and Belani, 2011; Jawad and Sulong, 2013).

Some approaches are just modifications of exiting techniques to improve their performance when applied to bulk data in general and images in particular. Other remarkable approaches utilize chaos theory and biologically-inspired approaches (Delman, 2004; Mao and Chen, 2005; Kumar and Ghose, 2009; Agarwal, 2012; Ratan, 2014). The principal idea of image encryption is *confusion* of image pixels and *diffusion* of pixel values to become more immune for the common attacks on cryptographic systems. Chaotic-based cryptography is one of the rapidly growing areas with several proposals for image encryption (Kocarev, 2001; Vohra and Patel, 2012). Thus, image encryption can take advantage of the fascinating properties of a chaotic dynamic system including randomness, and high sensitivity to system parameters and initial conditions. Biological processes, which are evolution-based (such as genetic algorithms, differential evolution and memetic algorithms), swarm based (such as particle swarm, ant colony, and immune systems), or neurosystem-based (such as artificial neural networks) have inspired many powerful computational algorithms for optimization, function approximation, learning or soft computing. These approaches have found promising applications in many complex systems including cryptography and cryptanalysis (Olariu and Zomaya, 2005; Laskari et al. 2005; Dadhich and Yadav, 2014).

In this chapter, after a brief background on chaos theory, we are going to first review the state-of-the-art of image cryptosystems with focus on chaotic-based and biologically-inspired approaches, whether used separately or combined. Although several approaches are reviewed and cited, this chapter is not meant to be comprehensive. We then provide a case study for image encryption utilizing ideas of genetic evolution such as mutation and crossover. We share some empirical results demonstrating and motivating the reader into this research field.

BACKGROUND: CHAOS THEORY

Over years since the early work of Herni Poincare in 1890, several attempts have been made toward developing understating of behavioral patterns associated with complex natural phenomena that are apparently unpredictable in the long term (Ditto and Munakata, 1995; Ott, 2002). Common characteristics of such phenomena are recurrence and extreme sensitivity to initial conditions, which is popularly referred to as a butterfly effect (this term is coined by Edward Lorenz to describe the potential influence on a hurricane caused by flapping the wings of a distant butterfly). Various systems have been investigated in the discrete and continuous time domains. Among the popular chaotic systems are:

- Chaotic maps (e.g. logistic map, Henon map, Arnold's cat map, Baker's map),
- Strange attractors (e.g. Lorenz weather model, Chau's circuit, Rossler attractor), and
- Double pendulum.

Figure 1. Trajectory simulation of Chau's circuit.

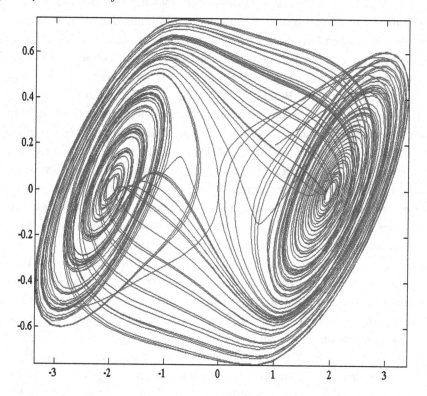

Figure 1 shows an example trajectory for a Chau's circuit. Recently, there has been mutual interest in hybrid systems involving various chaotic systems with neural networks, fuzzy logic, and evolutionary algorithms (Zelinka et al., 2010).

Although chaos development has started with meteorology for weather forecasting, the theoretical concepts have found many applications in several other areas such as engineering, computer science, economic and financial sciences, politics, psychological aspects of human behavior, quantum physics, celestial mechanics, and fluid turbulence. Some examples of computer science applications are cryptography, DNA computing, and robotics. In the following subsections, we will provide more details on work related to image encryption in particular.

IMAGE CRYPTOSYSTEMS: REVIEW

In this section, we review the research proposals for image encryption and concentrate on chaotic-based and biologically-inspired approaches. We divide the techniques into four subsections. The first subsection reviews the straightforward techniques and some of the modifications that been proposed to make them applicable for image encryption with reasonable performance. Then, in the following subsection, we review several proposals for chaotic-based image encryption approaches. In the third subsection, we discuss approaches that are biologically inspired. Finally, we review techniques that involve both ideas; this subsection is entitled hybrid cryptosystems.

Conventional and Modified Cryptosystems

Perhaps the straightforward approach is to treat images as regular data and use any of the conventional symmetric or asymmetric cryptosystems. Over years, several standard have been developed for data encryption such as Data Encryption Standard (DES), Triple-DES, Advanced Encryption Standard (AES), International Data Encryption Algorithm (IDEA), Rivest-Shamir-Adleman (RSA), and techniques based on Elliptic Curve Cryptography (ECC) (Forouzan, 2007; Menezes et al., 2010). However, as mentioned earlier these techniques are generic and do not take into consideration the inherent characteristics of images including bulk size, and pixel correlation and redundancy. Thus, they turn out to be impractical and less efficient for image encryption. One direct approach is to combine compression with encryption (Bourbakis, 1997). The compressed image has smaller size and low redundancy. Consequently, it might be more reasonably handled by exiting data encryption techniques. Figure 2 shows a typical framework for a cryptosystem that performs encryption after compressing the image. On the decryption side, the order is reversed where decryption is performed first followed by image decompression to retrieve the Plain-Image. Other approaches try to balance the security requirement and the computational requirement by encrypting only significant regions of the plain-image rather than encrypting the full image (Yuen and Wong, 2011; Jawad and Sulong, 2013).

Some authors have proposed various changes to Advanced Encryption Standard (AES) to enhance its performance for images, e.g. (Zeghid et al., 2007; Bashir et al., 2012). Younes and Jantan (2008) introduced a new image encryption approach based on a combination of permutation and Rijndael encryption algorithm. The Plain-Image is first divided into 4×4 blocks which are permutated then encrypted. It was demonstrated that the proposed approach has led to significant reduction of the correlation between image elements and high entropy. A direct encryption approach has been proposed by Pareek et al. (2013) using diffusion-substitution for gray images. The plain image goes through a mixing process then 16 rounds where in each round the image is divided into key-dependent blocks that undergo through permutation and substitution.

Figure 2. General structure of image cryptosystem.

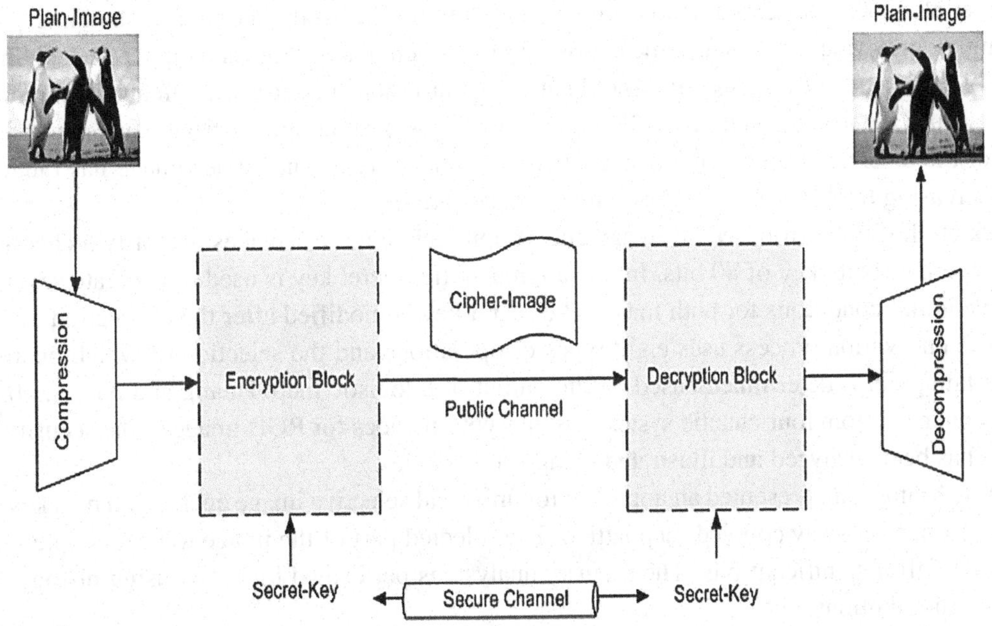

Several attempts have also considered image encryption in some frequency domain including discrete Fourier transform (DFT), discrete cosine transform (DCT), and wavelet transform, e.g. (Yuen and Wong, 2011; Tedmori and Al-Najdawi, 2014).

Chaotic-Based Cryptosystems

One of the successful techniques that has recently attracted the attention of many researchers is chaos-based encryption. Recall that chaos theory is an early developed field for studying the behavior of dynamic systems that are very sensitive to initial conditions and pseudo-randomness generated by deterministic equations (Gilmore and Lefranc, 2008). With the developments made in cryptography and chaos theory, several encryption approaches have been proposed in the literature over the past fifteen years. To provide more efficient and secure solutions, these approaches make use of the properties of chaotic systems including ergodicity, sensitivity to initial conditions, and sensitivity to system parameters. Several examples of these approaches can be found in (Guo, 2000; Kocarev, 2001; Mao and Chen, 2005; Guan et al., 2005; Pareek et al. 2006; Kocarev and Lian, 2011).

Starting in 1989, Matthews has published a paper on the derivation of a chaotic encryption algorithm where a stream cipher has been proposed based on a one-dimensional chaotic map (Matthews, 1989). Following these early attempts, the field has grown with many systems developed based on multidisciplinary ideas from mathematics, physics and electronics. Another approach has been proposed for symmetric block encryption using two-dimensional chaotic maps by Fridrich (1998). With the computer simulation, the author has shown the good diffusion properties of the proposed approach. A discussion of the link between cryptography and chaos theory is presented in (Kocarev and Jakimoski, 2001). This paper also provided an example of encryption based on a logistic map.

Chen et al. (2004) designed a real-time symmetric image encryption based on a generalization of the classical Arnold two-dimensional cat map to three-dimensional map. In their approach, two maps are used, one to shuffle the positions of image pixels whereas the other to confuse the relationship between the input plain-image and the output cipher-image. The authors demonstrated the high security and fast encryption of this approach through experimental work and security analysis.

Guan et al. (2005) presented another image encryption scheme that combines shuffling positions and changing gray values to confuse the relationship between plain-image and cipher-image. Shuffling positions is achieved with the use of Arnold cat map, but it does not affect the image histogram since the pixel values are not changed. In a following step, the pixel values are changed using a preprocessed version of the discrete output signal of the Chen's chaotic system. The cipher-image has random-like and by increasing the key space, the brute-force attacks are infeasible.

Pareek et al. (2006) proposed an image encryption technique that makes use of two chaotic maps with an external secret key of 80 bits. In this approach, the secret key is used to generate session keys and derive initial conditions for both maps. The secret key is modified after the encryption of each 16 pixels. The encryption process uses eight types of operations and the selection of which operation to use at certain pixel is determined based on the output of a logistic map. Huang and Nien (2009) used chaotic sequences from four chaotic systems as encryption codes for RGB images. The security of this approach has been analyzed and illustrated using some images.

In 2007, Xiang et al. presented an approach for universal selective image encryption by a key stream generated from a one-way coupled map lattice. The selected part of the image to be encrypted is composed of the left n significant bits. The security analysis is performed for $n = 4$ using histograms and correlation distributions.

Fu et al. (2011) proposed a chaos-based bit-level permutation for efficient and secure encryption of digital images. This approach uses a two-stage bit-level permutation using a chaotic sequence sorting algorithm and Arnold cat map. The authors made the claim that this approach can be a competitive alternative to permutation-diffusion type ciphers in terms of security, yet with much lower computational complexity. Thus, it can be a promising solution for real-time image communication applications. Zhang and Wang (2013) used piecewise linear chaotic map (PWLCM) to generate random sequences as part of a stream cipher for SPIHT compressed color images. Based on chaotic skew tent-map and S-box, Hussain et al. (2013) presented a technique that can cause confusion and diffusion for image encryption. Yuen and Wong (2011) applied chaotic based image encryption but in the frequency domain using Discrete Cosine Transform (DCT).

This research area is fast growing with several other approaches proposed in the last five years for image encryption based chaotic systems, e.g. (Mazloom and Eftekhari-Moghadam, 2009; Amin et al., 2010; Xia and Shih, 2010; Yoon and Kim, 2010; Ye, 2010; Chen and Chang, 2011; Kumar and Ghose, 2011; Mazloom and Eftekhari-Moghadam, 2011; Patidar et al., 2011; Peng et al., 2011; Wang et al., 2011; Kocarev and Lian, 2011; Wu et al., 2012; Huang, 2012; Chen et al., 2012; Fu et al., 2012; Seyedzadeh and Mirzakuchaki, 2012; Faragallah, 2012; Fu et al., 2013; Verma et al., 2013; Panduranga and Kumar, 2014; Parvin et al., 2014).

Wang and Wang (2014) proposed a more recent approach for image encryption based on chaos. In this approach, dynamic S-boxes are constructed using logistic and Kent chaotic maps where the initial conditions are generated using an external 256 bit key together with the last pixel of the plain-image. Encryption is performed on groups of pixels using S-boxes and the initial conditions are changed after each group of pixels. Through analysis of 256 gray images, this approach has demonstrated superiority in terms of speed and security.

With the increasing number of papers published on chaos-based cryptosystems, some researchers have tested their security against certain attacks. For instance, Wang et al. (2005) presented a successful chosen-plain text cryptanalytic attack against the 3D cat based symmetric image encryption. Using knowledge of symbolic dynamics and some specially designed plain-images, the authors were able to compute an equivalent initial condition of the diffusion process and subsequently rebuild a valid equivalent 3D cat matrix. With pointed out security weaknesses, it was recommended to use this approach only in limited applications. Further recent cryptanalysis of chaos-based cryptosystems can be found at (Solak et al., 2010; Wang and He, 2011; Solak, 2011; Rhouma and Belghith, 2011; Xing-Yuan and Guo-Xiang, 2012; Wang et al., 2014).

Biologically-Inspired Cryptosystems

Solutions for several complex practical problems have been attempted using nature-inspired algorithms. Information security and data encryption is not different. Rehan (2014) presented an overview on the applications of genetic algorithms to cryptology. Based on his work, the majority of research efforts was on cryptanalysis of classical ciphers and the design of crypto-primitives. Some attempts have been made to break various versions of data encryption standard (DES) using genetic algorithms or particle swarm (Garg, 2006; Song et al., 2007; Shahzad et al., 2009; Sathya et al., 2010; Abd-Elmonim et al., 2011). Several approaches for image encryption are based on genetic algorithms, e.g. (Al-Husainy, 2006; Afarin, R., & Mozaffari, 2013). Another approach based on particle swarm optimization for partial image encryption has been presented in (Kuppusamy and Thamodaran, 2012).

Bergmann (2007) conducted his doctoral thesis on the applications of natural-inspired algorithms for cryptanalysis. His focus was on genetic algorithms and particle swarm optimization. Another review of evolutionary computation for cryptanalysis can be found in (Laskari et al., 2005). An evolutionary approach using adaptive genetic algorithms for image encryption has been introduced in (Sharma et al., 2008). Another image encryption scheme based on evolutionary algorithms is developed in (Souici et al., 2011). But, this approach suffers from slow convergence. Dadhich and Yadav (2014) presented a recent review of the state-of-the-art of the applications of evolutionary algorithms, fuzzy logic and artificial immune systems to cryptography and cryptanalysis.

Differential evolution is another population-based evolutionary optimization approach for stochastic search that has been also applied to symmetric image encryption (Abuhaiba and Hassan, 2011). In this approach the authors used two-dimensional discrete Fourier transform and then applied differential evolution to manipulate the magnitude and phase. A linear feedback shift register was used to select image components for crossover and keyed mutation.

Several approaches based on cellular automata were also proposed for encryption including Hernández Encinas et al. (2002), Maleki et al. (2008), and Jin (2012).

Hybrid Cryptosystems

An overview that covers both genetic algorithms and chaotic systems for data encryption is presented in (Kumar and Ghose, 2009). In (Zelinka and Jasek, 2010), various versions of five evolutionary algorithms, namely differential evolution (DE), self-organizing migrating algorithm (SOMA), genetic algorithm (GA), simulated annealing (SA) and evolutionary strategies (ES) have been used for chaos synchronization to study the possibility of decrypting chaotically encrypted information. This idea has been tested under simplified assumptions using Clifford strange attractor to identify the control parameter of the chaos-based system. From the empirical study, it was found and concluded that chaotic-based encryption systems are probably unsolvable by such evolutionary techniques and consequently remains to be very safe.

A chaotic-based cryptosystem approach inspired by biological operations has been introduced for gray images in (Al-Utaibi and El-Alfy, 2010) and extended to color images in (El-Alfy and Al-Utaibi, 2011). In this approach the fusion and confusion of image pixels were implemented through mutation and crossover operations, respectively. Another hybrid approach for image encryption composed of a genetic algorithm and a chaotic function is proposed by Abdullah et al. (2012). In this approach, a genetic algorithm is used to search for the best encrypted image that has the highest entropy and lowest correlation coefficient from a population of chaotic-based encrypted images. The performance of this approach is evaluated and demonstrated that a high level of resistance to brute-force and statistical attacks is achievable. Wang et al. (2012) proposed designing substitution boxes (S-boxes) with good cryptographic properties based on chaotic maps and evolution processes. In this approach, the authors have first converted the problem of constructing S-box into the well-known traveling salesman problem before applying genetic algorithms.

Other techniques are based on combination of neural networks with chaotic systems have been proposed for image encryption (Lian et al., 2004; Lain, 2009; Bigdeli et al., 2012a). A chaotic neural network is composed of two layers: a chaotic neuron layer, for data diffusion, and linear neuron layer, for data confusion. Lian et al. (2004) applied this approach for JPEG 2000 image encryption by selecting some sensitive image components for encryption. It has been shown that this approach has good security with low computational requirements which makes it suitable for image encryption. This result has also been confirmed by the work proposed by Lian (2009). Bigdeli et al. (2012b) proposed another hybrid approach using Hopfield neural network and a chaotic system for image encryption.

A hybrid system using chaotic maps and DNA encoding is proposed for RGB color images by Liu et al. (2012). This approach can resist exhaustive and statistical attacks due to the large key space and the high key sensitivity. The image color frames R, G, and B are first encoded using DNA. Then, the resulting frames are added using DNA addition then complemented using DNA sequence matrix controlled by logistic map. Liu et al. (2013) proposed a color image encryption using Choquet fuzzy integral (CFI) and a hyper-chaotic system composed of a piecewise linear chaotic map (PWLCM) with the Lorenz system. The chaotic system generates parameters for the CFI which is then used to confuse and diffuse the color components of the image. Other hybrid approaches that combine DNA and chaotic maps have been lately proposed in (Zhang et al., 2010; SaberiKamarposhti et al., 2012; Enayatifar et al., 2014)

Chaotic-based systems have also been combined with reversible cellular automata in the approach proposed by Wang and Luan (2013) for image encryption. For confusion, each pixel is divided into 4-bit units and keyed mutation is performed using intertwining logistic map. For diffusion, a reversible cellular automata is applied for several rounds at the bit level.

CASE STUDY

Cryptosystem Framework

In this section, we present a case study for color image symmetric cryptosystem based on chaotic maps and genetic operations. An early version of this approach has been presented for gray images in (Al-Utaibi and El-Alfy, 2010) and tested for RGB color images in (El-Alfy and Al-Utaibi, 2011). A block diagram outlining the main steps of the considered case study follows the same general structure in Figure 2. As shown in this figure, the source side of the cryptosystem can first perform compression to reduce the image size before going through the encryption block to generate a Cipher-Image. The Cipher-Image is stored or transmitted over a public channel. At the destination side, the Cipher-Image goes through an inverse process. First, it will be decrypted using an inverse procedure to the one implemented in the encryption block. Both the source and the destination share a key secretly which is used in the encryption and decryption procedures. The details of the chaotic-based encryption block with genetic operations are shown in Figure 3. The system starts by taking a Plain-Image as input and decomposes it into various primary colors or channels such as RGB, HSV, CMYK, YUV, YCbCr, or YPbPr (Tkalcic and Tasic, 2003; Busin et al. 2008). Then image diffusion and confusion is achieved using crossover and mutation operations. The parameters for these processes are generated using chaotic maps and secret keys. The decryption block is similar to the encryption algorithm but in reverse order. Thus, the Cipher-Image undergoes first through a mutation operation then column-wise crossover followed by row-wise crossover. The controlling parameters for each operation are generated in a manner identical to their generation at the source side from the secret key.

Figure 3. Outline evolutionary encryption of color images based on chaos-based sequences.

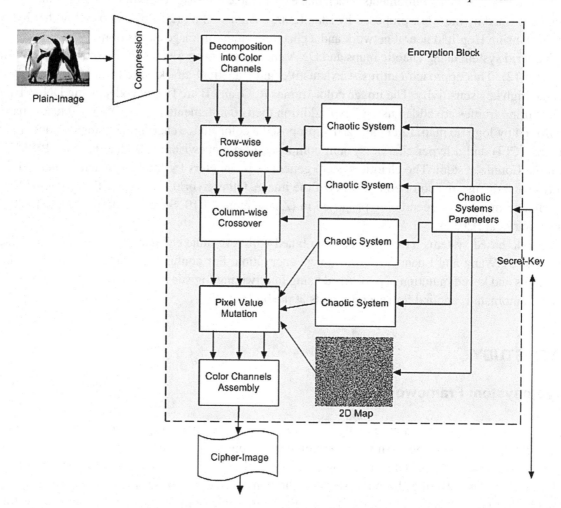

A. Chaotic Systems

In the presented framework, chaotic systems are used to generate chaotic sequences based on controlling parameters and initial conditions. Without loss of generalization, we can use a variety of chaotic systems such as logistic maps, tent maps, Arnold's cat map, horseshoe map, Chua's circuit attractor, Baker's map, Henon's attractor, Rossler's attractor, and Lorenz attractor (Alligood et al. 1997; Gilmore and Lefranc, 2008). However, we used logistic maps in the described test case. For more details on this type of maps, we refer the reader to (Coiteux and Coskey, 2014). Each logistic map is simply defined by the following one-dimensional quadratic recurrence relation:

$$x_t = \mu x_{t-1}(1 - x_{t-1})$$

where μ is a controlling parameter with value in the range $3.569955672 < \mu \leq 4$, and x_t is a real number in the range [0,1]. Figure 4 shows 20 iterations of a typical logistic map with $\mu = 3.9$ and $x_0 = 0.1$. Given values for the controlling parameter μ and the initial condition x_0, a real-valued chaotic sequence

Figure 4. A typical graph showing 20 iterations of a logistic map with μ = 3.9 and x₀ = 0.1

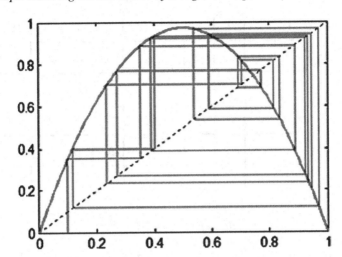

is generated. Due to the sensitivity of the sequence to the values of μ and x_0 and the infinite number of possibilities of the real values, encrypted images are very difficult for brute-force attack (that needs to try all possibilities).

The values of μ and x_0, and subsequently the chaotic sequence, can be used for encrypting the whole image or the image can be divided into blocks and different sequences are used for different blocks. They can also be fixed for all color channels or changed for each color channel.

In the empirical study below, this chaotic map is used four times for each color channel with different parameters similar to the work by (El-Alfy and Al-Utaibi, 2011; Fu and Zhu, 2008) to generate four real-valued chaotic sequences S_1, S_2, S_3, S_4. The sequences S_1 and S_3 are of length M and the other two sequences S_2 and S_4 are of length N where $M \times N$ is the size of the Plain-Image in pixels. The real-valued sequences are mapped to integer/binary sequences in a variety of ways including normalization, thresholding, or sorting. In our case, we sorted the elements in the chaotic sequence in ascending order and took the position indices in the sorted sequence as the key streams (which will be referred to as K_1, K_2, K_3 and K_4). These key streams are then used to control the confusion and diffusion procedures through crossover and mutation operations.

Two other chaotic systems can be optionally used. One to generate a 2D map that will be used as input to the pixel value mutation box; yet this system can be replaced by a shared secret image that is known for both the sender and the receiver. The second chaotic system is used to generate the parameters for all other chaotic systems from the input secret key. Alternatively, this system can be omitted if the parameters are again shared secretly with the receiver.

B. Confusion by Crossover

Image confusion is achieved by scrambling the image pixels row-wise and then column-wise using a biologically inspired multi-point crossover operation. The exchange of pixel locations is determined by the two-key streams K_1 and K_3 where the first is used for row-wise crossover and the second is used for column-wise crossover. Whether the operation is performed row-wise or column-wise, it

Figure 5. Illustration of crossover operation of two pixel sequences.

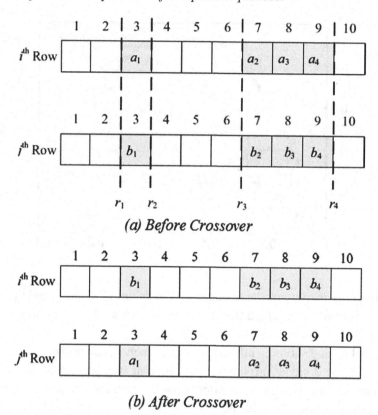

is similar except that the inputs are selected from image rows or columns. Hence, we only explain row-wise crossover. This process iteratively selects two rows and performs multi-point crossover on them. The locations of the crossover points are determined by the value in the key, then pixel values are exchanged between the two rows as demonstrated in Figure 5 which is adopted from (El-Alfy and Al-Utaibi, 2011).

C. Diffusion by Mutation

To diffuse the image pixel, we imitate the biological mutation operation. This operation masks the intermediate image resulting from crossover with a randomly-generated image using an XOR operation. For this purpose, the sender and receiver must first agree on some randomly generated image and keep it secret or agree on a way to generate it. In our case, it is generated using a chaotic map with known parameters to the sender and receiver. The XOR operation is performed pixel by pixel but using two key streams K_3 and K_4 which determine which pixels to XOR next. For instance, pixel $I_m(i, j)$ in the cipher image is obtained by XORing pixel $I_c(i, j)$ in the image resulting from crossover with pixel $K_s(v_i, v_j)$ of the secret image, where $v_i \in K_3$ and $v_j \in K_4$. Thus, $I_m(i, j) = I_c(i, j) \oplus K_s(v_i, v_j)$. This process is explained in Figure 6 by means of a simple example of 4×4 image adopted from (El-Alfy and Al-Utaibi, 2011).

Figure 6. Illustration of the mutation operation for one color channel of 4×4 block.

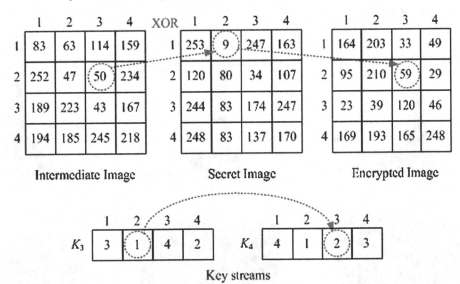

Intermediate Image   Secret Image   Encrypted Image

Key streams

Empirical Results

The code for the described framework is implemented in MATLAB and its performance is tested for a particular case to encrypt different color images. The parameters of the four logistic sequences used in encryption are generated using another logistic map with $\mu = 3.98$ and $x_0 = 0.3$. The selected values are used in an arbitrary order in encrypting all considered images in this chapter.

Figure 7. Examples of Plain-Images (top) and resultant Cipher-Images (bottom); Child is 256×256 24-bit color JPEG, Peppers is 512×512 24-bit color TIFF, and Penguins is 256×256 24-bit color JPEG.

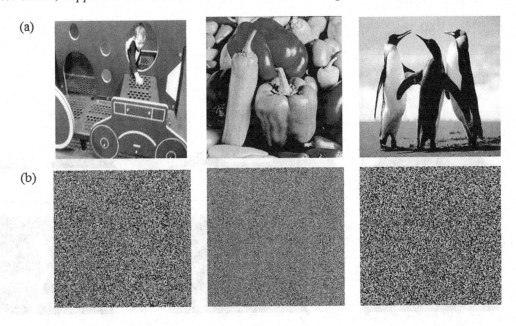

Figure 8. Histograms for the Red, Green and Blue color channels for the Child Plain (a) and Cipher (b) Images shown in Figure 7.

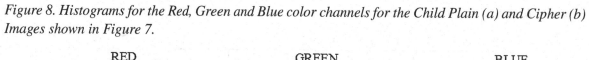

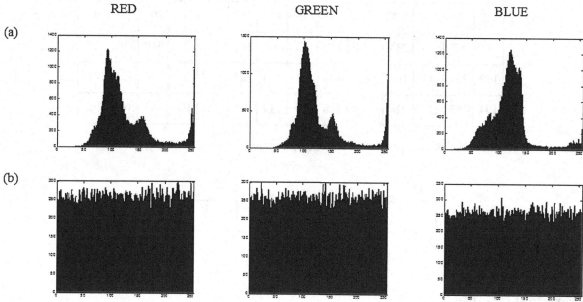

Figure 7 shows the resulting Cipher-Images for three 24-bit color Plain-Images. The first image is a 256×256 24-bit child photo in JPEG format, the second image is a 512×512 24-bit peppers image in TIFF format, and the third image is a 256×256 24-bit penguins photo in JPEG format. The top row in Figure 7 shows the original plain-images whereas the bottom row shows the corresponding cipher-images, which appear to be random.

Figure 9. Histograms for the Red, Green and Blue color channels for the Peppers Plain (a) and Cipher (b) Images shown in Figure 7.

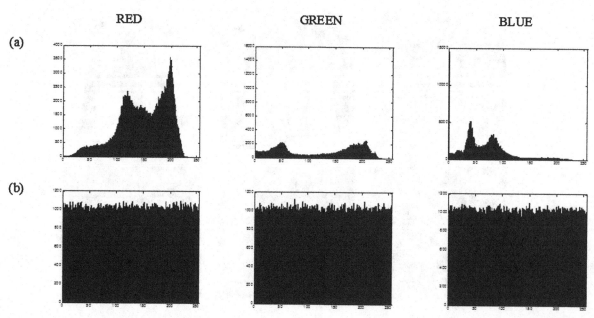

Figure 10. Histograms for the Red, Green and Blue color channels for the Penguins Plain (a) and Cipher (b) Images shown in Figure 7.

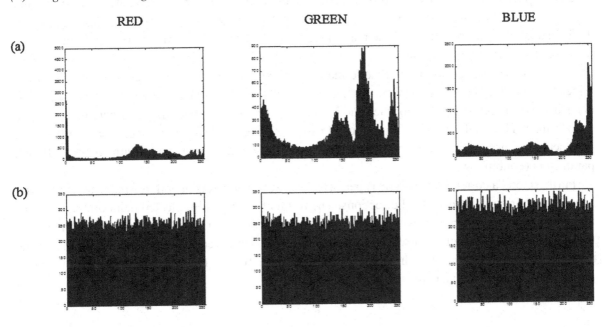

Figure 11. Sensitivity analysis: (a) correctly decrypted using the same parameters during encryption and decryption, (b) incorrectly decrypted using slightly different parameters than those used for encryption.

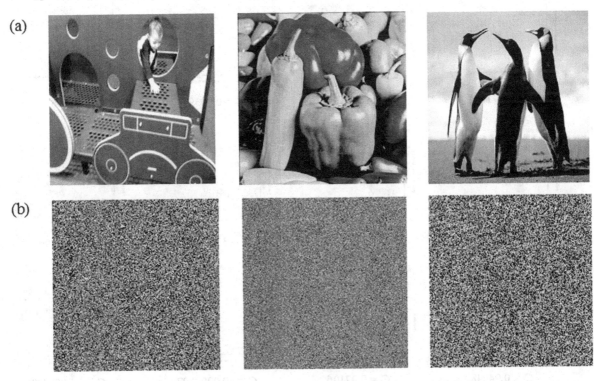

Recall that a histogram is a plot showing the distribution of pixel values of an image and is often used in cryptanalysis. We tested the histogram of various color channels before and after encryption and the results are shown in Figure 8, 9 and 10. Obviously, the histograms of the cipher images are almost uniform and different from those of the plain images; this indicates the difficulty of statistical analysis to attack the encryption algorithm.

As mentioned the sensitivity of chaotic maps to initial conditions makes them difficult for brute-force attack. To test the key sensitivity, we tried to decrypt the three considered images in two situations (1) using the correct parameters for the chaotic map, and (b) using slightly different parameters for the chaotic map. The results are shown in Figure 11 for the correctly decrypted images that use the same parameters in encryption and decryption (top row) and those that are decrypted with slightly different parameters (bottom row).

Furthermore, a correlation analysis is performed for adjacent pixels in both the plain and cipher images in the horizontal and vertical directions. The results for randomly selected pairs of pixels for the three considered images are shown in Figure 12. It is clear from the first two columns in the figure that the adjacent pixels are highly correlated in the plain images. However, for encrypted images there is no clear correlation as indicated in the last two columns in the figure. This can be attributed to the near-uniform distribution of pixels in the encrypted images.

Figure 12. Correlation analysis: (a) Child image, (b) Peppers image, (c) Penguins image.

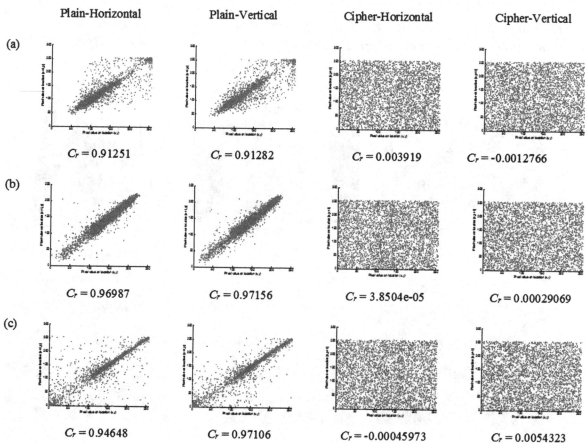

	Plain-Horizontal	Plain-Vertical	Cipher-Horizontal	Cipher-Vertical
(a)	$C_r = 0.91251$	$C_r = 0.91282$	$C_r = 0.003919$	$C_r = -0.0012766$
(b)	$C_r = 0.96987$	$C_r = 0.97156$	$C_r = 3.8504e-05$	$C_r = 0.00029069$
(c)	$C_r = 0.94648$	$C_r = 0.97106$	$C_r = -0.00045973$	$C_r = 0.0054323$

CONCLUSION

This chapter has intensively reviewed several approaches for image encryption based on ideas from chaos theory and biologically-inspired algorithms. With the vast amount of publications in these areas, this chapter is not intended to cover all aspects but to motivate the reader in these research directions. A case study has been presented which uses mutation and crossover for image diffusion and confusion to hide the content and decrease the correlation between pixels. The mutation and crossover operations are performed in certain order based a key stream generated using a chaotic map. With the high sensitivity of key streams generated from the chaotic map, the brute-force attack will much more difficult. Experimental work is provided for three RGB color images. The security is demonstrated using histograms, correlation, and sensitivity analyses.

REFERENCES

Abd-Elmonim, W. G., Ghali, N. I., & Abraham, A. (2011). Known-plaintext attack of DES-16 using Particle Swarm Optimization. In *Third World Congress on Nature and Biologically Inspired Computing (NaBIC)*. doi:10.1109/NaBIC.2011.6089410

Abdullah, A. H., Enayatifar, R., & Lee, M. (2012). A hybrid genetic algorithm and chaotic function model for image encryption. *International Journal of Electronics and Communications, 66*(10), 806–816. doi:10.1016/j.aeue.2012.01.015

Abuhaiba, I. S. & Hassan, M. A. (2011). Image encryption using differential evolution approach in frequency domain. *Signal and Image Processing: An International Journal, 2*(1).

Afarin, R., & Mozaffari, S. (2013). Image encryption using genetic algorithm. In *8th Iranian Conference on Machine Vision and Image Processing (MVIP)*.

Agarwal, A. (2012). Secret key encryption algorithm using genetic algorithm. *International Journal of Advanced Research in Computer Science and Software Engineering, 2*(4), 216–218.

Al-Husainy, M. A. (2006). Image encryption using genetic algorithm. *Information Technology Journal, 5*(3), 516–519. doi:10.3923/itj.2006.516.519

Al-Utaibi, K., & El-Alfy, E.-S. (2010). A bio-inspired image encryption algorithm based on chaotic maps. In *IEEE Congress on Evolutionary Computation*. doi:10.1109/CEC.2010.5586463

Alligood, K. T., Sauer, T. D., & Yorke, J. A. (1997). *Chaos: An Introduction to Dynamical Systems*. Springer. doi:10.1007/978-3-642-59281-2

Amin, M., Faragallah, O. S., & Abd El-Latif, A. A. (2010). A chaotic block cipher algorithm for image cryptosystems. *Communications in Nonlinear Science and Numerical Simulation, 15*(11), 3484–3497. doi:10.1016/j.cnsns.2009.12.025

Bashir, A., Hasan, A. S. B., & Almangush, H. (2012). A new image encryption approach using the integration of a shifting technique and the AES algorithm. *International Journal of Computers and Applications, 42*(9).

Bergmann, K. P. (2007). *Cryptanalysis using nature-inspired optimization algorithms.* (Doctoral dissertation). University of Calgary.

Bhowmik, S., & Acharyya, S. (2011). Image cryptography: the Genetic algorithm approach. In *IEEE International Conference on Computer Science and Automation Engineering (CSAE)*, (Vol. 2, pp. 223-227). IEEE.

Bigdeli, N., Farid, Y., & Afshar, K. (2012a). A novel image encryption/decryption scheme based on chaotic neural networks. *Engineering Applications of Artificial Intelligence, 25*(4), 753–765. doi:10.1016/j.engappai.2012.01.007

Bigdeli, N., Farid, Y., & Afshar, K. (2012b). A robust hybrid method for image encryption based on Hopfield neural network. *Computers & Electrical Engineering, 38*(2), 356–369. doi:10.1016/j.compeleceng.2011.11.019

Bourbakis, N. G. (1997). Image data compression-encryption using g-scan patterns. In *Proc. IEEE International Conference on Systems, Man, and Cybernetics: Computational Cybernetics and Simulation* (vol. 2, pp. 1117–1120). IEEE.

Busin, L., Vandenbroucke, N., & Macaire, L. (2008). Color spaces and image segmentation. *Advances in Imaging and Electron Physics, 151*, 66.

Chen, C. P., Zhang, T., & Zhou, Y. (2012). Image encryption algorithm based on a new combined chaotic system. In *IEEE International Conference on Systems, Man, and Cybernetics (SMC)*. doi:10.1109/ICSMC.2012.6378120

Chen, D., & Chang, Y. (2011). A novel image encryption algorithm based on Logistic maps. *Advances in Information Science and Service Sciences, 3*(7), 364–372. doi:10.4156/aiss.vol3.issue7.43

Chen, G., Mao, Y., & Chui, C. K. (2004). A symmetric image encryption scheme based on 3D chaotic cat maps. *Chaos, Solitons, and Fractals, 21*(3), 749–761. doi:10.1016/j.chaos.2003.12.022

Chen, R. J., Lu, W. K., & Lai, J. L. (2005). Image encryption using progressive cellular automata substitution and SCAN. In *IEEE International Symposium on Circuits and Systems, ISCAS*. doi:10.1109/ISCAS.2005.1464931

Coiteux, K., & Coskey, S. (2014). *An Introductory Look at Deterministic Chaos.* (Senior Thesis). Boise State University.

Dadhich, A., & Yadav, S. K. (2014). Evolutionary Algorithms, Fuzzy Logic and Artificial Immune Systems applied to Cryptography and Cryptanalysis: State-of-the-art review. *Optimization, 3*(6).

Ditto, W., & Munakata, T. (1995). Principles and applications of chaotic systems. *Communications of the ACM, 38*(11), 96–102. doi:10.1145/219717.219797

El-Alfy, E. S., & Al-Utaibi, K. (2011). An Encryption Scheme for Color Images Based on Chaotic Maps and Genetic Operators. In *The Seventh International Conference on Networking and Services, ICNS*.

Enayatifar, R., Abdullah, A. H., & Isnin, I. F. (2014). Chaos-based image encryption using a hybrid genetic algorithm and a DNA sequence. *Optics and Lasers in Engineering, 56*, 83–93. doi:10.1016/j.optlaseng.2013.12.003

Faragallah, O. S. (2012). An enhanced chaotic key-based RC5 block cipher adapted to image encryption. *International Journal of Electronics*, *99*(7), 925–943. doi:10.1080/00207217.2011.651689

Forouzan, B. A. (2007). *Cryptography & Network Security*. McGraw-Hill, Inc.

Fridrich, J. (1998). Symmetric ciphers based on two-dimensional chaotic maps. *International Journal of Bifurcation and Chaos in Applied Sciences and Engineering*, *8*(06), 1259–1284. doi:10.1142/S021812749800098X

Fu, C., Chen, J. J., Zou, H., Meng, W. H., Zhan, Y. F., & Yu, Y. W. (2012). A chaos-based digital image encryption scheme with an improved diffusion strategy. *Optics Express*, *20*(3), 2363–2378. doi:10.1364/OE.20.002363 PMID:22330475

Fu, C., Lin, B. B., Miao, Y. S., Liu, X., & Chen, J. J. (2011). A novel chaos-based bit-level permutation scheme for digital image encryption. *Optics Communications*, *284*(23), 5415–5423. doi:10.1016/j.optcom.2011.08.013

Fu, C., Meng, W. H., Zhan, Y. F., Zhu, Z. L., Lau, F., Tse, C. K., & Ma, H. F. (2013). An efficient and secure medical image protection scheme based on chaotic maps. *Computers in Biology and Medicine*, *43*(8), 1000–1010. doi:10.1016/j.compbiomed.2013.05.005 PMID:23816172

Fu, C., & Zhu, Z. (2008). A chaotic image encryption scheme based on circular bit shift method. In *The 9th International Conference for Young Computer Scientists, ICYCS* (pp. 3057-3061). doi:10.1109/ICYCS.2008.522

Garg, P. (2006). Genetic algorithm attack on simplified data encryption standard algorithm. *Special Issue: Advances in Computer Science and Engineering*, *23*, 139–174.

Gilmore, R., & Lefranc, M. (2008). *The topology of chaos: Alice in stretch and squeezeland*. John Wiley & Sons.

Guan, Z.-H., Huang, F., & Guan, W. (2005). Chaos-based image encryption algorithm. *Physics Letters. [Part A]*, *346*(1), 153–157. doi:10.1016/j.physleta.2005.08.006

Guo, J. I. (2000). A new chaotic key-based design for image encryption and decryption. In *Proceedings of the 2000 IEEE International Symposium on Circuits and Systems*. IEEE.

Hernández Encinas, L., Martín del Rey, Á., & Hernández Encinas, A. (2002). *Encryption of images with 2-dimensional cellular automata*. Academic Press.

Huang, C. K., & Nien, H. H. (2009). Multi chaotic systems based pixel shuffle for image encryption. *Optics Communications*, *282*(11), 2123–2127. doi:10.1016/j.optcom.2009.02.044

Huang, X. (2012). Image encryption algorithm using chaotic Chebyshev generator. *Nonlinear Dynamics*, *67*(4), 2411–2417. doi:10.1007/s11071-011-0155-7

Hussain, I., Shah, T., & Gondal, M. A. (2013). Application of S-box and chaotic map for image encryption. *Mathematical and Computer Modelling*, *57*(9), 2576–2579. doi:10.1016/j.mcm.2013.01.009

Jawad, L. M., & Sulong, G. B. (2013). A review of color image encryption techniques. [IJCSI]. *International Journal of Computer Science Issues*, *10*(6).

Jin, J. (2012). An image encryption based on elementary cellular automata. *Optics and Lasers in Engineering, 50*(12), 1836–1843. doi:10.1016/j.optlaseng.2012.06.002

Kocarev, L. (2001). Chaos-based cryptography: A brief overview. *IEEE Circuits and Systems Magazine, 1*(3), 6–21. doi:10.1109/7384.963463

Kocarev, L., & Jakimoski, G. (2001). Logistic map as a block encryption algorithm. *Physics Letters. [Part A], 289*(4), 199–206. doi:10.1016/S0375-9601(01)00609-0

Kocarev, L., & Lian, S. (Eds.). (2011). *Chaos-based Cryptography: Theory, Algorithms and Applications* (Vol. 354). Springer. doi:10.1007/978-3-642-20542-2

Kumar, A. & Ghose, M. (2009). Overview of information security using genetic algorithm and chaos. *Information Security Journal: A Global Perspective, 18*(6), 306–315.

Kumar, A., & Ghose, M. K. (2011). Extended substitution–diffusion based image cipher using chaotic standard map. *Communications in Nonlinear Science and Numerical Simulation, 16*(1), 372–382. doi:10.1016/j.cnsns.2010.04.010

Kuppusamy, K., & Thamodaran, K. (2012). Optimized partial image encryption scheme using PSO. In *International Conference on Pattern Recognition, Informatics and Medical Engineering (PRIME)*. doi:10.1109/ICPRIME.2012.6208350

Laskari, E. C., Meletiou, G. C., Stamatiou, Y. C., & Vrahatis, M. N. (2005). Evolutionary computation based cryptanalysis: A first study. *Nonlinear Analysis: Theory, Methods & Applications, 63*(5).

Lian, S. (2009). A block cipher based on chaotic neural networks. *Neurocomputing, 72*(4), 1296–1301. doi:10.1016/j.neucom.2008.11.005

Lian, S., Chen, G., Cheung, A., & Wang, Z. (2004). A chaotic-neural-network-based encryption algorithm for JPEG2000 encoded images. In *Advances in Neural Networks-ISNN 2004* (pp. 627–632). Springer Berlin Heidelberg. doi:10.1007/978-3-540-28648-6_100

Liu, H., Wang, X., & Kadir, A. (2013). Color image encryption using Choquet fuzzy integral and hyper chaotic system. *Optik-International Journal for Light and Electron Optics, 124*(18), 3527–3533. doi:10.1016/j.ijleo.2012.10.068

Liu, L., Zhang, Q., & Wei, X. (2012). A RGB image encryption algorithm based on DNA encoding and chaos map. *Computers & Electrical Engineering, 38*(5), 1240–1248. doi:10.1016/j.compeleceng.2012.02.007

Maleki, F., Mohades, A., Hashemi, S. M., & Shiri, M. E. (2008). An image encryption system by cellular automata with memory. In *Third International Conference on Availability, Reliability and Security*. doi:10.1109/ARES.2008.121

Mao, Y., & Chen, G. (2005). Chaos-based image encryption. In *Handbook of Geometric Computing* (pp. 231–265). Springer Berlin Heidelberg. doi:10.1007/3-540-28247-5_8

Mazloom, S., & Eftekhari-Moghadam, A. M. (2009). Color image encryption based on coupled nonlinear chaotic map. *Chaos, Solitons, and Fractals, 42*(3), 1745–1754. doi:10.1016/j.chaos.2009.03.084

Mazloom, S., & Eftekhari-Moghadam, A. M. (2011). Color image cryptosystem using chaotic maps. In *IEEE Symposium on Computational Intelligence for Multimedia, Signal and Vision Processing (CIMSIVP)*. IEEE.

Menezes, A. J., Van Oorschot, P. C., & Vanstone, S. A. (2010). *Handbook of applied cryptography*. CRC Press.

Olariu, S., & Zomaya, A. Y. (Eds.). (2005). *Handbook of bioinspired algorithms and applications*. CRC Press. doi:10.1201/9781420035063

Ott, E. (2002). *Chaos in dynamical systems*. Cambridge university press. doi:10.1017/CBO9780511803260

Panduranga, H. T., & Kumar, S. N. (2014). Image encryption based on permutation-substitution using chaotic map and Latin Square Image Cipher. *The European Physical Journal. Special Topics*, 1–15.

Pareek, N. K., Patidar, V., & Sud, K. K. (2006). Image encryption using chaotic logistic map. *Image and Vision Computing*, 24(9), 926–934. doi:10.1016/j.imavis.2006.02.021

Pareek, N. K., Patidar, V., & Sud, K. K. (2013). Diffusion–substitution based gray image encryption scheme. *Digital Signal Processing*, 23(3), 894–901. doi:10.1016/j.dsp.2013.01.005

Parvin, Z., Seyedarabi, H., & Shamsi, M. (2014). A new secure and sensitive image encryption scheme based on new substitution with chaotic function. *Multimedia Tools and Applications*, 1–18.

Patel, K. D., & Belani, S. (2011). Image encryption using different techniques: A review. *International Journal of Emerging Technology and Advanced Engineering*, 1(1), 30–34.

Patidar, V., Pareek, N. K., Purohit, G., & Sud, K. K. (2011). A robust and secure chaotic standard map based pseudorandom permutation-substitution scheme for image encryption. *Optics Communications*, 284(19), 4331–4339. doi:10.1016/j.optcom.2011.05.028

Peng, J., Zhang, D., & Liao, X. (2011). A novel algorithm for block encryption of digital image based on chaos. *International Journal of Cognitive Informatics and Natural Intelligence*, 5(1), 59–74. doi:10.4018/jcini.2011010104

Ratan, R. (2014). Applications of Genetic Algorithms in Cryptology. In *Proceedings of the Third International Conference on Soft Computing for Problem Solving* (pp. 821-831). Springer India. doi:10.1007/978-81-322-1771-8_71

Rhouma, R., & Belghith, S. (2011). Cryptanalysis of a chaos-based cryptosystem on DSP. *Communications in Nonlinear Science and Numerical Simulation*, 16(2), 876–884. doi:10.1016/j.cnsns.2010.05.017

SaberiKamarposhti, M., AlBedawi, I., & Mohamad, D. (2012). A new hybrid method for image encryption using DNA sequence and chaotic logistic map. *Australian Journal of Basic and Applied Sciences*, 6(3), 371–380.

Sathya, S. S., Chithralekha, T., & Anandakumar, P. (2010). Nomadic genetic algorithm for cryptanalysis of DES 16. *International Journal of Computer Theory and Engineering*, 2(3), 1793–8201.

Seyedzadeh, S. M., & Mirzakuchaki, S. (2012). A fast color image encryption algorithm based on coupled two-dimensional piecewise chaotic map. *Signal Processing, 92*(5), 1202–1215. doi:10.1016/j.sigpro.2011.11.004

Shahzad, W., Siddiqui, A. B., & Khan, F. A. (2009). Cryptanalysis of four-rounded DES using binary particle swarm optimization. In *Proceedings of the 11th Annual Conference Companion on Genetic and Evolutionary Computation Conference.* doi:10.1145/1570256.1570294

Sharma, M., Kowar, M. K., & Sharma, M. (2008). An improved evolutionary algorithm for secured image using adaptive genetic algorithm. *Journal of Discrete Mathematical Sciences and Cryptography, 11*(6), 673–683. doi:10.1080/09720529.2008.10698397

Solak, E. (2011). Cryptanalysis of chaotic ciphers. In *Chaos-Based Cryptography* (pp. 227–256). Springer Berlin Heidelberg. doi:10.1007/978-3-642-20542-2_7

Solak, E., Rhouma, R., & Belghith, S. (2010). Cryptanalysis of a multi-chaotic systems based image cryptosystem. *Optics Communications, 283*(2), 232–236. doi:10.1016/j.optcom.2009.09.070

Song, J., Zhang, H., Meng, Q., & Wang, Z. (2007). Cryptanalysis of four-round DES based on genetic algorithm. In *International Conference on Wireless Communications, Networking and Mobile Computing, WiCom.* doi:10.1109/WICOM.2007.580

Souici, I., Seridi, H., & Akdag, H. (2011). Images encryption by the use of evolutionary algorithms. *Analog Integrated Circuits and Signal Processing, 69*(1), 49–58. doi:10.1007/s10470-011-9627-4

Tedmori, S., & Al-Najdawi, N. (2014). Image cryptographic algorithm based on the Haar wavelet transform. *Information Sciences, 269,* 21–34. doi:10.1016/j.ins.2014.02.004

Tkalcic, M., & Tasic, J. F. (2003). *Colour spaces: perceptual, historical and applicational background.* Eurocon.

Verma, O. P., Nizam, M., & Ahmad, M. (2013). Modified multi-chaotic systems that are based on pixel shuffle for image encryption. *Journal of Information Processing Systems, 9*(2), 271–286. doi:10.3745/JIPS.2013.9.2.271

Vohra, R., & Patel, B. (2012). An efficient chaos-based optimization algorithm approach for cryptography. *International Journal of Communication Network Security, 1*(4), 75–79.

Wang, K., Zou, L., Song, A., & He, Z. (2005). On the security of 3D Cat map based symmetric image encryption scheme. *Physics Letters. [Part A], 343*(6), 432–439. doi:10.1016/j.physleta.2005.05.040

Wang, X., & He, G. (2011). Cryptanalysis on a novel image encryption method based on total shuffling scheme. *Optics Communications, 284*(24), 5804–5807. doi:10.1016/j.optcom.2011.08.053

Wang, X., & Luan, D. (2013). A novel image encryption algorithm using chaos and reversible cellular automata. *Communications in Nonlinear Science and Numerical Simulation, 18*(11), 3075–3085. doi:10.1016/j.cnsns.2013.04.008

Wang, X., Luan, D., & Bao, X. (2014). Cryptanalysis of an image encryption algorithm using Chebyshev generator. *Digital Signal Processing, 25,* 244–247. doi:10.1016/j.dsp.2013.10.020

Wang, X., & Wang, Q. (2014). A novel image encryption algorithm based on dynamic S-boxes constructed by chaos. *Nonlinear Dynamics, 75*(3), 567–576. doi:10.1007/s11071-013-1086-2

Wang, Y., Wong, K. W., Li, C., & Li, Y. (2012). A novel method to design S-box based on chaotic map and genetic algorithm. *Physics Letters. [Part A], 376*(6), 827–833. doi:10.1016/j.physleta.2012.01.009

Wang, Y., Wong, K. W., Liao, X., & Chen, G. (2011). A new chaos-based fast image encryption algorithm. *Applied Soft Computing, 11*(1), 514–522. doi:10.1016/j.asoc.2009.12.011

Wu, Y., Yang, G., Jin, H., & Noonan, J. P. (2012). Image encryption using the two-dimensional logistic chaotic map. *Journal of Electronic Imaging, 21*(1), 013014–1. doi:10.1117/1.JEI.21.1.013014

Xiang, T., Wong, K. W., & Liao, X. (2007). Selective image encryption using a spatiotemporal chaotic system. Chaos: *An Interdisciplinary. Journal of Nonlinear Science, 17*(2), 023115.

Xiao, D., & Shih, F. Y. (2010). Using the self-synchronizing method to improve security of the multi chaotic systems-based image encryption. *Optics Communications, 283*(15), 3030–3036. doi:10.1016/j.optcom.2010.03.063

Xing-Yuan, W., & Guo-Xiang, H. (2012). Cryptanalysis on an image block encryption algorithm based on spatiotemporal chaos. *Chinese Physics B, 21*(6), 060502. doi:10.1088/1674-1056/21/6/060502

Ye, G. (2010). Image scrambling encryption algorithm of pixel bit based on chaos map. *Pattern Recognition Letters, 31*(5), 347–354. doi:10.1016/j.patrec.2009.11.008

Yoon, J. W., & Kim, H. (2010). An image encryption scheme with a pseudorandom permutation based on chaotic maps. *Communications in Nonlinear Science and Numerical Simulation, 15*(12), 3998–4006. doi:10.1016/j.cnsns.2010.01.041

Younes, M. A. B., & Jantan, A. (2008). An image encryption approach using a combination of permutation technique followed by encryption. *International Journal of Computer Science and Network Security, 8*(4), 191–197.

Yuen, C. H., & Wong, K. W. (2011). A chaos-based joint image compression and encryption scheme using DCT and SHA-1. *Applied Soft Computing, 11*(8), 5092–5098. doi:10.1016/j.asoc.2011.05.050

Zeghid, M., Machhout, M., Khriji, L., Baganne, A., & Tourki, R. (2007). A modified AES based algorithm for image encryption. *International Journal on Computer Science and Engineering, 1*(1), 70–75.

Zelinka, I., Celikovsk`y, S., Richter, H., & Chen, G. (Eds.). (2010). *Evolutionary algorithms and chaotic systems* (Vol. 267). Springer. doi:10.1007/978-3-642-10707-8

Zelinka, I., & Jasek, R. (2010). Evolutionary decryption of chaotically encrypted information. In *Evolutionary Algorithms and Chaotic Systems* (pp. 329–343). Springer Berlin Heidelberg. doi:10.1007/978-3-642-10707-8_10

Zhang, Q., Guo, L., & Wei, X. (2010). Image encryption using DNA addition combining with chaotic maps. *Mathematical and Computer Modelling, 52*(11), 2028–2035. doi:10.1016/j.mcm.2010.06.005

Zhang, X., & Wang, X. (2013). Chaos-based partial encryption of SPIHT coded color images. *Signal Processing, 93*(9), 2422–2431. doi:10.1016/j.sigpro.2013.03.017

ADDITIONAL READING

Banerjee, S. (2011). *Chaos Synchronization and Cryptography for Secure Communications: Applications for Encryption*. IGI-Global. doi:10.4018/978-1-61520-737-4

Banerjee, S. (2012). A Cryptographic Scheme Based on Chaos Synchronization and Genetic Engineering Algorithm. In *Applications of Chaos and Nonlinear Dynamics in Science and Engineering-Vol. 2* (pp. 249–270). Springer Berlin Heidelberg. doi:10.1007/978-3-642-29329-0_10

de Castro, L. N. (2007). Fundamentals of natural computing: An overview. *Physics of Life Reviews*, *4*(1), 1–36. doi:10.1016/j.plrev.2006.10.002

Delman, B. (2004). Genetic algorithms in cryptography. Master's thesis, Rochester Institute of Technology.

Guyeux, C., & Bahi, J. (2010). A new chaos-based watermarking algorithm. In*SECRYPT'10, Int. conf. on security and cryptography* (pp. 455-458).

Kekre, H. B., Sarode, T., Halarnkar, P. N., & Mazumder, D. (2014). Image Encryption using Hybrid Transform Domain Scrambling of Coefficients. *International Journal (Toronto, Ont.)*, *2*(6).

Kocarev, L., & Galias, Z. (2009). *Intelligent computing based on chaos* (Vol. 184). Heidelberg: Springer. doi:10.1007/978-3-540-95972-4

Li, C.-G., & Han, Z.-Z. (2003). The new evolution of image encryption techniques. *Information and Control-Shenyang*, *32*(4), 339–343.

Li, S., Chen, G., & Zheng, X. (2006). Chaos-Based Encryption for Digital Image and Video. *Multimedia Encryption and Authentication Techniques and Applications*, 129.

Maniccam, S. S., & Bourbakis, N. G. (2004). Image and video encryption using SCAN patterns. *Pattern Recognition*, *37*(4), 725–737. doi:10.1016/j.patcog.2003.08.011

Nien, H. H., Huang, W. T., Hung, C. M., Chen, S. C., Wu, S. Y., Huang, C. K., & Hsu, Y. H. (2009). Hybrid image encryption using multi-chaos-system. In *7th International Conference on Information, Communications and Signal Processing, ICICS*.

Ou, C. M. (2008). Design of block ciphers by simple chaotic functions. *Computational Intelligence Magazine, IEEE*, *3*(2), 54–59. doi:10.1109/MCI.2008.919074

Petras, I. (2011). *Fractional-order nonlinear systems: modeling, analysis and simulation*. Springer. doi:10.1007/978-3-642-18101-6

Sadeg, S., Gougache, M., Mansouri, N., & Drias, H. (2010, October). An encryption algorithm inspired from DNA. In *International Conference on Machine and Web Intelligence (ICMWI)*, (pp. 344-349).

Salleh, M., Ibrahim, S., & Isnin, I. F. (2003). Enhanced chaotic image encryption algorithm based on Baker's map. In *Proceedings of the 2003 International Symposium on Circuits and Systems, ISCAS'03*. (Vol. 2, pp. II-508). doi:10.1109/ISCAS.2003.1206022

Shih, F. Y. (Ed.). (2012). *Multimedia Security: Watermarking, Steganography, and Forensics*. CRC Press. doi:10.1201/b12697

Taneja, N., Raman, B., & Gupta, I. (2011). Selective image encryption in fractional wavelet domain. *AEÜ.* *International Journal of Electronics and Communications, 65*(4), 338–344. doi:10.1016/j.aeue.2010.04.011

Tang, Z., & Zhang, X. (2011). Secure image encryption without size limitation using Arnold transform and random strategies. *Journal of Multimedia, 6*(2), 202–206. doi:10.4304/jmm.6.2.202-206

Wang, L., Ye, Q., Xiao, Y., Zou, Y., & Zhang, B. (2008). An image encryption scheme based on cross chaotic map. In *IEEE Congress on Image and Signal Processing*, CISP'08, volume 3, pages 22–26. doi:10.1109/CISP.2008.129

Xu, S., Wang, Y., Wang, J., & Tian, M. (2008). Cryptanalysis of two chaotic image encryption schemes based on permutation and XOR operations. In *International Conference on Computational Intelligence and Security, CIS'08*. doi:10.1109/CIS.2008.146

Zhang, H., Feng, X., Qin, Z.-P., & Liu, Y.-Z. (2002). Evolutionary cryptosystems and evolutionary design for DES. *Journal-China Institute of Communications, 23*(5), 57–64.

Zhang, L., Liao, X., & Wang, X. (2005). An image encryption approach based on chaotic maps. *Chaos, Solitons, and Fractals, 24*(3), 759–765. doi:10.1016/j.chaos.2004.09.035

Zhang, L. Y., Li, C., Wong, K.-W., Shu, S., & Chen, G. (2012). Cryptanalyzing a chaos-based image encryption algorithm using alternate structure. *Journal of Systems and Software, 85*(9), 2077–2085. doi:10.1016/j.jss.2012.04.002

Zhang, W., Wong, K. W., Yu, H., & Zhu, Z. L. (2013). An image encryption scheme using reverse 2-dimensional chaotic map and dependent diffusion. *Communications in Nonlinear Science and Numerical Simulation, 18*(8), 2066–2080. doi:10.1016/j.cnsns.2012.12.012

Zhang, Y., Li, C., Li, Q., Zhang, D., & Shu, S. (2012). Breaking a chaotic image encryption algorithm based on perceptron model. *Nonlinear Dynamics, 69*(3), 1091–1096. doi:10.1007/s11071-012-0329-y

KEY TERMS AND DEFINITIONS

Chaos Theory: The study of complex nonlinear behavior of dynamic systems that is sensitive to initial conditions and apparently random or unpredictable though described by simple deterministic mathematical equations. It has applications in various disciplines including engineering, physics, biology, sociology, economics, politics and meteorology.

Cryptanalysis: Analysis of cryptographic algorithms for revealing weaknesses and utilizing them to break the security and gain access to the message content or the cryptographic key.

Cryptosystem: A system that involves a pair of algorithms for encrypting plaintext into ciphertext and decrypting ciphertext back to the original plaintext. It is an alternative term for a cryptographic system.

Evolutionary Algorithm: A class of population-based meta-heuristic search methodologies for effectively sampling the search space and approximating optimal solutions. It is inspired by principles and operations in biological evolution such as recombination, mutation and natural selection. This class encompass methods such as genetic algorithms, evolution strategies and genetic programming.

Nature-Inspired Computation: A set of computational models and algorithms inspired by natural processes to solve real-world problems in various disciplines including engineering and science.

Particle Swarm Optimization: A population-based stochastic optimization technique inspired by the movement of social organisms such as bird flocking or fish schooling. It shares similarity to evolutionary algorithms in the sense that it starts with a population of particles that are iteratively moved around the space searching for the best solution.

Section 3
Intelligent Intrusion Detection

This section illustrates the approaches utilized to build optimal, adaptive and comprehensive intrusion detection systems.

Chapter 5

The Conceptual and Architectural Design of an Intelligent Intrusion Detection System

Mradul Dhakar
ITM University Gwalior, M.P., India

Akhilesh Tiwari
Madhav Institute of Technology and Science, Gwalior, India

ABSTRACT

The tremendous work in the field of security has made enormous efforts towards the ascertainment of innovative ideas along with their practical applicability. These motivated the security agencies to adopt them practically. But adequate remedies are not accomplished yet due to the enhanced technological aspects even in the unlawful communities. These communities have become a major concern for the security agencies and can be considered as unaddressed issue. This concern led to the introduction of Intrusion Detection Systems (IDSs). The IDS is a means for detecting the intrusive events concealed among the activities of normal users. Additionally, such systems also provide necessary assistance in preventing future intrusions. The present chapter focuses on improving the performance of the IDS in order to meet the contemporary progression by proposing a system that is able to achieve a system that is effective, adaptive and intelligent in nature and is able to remarkably detect intrusions. In order to accomplish the desired system, the chapter involves development of intelligent IDS.

INTRODUCTION

Now-a-days, revolution of the internet has made it possible to connect all the corners of the world and empowers the user to share data in an easy and fastest manner. Although this is a convenient mode of communication but it requires much of data to be stored on the web with the necessity of being secured.

DOI: 10.4018/978-1-4666-9426-2.ch005

The increased number of adverse attacks on web resources has called forth the security concerns. This led to the successful implementation of a system capable of detecting abnormalities (generally referred as intrusions). This detection system is recognized as Intrusion Detection System (IDS).

The process of surveillance of the user's network activities and then identifying and distinguishing the normal and abnormal activities is termed as intrusion detection whereas the dedicated system used for intrusion detection is known as Intrusion Detection System (IDS). Whenever an intruder attempts to compromise the availability, integrity or confidentiality of the system or the whole network itself, the IDS monitors and identifies the prohibited activities and forbids the illicit users from accessing services or resources of the computer system or the network. The system performs the relevant actions by taking various predefined anticipations into consideration.

Intrusion Detection System (Mohammad, Sulaiman & Muhsin, 2011; Parekh, Madan & Tugnayat, 2012) is basically software or the combination of software and hardware that automates the process of tracking and analyzing of events on the web. The IDS has the capability to detect the intrusion in network by being in charge of taking action against any intrusion sensed. It generates an alarm whenever any intrusion is detected in the traffic. But sometimes there are the cases when a user is accidently detected as intruder as much of his/her activities match the abnormal behavior and as a result generates the alarm. This type of generation of alarm is named as a false alarm.

In order to decrease the rate of false alarm IDS was amalgamated with various Artificial Intelligence (AI) techniques. Despite of available promising AI techniques such as rule based expert system, genetic algorithm, inductive sequential patterns, state transition analysis and artificial neural network in IDS; the IDS is still facing problems in effective pattern recognition and classification. Data mining with its techniques in this context have proved itself as the most prominent way for handling these problems.

The key ideas are to use data mining techniques to discover consistent and useful patterns of system features that describe the program and user behavior, and use the set of relevant system features to compute (inductively learned) classifiers that can recognize anomalies and known intrusions (Lee & Stolfo, 1998). With this thought, data mining based IDS has come out as the frequently preferred approach.

When applying data mining technology to intrusion detection systems, it can mine the features of new and unknown attacks well, which is a maximal help to the dynamic defense of intrusion detection system (Song & Ma, 2009). Data mining based IDS has the advantage of potentially being able to detect new attacks and prevent the attack on a network (Raut & Gawali, 2012). This enables the system to cope up with the advancements. Furthermore, use of data mining techniques for intrusion detection helps in identifying the trends within data that go beyond simple analysis (Feruza & Yusufovna, 2008).

In order to provide greater security policies, IDS is classified into Misuse and Anomaly Detection categories, discussed in further section.

TYPES OF ATTACK

This Section describes the major types of attack that are being detected by an intrusion detection system. There are four major attack categories (Peddabachigari, Abraham, Grosanc & Thomas, 2007; Jiang, Song, Wang, Han & Li, 2006) in general and are described in the following subsections.

- **Denials-of-Service (dos):** Denial of Service is the type of attack where the legitimate users are restrained from accessing the services of a host or network resources. The attacker makes the resources either too busy or overflow by sending a persistent request which as a consequence restrict the host or network drops the requests received resulting in poor service handling.
- **Probing/Surveillance:** Probing or Surveillance are the attacks in which the attacker tries to compromise the services either performed by probing or gaining knowledge about the network configuration and its vulnerabilities with the motive to harm or retrieve information regarding the resources of the comprised system or network.
- **User-to-Root (U2R):** User-to-Root attacks are attempts by an attacker who is non-privileged user and aims to gain administrative privileges i.e. the attacker / intruder is a local user tries to gain access onto a computer system as a root administrator for compromising the vulnerabilities of the system.
- **Remote-to-Local (R2L):** Remote-to-Local attack is another kind of intrusion attack where the remote user who is an intruder consistently sends packets/requests to a machine set-up locally in order to acquire access as a local user. The intruder tries to explore the vulnerabilities by exploiting the acquired privileges of a local user.

INTRUSION DETECTION SYSTEM: AN OVERVIEW

The consistently upgraded system which is meant typically for identifying the intrusive activities by the tracking the on-going activities on the web, such an abnormality detection system is familiarized as IDS. An intrusion detection system (IDS) inspects all inbound and outbound network activities and identifies suspicious patterns that may indicate a network or system attack from someone attempting to break into or compromise a system (Parekh, Madan & Tugnayat, 2012). The Intrusion Detection System performs the process of monitoring the events which are occurring in a computer system or network and analyzing them for signs of possible incidents (Jain & Upendra, 2012).

Intrusions are the illegal activities which are performed in order to gain unauthorized access of a secured system or network. In relation to intrusion, intrusion detection is a process to detect events (activities) which are suspicious in nature. Intrusion Detection System (IDS) is an important detection used as a countermeasure to preserve data integrity and system availability from attacks (Z. Rehman, S. Rehman & Khan, 2009). Whenever there is a case that an intruder attempts to compromise the availability, integrity or confidentiality of the network resources or a system, the IDS monitoring the activities, detects the abnormal events and restricts the illegitimate users from utilizing resources or services of the computer system. In addition performs the suitable actions by considering various available predefined anticipations.

In general, an IDS monitors and records events in a computer system, performs analysis to determine if the events are security incidents, alerts security practitioners regarding potential threats, and produces event reports (National Institute of Standards and Technology, 2007). Henceforth IDS has come out as the most crucial step towards the system and network security, where data and resource protection is of utmost importance.

The advancement of IDS over firewall and antivirus can be well understood with the help of comparison shown in Table 1.

Table 1. Different Characteristics Posed by Firewall, Antivirus and IDS

Characteristics	Firewall	Anti-Virus	IDS
Internal attacks handling	Not Available	Limited way	Available
Prevention from intrusive activities	Not Available	Limited way	Available
Recording previous intrusive attempts	Not Available	Available	Available
Alert generation	Not Available	Not Available	Available
Detection of abnormal activities	Not Available	Limited way	Available
Responding to intrusive activities	Not Available	Limited way	Available

It can be viewed from the Table 1 that the crucial characteristics which are the necessity of efficient detection of abnormalities are not preliminary fulfilled by the firewall while antivirus has limitation for: ability to control internal attacks, ability to log intrusion attempts, ability to detect attacks and ability to handle new attacks. When the discussed characteristics are viewed in context of IDS, it is found that IDS satisfies all of the necessities.

TYPES OF INTRUSION DETECTION SYSTEM

Intrusion detection is fundamentally classified into two types in accordance with the strategy of detection: Intrusion detection based on detection process and data analyzed and stored. The illustrations of these two types are as follows:

Intrusion Detection: Based on Detection Process

Intrusion detections considering their detection process are sub-categorized into Misuse / Signature-based intrusion detection and Anomaly-based intrusion detection. Intrusion detection techniques can be categorized into misuse detection, which uses patterns of well known attacks or weak spots of the system to identify intrusions; and anomaly detection, which tries to determine whether a deviation from the established normal usage patterns can be flagged as intrusions (Lee & Stolfo, 1998). Here is the detailed discussion of both detection types:

Signature/Misuse Detection

Misuse Detection, also known as Signature-based Detection, is the approach where the known attack patterns are stored for performing detection. This technique searches for signature patterns of already known attacks in a network traffic. It uses patterns of well known attacks or weak spots of the system to identify intrusions. The idea of misuse detection is to represent attacks in the form of a pattern or a signature so that the same attack can be detected and prevented in the future (Mukkamala, Sung & Abraham, 2005).

The misuse detection is the technique which based on the extensive knowledge of previously learned patterns provided by human experts and detects the intrusive activities. A periodically updated database is usually used to store the known attack signatures and is more similar to the working of anti-virus software. The detection in misuse is performed by matching features acquired through the attacking feature library and confirming the attack incidents. The key advantage of misuse detection system is that once the patterns of known intrusions are stored, future instances of these intrusions can be detected effectively and efficiently (Raut & Gawali, 2012). The misuse detection though finds its way in the detection process by detecting even negligible intrusion with less false alarm rate; it fails in detecting attacks new or unknown to it. Example of misuse system is IDIOT (Kumar & Spafford, 1995) and STAT (Ilgun, Kemmerer & Porras, 1995).

Anomaly Detection

Anomaly detection or the statistical intrusion detection is the detection process which analyzes audit-log data for abnormal user and system behavior. It is also referred to as behavior based detection or generic intrusion detection model. Anomaly detects intrusion as the deviation of user activities from the normal threshold on the web. This technique is based on the detection of traffic anomalies (Lappas & Pelechrinis, n.d.).

In anomaly detection, profiles for normal network behavior are defined which can be used to detect the abnormality within the network. It is the technique which is able to identify new intrusion types because of the deviation from normal activity. A threshold value (or a limiting factor) is set for deciding intrusion. If the divergence is much larger than a preset threshold then such an activity is considered as intrusive. The key advantages of anomaly detection systems are that they can detect unknown intrusion since they require no a priori knowledge about specific intrusions (Raut & Gawali, 2012). Anomaly detection contrarily to misuse detection fails to detect negligible intrusion along with high false alarm rate. Example of anomaly system is IDES (SRI International, 1992).

Intrusion Detection: Based on Data Analyzed and Stored

On the basis of the data which is being analyzed and stored for intrusion detection, IDS can be classified into Host-based intrusion detection (HIDS) and Network-based intrusion detection (NIDS). In HIDS data to be protected is collected from the host (or system) in the network while NIDS collects data in the form of packets directly from the network.

Host-Based Intrusion Detection System (HIDS)

Host-based IDS analyze host-bound audit sources such as operating system audit trails, system logs, and application logs (Joo, Hong & Han, 2003). HIDS is recognition approach in which a host or system gathers the records of different activities of host including system logs, NT event logs etc as data. As the system surveillances only the agent or host, it is able to determine intrusions more accurately. As all the critical data is on the host, no additional hardware or software is needed to be installed. However redundancy is one of the crucial concerns especially when it is desirable to install the system for a network and a HIDS is required to be installed individually for each host.

Software abstract is loaded onto a system for the detection of intrusion. The data required to be secured is collected from the host (or system) in the network. This software persistently monitors the event logs and file attributes generated by various applications and operating system. The software then checks the integrity of system files (Raut & Gawali, 2012). The system lacks detecting the attacks such as DoS and DDoS where network monitoring is required. The efficiency in terms of speed decreases whenever a large number of host need to be deployed and henceforth, the system cost also increases. HIDS are efficient in detecting buffer overflow attacks. These are OS dependent and as a prerequisite require planning before performing the implementation.

Network-Based Intrusion Detection System (NIDS)

Network-based IDS analyze network packets that are captured on a network (Joo, Hong & Han, 2003). NIDS is an approach where detection is performed on the network. It is the detection process in which the system collects data in the form of packets from the network being monitored rather than collecting it from a particular host/agent directly. The system provides enhanced security against the DoS type of attacks in comparison to HIDS. There is no need for installing the software on several surveillance systems and hence they are not much expensive. The only drawback is that it lacks accuracy due to loss of some data during the detection process. The large network scalability is still a problem which needs to be addressed.

NIDS in place of installing software to a particular system installs it in a network for detecting intrusions. The data for detection is analyzed directly from the network which is in the form of packets. NIDS is OS independent and fails to scan protocol or content if the traffic is encrypted however provides better security against denial of service attacks. They parse the packets, analyze them and extract useful information from them (Raut & Gawali, 2012). NIDS is considered well in providing security against the DoS type of attacks. Also, NIDS are OS independent and are easy to deploy.

RELATED WORK

The manifesting attempt for preserving a computer system or its information from being compromised was very first enlighten in 1980 by James Anderson. He had defined the intrusion detection system as a remedy to computer as well as the information security. He recommended the need of auditing the data containing vital information focusing governmental organization. He suggested keeping surveillance of data and detecting the misuse along with the understanding of user behaviour.

This step of Anderson towards the intrusion detection brought a revolution in computer security where tremendous efforts are being made to prohibit penetration of the illicit people who aim to violate the intimacy of the genuine usage of internet.

There are various Artificial Intelligence (AI) techniques which has been unified to develop the intrusion detection system such as artificial neural network, genetic algorithm, inductive sequential patterns, state transition analysis, rule based experts system; the IDS is still facing problems in effective pattern recognition and classification. In this context, data mining with its techniques have proved itself as the most prominent way for handling the problem. To extract useful patterns from massive amount data that ever-increasing, data mining plays an outstanding role.

Intrusion Detection System had been coming forth with data mining techniques in 1998. Lee and Stolfo (1998) incorporated Data Mining techniques in Intrusion Detection and since then a number of researchers have developed intrusion detection systems with the incorporation of data mining techniques.

The benchmark in the Intrusion Detection System technology was provided by Denning (1986) with the development of the first model for intrusion detection i.e. Intrusion Detection Expert System (IDES). This Model utilized system's audit records by monitoring it for the detection of abnormal patterns. By providing a general purpose framework, IDES was likely to be independent of the application environment, system vulnerability or type of intrusion.

The concept of Network-based Intrusion Detection system (NIDS) was proposed by Heberlein et al. (1990). The system was earlier named as Network Security Monitor (NSM) and was used for prominent government installations in order to gain excessive information by monitoring network traffic. Heberlein is also known for his contribution for extending DIDS that involved the new concept of hybrid intrusion detection systems. The development of Network Security Monitor led the intrusion detection system to the commercial world.

Debar, Becker and Siboni (1992) proposed intrusion detection system by using neural network. The proposal stated that neural network alone was useful so it required to be integrated with any expert system which has a knowledge base containing identified intrusion scenarios. This system constituted five main functional blocks: Data Acquisition, Data Formatting, Artificial Neural Network, Expert System – Neural Network Analysis and Control and Expert System – Analysis and Decision. The advantages of this approach over IDES are: Statistical methods sometimes depend on some assumptions about the underlying distributions of subject behavior. A neural network approach will have the effect of relaxing these assumptions on the data distribution and the neural network model can be easily modified in comparison to the statistical model. The trial and error method that is used to determine parameters for neural networks, consumes much time which was its disadvantage.

Ko (2000) developed a reliable intrusion detection system that built specification in a first order of valid behavior by the utilization of Inductive Logic programming. This approach was the combination of anomaly detection and specification based detection. Firstly, to determine the attacks, analyzable and formal specifications were utilized afterwards with the help of little physical involvement rules for the detection of system independent abnormalities were produced. The rules were represented in such a simple manner that can be understandable by human and also susceptible to analysis. The system can be able to detect attacks efficiently with low false positives. But the system was inefficient to detect DoS and probe type of attacks.

Sekar, Bendre, Dhurjati and Bollineni (2001) presented learning program behavior based intrusion detection system. Sequence of system calls had been captured, in this method which was then represented as finite state automata (FSA). To recognize variations of behavior that was learnt at the time of training, the system took into consideration the looping structure and branching structure of the program. As the system utilized FSA approach hence it was having state information which permitted the program to perform classification in a more effective manner of odd segments of code. The system was mainly aimed to focus on the behaviors of program that can be utilized to decrease training time and memory requirements. The advantage of this approach was that it decreased the false positives significantly. The disadvantage of this approach was that cannot able to detect attacks that have call arguments and that cannot change the program's behavior.

Han and Cho (2003) proposed an anomaly-based detection technique that uses multiple measures and models. Four detection methods had been developed that use system call events, resource usage of process, file access events as the measure of normal behavior, with the three modeling methods. To integrate all these, another approach was proposed which utilized a rule based approach. The system can model normal behaviors; hence it was expected to perform better.

Boukerche, Jucá, Sobral and Notare (2004) proposed a fraud detection mechanism for tracking intrusive activities both in computer system and mobile telecommunication network. The neural immune human system was the basis of this system. The main task of this system was the analysis of critical services and their utilization during the surveillance for the intrusive activities and misuse of the systems.

Jiang, Song and Dai (2005) presented an intrusion detection system called HPMoniter having high performance. This system involved a dynamic load balancing algorithm namely dynamic least load first (DLLF) algorithm. Also it used Shift max algorithm (SMA) for string matching. To process the incoming data, distributed analyzers are used and in each analyzer a data stream was fed for the detection of a subset of all scenarios.

Amini, Jalili and Shahriari (2006) introduced Real-Time Unsupervised Neural-Net-based Intrusion Detector for real time intrusion detection. For intrusion detection the system employed with unsupervised neural nets. Also the system can be able to train, test and tune the neural nets. This system had five main components: sniffer, preprocessor, UNN-engine, responder and manager, and controller. The first component was used to collect data from network traffic. Then the numerical features had been mined from the collected data and convert them in the binary and normalized form and passed them to the next component i.e. UNN-engine. After getting the data, UNN-engine used it for the training of neural network. Further in the operation phase this data was used for the detection of attacks.

Khan, Awad and Thuraisingham (2007) opted support vector machine and a modified version of hierarchical clustering i.e. Dynamically Growing Self-Organizing Tree (DGSOT), for the development of intrusion detection system which was indented for anomaly detection. First the training time of support vector machine was reduced by using a cluster analysis technique. The DGSOT algorithm used to generate cluster structures in the initial to expend training set progressively. In order to reduce the training set and for the betterment of the accuracy of this system a Clustering Tree based on SVM (CTSVM) method had been proposed. The system gave better performance by increasing the true positives and reducing the false alarms.

Munz, Li and Carle (2007) presented a K-means clustering based algorithm to extract feature datasets from flow records. In the training dataset the normal and anomalous traffic was separated out by this data mining approach. This method was allowed to deploy it in real time detection because the cluster centroids generated by K-means algorithm utilized in the fast anomaly detection. To improve the detection rate the clustering algorithm was applied individually for different services.

Panda and Patra (2007) presented a Naïve Bayes algorithm based framework for network intrusion detection system. The data set labeled by network services utilized by the framework to breed the patterns of services. Afterward the Naïve Bayes classifier made use of these patterns for the detection of attack available in dataset. Although this method provided better detection rate, consume less time but generated high false positive rate than neural network based system.

Peddabachingari, Abraham, Grosanc and Thomas (2007) presented two hybrid intrusion detection approaches. First was a hierarchical intelligent intrusion detection system had been developed which involved the combination of decision tree and support vector machine. Second was an ensemble approach based intrusion detection system which combined the base classifiers. In order to increase the detection rate and decrease the computational complexity hybrid classifiers had been combined with base classifiers.

Xiang, Yong and Meng (2008) proposed a hybrid multiple-level classifier for intrusion detection. A supervised tree classifier had been combined with an unsupervised Bayesian based clustering in order to detect intrusions. For the hybrid classification a four stage intrusion detection model had been developed. In the first stage utilized the C4.5 algorithm to mine Normal, U2R and R2L type of connections as accurately as possible. In the second stage Bayesian Clustering (AutoClass) was used to effectively isolate the U2R, R2L and Normal connections. In stage three U2R and R2L connections were separate out with the utilization of decision trees. The last stage involved C4.5 decision tree for further classification of all classes of attacks in their particular attack types. The outcome of last stage provides detailed analysis of each attack type to the system administrator and helped them to understand that which attack was involved to compromise the system security.

Song and Ma (2009) developed an Intrusion Detection System which utilized Data Mining technique. The system was having following modules: data collecting and preprocessing module, association rule mining module and intrusion detection analysis module, etc. The task of the data collecting and preprocessing module was to remove inconsistent information, missing values and redundant values i.e. data cleaning and selecting relevant features. The association rule mining module involved producing association rules by mining of patterns of intrusive behavior and this led the system to detect unknown intrusions. The intrusion detection analysis module used K-Mean clustering algorithm to classify the attacks.

Muda, Yassin, Sulaiman and Udzir (2011) proposed a hybrid approach by combining a clustering and a classification algorithm for better accuracy and named as KMNB. The K-Means algorithm was utilized as clustering algorithm while naïve bayes classifier as classification algorithm. In the first stage K-Means is employed to categorize sets of samples that act maliciously and no-maliciously while in subsequent stage Naïve Bayes is applied to classify all data into correct class categories.

Mohammad and Awadelkarim (2011) proposed a framework that used data mining for building network intrusion detection system for Sudan University of Science and Technology (SUST) network. The Proposed system was a hybrid technique which combined both misuse and anomaly detection. It incorporated two data mining techniques i.e. decision tree (C5.0 algorithm) and distance based clustering (Two-steps algorithm). The framework had consist four main phases i.e. data collection phase, data filtering phase, feature extraction phase and Data mining phase. In the data collection phase a sniffer was used to capture all packets and stores its header in MySQL database. In data filtering phase the captured data were filtered in order to remove network traffic non relevant for analysis. In data extraction phase new features were extracted to prepare for mining step. And in the data mining phase the mining was performed in two steps. In the first step known attacks are detected using C5.0 classification algorithm while in the second step clustering technique was used to discover new attacks not detected as intrusions in the first step by using a two step clustering algorithm.

Panda, Abraham and Patra (2012) proposed to use a hybrid intelligent approach for network intrusion detection. Firstly an unsupervised or supervised algorithm was used for feature selection i.e. selection of significant features. Afterwards classification or clustering technique was utilized to develop an intrusion detection system. Initially, a clustering or classification technique was applied to the training set to filter data. Subsequently, the filtered data had been passed to the final classifier to get the final outcome. And to assess the performance of the proposed approach, the final outcome had been verified by 10-fold cross validation technique. The distribution of probability obtained by this approach assist that how the proposed technique was taking an intelligent decision.

Altwaijry and Algarny (2012) utilized Bayesian Probability for the development of an intrusion detection system. To increase the detection rate of r2l types of attack was the motive of this research. To accomplish it, several Bayesian filters in parallel were used with each filter optimized to detect one type of record. An anomaly based Naïve Bayesian classifier had been developed to identify normal and attacks TCP traffic by their different probabilities. The classified traffic had been utilized for the training of this classifier and fine-tuned the probabilities. Further, it classified each TCP connection as either an attack or normal traffic by the estimation of probabilities.

Koc, Mazzuchi and Sarkani (2012) proposed a multinomial classifier intrusion detection model that was used to classify normal or attack events of network events. A data mining method i.e. Hidden Naïve Bayes (HNB) was utilized in the development of this model. To improve the accuracy and limit the requirement of resources of intrusion detection system, Naïve Bayes and structurally extended Naïve Bayes techniques had been improvised with the involvement of feature selection method and dicretiztion.

Elbasiony, Sallam, Eltobely and Fahmy (2013) proposed a hybrid network intrusion detection framework based on random forests and weighted k-means to overcome the drawbacks of both misuse and anomaly detection. Feature importance values calculated by the random forests algorithm are used in the misuse detection part to improve the detection rate of the anomaly detection part. A supervised method is proposed to improve the anomalous cluster determination by injecting known attacks into the uncertain data before being clustered, and using these known intrusions in determining the anomalous clusters.

Nadiammai and Hemalatha (2014) proposed four algorithms i.e. EDADT algorithm, Hybrid IDS model, Semi-Supervised Approach and Varying HOPERAA Algorithm for resolving the issues like Classification of Data, High Level of Human Interaction, Lack of Labeled Data, and Effectiveness of Distributed Denial of Service Attack. The EDADT i.e. Efficient Data Adapted Decision Tree algorithm proposed for classification of data reduced the actual size of the dataset and helped the administrator to analyze the ongoing attacks efficiently with less false alarm rate respectively. The Hybrid IDS model was proposed for reducing the human interaction involved combinations of different statistical methods like Packet Header Anomaly Detection (PHAD), Network Traffic Anomaly Detector (NETAD), Application Layer Anomaly Detector (ALAD) and Learning Rules for Anomaly Detection (LERAD) with SNORT. Out of these, SNORT+ALAD+LERAD gave better performance when compared with others. To overcome the overwhelming problem of supervised and unsupervised methods, the semi-supervised method had been proposed. It required a small amount of labeled data and large amount of unlabeled data. Finally, Hopping Period Alignment and Adjustment (HOPERAA) algorithm proposed for effective detection of distributed denial of service attack.

Feng, Zhang, Hu, Huang and Jimmy (2014) proposed a new machine learning data classification algorithm named Combining Support Vector with Ant Colony (CSVAC). As the name suggests, it utilized modified versions of two well known techniques i.e. support vector machine (SVM) and Self-Organized Ant Colony Network (CSOACN) to achieve improved performance in both accuracy and running time.

ISSUES AND CHALLENGES IN THE CURRENTLY USED IDSs

As a result of critical analysis of the existing literature, following gaps/shortcomings have been identified. These gaps/shortcomings constitute the scope of the present research work.

1. Most of the currently used intrusion detection systems are not able to detect R2L and U2R types of attack effectively.

2. Most of the existing intrusion detection systems are not adaptive in nature i.e. they are not able to adapt the information of additional intrusions. Hence, there is a need for the incorporation of adaptability.

3. Though many of the useful improvements have been performed by various researchers for reducing false alarm rates; still there is a possibility to handle this issue in a more effective manner.

4. Most of the existing intrusion detection systems are not able to detect attacks with desired accuracy level. Hence there is a need to incorporate such a mechanism which will assist in improving the overall accuracy.

PROPOSED INTELLIGENT INTRUSION DETECTION SYSTEM

In order to overcome the issues discussed in aforesaid section, a new intelligent intrusion detection system has been proposed and shown in Figure 1. Intelligent IDS is a blend of specialized features of Tree Augmented Naïve Bayes (TAN) classifier and Reduced Error Pruning (REP) classifier. Both the classifiers work subsequently viz. TAN classifier is used as a base or primary classifier and the other REP classifier as a Meta classifier as the secondary classifier. The Meta classifier utilized the concept of Meta classification which is a learning technique that learns from the Meta data generated intermediately and judges the correctness of the classification of every instance by base classifier. The judgment from each classifier for each class is treated as a feature and then builds another classifier, i.e. a meta-classifier, to make the final decision (Lin & Hauptmann, 2003).

The Intelligent Intrusion Detection System involves following phases:

Dataset

As discussed earlier, the dataset used for the experimentation purpose is the standard KddCup'99. For the experimental comfort, instead of using the whole instances of KDDCup'99 dataset only 10% of it has been used for training and testing of the implemented system. The 10% of the KddCup'99 dataset comprise 494021 instances.

Preprocessor and Splitter

Preprocessor

From the KDDCup'99 dataset (discussed later in experimentation section), among the 42 features, the 42nd feature which implies class label is broadly categorized into five major categories in the preprocessing module for the sake of moderating the complexity of performance evaluation of the developed system. The actual KddCup'99 dataset consists of 22 types of attack labels hence it becomes inconvenient to evaluate the performance of the classification system. The attack labels in the preprocessing phase are categorized into their respective the class labels viz. DoS, Probe, R2L, U2R and Normal are facilitating the ease of experimentation.

Figure 1. Architectural Design of Intelligent Intrusion Detection System

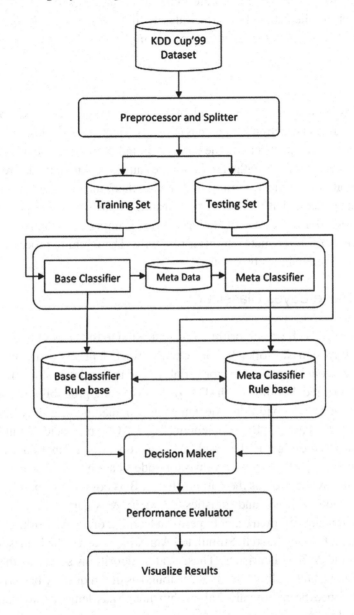

Splitter

After the receipt of the outcome of the preprocessing phase as five attack categories, the Dataset Splitter module of the proposed system partitions the entire dataset into two proportions- training part and testing part. The partitioning of the dataset is done by using a method recalled as holdout method. In the holdout method, the given data are randomly partitioned into two independent sets, a training set and a test set (Han, Kember, Pei, 2006). In the model, 66% of the dataset is used as the training set and the left over 34% of the dataset is used as the testing set. The training set is used to make the system learn about the attacks while the test set is used to determine the accuracy of the derived system. On passing the KddCup'99 dataset via the data splitting module, the dataset gets partitioned into the training set consisting of 326054 instances and the testing set consisting of 167967 instances.

Learning Phase

Learning phase enables the system to learn and adapt the multiple types of attacks possible. The learning phase of Intelligent Intrusion Detection System has two classifiers i.e. base classifier and meta classifier. The training set generated after propagating the dataset through Splitter phase has been applied as input to base classifier. The base classifier in the model utilizes an algorithm named, Tree Augmented Naïve Bayes for the generation of classification rules and storing them in base classifier rule base for further process. The meta data generated as a result of the learning of base classifier passes to meta classifier. The meta classifier thereafter makes use of Reduced Error Pruning decision tree for the production of classification rules and stock up in meta classifier rule base. The learning processes of both the classifiers are described in the following subsections:

Tree Augmented Naïve Bayes Classifier

Tree Augmented Naïve (TAN) Bayes algorithm is an extension to the Naïve Bayes algorithm and based on Bayesian network. Bayesian Network (BN) or Belief Network or probabilistic directed acyclic graphical model is a statistical model implemented for variables and their relationships. It is generally a search algorithm that uses a Directed Acyclic Graph (DAG) for answering probabilistic queries representing a set of random variable and their conditional dependencies. In data mining, BayesNet comes under the classification method that is based on Bayes Theorem. The DAG here considers random variables as the nodes and dependencies as the edges in the graph. Also, a probabilistic function is associated with each node that takes the input as a particular set of values for node's parent variables and gives the probability of a variable represented by the node as the output. Hence, BNs combine principles from graph theory, probability theory, computer science, and statistics (Altwaijry & Algarny, 2012).

BayesNet uses a search algorithm in order to perform learning of the network. The search algorithms such as K2, Hill Climber, Genetic Search, Stimulated Annealing etc. are the heuristic search algorithms that are confined to some defined heuristics. These search algorithms serves as the basis for the DAG obtained as a result of the analysis. In the study K2 is found as the frequently preferred search algorithm for intrusion detection. Since the traditional K2 algorithm though has demonstrated satisfactory outcomes, but the restriction faced is the dependency on the order imposed on the nodes. While the advantage of the search algorithm in the proposed system i.e. TAN is, that the dependencies among variables, along with the parent class variables, are also taken into account.

According to Friedman, Giegar and Goldszmidt (1997), TAN approximates the interactions between attributes by using a tree structure imposed on the Naïve Bayesian structure. Based on Bayes theorem, Naïve Bayes is a probabilistic classifier structure having naïve (or strong) independence assumptions. The structure generated using Naïve Bayes encodes the strong conditional independence assumption among attributes. This means that the class node is itself the parent node for each and every attribute node having no parent node defined for it. Thus the joint probability as represented by:

$$p(c, v_1, v_2, ... v_n) = p(c) \prod_i p(v_i \mid c)$$

The TAN network is an improvement to Naïve Bayes where the strong conditional independence assumptions do not taken into consideration. In fact, the TAN is an extension of Naïve Bayes which allows additional edges between the attributes of the network in order to capture correlations among them (Carvalho, Oliveira & Sagot, 2007). Similar to Naïve Bayes, each attribute in TAN have class node known as augmenting edge pointing towards it. These augmenting edges are responsible for encoding statistical dependencies among attributes. Thus, the joint probability in TAN depends on probabilities conditioned on class in-fact and on an attribute parent node pa_{v_i} well.

$$p(c, v_1, v_2, ..., v_n) = p(c) \prod_{i=1}^{n} p(v_i \mid pa_{v_i}, c)$$

From these network structures and corresponding joint distributions class predictions $\hat{C}(V)$ can be computed

$$\hat{C}(V) = \arg \max_c P(C \mid V) \propto P(C) \prod_i P(V \mid C)$$

The network structure in Naïve Bayes is known in advance whereas network structures in TAN need to be learned. The conditional mutual information function finds the maximal weighted spanning tree in a graph in order to construct the maximum-likelihood tree. The function between two attributes is calculated and is made to be learnt.

The functioning of TAN can be understood by considering the steps discussed in Singh A. (2006):

1. Between each pair of distinct variables, compute the conditional mutual information given C,

$$I(X_i; X_j \mid C) = \sum_{x_i, x_j, c} \widetilde{P}(x_i, x_j, c) \log \frac{\widetilde{P}(x_i, x_j \mid c)}{\widetilde{P}(x_i \mid c)\widetilde{P}(x_j \mid c)}$$

where $\widetilde{P}(\cdot)$ is an empirical distribution (computed using the training data).

2. Intuitively, this quantity represents the gain in information about adding X_i as a parent of X_j given that C is already a parent of X_j.
3. Build a complete undirected graph on the features $X_1, ..., X_n$ where the weight of the edge between X_i and X_j is $I(X_i; X_j \mid C)$ Call this graph G_F.
4. Using Kruskal or Prim's algorithm, find a maximum weighted spanning tree on G_F. Call it T_F.
5. Pick an arbitrary node in T_F as the root and set the direction of all the edges in T_F to be outward from the root. Call the directed tree T'_F.
6. The structure of the TAN system consists of a Naive Bayes model on the joint probability $P(C, X_1, ..., X_n)$ augmented by the edges in T'_F.

Reduced Error Pruning Classifier

A REP acronym for Reduced Error Pruning is a fast decision tree learner classifier under data mining techniques. REP uses a set known as validation data set for estimating generalization error which is to be pruned. The error is pruned for a node having highest reduced error rate. This is done almost for each node in the tree.

Pruning is a technique which aims at reducing the size of a decision tree. This is done by removing (pruning) parts of a tree allowing better classification of instances. Hence leading to reduced classification complexity and increased accuracy. The accuracy is incremented by the trimming of overfitting and by elimination of the parts that may be based on noisy or erroneous data. Hence, a pruning of a tree has been a subtree of the original tree with just zero, one or more internal nodes changed into leaves (Elomaa & Kääriäinen, 2001).

The REP performs pruning of leaves of the tree by replacing each node with its most popular class. First, the training data are split into two subsets: a growing set (usually 2/3) and a pruning set (1/3) (Fürnkranz, 1997). The growing phase built up the rules for constructing classification tree whereas on the other side pruning phase executes pruning.

The number of instances misclassified while performing analysis on validation or pruning set by propagating errors upward from the leaf nodes reveals error rate for each node. The difference in error is estimated in order to judge which node can be pruned. The difference is calculated by replacing the most common class resulting from a node. If this difference result is a reduction in error then the subtree below the node can be considered for pruning.

The primary benefits of the REP classification technique are its simplicity and computation speed of decision learning. The only shortcoming faced with this technique is that it requires large data for performing pruning.

Testing Phase

To assess the performance of Intelligent Intrusion Detection System the test set generated during Splitter phase has been applied to both the rule base i.e. base classifier rule base and meta classifier rule base. Further the outcomes of both the classifier passes to Decision Maker phase.

Decision Maker

The Decision Maker is the most significant phase of the proposed model. It is the ultimate judge of the identifying the class of attack which has been detected. It is responsible for taking the final decision over the identifications of attacks detected by the two detection algorithms. This is generally performed by comparing the outcomes of base classifier and meta classifier.

Performance Evaluator

The Classifier Performance Evaluator module facilitates the calculation of various classification performance measures in order to judge the accuracy of the proposed systems. These measures serve as a base for determining the correctness of a system. These measures are as follows:

Table 2. Confusion Matrix for TN, TP, FP and FN

	Correctly Classified	**Incorrectly Classified**
Valid Record	True Negative (TN)	False Positive (FP)
Attack Record	True Positive (TP)	False Negative (FN)

True Positive Rate (TPR):

$$TPR = \frac{TP}{TP + FN}$$

False Positive Rate (FPR):

$$FPR = \frac{FP}{FP + TN}$$

where TP (True Positive), FN (False Negative), FP (False Positive) and TN (True Negative) can be defined as follows as describes in Han, Kamber and Pei (2006):

1. **True Negative (TN):** Negative tuples, correctly labeled by the classifier.
2. **True Positive (TP):** Positive tuples, correctly labeled by the classifier.
3. **False Positive (FP):** Negative tuples, incorrectly labeled as positive.
4. **False Negative (FN):** Positive tuples, mislabeled as negative.

A confusion matrix is constructed considering these four terms, shown in Table 2. A confusion matrix is a tabular representation defining performance of an algorithm. The column describes the instances of a prediction class while the row describes the instances of an actual class.

Visualize Result

This phase provides mandatory assistance for obtaining the classification details such as the time used for evaluation, accuracy of the algorithm and other performance measurements. The outcomes of all the experimentations performed are analyzed through this phase. These results may be produced in the form of a text file, graph, etc.

EXPERIMENTATION ENVIRONMENT

This section explores the experimentation that has been done on developed Intelligent Intrusion Detection System.

Dataset Description

The KDDCup'99 dataset (Information and Computer Science, 1999) has been the most widely used datasets since 1999. It has become a preferred dataset used in intrusion detection system to evaluate the effectiveness of IDS models. The KDDCup'99 dataset was originated from processing the tcpdump segment of DARPA 1998 evaluation dataset. The KDDCup'99 data set consists of 41 features and a separate feature (42nd feature) that labels the connection as 'normal' or a type of attack. The normal behavior refers to the genuine activities on the web whereas the abnormal behavior refers to the various intrusions or attacks performed.

The data set contains a total of twenty two attack types (connections) that fall into four major categories i.e. Denial of service (Dos), Probe, User to Root (U2R), and Remote to User (R2L). Table 3 shows the classification of twenty two attack categories into their respective categories.

Kddcup'99 dataset has two variations of training dataset; one is a full training set having 5 million connections and the other is 10% of this training set having 494021 connections. The 10% KDDCup'99 dataset similar to the original KDDCup'99 consists of all 41 attributes along with the additional class label as the 42nd attribute, and 22 types of attacks. The applicability of the data usage depends upon the user who performs the analysis of IDS that whether the 10% of the dataset is quite enough for the analysis or not.

Since the KDDCup'99 data set consists of a huge number of data records of the training and testing of the intrusion detection system, difficulty is faced in analyzing the dataset as a whole. Henceforth the dataset utilized for the analysis of the proposed system is only 10% of the original dataset.

Experimental Setup

The experimental setup includes the benchmark WEKA tool. WEKA (Waikato Environment for Knowledge Analysis) (Hall et al., 2009) is a data mining and machine learning tool designed by The University of Waikato, New Zealand. The tool is defined as the collection of state-of-the-art machine learning algorithms and data processing tools implemented in Java. It is open source software which is licensed under the GNU General Public License. The tool is considered well suited for data mining applications because of its support to predictive modeling and data analysis algorithms. The tool also aids in visualization due to its graphical user interface. Hence the tool is also regarded as the gathering of visualization tools along with data analysis and predictive modeling algorithms implemented. The backbone support of java makes the tool preferred function on any of the modern computing platforms. The data in the WEKA tool are always maintained in form a relation or a flat file stored in the ARFF

Table 3. Subclasses of Major Attack Categories

Class	Attacks
DoS	back, land, Neptune, pod, smurf, teardrop
U2R	buffer_overflow, loadmodule, perl, rootkit
R2L	ftp_write, guess_passwd, imap, multihop, phf, spy, warezclient, warezmaster
Probe	ipsweep, nmap, portsweep, satan

(Attribute Relationship File format) file, CSV (Comma Separated Values) file, etc. The data can also be fetched from a URL or from SQL database (using JDBC). The audit data can be prepared either by using the command line interface present with the tool or simply using any of the supporting formats.

The WEKA simulation tool has been installed on a system configured with Xenon 2.4 GHz processor and 4GB RAM. The Java heap size for WEKA has been set to 2048 MB.

EXPERIMENTATION WITH KDDCUP'99 DATASET USING WEKA SIMULATION ENVIRONMENT

This Section explores the experimental outcomes obtained through the developed Intelligent Intrusion Detection Systems. All the experiments have been performed using the KDDCup'99 dataset in the WEKA simulation environment.

Figure 2 shows the outcomes of Intelligent Intrusion Detection System. When the testing set has been applied to Intelligent Intrusion Detection System, it has successfully classified the normal instances as 99.9%, DoS type of attacks as 100%, Probe type of attacks as 98.7%, R2L type of attacks as 97.1% and U2R type of attacks as 83.3%.

The overall performance of Intelligent Intrusion Detection System is shown in Table 4. The percentage, of Correctly Classified Instances is 99.9619% and Incorrectly Classified Instances is 0.0381%.

Figure 2. Experimental Outcomes of Intelligent Intrusion Detection System

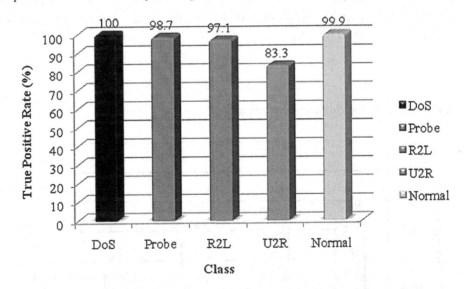

Table 4. Performance of Intelligent Intrusion Detection System

Parameter	Performance (in Percentage)
Correctly Classified Instances	99.9619
Incorrectly Classified Instances	0.0381

Figure 3. True Positive Rate for DoS type of attacks

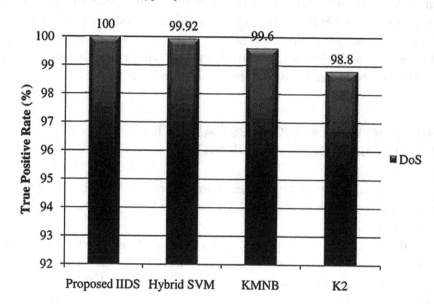

COMPARATIVE ASSESSMENT

This Section covers the in depth comparative experimental investigation of developed Intelligent Intrusion Detection System with Hybrid SVM as discussed in Peddabachigari, Abraham, Grosanc and Thomas (2007), KMNB as described in Muda, Yassin, Sulaiman and Udzir (2011) and K2-based IDS as analyzed in Dhakar and Tiwari (2013).

Figure 4. True Positive Rate for Probe type of attacks

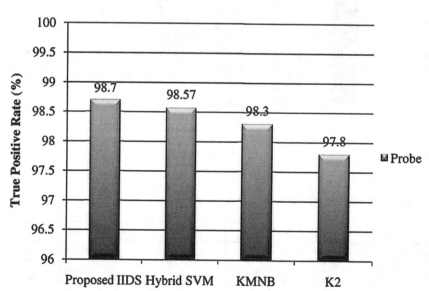

Figure 5. True Positive Rate for R2L type of attacks

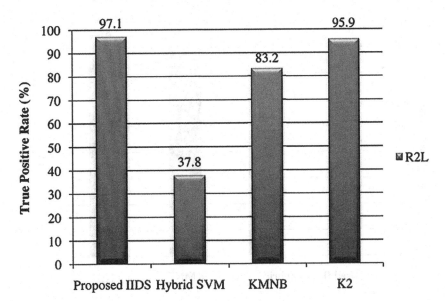

Figure 3 shows the True Positive Rate for the detection of DoS type of attacks. It can be observed that the performance of the developed IIDS is better than other systems. It is needless to write that the developed IIDS outperforms all the three systems by claiming the 100% detection rate of DoS types of attack.

Figure 4 shows the comparative estimation of True Positive Rate for Probe type of attacks. It can be observed that the IIDS provides highest detection rate i.e. 98.7%, then of Hybrid SVM, KMNB and K2 having detection rate of 98.57%, 98.3% and 97.8% respectively.

Figure 5 shows the True Positive Rate for R2L type of attacks. It can be noticed that IIDS has the most precise detection rate of 97.1% while Hybrid SVM, KMNB and K2 have detection rates of 37.8, 83.2 and 95.9% respectively.

Figure 6 shows the True Positive Rate for U2R type of attacks. In detecting the U2R type of attacks, the IIDS outperforms the Hybrid SVM, KMNB and K2-based IDSs while the detection rate for IIDS is 83.3%, for Hybrid SVM is 48%, for KMNB is 80% and for K2-based IDS is 81%.

Figure 7 shows the True Positive Rate for the detection of Normal instances. It can be observed that the developed IIDS has a detection rate of 99.9% and it outperforms the Hybrid SVM, KMNB and K2-based IDS with the detection rate of 99.7%, 99.5% and 98.5% respectively.

SCOPE FOR FUTURE WORKS

Though the proposed model is adequately able to surpass the desirable characteristics of a standard intrusion detection system, still there are some shortcomings which are considered as future work. These are:

1. There is a need to adequately detect the U2R and R2L type of attacks.
2. Still there is a need to suggest remedies for handling intrusion and fraud detection at the application level.

Figure 6. True Positive Rate for U2R type of attacks

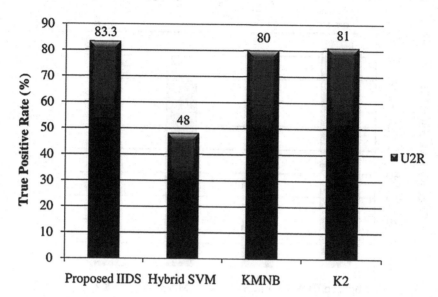

Figure 7. True Positive Rate for Normal type of instances

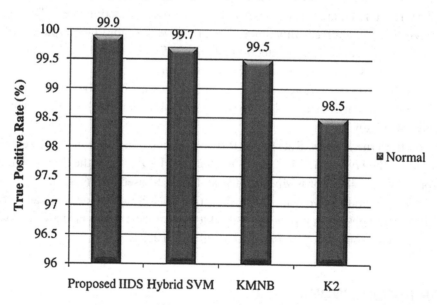

3. The system requires an automatic responding to any detected intrusion.
4. There is a need to work to detect R2L and U2R attacks at global level.
5. The KDDCup'99 dataset requires a revision in order to learn about the existing unknown type of attacks.

CONCLUSION

The experimental assessments performed throughout the research have successfully revolutionized the intrusion detection system performance. During conduction of experiments, it has been realized that IDS with Data Mining has significantly enabled the system to valuably detect the intrusions with greater accuracy level and also helps in the reduction of false alarm rate. With the purpose of improving the accuracy in the detection rate of different attacks, the Hybrid Intelligent Intrusion Detection system has been developed which aims to result in more effective outcomes such that IDS would more capably track and detect intrusions. The accuracy level obtained for the intelligent intrusion detection system is 99.9619% which is quite satisfactory. This system is able to intelligibly provide the efficient outcomes making the IDS as the helping hand for nailing the major concern about system and network security.

To witness the success of the development of IIDS, it is judged against the available data mining based IDS models. The comparison models include Hybrid Support Vector Machine (SVM), K-Means and Naïve Bayes (KMNB) and K2-based intrusion detection system. The end results prove that the IIDS surpasses the compared existing techniques of IDS in respect of Accuracy. Hence it can be concluded that the Intelligent Intrusion Detection System may be expected as the most influential framework meeting the requirements of the advance scenario.

REFERENCES

Altwaijry, H. & Algarny, S. (2012). Bayesian based intrusion detection system. *Journal of King Saud University – Computer and Information Sciences, 24*, 1–6.

Amini, M., Jalili, R., & Shahriari, H. R. (2006). RT-UNNID: A practical solution to real-time network-based intrusion detection using unsupervised neural networks. *Computer & Security Elsevier, 25*(6), 459–468. doi:10.1016/j.cose.2006.05.003

Boukerche, A., Jucá, K. R. L., Sobral, J. B., & Notare, M. S. M. A. (2004). An artificial immune based intrusion detection model for computer and telecommunication systems. *Parallel Computing Elsevier, 30*(5-6), 629–646. doi:10.1016/j.parco.2003.12.008

Carvalho, A. M., Oliveira, A. L., & Sagot, M. (2007). Efficient learning of Bayesian network classifiers: An extension to the TAN classifier. In *Proceedings of Advances in Artificial Intelligence* (pp. 16–25). Springer.

Debar, H., Becker, M., & Siboni, D. (1992). A Neural Component for an Intrusion Detection System. *In Proceedings of Symposium on Research in Security and Privacy* (pp. 240-250). IEEE. doi:10.1109/RISP.1992.213257

Denning, D. E. (1983). An Intrusion-Detection Model. In *Proceedings of the Seventh IEEE Symposium on Security and Privacy* (pp. 119–131). IEEE.

Dhakar, M., & Tiwari, A. (2013). Analysis of K2 based Intrusion Detection System. *Current Research in Engineering, Science and Technology (CREST) Journals, 1*(5), 129–134.

Elbasiony, R. M., Sallam, E. A., Eltobely, T. E., & Fahmy, M. M. (2013). A hybrid network intrusion detection framework based on random forests and weighted k-means. *Ain Shams Engineering Journal, 4*(4), 753–762. doi:10.1016/j.asej.2013.01.003

Elomaa, T., & Kääriäinen, M. (2001). An analysis of Reduced Error Pruning. *Journal of Artificial Intelligence Research, 15*, 163–187.

Feng, W., Zhang, Q., Hu, G., & Huang, J. X. (2014). Mining network data for intrusion detection through combining SVMs with ant colony networks. *Future Generation Computer Systems Elsevier, 37*, 127–140. doi:10.1016/j.future.2013.06.027

Feruza, S. & Yusufovna (2008). Integrating Intrusion Detection System and Data Mining. In *Proceedings of International Symposium on Ubiquitous Multimedia Computing* (pp. 256-259). IEEE.

Friedman, N., Giegar, D., & Goldszmidt, M. (1997). Bayesian Network Classifiers. *Machine Learning, 29*(2/3), 131–163. doi:10.1023/A:1007465528199

Fürnkranz, J. (1997). Pruning Algorithms for Rule Learning. *Machine Learning, Kluwer Academic Publishers, 27*(2), 139–172. doi:10.1023/A:1007329424533

Hall, M., Frank, E., Holmes, G., Pfahringer, B., Reutemann, P., & Witten, I. H. (2009). The WEKA Data Mining Software: An Update. *SIGKDD Explorations, 11*(1), 10–18. doi:10.1145/1656274.1656278

Han, J., Kamber, M., & Pei, J. (2006). *Data Mining: Concepts and Techniques.* San Francisco, CA: Morgan Kaufmann Publishers.

Han, S., & Cho, S. (2003). Detecting Intrusion with Rule-Based Integration of Multiple Models. *Computers & Security Elsevier, 22*(7), 613–623. doi:10.1016/S0167-4048(03)00711-9

Heberlein, L. T., Dias, G. V., Levitt, K. N., Mukherjee, B., Wood, J., & Wolber, D. (1990). A network security monitor. In *Proceedings of Computer Society Symposium on Research in Security and Privacy* (pp. 296-304). IEEE.

Ilgun, K., Kemmerer, R. A., & Porras, P. A. (1995). State transition analysis: A rule-based intrusion detection approach. *IEEE Transactions on Software Engineering, 21*(3), 181–199. doi:10.1109/32.372146

Information and Computer Science, University of California, Irvine. (1999). *KDD Cup 1999 Dataset* [Data file]. Available from http://kdd.ics.uci.edddatabases/kddcup99/kddcup99.html

International, S. R. I. (1992). *A Real-Time Intrusion Detection Expert System (IDES) - Final Technical Report.* Washington, DC: Author.

Jain, Y. K. & Upendra. (2012). An Efficient Intrusion Detection based on Decision Tree Classifier Using Feature Reduction. *International Journal of Scientific and Research Publication, 2*(1), 1–6.

Jiang, S. Y., Song, X., Wang, H., Han, J., & Li, Q. (2006). A Clustering-based Method for Unsupervised Intrusion Detection. *Pattern Recognition Letters Elsevier, 27*(7), 802–810. doi:10.1016/j.patrec.2005.11.007

Jiang, W., Song, H., & Dai, Y. (2005). Real-time intrusion detection for high-speed networks. *Computers & Security Elsevier, 24*(4), 287–294. doi:10.1016/j.cose.2004.07.005

Joo, D., Hong, T., & Han, I. (2003). The neural network models for IDS based on the asymmetric costs of false negative errors and false positive errors. *Expert Systems with Applications Elsevier, 25*(1), 69–75. doi:10.1016/S0957-4174(03)00007-1

Khan, L., Awad, M., & Thuraisingham, M. (2007). A New Intrusion Detection System using Support Vector and Hierarchical Clustering. *The VLDB Journal, 16*(4), 507–521. doi:10.1007/s00778-006-0002-5

Ko, C. (2000). Logic Induction of Valid Behavior Specifications for Intrusion Detection. In *Proceedings of the Symposium on Security and Privacy* (pp. 142-153). IEEE. doi:10.1109/SECPRI.2000.848452

Koc, L., Mazzuchi, T. A., & Sarkani, S. (2012). A network intrusion detection system based on a Hidden Naïve Bayes multiclass classifier. *Expert Systems with Applications Elsevier, 39*(18), 13492–13500. doi:10.1016/j.eswa.2012.07.009

Kumar, S., & Spafford, E. H. (1995). A software architecture to support misuse intrusion detection. In *Proceedings of the 18th National Conference on Information Security* (pp. 194–204).

Lappas, T., & Pelechrinis, K. (n.d.). *Data Mining Techniques for (Network) intrusion Detection Systems*. Retrieved from http://www.academia.edu/5016171/Data_Mining_Techniques_for_Network_Intrusion_Detection_Systems

Lee, W., & Stolfo, S. J. (1998). Data Mining Approaches for Intrusion Detection. In *Proceedings of the 7th USENIX Security Symposium*. San Antonio, TX: USENIX.

Lin, W., & Hauptmann, A. (2003). Meta-classification: Combining Multimodal Classifiers. In O. R. Zaïane, S. J. Simoff, & C. Djeraba (Eds.), Mining Multimedia and Complex Data (pp. 217–231). Berlin: Springer.

Mohammad, M. N., Sulaiman, N., & Muhsin, O. A. (2011). A Novel Intrusion Detection System by using Intelligent Data Mining in Weka Environment. *Elsevier, Procedia Computer Science, 3*, 1237–1242.

Mohammed, R. G., & Awadelkarim, A. M. (2011). Design and Implementation of a Data Mining-Based Network Intrusion Detection Scheme. *Asian Journal of Information Technology, 10*(4), 136–141. doi:10.3923/ajit.2011.136.141

Muda, Z., Yassin, W., Sulaiman, M. N., & Udzir, N. I. (2011). A K-Means and Naïve Bayes Learning Approach for Better Intrusion Detection. *Information Technology Journal, 10*(3), 648–655. doi:10.3923/itj.2011.648.655

Mukkamala, S., Sung, A. H., & Abraham, A. (2005). Intrusion detection using an ensemble of intelligent paradigms. *Journal of Network and Computer Applications, 28*(2), 167–182. doi:10.1016/j.jnca.2004.01.003

Munz, G., Li, S., & Carle, G. (2007). Traffic Anomaly Detection using K-Means Clustering. In *Proceedings of performance, reliability and dependability evaluation of communication networks and distributed systems*. 4 GI / ITG Workshop MMBnet.

Nadiammai, G. V., & Hemalatha, M. (2014). Effective approach toward Intrusion Detection System using data mining techniques. *Egyptian Informatics Journal*, *15*(1), 37–50. doi:10.1016/j.eij.2013.10.003

National Institute of Standards and Technology. (2007). *Guide to Intrusion Detection and Prevention Systems (Special Publication 800-94)*. Gaithersburg, MD: US Department of Commerce.

Panda, M., Abraham, A., & Patra, M. R. (2012). A Hybrid Intelligent Approach for Network Intrusion Detection. In *Proceedings of International Conference on Communication Technology and System Design*, (pp. 1-9). doi:10.1016/j.proeng.2012.01.827

Panda, M., & Patra, M. R. (2007). Network Intrusion Detection using Naïve Bayes. *International Journal of Computer Science and Network Security*, *7*(12), 258–263.

Parekh, S. P., Madan, B. S., & Tugnayat, R. M. (2012). Approach For Intrusion Detection System Using Data Mining. *Journal of Data Mining and Knowledge Discovery*, *3*(2), 83–87.

Peddabachigari, S., Abraham, A., Grosanc, C., & Thomas, J. (2007). Modeling Intrusion Detection System using Hybrid Intellegent System. *Journal of Network and Computer Applications*, *30*(1), 114–132. doi:10.1016/j.jnca.2005.06.003

Raut, R. G., & Gawali, Z. (2012). Intrusion Detection System using Data Mining Approach. *International Journal of Computer Science and Information Technology Research Excellence*, *2*(2).

Rehman, Z., Rehman, S. S. A., & Khan, L. (2009). *Survey Reports on Four Selected Research Papers on Data Mining Based Intrusion Detection System* [PowerPoint slides]. Retrieved from http://web2.uwindsor.ca/courses/cs/aggarwal/cs60564/surveys/ZillurRahmanKhan.ppt

Sekar, R., Bendre, M., Dhurjati, D., & Bollineni, P. (2001). A Fast Automation-Based method for Detecting Anomalous Program Behaviors. In *Proceedings of the Symposium on Security and Privacy* (pp. 144-155). IEEE.

Singh, A. (2006). *Tree-augmented naive bayes* [PDF Document]. Retrieved from Lecture Notes Online Web site: http://courses.cms.caltech.edu/cs155/

Song, C., & Ma, K. (2009). Design of Intrusion Detection System Based on Data Mining Algorithm. In *Proceedings of International Conference on Signal Processing Systems* (pp. 370-373). IEEE. doi:10.1109/ICSPS.2009.202

Xiang, C., Yong, P. C., & Meng, L. S. (2008). Design of Multiple-Level Hybrid Classifier for Intrusion Detection System using Bayesian Clustering and Decision Trees. *Pattern Recognition Letters Elsevier*, *29*(7), 918–924. doi:10.1016/j.patrec.2008.01.008

KEY TERMS AND DEFINITIONS

Attack: To compromise the system vulnerabilities in terms of integrity, confidentiality or availability.

Classification: To prognosticate a category for present observation from a set of predefined categories.

Data Mining: A process that used to mine knowledgeable patterns out of large amounts of data.

Dataset: A compilation of a set of related data records stored in the data repository.

Directed Acyclic Graph: A directed graph exclusive of cycles.

Intrusion: A course of action to acquire unauthorized access to information with illicit motives.

Meta Classifier: A classifier that uses meta data in order to learn patterns.

Pruning: A technique to purge redundant sub trees in the decision tree.

Chapter 6
Agents for Intrusion Detection in MANET:
A Survey and Analysis

Leila Mechtri
Badji Mokhtar University, Algeria

Fatiha Djemili Tolba
Badji Mokhtar University, Algeria

Salim Ghanemi
Badji Mokhtar University, Algeria

ABSTRACT

Mobile Ad-hoc NETworks (MANETs) are believed to be highly vulnerable to security threats due to the numerous constraints they present such as: the absence of a fixed infrastructure, the dynamic topology change, their dependence on cooperative communication, the unreliability of wireless links and most importantly the absence of a clear line of defense. Since intrusion detection and agent technology proved to offer several potential advantages, there has been a great tendency for using agents to build optimal, adaptive and comprehensive intrusion detection systems to fit MANET security requirements. This chapter presents a survey and analysis of the work that has been recently done for the deployment of agent technology in the area of MANET intrusion detection. In particular, recent advances in that field in terms of existing frameworks, architectures and implementations as well as a discussion of the obtained advantages in addition to the potentially introduced vulnerabilities are presented.

INTRODUCTION

Over the past years, Mobile Ad-hoc NETworks (MANETs) have raised several challenging security-related issues. The inherent nature of the wireless medium together with the distributive structure of these networks makes them susceptible to a wide variety of security threats ranging from passive eavesdropping to active interference. Moreover, these networks are highly resource constrained in terms of

DOI: 10.4018/978-1-4666-9426-2.ch006

network topology, memory and computational abilities, which complicated the design and deployment of security solutions. Considering these issues, securing MANETs by means of traditional security mechanisms such as firewalls and authentication is deemed unsatisfactory.

For that, there is always a need for intrusion detection systems (IDSs) to guarantee an acceptable security level. In MANET, IDSs are, generally, classified into four main classes (architectures), namely, stand-alone IDSs, distributed and cooperative IDSs, hierarchical IDSs and agent-based IDSs. Contrary to stand-alone IDSs, where the detection process is performed on each node, and there is no cooperation or data exchange between the network nodes, distributed and cooperative IDSs suggest that every node in the MANET must participate cooperatively in intrusion detection and response. Hierarchical IDSs, on the other hand, are the most suitable for multi-layered networks where the network is divided into clusters. The main idea behind this architecture is that instead of performing host-based intrusion detection at each node, a cluster head is selected to collect security-related information from nodes in a cluster and determines if an intrusion has occurred. The last architecture of MANET IDSs, denoted agent-based IDS architecture, is based on the distribution of the intrusion detection tasks amongst a number of agents.

It is worth noting that contrary to former IDS architectures (stand-alone, distributed and cooperative, and hierarchical) which were excessively used for the development of MANET IDSs, the studies that approach agent-based IDSs were quite few in the early years of IDS deployment in MANET. This is mainly due to: (i) the additional complexity involved in developing agent-based IDSs especially as this technology is known for introducing new challenges with respect to security mainly when dealing with mobile agents and (ii) the lack of experience in formulating agent-based solutions to applications. However, as they, recently, proved several advantages, agents are gaining great attention especially for their suitability for the building of distributed applications. This is what encourages many researchers to explore more possibilities for the application of agents in the context of MANET intrusion detection. This paper presents an up-to-date survey of the state of the art in the area of MANET intrusion detection with a great emphasis on the application of agent technology in this context.

This paper is organized as follows: section 2 outlines the basic features of IDSs, agents and agent-based technologies. Then, section 3 focuses on the recent advances, in terms of the proposed frameworks, architectures and implementations, for the application of agent technology to MANET intrusion detection. Section 4 presents and discusses the drawn conclusions about agent deployment in MANET intrusion detection, with respect to the studied frameworks. Finally, some concluding remarks are given in section 5.

BACKGROUND

In this section we introduce some concepts and terminology related to the field of agent-based intrusion detection.

Intrusion Detection

Intrusion detection is the process of monitoring and analyzing events of computer systems or networks in order to uncover any set of actions that attempt to compromise the integrity, confidentiality or availability of a resource (Hung-Jen, Chun-Hung, Ying-Chih, & Kuang-Yuan, 2013).

There are two main intrusion detection methods, namely anomaly detection and misuse (or signature-based) detection. Anomaly detection models normal behavior i.e., it compares observed data to normal behavior patterns, while misuse detection deals with attack behavior i.e., it compares observed data to known attack patterns. A hybrid intrusion detection that combines both anomaly and misuse detection can be considered as a third method of detection. Each of these methods has some advantages over the other one, but at the same time, they present some serious shortcomings. For instance, misuse detection is effective for accurately detecting known attacks but it generally fails to detect unforeseen attacks. Unfortunately, this inability to detect unknown attacks is deemed to generate a significant number of false negative alarms. Anomaly detection, on the other hand, allows the detection of new attacks since it focuses, during its analyses, on any deviation from the normal behavior of the supervised system rather than being limited to the search of some specific attack scenarios. However, this might lead to the generation of a significant number of false positive alarms since it is often difficult to perfectly model the system's normal behavior.

The source of data used by those methods can be either the host on which the intrusion detection system (IDS) is run or the network itself. Thus, we come to distinguish between two classes of IDSs which are Host-based IDSs (H-IDS) and Network-based IDSs (N-IDS).

The commonly used metrics for IDS evaluation are summarized in Table 1, where values of TP, TN, FP and FN are counted with respect to the relation between the predicted and actual classes of the audited profiles as illustrates Table 2.

Table 1. IDS evaluation metrics

Metric	Formula	Description
Accuracy	$(TP + TN)/(TP + TN + FP + FN)$	The probability that the IDS can correctly predict normal profiles and attacks
Precision	$TP/(TP + FP)$	the proportion of predicted attack cases that are real attacks
Specificity	$TN/(TN + FP)$	The proportion of normal profiles that are successfully identified as normal profiles
Detection rate (Recall)	$TP/(TP + FN)$	The proportion of attacks that are successfully identified as attack cases
False positive alarm rate	$FP/(FP + TN)$	The proportion of learned normal profiles that are considered as attacks
False negative alarm rate	$FN/(FN + TP)$	The proportion of attacks that are not successfully detected

Table 2. IDS confusion matrix

		Predicted Class	
		Normal Profile	**Attack**
Actual Class	**Normal Profile**	True negative (TN)	False positive (FP)
	Attack	False negative (FN)	True positive (TP)

Software Agents

An agent can be defined as a computer system that is able to execute autonomous actions in its environment, in a flexible and intelligent manner, in order to achieve a predefined goal. Therefore, a multi-agent system is a system that consists of a collection of autonomous agents that can interact together to learn or to exchange experiences. Agent-based systems usually encompass three main types of agent architectures, namely: reactive, deliberative and the hybrid architecture where aspects of both reactive and deliberative agents are combined.

Reactive agents do not have representations of their own environment and act using a stimulus/response type of behavior; they respond to the present state of the environment in which they are situated. They neither take history into account nor plan for the future. Reactive agents make decisions based on local information. Thus, they cannot take into consideration non-local information or predict the effect of their decisions on the global behavior of the multi-agent system. Moreover, they lack adaptability as they cannot generate an appropriate plan if faced with a state that was not considered a priori. Despite these limitations, reactive agents still have the advantage of being speed which necessarily makes them desired in rapidly changing environments.

The key component of a deliberative agent however is a central reasoning system that constitutes the intelligence of the agent. Thus, unlike reactive agents, deliberative agents maintain a model of the internal state and they are able of predicting the effects of their committed actions. More importantly, these agents are mainly characterized by their ability to generate plans that successfully lead to the achievement of their goals even in unforeseen situations. Unfortunately, a major problem with deliberative agents is that the sophisticated reasoning can slow them which may cause latency in the reaction time which is undesirable especially in case of real-time applications.

Basically, agents present several interesting features, among which we cite:

1. **Autonomy:** Agents operate without the direct intervention of humans or others, and have some kind of control over their actions and internal state. In other words, it takes actions based on its built-in knowledge and its past experiences;
2. **Social Ability:** Agents interact with other agents via some kind of agent-communication language;
3. **Reactivity:** Agents perceive their environment and respond in a timely fashion to changes that occur in it;
4. **Pro-Activeness:** Agents do not simply act in response to their environment, but they are able to exhibit goal-directed behavior by taking initiative;
5. **Negotiation:** The ability to conduct organized conversations to achieve a degree of cooperation with other agents;
6. **Adaptation:** The ability to improve its performance over time when interacting with the environment in which it is embedded.

With these interesting features in mind, many researchers sought to investigate this technology in developing optimal, adaptive and comprehensive intrusion detection systems to fit MANET security requirements. Agents exploited in intrusion detection can be either stationary agents, used mainly for monitoring purposes and for local intrusion detection, or mobile agents best suited for distributed operations such as: gathering network-related information, broadcasting detection results and performing global responses while offering several advantages like: network load reduction, dynamic adaption, robustness and flexibility.

AGENT-BASED IDSs

The need for effective, optimal and adaptive intrusion detection systems that fit MANET requirements caused agent-based IDSs to prevail though the complexity and challenges entailed by their deployment. Recently, new paradigms for agent-based MANET IDSs were explored.

Stationary Agent Based IDSs

FORK (Ramachandran, Misra, & Obaidat, 2008) is a two-pronged strategy to an agent-based intrusion detection system for ad-hoc networks, in which only those nodes that are capable of participating in the intrusion detection process, in terms of their available resources and their reputation level (which increases when the node successfully assists in intrusion detection tasks and decreases in case of failure) are allowed to compete for and get the IDS agent tasks. The authors base the task allocation process on principles of auctioning. Whenever one or more nodes detect certain changes in the network, they initiate an auction process by submitting auction requests to the rest of the network nodes. The interested nodes submit their bids to the initiating node(s) that, then, choose them based on several metrics including a battery power metric. Finally, the chosen nodes perform the intrusion detection tasks using a variation of the Ant Colony Optimization (ACO) algorithm. For instance, each network node contains all the modules (lightweight agents) required to perform the anomaly detection tasks such as: host and network monitoring (data collection), the decision making given a set of audit data, and the activation of defensive actions if malicious behaviors have been detected.

Experiments show that the proposed detection algorithm is effective in terms of the accuracy of rules formed and the simplicity in their content. It was also shown that detection rates were improved compared to other IDSs. Nevertheless, node mobility, which highly affects the detection accuracy, was not considered in this evaluation. On the other hand, the distribution of detection tasks among a set of carefully selected nodes helps conserving local resources, mainly battery power. However, this IDS seems to be insecure as no suggestions about securing the mobile agents were given. Also, the cooperative nature of the proposed detection scheme offers the opportunity to malicious nodes to cause resource-consumption-like attacks by initiating fake detection tasks.

The biological immune system was a source of inspiration for several agent-based IDS designers, who tried to take benefit of the analogy that exists between the two fields to approach the distinguished ability of the biological immune system to distinguish self from non-self and to protect the human body from this latter.

One example of such IDS architecture is presented in (Byrski and Carvalho, 2008). Here, A. Byrsky and M. Carvalho designed an immunological intrusion detection system based on the agent concept for securing MANET. This IDS consists of a set of autonomous agents, denoted detectors, distributed among the different network nodes. Each detector implements an anomaly intrusion detection approach based on the negative selection algorithm and monitors the communication of its neighboring nodes. For that, every node maintains both a set of self-patterns (characterizing normal behavior) and a set of non-self-patterns (characterizing potential anomalous behavior). Upon the observation of any kind of disturbance in the behavior of a node, the concerned detectors communicate with neighboring detectors in order to consult their observations. Then, a collective decision is undertaken based on the reliability weight of contributing detectors. This weight is applied by the super-detectors that represent the second level of detectors.

Although it seems simple and effective in detecting intrusions, this approach might have a negative effect on the nodes' performance mainly in networks with high mobility, where detectors and super-detectors have to regenerate neighbors' self-patterns and non-self-patterns as well as neighboring detectors' reliability weights each time the network topology changes. So far, the approach ensures a high level of reliability because even if the detectors cannot maintain contact among themselves, they still may react to the behavior they sense.

Some generic stationary agent-based IDSs that can be adopted for MANET were also proposed in the literature. For instance, Servin and Kudenko (2008) proposed a hierarchical architecture of distributed intrusion detection systems integrated by remote sensor agent diversity and reinforcement learning (RL) to detect and categorize DDoS Attacks.

This architecture is built from m cells with each cell composed of one central agent (RL-IDS) and n sensor agents. In RL, agents or programs sense their environment in discrete time steps and they map those inputs to local state information. Under this consideration, distributed sensor agents were configured to process the local state information and pass on short signals up a hierarchy of RL-IDS agents. That is, a sensor agent learns to interpret local state observations, and communicates them to a central agent higher up in the agent hierarchy.

Central agents, in turn, learn to send signals up the hierarchy, based on the signals that they receive.

Then, via the signals from the lower-level RL-IDS agents, the agent on top of the hierarchy learns whether or not to trigger an intrusion alarm. If the signal is in accordance with the real state of the monitored network, all the agents receive a positive reward. If the action is inaccurate, all the agents receive a negative reward. Thus, after a certain number of iterations of the algorithm, every agent would know for each state the action that they need to execute to obtain positive rewards. Also, the Q-learning technique and a simple exploration/exploitation strategy are used to enable the agents to learn an accurate signal policy and to maximize the obtained reward over the time.

The proposed approach was evaluated in an abstract network domain with different architectures varying the number of agents, the number of states per sensor agent, the exploration/exploitation strategy, the distribution of attacks as input information, and the agent architecture.

Clearly, a clustered MANET would be a good ground for such IDS architecture with clusters mapping the cells, cluster-heads running RL-IDS agents, and cluster-member nodes running sensor agents.

Mobile Agent Based IDSs

Mobile agents are special software agents that have the ability to roam through networks. Mobile agents offer several potential advantages over stationary agents when used to design MANET applications with respect to load reduction, dynamic and static adoption, and bandwidth conservation. In this overview, Roy and Chaki (2011) introduced a totally mobile agent based IDS to detect the blackhole attack in MANET. This IDS, referred to as MABHIDS, defines two types of agents: a mobile agent and a specialized agent. First, the source node (willing to communicate with another node) generates a mobile agent and forwards it to the next hop node in the route to the intended destination. The mobile agent has to collect the raw data from the host machine then it computes the packet delivery ratio (R_i) for the ith host. The specialized agent then compares the R_i value with a threshold ThR, predefined by the source node, and gives responses to the source node accordingly.

Although this approach was proven to be efficient in detecting the blackhole attack, it still too limited and needs to be extended so that to detect more attacks especially as the number of newly discovered attacks is always increasing. In addition, MABHIDS is based on merely mobile agents and their ability to roam in the network, but no security mechanism was integrated to protect them from attacks though they are well known for their security vulnerabilities.

Ping, Futai, Xinghao, and Jianhua (2007) also proposed an intrusion detection and response system for MANET based on mobile agents. It is composed of a monitor agent residing on every network node, a decision agent, and a collection of block agents. Each monitor agent collects information of its neighbor nodes' behavior, filters it from unnecessary information, and sends this information after coding to the decision agent upon receiving a query message from this latter.

The decision agent, then, detects intrusions by analyzing monitor agents' information. Due to resource constraints in MANET, decision agents are distributed over only some nodes. However, network dynamics may cause a decision agent to move with its node thereby leaving the zone without any supervision. To tackle this problem, the authors suggested that if monitor agents in a zone have not received the query packet for a long period, a new node will be selected to run the decision agent.

If an intrusion is detected, the decision agent will produce block agents that will be sent to the neighbor nodes of the intruder to form the mobile firewall and isolate the intruder. To finish, a process of local repair will be executed to find new routes to replace all paths that include the intruder.

Though it succeeded in automating the response process, the proposed approach adopted no mechanism to prevent malicious or compromised nodes from initiating blackmail attacks through the generation of fake query messages.

Detection of unknown attacks together with the ability to detect attacks at different network layers is indispensable for a comprehensive IDS.

Realizing that, Devi and Bhuvaneswaran (2011) proposed an efficient cross layer anomaly-based intrusion detection architecture. This architecture implements a fixed width clustering algorithm for the training phase in order to build the normal profiles database. A data mining technique is then used by the intrusion detection module to distinguish attacks from normal profiles. This technique uses an association algorithm (Fast Apriori Algorithm) to extract necessary traffic features and to collect data streams from various network layers (physical, MAC, and network layers).

Data collection is usually followed by the local detection phase, in which the local detection module (consisting of an anomaly detection engine that uses the fixed width clustering algorithm) analyzes the local data traces gathered by the collection module for evidence of anomalies. If any detection rule deviates beyond the anomaly threshold and if the local detection module has a high accuracy rate, it can independently determine that the network is under attack and thus, it initiates the alert management agent. However, if the support and confidence level is low or intrusion evidence is weak and inconclusive in the detecting node then it can make collaborative decision by gathering intelligence from its surrounding nodes via protected communication channel. The decision of the cooperative detection is based on the majority of the voting of the received reports indicating an intrusion or anomaly. Upon receiving alerts (either from local detection or cooperative detection agents), the alert management agent collects them in the alert cache for t seconds. If there are more abnormal predictions than the normal predictions then it is regarded as abnormal and with adequate information an alarm is generated to inform that an intrusive activity is in the system.

Evaluation of the proposed approach revealed that it has some advantages. For instance, the way in which generated alerts are treated reduces both false positive and false negative alarms. Also, the use of the fixed width algorithm helps in detecting attacks at different layers while the fast apriori algorithm increased the speed of detecting them significantly. Nevertheless, this approach implicates that the nodes should have considerable computational capabilities to run such algorithms. In addition, the authors considered that a protected channel is used as a means of communication between neighboring nodes but no description of how to protect the channel was provided. Furthermore, the initialization of a cooperative detection depends on the level of intrusion evidence within the local detection module but there is no specification about when intrusion evidence is deemed weak or strong.

While some researchers use agents to build distributed agent-based IDSs, others (Li & Qian, 2010; Sen, 2010; Farhan, Zulkhairi, & Hatim, 2008; Pattanayak & Rath, 2014) prefer the use of agents to build hierarchical IDSs so that to get benefit of the specific characteristics offered by both architectures such as load balancing especially in networks where not all the nodes are capable of performing detection tasks.

In (Li & Qian, 2010) the authors proposed an agent-based intrusion detection model for MANET that forms a cluster head-centered backbone network by using a decision mode of joint detection used among cluster heads and vote by ballot in partial cluster heads. More specifically, the proposed model adopts a clustering algorithm for the building of nodes clusters, which form the platform for the agent-based intrusion detection. Intrusion detection agents are activated on elected cluster head nodes at the same time of cluster formation. These agents use a parameter based intrusion detection method that allows to detect any abnormal activities within a cluster and to generate local response in case of intrusion detection. In case of uncertainty, however, the cluster head node will trigger the joint detection among the cluster heads that will use a partial voting to determine malicious nodes. In case of an intrusion confirmed, a global network response in the form of blacklist broadcasting will be initiated. However, if the intruder is the cluster-head node itself, neighboring cluster-head nodes, in addition to screening the intruder, will split and merge its cluster, or assign a new cluster-head using the adopted clustering algorithm.

According to its authors, the proposed model has advantages of short computing time, low consumption of both bandwidth and power and high detection rates. Nevertheless, mobility might present a serious problem to the proposed model. Actually, nodes mobility leads to cluster reformation which, by the way, implies the regeneration of detection agents thereby, resetting the detection process. This might result in: delaying the detection and response to intrusions, network overhead and nodes' resource consumption especially if a node is always chosen as a cluster head. Also, no mechanism for preventing a compromised node from being a cluster head was proposed.

In (Sen, 2010) the architecture of the proposed signature-based IDS is, however, organized as a dynamic hierarchy in which the intrusion data is acquired by network nodes and is incrementally aggregated, reduced in volume, and analyzed as it flows upwards to the cluster-head.

It mainly consists of two broad modules: the Cluster-Head Module (CHM) running only on cluster-head nodes and the Cluster-Member Module (CMM) running on all the network nodes i.e., both cluster-heads and cluster-member nodes.

Every CMM maintains a database denoted intrusion interpreter base in which attacks' signatures and related thresholds are stored.

It detects intrusions locally and may request the cluster-head node for initiating a cooperative intrusion detection and response action if additional information or a global response is required. In case of a cooperative intrusion detection, the cluster-head dispatches mobile agents to gather information from other members in the same cluster and other clusters, and then processes the gathered information to detect any intrusion in a global scale.

If an intrusion is detected by a CMM, it initiates a local response and, if need be, it communicates its response to its cluster head. This latter, via its CHM, logs the event and informs the nodes within its cluster and the adjacent cluster-heads (which in turn inform their cluster members) to isolate the offending node from the network.

Intrusion related message communication is handled by mobile agents. Cluster-heads can create, dispatch and process the results returned by the mobile agents.

A database is maintained for the mobile agents that are created and dispatched. They are created only at the time of cooperative intrusion detection and are destroyed immediately after accomplishing the designated tasks successfully or if the associated timer expires.

Pattanayak and Rath (2014) proposed that a cluster head is to be elected, at the initiation of each application, based on a battery power metric. A dedicated mobile agent, consisting of a registration module (RM), a service agreement (SA), a detection module (DM) and a prevention module (PM), is incorporated in each cluster. During the initiation of a new application, all the nodes in the cluster need to register with the mobile agent and to accept a service agreement specific to the initiated application. The mobile agent, on its own, maintains a list of registered nodes in its registration module and uses the detection module to monitor each packet routed through the cluster head. If a mismatch occurs in source and destination addresses, the mobile agent will inform the cluster head to drop the packet and to block the respective node. If the mismatch occurs in the application ID or the packet length exceeds the threshold, then only the packet will be dropped by the cluster head.

This approach is time and resource consuming for all the packets are routed and monitored by the CH (mainly in case of several concurrent applications). Hence, a battery power metric is not sufficient to choose a reliable CH able of handling all the cluster communications in addition to performing intrusion detection tasks. Also, a node is not allowed to leave its cluster until the application is finished which is not the case of real world MANETs.

Another way of modeling the hierarchical agent-based IDS architecture was explored in (Farhan et al., 2008). Here, a zone-based framework is used to divide the whole ad hoc network into non overlapping zones. Nodes in a zone are either gateway nodes (inter-zone nodes), if a connection to a node in the neighboring zone exists, or intra-zone nodes, otherwise.

In the proposed IDS framework, called MAZIDS, every intra-zone node runs a LIDS (Local Intrusion Detection System) locally to perform local data collection, anomaly detection and to initiate local response using mobile agents while gateway nodes will run GIDS (Gateway Intrusion Detection System).

GIDS are in charge of initiating global and zone intrusion detection and response. If a node detects an intrusion locally, it will initiate a local alarm, by sending an alarm message to the nearest GIDS, which in turn will trigger either cooperative agents or local and global response agents depending on the strength of evidence in the intrusion. Then, the GIDS, through its manager agent stores the alarm in the long term memory (LTM) if the intrusion is detected with strong evidence or in the short term memory (STM) in case of weak or inconclusive evidence, for future reference.

Not so far from clustered MANETs, the ad hoc network in (Mohamed & Abdullah, 2009) is divided into domains with each domain controlled by a master (server) node chosen based on relevant capabilities such as processing ability, battery power, and signal strength. In order not to exhaust the server's resources, a management method for dynamically changing the role of a domain node to act as a server is specified.

The proposed security approach defines four agents and is handled in two phases. First, the network domains pass with a recognition phase during which all of the four agents reside on the server side. This is a simulation of the maturation phase that takes place in thymus in the biological immune system. For instance, the monitor agent will learn to distinguish between the self (normal behavior) and non-self patterns (anomalous behavior) until it gets matured enough to detect intruders.

Following the recognition phase, the manager agent will release monitor and replicate agents in the domain and shifts to a listen state. While listening, the manager agent will act according to the notifications it receives from the monitor and replicate agents. Every monitor agent will supervise the packets passing through its node using a combination of both negative selection and danger theory. In case of suspicion, it will block the packets and will update the local database.

Recover agent is used in an attempt to add self-healing capability to the network. For instance, a restore point is periodically created for each node inside the domain and the healing process can be triggered automatically, using information reported by the monitoring agents, to correct nodes problems.

TraceGray (Taggu & Taggu, 2011) is an application layer scheme that uses mobile agents to detect grayholes in a DSR-based (Dynamic Source Routing) MANET. Actually, this IDS scheme invokes a mobile agent, which while migrating from its home context (the node on which the agent was created) towards the destination context, reports any grayhole it found on its path. For that, the authors defined five states for an agent:

1. **Initial:** Refers to the agent's state at the time of its creation at its home context.
2. **1st Hop:** The agent changes its state to the 1st hop state upon successful migration to the next hop node from the source node.
3. **2nd Hop:** Reaching this state means that two hops from the home context have been successfully traversed and the mobile agent have to migrate backwards to its home context.
4. **Analysis:** The mobile agent reaches the analysis state upon successful return to the home context. If the second hop node is the destination context then this will imply that no grayholes were found. However, if the second hop node is not the destination context, then the mobile agent sets its new home context to the first hop node and restarts the whole traversal process by changing its state to the initial state. Whenever the return flow from second hop to the home context is not successful as indicated by timer expiry, a grayhole at the first hop node is announced.
5. **Dispose:** The mobile agent arrives at this state whenever ROUTE BROKEN condition occurs or timer expires

The deployment of such a solution is fairly easy and does not require any modification of the routing protocol but it is worth noting that it generates a considerable load and bandwidth consumption as well as a significant delay in attack reporting especially for the detection of grayholes over long paths. Moreover, the approach considers only one routing protocol (DSR), what makes it improper for other routing protocols like OLSR (Optimized Link State Routing) and AODV (Ad-hoc On-demand Distance Vector).

In (Hong-song, Zhenzhou, Mingzeng, Zhongchuan, & Ruixiang, 2007; Hong-Song, Jianyu, & Lee, 2008) two novel multi-agent-based dynamic lifetime intrusion detection and response schemes are proposed to protect AODV-based MANETs from blackhole and DoS attacks. In both schemes, agents are designed so as to dynamically adapt their creation, execution and expiration to the routing process status and are related to one RREQ–RREP stream. In (Hong-song et al., 2007) each agent is responsible for the monitoring of nodes within a three-hop zone. When the RREQ or RREP messages are out of this zone, a new agent is generated to execute the detection algorithm so as to avoid the delay in listening the routed packets. Once created, the current agent executes the intrusion detection algorithm based on the related link list and MAC-IP control table. In (Hong-song et al., 2008), however, only link list data is used by the IDS agent, implemented as a thread in network processor.

If the agent finds the node itself has malicious behavior, it can migrate to another high trustworthy node. Finally, if there is no RREQ–RREP stream in the network for some time, the related agent expires and the detection information is saved by the agent node for future detection.

While they efficiently improve trustworthiness, decrease computing complexity and save energy consumption, both approaches badly affect the network performance especially when many nodes initiate routing operations simultaneously. More specifically, the association of a new agent to every RREQ-RREP stream might overload the nodes (mainly those that are involved in many routes) with heavy extra processing loads entailed by the different detection agents.

Hybrid-Agent Based IDSs

While the previously discussed IDSs were comprised of collections of merely stationary or mobile agents, other works like (Bourkache, Mezghiche, & Tamine, 2011; Mechtri, Djemili, & Ghanemi, 2012; Stafrace & Antonopoulos, 2010; Ye & Li, 2010; Chang & Shin 2010) were looking forward to enhancing the IDSs' fault tolerance and scalability through the combination of both stationary and mobile agents.

In (Bourkache et al., 2011), the authors proposed a new model for the building of a distributed and intelligent real-time intrusion detection system that fits MANET security requirements. The proposed IDS model is composed of multiple local IDS agents distributed among the different network nodes. Each local IDS is responsible for detecting intrusions locally using its three constituent agents, namely collector, the detection agent and the response agent. It implements a classification method as an anomaly detection engine in which classes of normal behavior in the form of data vectors together with detection thresholds are built during the learning stage. In the test stage, however, the detection of local anomalies starts by collecting data using collector. Then, the detection agent builds a vector characterizing the audited activity to be compared with the centers of gravity of the various classes of normal behavior using the Euclidean distance. Finally, the system administrator, based on the predefined thresholds, can decide whether the audited activity presents an anomaly or not. To have a global vision of the network's security state and to defend against distributed attacks, collector agents were, further, designed so that to roam in the network to collect data from other network nodes.

The main disadvantage of this approach is that it relies on the network administrator to accomplish the final step of the detection process i.e., to decide about the presence of an anomaly. Also, no response mechanism was described though the use of a response agent.

MASID (Multi-Agent System for Intrusion Detection) (Mechtri et al. 2012) is another agent-based intrusion detection system, in which a collection of both stationary and mobile agents is in charge of performing a distributed and cooperative intrusion detection. Each network node is provided with a Local IDS (LIDS) running independently and monitoring local activities. Each LIDS detects intrusions from local traces and initiates local and global response. If an anomaly is detected in the local data, or if there are signs of intrusion and there is not enough evidence, neighboring local IDSs will cooperatively participate in the detection process, either by participating actively in the response or by, simply, providing some additional information, respectively. Each LIDS is comprised of five different but complementary agents, namely: collector, the detection agent, collaborator, the response agent and the SNMP (Simple Network Management Protocol) agent. By using agents, a complete automation of the detection process together with low use of both host and network resources and time were achieved.

Considering resource constraints in MANET, the behavior of MASID was adapted to the node's state (i.e., whether it is under attack or not) by creating a kind of active/sleep transition in state for each of MASID's constituent agents. Sleep refers to a state where the concerned agent is not performing any actions. In such a situation, the agent will free all its pre-allocated resources. Active state, however, refers to the agent's state when performing the required tasks. This way, both system and network resources were conserved to the maximum possible. Also, the parallel execution of the different intrusion detection tasks, through the use of several agents, each performing a specific detection subtask, permits a considerable reduction of the runtime thereby, leading to faster detection and response to attacks.

On the other hand, MASID is supposed to be enhanced so that to recover some weaknesses such as: (i) considering nodes' mobility effects on the distributed detection process, (ii) enhancing the system's fault tolerance, and (iii) securing mobile agents and their communication.

Chang and Shin (2010) focused on the detection of intrusions at the application layer. Similarly to many other agent-based IDSs, they used a local IDS, consisting on a monitoring and detection agent, a response agent, and a communication agent to detect intrusions at every network node. Their main contribution is the use of mobile agents to augment each node's intrusion-detection capability. Specifically, they equipped the network with a mobile agent server capable of creating and dispatching three types of mobile agents: update, analysis, and verification agents.

If a local IDS fails to identify a suspicious behavior, its response agent will request the mobile agent server to send analysis agents for further investigation. The analysis agent is capable of a more detailed analysis and diagnosis compared to the local IDS as it can launch multi-point network-based anomaly detection. Once the investigation completed, the analysis agent will report the results to the mobile agent server. Hence, if a new attack type is detected or the suspicious activity is judged as a change in the node's behavior, an update agent will be created to update local IDSs' databases with the new attack signature or normal profile.

Further, the mobile agent server periodically checks the status of local IDSs using verification agents. If a vulnerability is detected, it will patch and install programs on the concerned mobile nodes via its update agents.

Clearly, mobile agents can overcome network latency and reduce the network load related to intrusion detection. Also, this approach was a step forward in enhancing agent-based IDSs' fault tolerance, but it might lead to further problems. For instance, the mobile agent server might exhaust the node's resources (mainly processing and storage) in addition to being a single point of failure.

In (Ye & Li, 2010), a multi-agent system is again used to mimic the biological immune system in an attempt to secure a network after dividing it into independent logical zones.

The proposed security architecture defined two types of immune agents: detection agents uniformly distributed in the network and counterattack agents, residing on all the nodes.

Nodes, carrying out the detection agents, initiate zone creation through sending query messages to their one-hop neighbors. The other nodes will join the zone of the originator of the first query message they receive. A newly coming node sends a request message to its one-hop neighbors to join a detection zone. Detection agents that receive the request respond to it and the node will join the zone of the originator of the first response message it receives. If none of the neighbors is carrying a detection agent, the request message will be forwarded until it reaches a node with a detection agent. This latter copies itself and then moves to the new node.

Once the detection zones established, detection agents start data collection from the nodes within their zones and look for any matches with the records in their immune memories (misuse detection). If no matches are found, the agent will contrast the codes of the audited node's acts with protocols in its immune strategy library (anomaly detection).

If an intrusion is detected, the detection agent, through its communication module, will trigger dormant counterattack agents on the intruder's neighbor nodes to surround and isolate the intruder. Isolation is achieved through refraining from sending and receiving packets from the invader until it leaves the network or its power is exhausted.

This approach is simple but spends huge network resources for the management of detection zones (exponential to nodes' mobility).

A different artificial immune system based IDS for MANET was proposed in (Kumar & Reddy, 2014). Here, each node was equipped with two agents: A mobile agent and a master agent. The mobile agent is in charge of gathering information related to bandwidth, packet delivery rate and delay from neighboring nodes.

Collected information will be reported to the master agent residing on the mobile agent's home node that will use it to run the artificial immune system to generate and /or update normal profiles patterns. Upon receiving new packets, a node calculates parameters like packet delivery rate and delay. If the calculated parameters match with the patterns generated by the master agent, then the connection is considered as valid. Otherwise, an alert is generated and carried by the communication agent to the source node. This latter halts the on-going transmission and resumes it after a stipulated period of time.

The detection approach is simple and the way normal patterns are generated ensures normal profiles patterns to be updated constantly. However, this way can be misleading, thereby causing the IDS to generate false alarms.

da Cunha Neto, Zair, Fernandes, and Froz (2013) presented a model of a wireless intrusion detection system (WIDS) aiming to expand Botnet detectors by using a set of agents that interact directly or indirectly to collect (through the monitoring agent) and analyze packets in wireless networks. The model, via the filtering agent, uses packet filtering through the WhiteList and BlackList, besides carrying the signature and anomaly analysis (via the signature analysis and anomaly analysis agents, respectively), to minimize the false positives.

If a security incident is detected, appropriate countermeasures are taken in accordance with the reaction database (notifying or blocking the signal from an intruder). In addition to the reaction database, a set of specialized databases (Collection Database, WhiteList Database, BlackList Database, Signature Database, and a Knowledge Database) is used for maintaining the persistent information from each agent.

Evaluation of the proposed approach revealed that WIDS can identify attacks with great efficiency and speed, due to the possibility of eliminating packages not needed to evaluation using the filter agent.

Another different way of approaching agent-based IDS solutions in ad-hoc networks is to visualize the network as an urban hostile zone, where the agents collaboratively follow specific tactics to police the zone. From this perspective, Stafrace and Antonopoulos (2010) presented the design of an agent framework modeled over a military command structure and an agent behavioral model, which employs adapted military tactics to police routes, and detect intruders in wireless ad-hoc networks.

The proposed detection solution works as follows: A Command Post (CP) is set up on Node S to control the route to Node D. The Command Post is a process that periodically orders a patrol mission along the route. A patrol mission consists of an Active Reconnaissance Phase and a Route Patrol Phase. The detection mission commences with the active reconnaissance process such that node S begins counting the outbound data packets for the destination node D. The duration of the reconnaissance activity is based on the data packet throughput and route stability. This phase results in a Reconnaissance Snapshot containing the number of outbound packets grouped by the next hop address. Each packet that was counted during this phase is also tagged with a Snapshot ID. In addition, an Intelligence (INTEL) process consisting of a similar reconnaissance function is performed on each intermediate node along the supervised route. The final result of the INTEL process is thereby a Reconnaissance Snapshot containing the respective packet counts for every intermediate node. On successful completion of phase one, the CP initiates the second phase whereby a Scout Patrol Squad is deployed to police the controlled route. The tactical mobile agent squad consists of three units, namely the Scout Leader (SL) and two scouts: Scout A (SA) and Scout B (SB). Both scouts perform a data collection-like function, which is basically querying the INTEL process on their host nodes for specific reconnaissance snapshots. Then, the leader of the squad will evaluate the observation provided by the scouts. Finally, it will perform a threat assessment based on the outcome of the evaluation and take the required actions accordingly.

Since tactical agents follow a risk-based approach which means that the frequency of patrols is directly proportional to the risk factor of the route (which is in turn a factor of the route throughput and frequency of use), resources were conserved without impacting the effectiveness of the IDS. Also, the proposed solution is independent of the routing protocol i.e., it is applicable to wireless ad-hoc networks regardless of the routing protocol. Nonetheless, the CP constitutes a single point of failure. In addition, the solution does not offer the possibility to detect unknown attacks.

Because traditional security-centric mechanisms consume a large amount of network resources and thereby degrading its performance, Wang et al. (2013) designed a network performance-centric anomaly detection scheme for resource constrained MANETs. This scheme employs a fully distributed multi-agent framework. More specifically, the system uses a platform of mobile agents to design the energy-aware and self-adaptive anomaly detection. In this concern, four kinds of agents, residing in every node, were defined, namely: the network tomography agent (NTA), the anomaly detection agent (ADA), the communication service agent (CSA), and the state detection agent (SDA).

The proposed anomaly detection system proceeds in two phases. The first phase aims at detecting link delay anomalies while the second phase tries to quickly detect and accurately localize malicious nodes on links. For instance, the detection is started by executing an energy-aware root election mechanism that selects the most cost-efficient node as the root that will sponsor system services. By the way, the NTA on that node will be considered as the root NTA that will be activated while other NTAs remain inactive to save resources. The root NTA performs the following functions: topology identification using a spatial time model, active probing, and inferring link delay distribution based on the Expectation Maximum method. Then, each ADA independently undertakes to set up the delay distribution profile of the link on which it is located. Once the profile of a link delay characteristics is obtained, it can be compared to the inferred delay of the link delivered by the NTA. If the inferred results go beyond a threshold value, the link is considered as an anomalous link and an alarm is raised. Since each ADA performs local detection using local audit data, the ADAs around an anomalous link can cooperate locally to confirm the maliciousness of a node. Furthermore, this cooperation should be done through secure channels. For that, CSA agents, used for communication services among the different nodes, were configured so that to communicate only intrusion detection related information. Again, for the sake of security, SDA agents are used to check the validity of CSAs and NTAs in the cooperative mobile nodes using MANET security encryption mechanisms.

Although this approach seems interesting and solves the problems related to mobile agents' security, raised by other works (Ramachandran et al., 2008; Roy & Chaki, 2011; Li & Qian, 2010; Mechtri et al., 2012), but it is too limited as it detects only link delay related attacks.

DISCUSSION

Table 3 summarizes the main features of existing agent-based IDSs, their main contributions, and the issues they do not address.

Figure 1 provides a statistical analysis of agent-based MANET IDSs in the light of the studied IDS models.

According to these statistics, the network (or the neighboring environment) seems to be the most popular source of data used in agent-based intrusion detection. This is due to the fact that network related data provide a more global vision of the network status and allows for the detection of distributed attacks. Also, most existing agent-based MANET IDSs are based on computation-depended and artificial intelligence techniques (RL, rule based systems, and swarm intelligence), since they are best suited for deployment on agent basis. It is also worth noting that IDS designers have made a great effort in mapping biological concepts to intrusion detection. For instance, they established the immunological metaphor by mapping T-cells, B-cells, antibodies, antigens, lymphocytes, maturation in thymus, and the immune memory to detection agents, decision agents, response agents, intrusions, mobile agents, training phase, and the agent's local database, respectively. Most of these techniques are designed to perform anomaly detection, which better fits MANET requirements in terms of resource conservation and detection of unknown attacks.

Figure 1. Statistical Analysis of Agent-based MANET IDSs

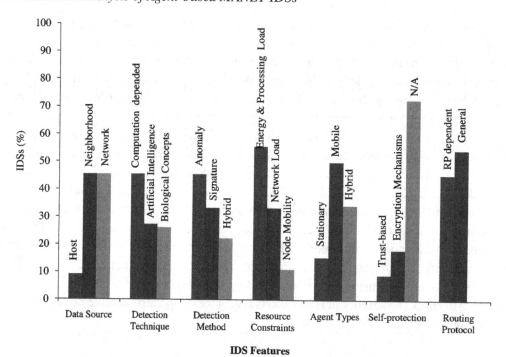

Table 3. Comparison of agent-based IDSs

	Detection Technique			Data Source			Response		Advantages	Disadvantages
	Anomaly Detection	Misuse Detection	Specification Based	Host	Neighbourhood	Network	Passive	Active		
Ramachandran et al. (2008)	✓					✓		✓	• Accuracy and simplicity of rules • Improves detection rates • Energy conservation	• Mobility of nodes not addressed • IDS security issues not addressed
Byrski and Carvalho (2008)	✓				✓		✓		Simple and reliable	High computational cost under high mobility
Servin and Kudenko (2008)				✓		✓	✓		Accuracy enhanced over time through learning	• High Communication overhead • Single point of failure
Roy and Chaki (2011)		✓			✓		✓		• Simple • Lightweight	• Detects only blackhole attack • Security of mobile agents not addressed
Ping et al. (2007)	✓				✓			✓	• Automated response • Considers node mobility and resource limitations	Vulnerable to blackmail attacks
Devi and Bhuvaneswaran (2011)	✓			✓			✓		• Detection of attacks at different layers • Reduces FPR and FNR • Fast detection	High computational load
Li and Qian (2010)		✓		✓				✓	• Reduced Energy and bandwidth consumption • Fast detection • FPR reduction	• High architecture maintenance cost under mobility • Single point of failure
Sen (2010)		✓		✓				✓	Detection of distributed attacks	High bandwidth consumption
Pattanayak and Rath (2014)			✓		✓		✓		High protection level	• Time and resource consuming • The method is not consistent due to unrealistic assumptions on nodes mobility
Farhan et al. (2008)	✓			✓			✓		• Dynamic adaption to environment changes • Scalable and robust	Single point of failure (GIDS)
yasir and Azween (2009)	✓			✓				✓	The self-healing capability	Single point of failure (Master nodes)
Taggu and Taggu (2011)		✓				✓	✓		Simple and easy to deploy	• High resource and bandwidth consumption • Cause detection and response latency even when there is enough evidence locally • Routing protocol dependent
Hong-song et al.. (2008)		✓				✓		✓	• Considers security of IDS agent • Low computional complexity • Saves energy	• Routing protocol dependent • Overload nodes if the number of RREQ/RREP increases
Mechtri et al. (2012)	✓	✓		✓		✓		✓	Considers resource limitation	Security of mobile agents not addressed
Chang and Shin (2010)	✓	✓		✓			✓		Enhances IDS fault-tolerance	Single point of failure (the mobile agent server)
Ye and Li (2010)	✓	✓			✓			✓	The active response mechanism	High architecture maintenance cost under mobility

continued on following page

Table 3. Continued

	Detection Technique			Data Source			Response		Advantages	Disadvantages
	Anomaly Detection	Misuse Detection	Specification Based	Host	Neighbour-hood	Network	Passive	Active		
Wang et al. (2013)	✓			✓				✓	• Considers security issues of mobile agents • Considers resource constraints	Detects only link delay related attacks
Cunha Neto et al. (2013)	✓	✓				✓		✓	Fast detection due to the possibility of eliminating packages not needed to evaluation using the filter agent	Overload nodes

Further, stationary agents are rarely adopted by these IDSs though the simplicity and low cost of their deployment. Contrary, mobile agents were extensively used to build agent-based IDSs, though they were deemed to introduce additional vulnerabilities to the network, for their capabilities of roaming and resource conservation. Nonetheless, there has been recently more tendency for the use of multiple agent types within the same IDS so that to have better overall control of the network. The study revealed also that while designing agent-based IDSs, the designers' main focus is to reduce energy consumption and the network load generated by the IDS, leaving crucial issues like node mobility and the IDSs' security problems open. Finally, evaluation of these IDSs shows that almost all of them do require neither high processing capabilities nor high memory storage.

Building on the studied approaches and their analysis, it is clearly seen that agent-based MANET IDSs have some common features:

1. Distribution of the detection tasks on a group of collaborating agents distributed over the network;
2. Use of mobile agents for both communication (collaboration) and data collection on remote hosts;
3. Approaching real-time detection and response;
4. Besides, almost all these IDSs are lightweight, flexible and present an exceptional ease in maintenance (modifications and extensions can be made without halting the whole system).

Table 4 summarizes some of the several advantages obtained when using agent technology for the building of MANET IDSs in particular and MANET applications in general, with respect to MANET requirements.

Nevertheless, in addition to the complexity of their deployment, these agents might bring new vulnerabilities to the network such as:

1. The security vulnerability introduced by mobile agents especially when they are operating in a hostile environment. In fact, in addition to their being vulnerable to security threats, they can be the source of new threats to the network. For instance, a compromised agent with some privileges

Table 4. Advantages of using agents for MANET intrusion detection

Agent Features	MANET Shortcomings	Description
Scalability	Constrained processing and energy power	Agents reduce the computational load and consumed energy by dividing the (detection) tasks over different hosts.
Mobility	Limited bandwidth and storage capacity	Instead of transferring huge amounts of data (audited data), the processing unit (detection agent) is moved to data.
Portability	Heterogeneity of devices	Agents run on agent platforms, thereby guaranteeing independence from the platform of the host.
Autonomous execution	Dynamic topology	If the network is segmented or some agents cease to function (under the threat of an attack), the rest of the agents can still continue to function (guaranteeing a proportional level of security).
Fault tolerance	Vulnerability to attacks	An attacker can disable a small finite number of backups but not all of them (agent-based applications use redundancy to protect their components).

(intrusion detection agents are usually given more privileges such as accessing to nodes' private information, accessing routing tables, and filtering routed packets) can cause serious damages without being suspected.

2. Code size may be too long (development of complex security solutions sometimes require large amounts of code), thereby causing latency in the processing time for static agents, slowing down the mobile agents in addition to network bandwidth high consumption.

3. Some of the proposed IDSs do not satisfy MANET requirements in terms of resource conservation and the dynamic topology change.

4. Some IDSs do not take into account mobility of the network. For instance, IDS architectures that are based on cluster-based approaches are costly to build and maintain in high mobility networks. The false positive rate may be greatly affected by the mobility level especially for anomaly-based IDSs.

5. Multi-agent systems are generally vulnerable to faults and system failures, thereby causing agent-based IDSs to be vulnerable and fault-prone.

6. Besides, some IDSs have critical points of failure (usually related to the cluster head).

Fortunately, security problems could be solved through the use of electronic signature, encryption and authorization methods. Also, trade-offs between security requirements and performance are often created so as to cope with performance related problems.

OPEN ISSUES, CHALLENGES, AND SCOPE FOR FUTURE WORK

The conducted study and analysis show the strong relevance to use agents in designing intrusion detection tools for MANET. In fact, many of the features offered by agents show an exceptional match with MANET's inherent characteristics (Table 4) and agents are best suited for applications that are decentralized, changeable, ill-structured and complex like MANET intrusion detection.

However, other features like fault-tolerance and adaptability have not been fully exploited and there are still other issues that have not been fully addressed in that field. In fact, there are only few works that consider the effect of mobility on the intrusion detection process; therefore, it is an interesting topic for future research.

In addition, there are not much works, done in the area, that fully address the resource constraints issue. Network and node capabilities should be given an appropriate weight when designing MANET IDSs. For example, nodes should be assigned detection tasks based on their resources and communication between IDS agents should be adapted to the wireless links bandwidth. In other words, it should be minimized for low bandwidth links and optimized otherwise.

Also, the great majority of works done in the field does not consider security issues related to the IDS itself or are limited to making assumptions about them. The security of IDS agents, their communication, and IDS data should be considered by future works to fulfill the ideal MANET IDS requirements.

Similarly, IDS' fault-tolerance is almost absent in existing works. IDS' fault-tolerance is crucial for IDS and network survivability. It can be enhanced using, among others, techniques like replication of software agents, fault detection using heartbeat messages, and integrity checking for self-healing.

Besides, most existing IDSs can detect intrusions with high accuracy but fail to eliminate their source. The best they can do is to generate passive or proactive responses in terms of alarms or blacklist generation. Development of corrective responses seems more consistent and can help enhancing the network's survivability and healing ability.

Finally, most of the proposed IDSs have not been tested or evaluated. Hence, it is necessary to define evaluation criteria, datasets, and tools to guarantee the advancement of the field.

CONCLUSION

This paper presented a survey and analysis of the work that has been recently done for the deployment of agent technology in the area of MANET intrusion detection.

This study revealed that the scalability, performance and fault tolerance can be improved through the use of agents to perform intrusion detection tasks in MANET. In addition, agents proved their utility in overcoming some frustrating MANET related problems such as the constrained resources and the heterogeneity of platforms.

Nevertheless, the study revealed, also, that the use of agents and mainly mobile agents might bring new vulnerabilities to the network. For instance, during its roaming, a mobile agent may be subjected to alteration or worse yet destruction by a malicious node. Also, complex security mechanisms sometimes necessitate large amounts of code which inevitably affects the desired fast roaming of mobile agents between the different network hosts.

Therefore, future research works on that appealing subject are to be carefully designed so that to take major profit of the offered agents' capabilities while controlling the potentially introduced vulnerabilities.

REFERENCES

Bourkache, G., & Mezghiche, M., & Tamine, k. (2011). A Distributed Intrusion Detection Model Based on a Society of Intelligent Mobile Agents for Ad Hoc Network. In *Proceedings of the IEEE 2011 Sixth International Conference on Availability, Reliability and Security (ARES)* (pp. 569-572). Vienna: IEEE. doi:10.1109/ARES.2011.131

Byrski, A., & Carvalho, M. (2008). Agent-Based Immunological Intrusion Detection System for Mobile Ad-Hoc Networks. In *Proceedings of the International Conference on Computational Science* (584-593). Kraków, Poland: LNCS. doi:10.1007/978-3-540-69389-5_66

Chang, K., & Shin, K. G. (2010). Application-Layer Intrusion Detection in MANETs. In *Proceedings of the 43rd Hawaii International Conference on System Sciences* (1-10). Honolulu, HI: IEEE.

da Cunha Neto, R. P., Zair, A., Fernandes, V. P. M., & Froz, B. R. (2013). Intrusion Detection System for Botnet Attacks in Wireless Networks Using Hybrid Detection Method Based on DNS. In T. Sobh & K. Elleithy (Eds.), Emerging Trends in Computing, Informatics, Systems Sciences, and Engineering, Lecture Notes in Electrical Engineering 151 (pp. 689-702). Springer. doi:10.1007/978-1-4614-3558-7_59

Devi, V. A., & Bhuvaneswaran, R. S. (2011). Agent Based Cross Layer Intrusion Detection System for MANET. In D. C. Wyld et al. (Eds.), *CNSA 2011, CCIS 196* (pp. 427–440). Springer Verlag-Berlin.

Farhan, A. F., Zulkhairi, D., & Hatim, M. T. (2008). Mobile Agent Intrusion Detection System for Mobile Ad Hoc Networks: A Non-overlapping Zone Approach. In *Proceedings of the 4th IEEE/IFIP International Conference on Internet* (pp. 1-5). Tashkent: IEEE. doi:10.1109/CANET.2008.4655310

Hong-Song, C., Jianyu, Z., & Lee, H. W. J. (2008). A novel NP-based security scheme for AODV routing protocol. *Journal of Discrete Mathematical Sciences and Cryptography*, *11*(2), 131–145. doi:10.1 080/09720529.2008.10698172

Hong-song, C., Zhenzhou, J., Mingzeng, H., Zhongchuan, F., & Ruixiang, J. (2007). Design and performance evaluation of a multi-agent-based dynamic lifetime security scheme for AODV routing protocol. *Elsevier Journal of Network and Computer Applications*, *30*(1), 145–166. doi:10.1016/j.jnca.2005.09.006

Hung-Jen, L., Chun-Hung, R. L., Ying-Chih, L., & Kuang-Yuan, T. (2013). Intrusion detection system: A comprehensive review. *Elsevier Journal of Network and Computer Applications*, *36*(1), 16–24. doi:10.1016/j.jnca.2012.09.004

Kumar, P., & Reddy, K. (2014). An Agent based Intrusion detection system for wireless network with Artificial Immune System (AIS) and Negative Clone Selection. In *Proceedings of the International Conference on Electronic Systems, Signal Processing and Computing Technologies* (pp. 429-433). India: IEEE. doi:10.1109/ICESC.2014.73

Li, Y., & Qian, Z. (2010). Mobile agents-based intrusion detection system for mobile ad hoc networks. In *Proceedings of the International Conference on Innovative Computing and Communication and 2010 Asia-Pacific Conference on Information Technology and Ocean Engineering* (pp. 145-148). Macao, China: IEEE. doi:10.1109/CICC-ITOE.2010.45

Mechtri, L., Djemili, F. T., & Ghanemi, S. (2012). MASID: Multi-agent system for intrusion detection in MANET. in *Proceedings of the Ninth International Conference on Information Technology - New Generations (ITNG'12)* (pp. 65-70).Washington, DC: IEEE. doi:10.1109/ITNG.2012.18

Pattanayak, B. K., & Rath, M. (2014). A Mobile Agent Based Intrusion Detection System Architecture for Mobile Ad Hoc Networks. *Journal of Computer Science, 10*(6), 970–975. doi:10.3844/jcssp.2014.970.975

Ping, Y., Futai, Z., Xinghao, J., & Jianhua, L. (2007). Multi-agent cooperative intrusion response in mobile adhoc networks. *Elsevier Journal of Systems Engineering and Electronics, 18*(4), 785–794. doi:10.1016/S1004-4132(08)60021-3

Ramachandran, C., Misra, S., & Obaidat, M. S. (2008). A novel two-pronged strategy for an agent-based intrusion detection scheme in ad-hoc networks. *Elsevier Comput. Commun, 31*(16), 3855–3869. doi:10.1016/j.comcom.2008.04.012

Roy, D. B., & Chaki, R. (2011). MABHIDS: A New Mobile Agent Based Black Hole Intrusion Detection System. In N. Chaki & A. Cortesi (Eds.), *CISIM 2011, CCIS 245* (pp. 85–94). Springer Verlag-Berlin. doi:10.1007/978-3-642-27245-5_12

Sen, J. (2010). An Intrusion Detection Architecture for Clustered Wireless Ad Hoc Networks. In *Proceedings of the Second International Conference on Computational Intelligence, Communication Systems and Networks* (pp. 202-207). Liverpool, UK: IEEE. doi:10.1109/CICSyN.2010.51

Servin, A., & Kudenko, D. (2008). Multi-agent Reinforcement Learning for Intrusion Detection. In K. Tuyls et al. (Eds.), *Adaptive Agents and Multi Agent Systems III: Adaptation and Multi Agent Learning* (pp. 211–223). Springer-Verlag Berlin Heidelberg. doi:10.1007/978-3-540-77949-0_15

Stafrace, S. K., & Antonopoulos, N. (2010). Military tactics in agent-based sinkhole attack detection for wireless ad hoc networks. *Elsevier Comput. Commun., 33*(5), 619–638. doi:10.1016/j.comcom.2009.11.006

Taggu, A., & Taggu, A. (2011). TraceGray: An Application-layer Scheme for Intrusion Detection in MANET using Mobile Agents. In *Proceedings of the IEEE 3rd International Conference on Communication Systems and Networks (COMSNETS)* (pp. 1-4). Bangalore: IEEE. doi:10.1109/COMSNETS.2011.5716475

Wang, W., Wang, H., Wang, B., Wang, Y., & Wang, J. (2013). Energy-aware and self-adaptive anomaly detection scheme based on network tomography in mobile ad hoc networks. *Elsevier Information Sciences, 220*(20), 580–602. doi:10.1016/j.ins.2012.07.036

Yasir, M. A., & Azween, B. A. (2009). Biologically Inspired Model for Securing Hybrid Mobile Ad hoc Networks. In *Proceedings of the International Symposium on High Capacity Optical Networks and Enabling Technologies* (187-191). Penang: IEEE.

Ye, X., & Li, J. (2010). A Security Architecture Based on Immune Agents for MANET. In *Proceedings of the International Conference on Wireless Communication and Sensor Computing* (pp. 1-5). Chennai: IEEE.

KEY TERMS AND DEFINITIONS

AODV: The Ad-hoc On-demand Distance Vector is a reactive routing protocol that enables multi-hop, self-starting and dynamic routing in MANET.

Blackhole: An active DoS (Denial of Service) attack in which a malicious node exploits the routing protocols such as AODV to advertise itself as having a valid and good path to the destination node with the goal of dropping the absorbed packets.

DSR: The Dynamic Source Routing is similar to AODV but has the additional feature of source routing.

False Negatives: Cases where no alerts are raised when real intrusion attempts are present.

False Positives: IDS alerts that are raised on non-intrusive behaviors.

Grayhole: A variation of the blackhole attack in which the malicious node adopts a selective packet dropping.

Intrusion: Any set of actions that attempt to compromise the integrity, confidentiality or the availability of a resource.

Intrusion Detection System: A software or hardware system that automate the process of monitoring the events occurring in a computer system or network, analyzing them for signs of security problems. It can monitor and collect data from a target system (host or network), process and correlate the gathered information, and can initiate responses when evidence of an intrusion is detected.

MANET: A network consisting of a collection of mobile nodes that communicate with each other via wireless links without the help of any pre-existing infrastructure.

True Negatives: Cases where no alerts are raised and no intrusion attempts are present.

True Positives: IDS alerts that are raised for real intrusion attempts.

Section 4
Authentication

This section discusses entity and message authentication utilizing cryptography. It covers digital signature certificates and biometric authentication.

Chapter 7
Applications of Digital Signature Certificates for Online Information Security

Mohammad Tariq Banday
University of Kashmir, India

ABSTRACT

Information security has been the focus of research since decades; however, with the advent of Internet and its vast growth, online information security research has become recurrent. Novel methods, techniques, protocols, and procedures are continuously developed to secure information from growing threats. Digital signature certificates, currently offers one of the most trusted solutions to achieve CIA-trio for online information. This chapter discusses online information security through cryptography. It explains digital signature certificates; their benefits, the underlying standards, involved techniques, procedures, algorithms, processes, structure, management, formats, and illustration of their working. It highlights the potential of digital signatures and certificates in information security across different devices, services, and applications. It introduces a few useful tools to learn, train, and implement digital signature certificates.

INTRODUCTION

With the advent of digital storage and communication technologies the entire spectrum of storage and communication system has been revolutionized as digital information can be easily stored, copied, changed, and transported. More and more people and organizations are using digital documents instead of paper documents to conduct day-to-day transactions. These desirable properties of digital information are very useful but owing to easy and almost undetected modification of digital data, they have raised several security concerns. Therefore, digital data is regarded as unreliable in areas where privacy, authentication, and integrity of data are of concern unless some security procedure is attached to it. These are areas like contracts, receipts, approvals and others where users have severe and genuine concerns of unauthorized modification or disclosure of data. Hand signatures do not change this situation, because

DOI: 10.4018/978-1-4666-9426-2.ch007

it is easy to transfer a hand signature from one digitized document to another or to modify a digitized document that is hand signed. The risk of data misuse has increased many folds with the advent of networking and wireless communication as many users can gain access to the data if not secured. A solution to all these issues is digital signature. A digital signature is not a digitized hand signature, but a special kind of check-sum. Secret information ensures that a digital signature cannot be forged, while public information enables the verification of the signature. Digital signature ensures prevention of unauthorized access to data while ensuring accurate authentication to data without interference.

Different forms of encryption techniques are being used to ensure privacy of data transmitted over Internet. In addition to encryption, a digital signature of the message can be created and send along with the message by the sender. A digital signature is a checksum produced by a cryptographic transformation of data by the message sender to bind message data to the sender's identity. When properly implemented, it provides mechanisms to authenticate originator, verify data integrity, and permit signatory non-repudiation. A digital signature is an electronic, encrypted, stamp of authentication on digital information such as e-mail messages, macros, or electronic documents. A signature confirms that the information has originated from the signer and it has not been altered. Encryption and digital signature ensure information security but it is difficult to distribute and manage keys for systems that are large, heterogeneous, and geographically distributed. Public key infrastructure permits such systems to take advantages of encryption and digital signature through digital signature certificates. A digital signature certificate such as standard ITU-T X.509 certificate is a data structure signed by some trusted certification authority that binds a public key to a person, device, program, process, e-mail address, etc. Diverse types of digital signature certificates such as general purpose personal certificates, personal and enterprise e-mail certificates, SSL certificates, SSL wildcard certificates, SSL multi-domain certificates, code signing certificates, mobile device and App certificates, citizen eID and ePassports, etc. on servers, desktops, mobiles and other devices are used to secure data of various applications, services and access to devices. In addition, certificate management and certificate discovery services are used for PKI management. In addition, trusted time stamping services are integrated within digital signature certificates to authenticate time of creation of digital data. Digital signatures and digital signature certificates have tremendous prospectus and applications for information security in the era of Internet and mobility.

INFORMATION SECURITY

The term information security as defined by the US Code (2012) means *"protecting information and information systems from unauthorized access, use, disclosure, disruption, modification, or destruction in order to provide: (a) integrity, which means guarding against improper information modification or destruction, and includes ensuring information nonrepudiation and authenticity; (b) confidentiality, which means preserving authorized restrictions on access and disclosure, including means for protecting personal privacy and proprietary information; and (c) availability, which means ensuring timely and reliable access to and use of information"*. In recent years, the scope and dimensions of information security has evolved significantly. The area of information security besides covering security of data and information extends to security of networks and allied infrastructure. It has emerged as a profession across hardware, software and communication technologies for securing applications, databases and websites; security testing; information systems auditing; business continuity planning; digital forensics and crime investigations; network, and web penetration testing; incident responding; security architecture designing; security analysis; intrusion analysis; vulnerability research; disaster recovery; etc. To identify problem areas, develop necessary solutions to information security problems and for security policy development, a venerable model named *CIA Triad* has been conceived some two decades before. The *CIA Triad* has three main components namely confidentiality, integrity, and availability at three levels or layers: physical, personal and organizational; each of which represents a fundamental objective of information security. It is sometimes also referred to as the *AIC Triad,* or *PAIN*, which stands for privacy, availability/authentication, integrity, and non-repudiation. These are four key factors to achieve information security (Canava, 2001).

- **Confidentiality:** Also known as privacy, guarantees non-disclosure of information to unauthorized persons. It protects the right of individuals to control or influence what information related to them may be collected and stored, by whom, and to whom that information may be disclosed. Privacy guarantees the prevention of unauthorized access and its manipulation. It means that a transaction between businesses cannot be viewed or interfered with by an outside party. Loss of confidentiality is a security breach wherein information is read or copied by someone not authorized to do so. Loss of confidentially can be very serious issue in situations where information privacy is an important attribute. These may include information pertaining to bank records, insurance records, new product specifications, internal policies, investment strategies, etc. Often such an information is protected by privacy laws and their disclosure besides causing financial or other damages may invoke legal issues.

- **Integrity:** Ensures that the information is not changeable except by an authorized agent. Integrity as a concept means that there is resistance to alteration or substitution of data, and/or that such changes are detected and provable. Integrity guarantees security against forgery, which includes policies to stop distribution of software and data, contaminated with viruses, Trojans, Spywares, etc. This usually involves the use of checksums, one-way hashes, or other algorithmic validation of the data. Whether the data might be changed by accident or malice, preventing that change is the foremost concern, and detecting it is second. Integrity can be maintained at many levels, from the hardware all the way to the application logic. At first glance, it might seem that authenticity is included in the concept of Integrity but it is more specifically about the content of the data itself. Loss of integrity is any unexpected or unauthorized change made to information, whether by intentionally such as tampering or unintentional such as through human error. In certain systems such as air traffic control, electronic funds transfer, etc. even a small percentage of loss of integrity cannot be tolerated.

- **Authentication:** Is the security process that validates the identity of a communicating party and thus ensures that the document or software is genuine. In the simplest implementation, this takes the form of a password. Passwords can be easily compromised through indiscretion and typically, it is difficult to ascertain who actually is entering the password. Another variant of authentication is known as strong authentication wherein authentication is provided by a digital signature, which is an encrypted value, provided by an entity, requesting authentication that can only be decoded by the public key of the signature's owner. The act of determining whether a particular user or system has the right to carry out a certain activity, such as reading a file or running a program is **Authorization**. The system authenticates users before permitting them to carry out activity they are authorized to perform; therefore, authentication and authorization often go hand in hand.

- **Non-Repudiation:** Is a security service that prevents a party from falsely denying having been the source of data that it did indeed create. Non- repudiation means the ability to prove that a transaction originated from a particular party. So that party cannot deny that, it performed a certain transaction. A receiver cannot deny that he received a certain message from a sender, and a sender cannot deny that he sent a message to the receiver. Non-repudiation strengthens security, as means of authentication cannot later be refuted.

- **Availability:** Is a highly desired feature of information systems. To serve its purpose the system used to store and process the information, the communication channels used to access it and the security controls used to protect it must be functioning correctly so that it is available when needed. Highly available systems such as airline schedules, online inventory systems, etc. remain available all the times and their availability remains unaffected by disruptions such as hardware failures, power outages, system upgrades, and from attacks such as DOS attacks. Availability is challenging in collaborative environments where information requests cannot be delayed even while maintaining the system. Redundant systems and cloud concepts are widely used to guarantee availability of service in highly available systems.

The integrity, confidentiality and availability of information may be vulnerable to threat forms ID theft, data security breaches, human error or failure (accidents, employee mistakes, etc.), compromises to intellectual property (piracy, copyright infringement, etc.), espionage or trespass (unauthorized access and/or data collection), information extortion (blackmail of information disclosure), sabotage or vandalism (destruction of systems or information), information theft (illegal confiscation of information), software attacks (viruses, worms, macros, denial of service, etc.), natural disaster (fire, flood, earthquake, lightning, etc.), hardware failures or errors, software failures or errors (bugs, code problems, unknown loopholes, etc.), technological obsolescence (antiquated or outdated technologies), e-mail and messaging threats, Web threats, hacking tools, packet sniffing, social engineering and many more. Mitigating information security threats is an ongoing battle, as unique threats get prevalent swiftly, therefore, security administrators must begin with an understanding of the threats facing the information, and then must examine the vulnerabilities inherent in the systems that store, process, and transmit the information possibly subjected to those threats. Continuous identification of most serious vulnerabilities, possible threats to information and their rapid mitigation can prevent an organization from falling prey to any such threat.

INFORMATION SECURITY THROUGH CRYPTOGRAPHY

The growing and massive requirement of sending confidential information securely over open networks such as Internet has influenced the rapid development of security procedures. Nearly all security mechanisms are based on encryption and authentication. Encryption is used to keep secrets and authentication proves identity of individuals and systems. Though cryptography dates back to circa 1900 B.C., when Egyptians began using hieroglyphics in inscriptions, however, with the advances in mathematical techniques it has undergone radical changes. The complexity of cryptographic algorithms have increased many folds making them so powerful that it is considered impossible to break certain ciphers. However, besides security level, feasibility, cost of implementation, interoperability, application areas, speed, etc.

of a particular technique are also taken into consideration before deploying it for some practical use. Cryptographic algorithms protect data by converting it into unreadable form before transmission and then back at the desired destination. These processes called encryption and decryption ensure security of sensitive data such as financial and personal data while being transmitted on the information and communication systems. These procedures provide means to verify authenticity, integrity, and confidentiality of data. They also permit establishment of evidence to identify culprit in case of misuse of data.

In cryptography, the message that is to be transmitted is called *plaintext*. A process named *encryption* encodes this *plaintext* into encrypted form called *cipher-text* so that it cannot be understood by intermediate parties who do not know the key to decrypt it (Schneier, 1996). The purpose of encryption is to keep secrets. It has other uses such as protecting data in storage but encryption was first used to protect messages so that unauthorized person could not decode the message. An encryption function combines the message and the encryption key to produce an encrypted result. Without prior knowledge of the secret key, the result makes no sense. An algorithm used for encryption is called *Cipher* and the encoded message is called *Cipher text*. Some words, numbers, or phrases called *keys* are used by encryption algorithms and decryption algorithms called *deciphers* to encode and decode *plain messages* into *cipher-text* and vice versa. Some *Hash Algorithm* may also be used to create a fixed length *abstract* also called *digest*, which is small and unique representation of the message enabling message integrity. A computing system that implements one or more specific encryption algorithms is called *Cryptosystem*. The complimentary of cryptography is *cryptanalysis*, in which study of techniques to break cipher are entertained.

Secret Key Cryptography

In secret key cryptography, the same key called secret key or private key is used for both encoding (encryption) and decoding (decryption) of the plain message (Schneier, 1996). It is also called Symmetric Key Encryption, Shared Key Encryption, and Private Key Encryption. The secret key must be kept secret by all parties because it is used to both encrypt and decrypt message. Its disclosure enables anyone to decrypt the encoded information and as such can compromise information security. An algorithm that implements Secret Key Encryption is called Symmetric Algorithm. Symmetric algorithms are arithmetic algorithms that are easy to reverse so that they can be used for both decoding and encoding. Classic symmetric encryption (Schneier, 1996) can be achieved using techniques such as *Caesar, Vigenère, Hill, Monoalphabetic substitution, Playfair, ADFGVX, Byte Addition, Exclusive-OR, Vernam, homophonic substitution, permutation,* and *Solitaire*. Classical symmetric algorithms may seem too simple but similar techniques are used in modern symmetric encryption algorithms, however, these algorithms are complex and the size of the key is very large. Modern Symmetric Encryption (Schneier, 1996) can be achieved using techniques such as *IDEA, RC2, RC4, DES* in *ECB* mode, *DES* in CBC mode, *Triple-DES* in ECB mode, *Triple-DES* in CBC mode, *Rijndael,* and *AES* (self-extracting). Secret Key Encryption techniques require sophisticated mechanism to distribute key securely to all parties. There is no secure method to transfer symmetric key electronically between parties. However, they are faster than asymmetric key encryption algorithms and play a very vital role in the implementation of Public Key Cryptography (PKC). Public key cryptography provides secure means to exchange symmetric key used in certain operations of public key cryptography.

Figure 1. Encryption and decryption

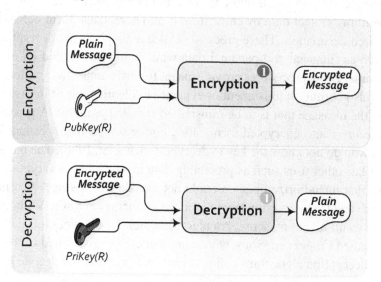

Public Key Cryptography

In public key cryptography, asymmetric encryption called Public Key Encryption (PKE) provides secure encryption of confidential messages and transactions. Public key encryption (Zheng et al, 2007) is an encryption methodology that uses asymmetric key pair (**Public Key** and **Private Key**) from which one key is used for encryption and the other is used for decryption. It allows the distribution of an encryption key that does not compromise the secrecy of the decrypting Private Key due to the utilization of a related pair of one-way functions. The Public Key is made public and is distributed widely and freely. The Private Key is never distributed and must be kept secret. Given a key pair, data encrypted with the Public Key can only be decrypted by its corresponding Private Key and conversely data encrypted with the Private Key can only be decrypted with the corresponding Public Key. This characteristic is used to implement encryption and digital signature.

In public key cryptography, encryption is achieved by encoding the plain message using some public key encryption algorithm employing public key of the intended recipient, which is decrypted, by the recipient by using the same encryption algorithm employing his private key. The functioning of encryption and decryption is illustrated in Figure 1.

The operations performed in each step are given in Table 1.

Table 1.

Process: Encryption	
Steps	**Operation**
1	The Plain message is transformed into encrypted message by encrypting it using the Public Key of the intended recipient.
Process: Decryption	
Steps	**Operation**
1	The received encrypted message is decrypted into the plain message by using Private Key of the recipient

Figure 2. Signing and verification

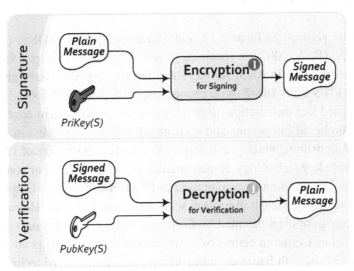

The encrypted message can only be transformed to plain text by using Private Key that corresponds to Public Key used for encrypting it. Any attempt to decrypt the encrypted message with wrong Private Key will be unsuccessful, thus ensuring privacy of the message. This scheme however does not ensure authentication, integrity, and non-repudiation.

In public key cryptography, plain message is signed by encoding it using some public key encryption algorithm employing private key of the signee, which is verified, by the recipient by using the same encryption algorithm employing public key of the sender. The functioning of signing and signature verification is illustrated in Figure 2.

The operations performed in each step are given in Table 2.

The signed message can only be decrypted to plain message by using Public Key that corresponds to Private Key used for signings it. The Public Key is typically attached to the signed message. Any attempt to decrypt the signed message with wrong Public Key will be unsuccessful, thus ensuring authentication, and non-repudiation. This scheme however, does not ensure privacy and integrity because anybody getting access to the signed message can decrypt it, as the Public Key of the sender is available freely and widely.

Table 2.

Process: Encryption (for Signing)	
Steps	**Operation**
1	The Plain message is transformed into encrypted form called signed message by encrypting it using the Private Key of the sender.
Process: Decryption (for Verification)	
Steps	**Operation**
1	The received signed message is decrypted into the plain message by using Public Key of the sender.

Asymmetric Encryption Algorithms

Asymmetric encryption algorithms include Digital Signature Standard (DSS) (FIPS, 1996), Rivest-Shamir-Adleman (RSA) (RSA, 2002) as specified in ANSI X9.31 and Elliptic Curve DSA (ECDSA) (ANSI X9.62, 1999) as specified in ANSI X9.62. These are also called digital signature algorithms and have been captured in FIPS PUB 186-2 (with change notice 1, dated 5 October 2001). They offer key advantages like simplified key distribution, digital signature, and long-term encryption. DSS is based on SHA1 hash, unencumbered (no patents and no license), and uses a minimum key size of 1024 bits. RSA is FIPS approved algorithm, which previously used a minimum key size of 1024 bits. The ECDSA is based on elliptical cure key technology. It uses smaller key sizes in comparison to other asymmetric encryption algorithms. The minimum key size used in ECDSA is 160 bits. Elliptic Curve Cryptography (ECC) is by far the most efficient algorithm with respect to key size. However, many aspects of elliptic curve technology have been patented by Certicom (www.certicom.com) and therefore licenses may have to be obtained as Certicom claims over 300 patents (and patents pending) various 'efficient implementations of ECC' in both hardware and software of elliptic curve technologies. It also holds patents on ECC key agreements, etc. There are open-source elliptic curve libraries that are available for use royalty-free and license-free (e.g. libecc, a C++ open source ECC crypto library available at http://libecc.sourceforge.net/). RSA had been patented by RSA but the patents have expired.

Hashing Algorithms

A one-way mathematical function called hashing function (Schneier, 1996) can be used to compute a small and fixed length message digest also called fingerprint, hash, or message abstract to ensure faster signing because signing a lengthy plain message can be time consuming. A hash function is a function that maps a bit string of arbitrary length to a fixed length bit string. Simple hash functions are often called checksums. These hash algorithms are not appropriate for security control because several plain text may produce same results. Approved hash functions are designed to satisfy the following properties: a) One-way: It is computationally infeasible to find any input that maps to any new pre-specified output, and b) Collision resistant: It is computationally infeasible to find any two distinct inputs that map to the same output. The advantages of using a hash function include:

1. Hashing is a one-way function and thus it is not possible to compute the original message from its hash;
2. Any change in the message will also change the message abstract – thus changes can be immediately detected;
3. Hash function receives messages of any length and produces hash of fixed length which is smaller than the message itself; and;
4. Hashing algorithms are faster than any symmetric and asymmetric encryption algorithms.

Hash functions do not have reciprocal functions, therefore, cannot be used to encode or decode information. However, they are useful to determine whether two parties know a particular key or not. For instance, instead of storing a user password in raw form in the underlying database, a hash of the password may be computed and stored. During login, the system computes hash of the user supplied password using the same hashing algorithm. The two hashes are compared to decide whether to grant

Figure 3. Signing and verification with hashing

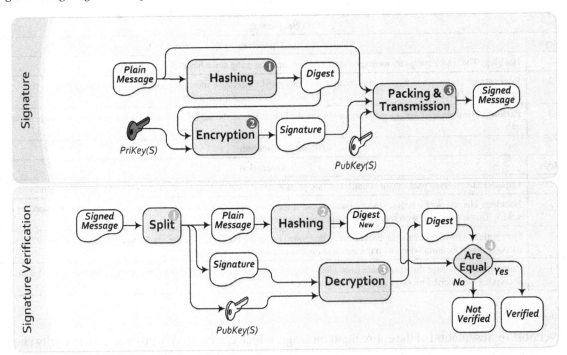

or deny the request. Since only hashes are stores in the underlying database, therefore, there is no security lapse even if the list of hashes from the underlying database is stolen, as passwords cannot be reconstructed from the hashes.

In public key cryptography, the sender uses a hash function to compute message digest and then encrypts the digest using his private key to get message signature. Since the signature is based on digest and not the plain message, it is not possible to reconstruct the message from the signature. Thus, this signature is appended to plain message and is transmitted over any transmitting medium. The public key is typically attached to the signed message. The recipient separates the plain message from the signature and the public key and then using same hashing function computes message digest of the plain message received, the received signature is decrypted into digest using public key of the sender. The two digests are compared to determine authenticity of sender. Any change in the plain message will also change the message abstract and thus unauthorized changes can be easily detected. The functioning of signing and verification is illustrated in Figure 3 and the operations performed in each step are given in Table 3.

The message digest obtained by decrypting the received signature and digest computed by hashing received plain message are same if plain message has not been modified and correct Public Key is used to decrypt the signature. If the two digests are same, the signature is verified, otherwise not. This scheme achieves authentication, integrity and non-repudiation but not privacy.

The cryptographic hash algorithm, Secure Hash Algorithm 1 (SHA-1) (SHA, 1995) is 168 bits and Message Digest 5 (MD5) (Rivest, 1992) is 128 bits. They are FIPS approved and were most commonly used functions that take an arbitrary length input message and return a unique fixed length output value known as the message digest. Other version of secure hash algorithm such as SHA-2 (SHA-224, SHA-256, SHA-384, and SHA-512) provide longer outputs. The digest is effectively a compressed but

Table 3.

Process: Signing	
Steps	**Operation**
1	**Hashing:** The sender computes message digest of plain message using some hash function like MD5, etc.
2	**Encryption:** The message digest is transformed into encrypted form called message signature by encrypting it using the Private Key of the sender.
3	**Packing:** The plain message, message signature and the Public Key of the sender are packed together to form a single packed unit.
Process: Verification	
Steps	**Operation**
1	**Unpack:** The received packed unit is unpacked into plain message, message signature, and the Public Key of the sender.
2	**Hashing:** The recipient computes the message digest of the plain message received using same algorithm that was used by the sender. This is compared with received message digest in step 4.
3	**Decryption:** The received message signature is decrypted using the Public Key of the sender to computer the original message digest for comparison with the message digest computed by the recipient.
4	**Comparison:** Message digest compute from plain message received by the recipient and the message digest obtained after decrypting the received message signature are compared.

irreversible representation of the entire input message, which can be used to provide data integrity checking, since changes in the digest indicate the message has also changed. This property has many useful applications such as the Digital Signature Standard (FIPS 186-3). When used to implement a Hash-based Message Authentication Code (HMAC) to FIPS 198, the hash function is keyed to provide a means of data authentication used in many secure protocols e.g. IPsec, TLS/SSL. The Secure Hash Algorithms (SHA) was developed by the US National Institute of Standards and Technology (NIST) as defined in FIPS 180-3. This describes the original SHA-1 hash as well as the SHA-2 family of algorithms. SHA-1, SHA-224, and SHA-256 are all 32-bit hash algorithms that generate 160-bit, 224-bit, and 256-bit digests respectively. The 64-bit SHA-384 and SHA-512 hash algorithms provide even greater security and generate 384-bit and 512-bit digests. The MD5 hash algorithm (developed by Ron Rivest) described in RFC 1321 is a legacy 32-bit hash algorithm that generates a 128-bit digest. Its potential weakness is that it can be used as a keyed hash. Other algorithms include RACE integrity (RIPEMD-160) (RIPE, 1995) and TIGER hash (Anderson and Biham, 1996). RIPEMD-160 is 160 bits while as TIGER hash is 192 bits. RIPEMD-160 is developed as part of the EC's research and development in advanced communications technology in Europe (RACE). TIGER hash has been designed for efficient operation on 64-bit platform. Both SHA-1 and SHA-2 hashing algorithms use an engine named "Merkle-Damgard" to process message text. Therefore, a successful attack on SHA-1 can become a potential threat to SHA-2. Some attacks have been successful to break SHA-1 to some extent; however, no successful attack against a full-round SHA-2 hash algorithm has been announced. Nevertheless, there is no guarantee that such attack mechanisms are not being developed in private. This is one reason that NIST sponsored the SHA-3 competition, which led to the development and recent adoption of KECCAK, which uses an innovative engine named "sponge engine" to hash the message text.

Figure 4. Functioning of digital signature

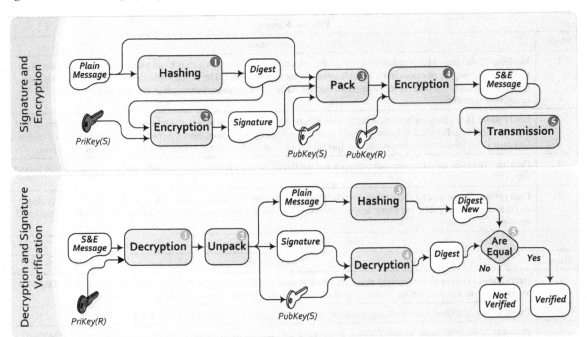

Digital Signature

Encryption and signing along with hashing can be combined to ensure privacy, integrity, authentication and non- repudiation. The plain message is hashed to compute a message digest, which is encrypted using Private Key of the sender to generate the message signature. The plain message, the message signature and the Public Key of the sender are packed together which is transformed into signed and encrypted message using the Public Key of the recipient. The recipient unpacks received message, which is the signed and encrypted message after which same hashing function is used to compute message digest of the received message, which is compared to the decrypted signature. The functioning of signing and verification is illustrated in Figure 4.

The operations performed in each step are given in Table 4.

Signed and encrypted messages can only be decrypted by the correct Private Key of the recipient thus ensuring privacy and at the same time hashing and signature verification by digest comparisons offer authenticity, integrity and non- repudiation.

The digital signature can be used to provide assurance that the claimed signatory signed the information. In addition, it may be used to detect whether or not the information was modified after it was signed. These assurances may be obtained whether the data was received in a transmission or retrieved from storage.

Digital Signature Using Symmetric Key

Encryption and decryption algorithms using asymmetric keys are too slow to be used for long messages, thus a symmetric key is generated and is used in Digital Signatures to encrypt the packed unit (plain message, the message signature and Public Key of sender). The Symmetric Key is encrypted using

Table 4.

	Process: Signing
Steps	**Operation**
1	**Hashing:** In this step, a hashing function is used to compute message digest, which is small and unique representation of the message. The purpose of evaluating a digest is to ensure message integrity. The digital signature is applied on the message digest, which is smaller than the message itself. Further, hashing functions are faster than symmetric and asymmetric encryption algorithms.
2	**Encryption:** In this step encryption, using Private Key of the sender is used to sign the message digest. Signing is performed to obtain non- repudiation. The message digest can be recovered by decrypting the encrypted message digest called message signature using the corresponding public key (public key of sender). Several algorithms have been proposed for signing.
3	**Packing:** The plain message, message signature and the Public Key of the sender are packed together to form a single packed unit.
4	**Encryption:** The packed message containing the plain message and the signature of the message in the form of encrypted digest along with the public key of the sender is encrypted using the public key of the recipient to form signed and encrypted message.
	Process: Signature Verification
Steps	**Operation**
1	**Decryption:** In this step, the received message, which is signed and encrypted, is decrypted using the private key of the receiver to form a packed message containing plain message, the signature and the public key of the sender.
2	**Unpack:** The decrypted message is unpacked into plain text, signature, and the public key of the sender.
3	**Hashing:** In this step, same hashing function that was used by the sender is used to compute message digest from the plain text message obtained after decrypting and unpacking the received message.
4	**Decryption:** In this step, the received message signature is decrypted using the received Public Key of the sender to obtain the message digest computed before transmitting the message.
5	**Comparison:** Message digest computed from plain message received by the recipient and the message digest obtained after decrypting the received message signature are compared.

the Public Key of the recipient so that it can only be decoded by the intended receiver who can use it to decrypt the packed unit before unpacking it and drawing semantics. The functioning of signing and verification is illustrated in Figure 5.

The operations performed in each step are given in Table 5.

The operation of this scheme is similar to that of digital signature without use of Symmetric Key and offers privacy, integrity, authentication and non- repudiation and simultaneously offers additional advantage of faster encryption and decryption. However, additional algorithm is required to evaluate Symmetric Key.

Public key authentication is often used when authentication should be performed automatically without user intervention. The systems involved can trade public keys and authentication information without the user interacting with the system (CGI Group Inc., 2004). For this reason, public key based authentication and its derivatives like certificate-based authentication are frequently used for machine authentication and for establishing anonymous encrypted sessions such as Secure Sockets Layer (SSL), Network Layer protocols, etc. It is also used in e-mail communications, document shearing, etc.

Figure 5. Functioning of digital signature (using symmetric key)

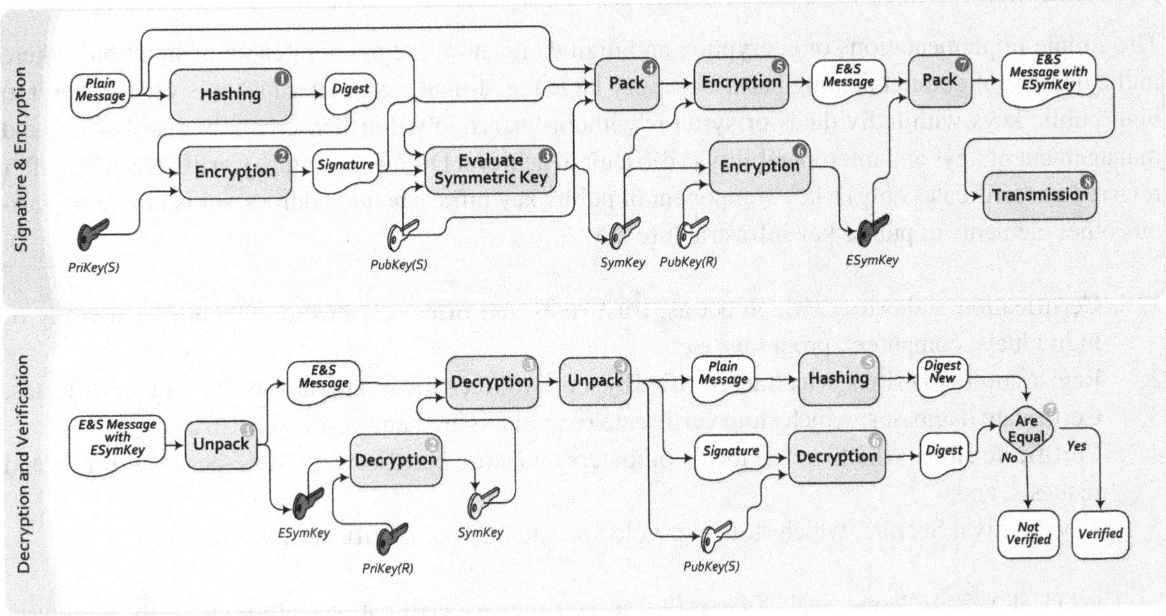

Table 5.

	Process: Signing
Steps	**Operation**
1	**Hashing:** This step is same as that for Digital Signature detailed in signed and encryption step 1 of section 4.2.3.
2	**Encryption:** This step is same as that for Digital Signature detailed in signed and encryption step 2 of section 4.2.3.
3	**Symmetric Key Evaluation:** A Symmetric Key is calculated using some algorithm based on plain message, message signature, and the public key of the sender. Any algorithm may be used for calculating the Symmetric Key.
4	**Packing:** The plain message, message signature and the Public Key of the sender are packed together to form a single packed unit.
5	**Encryption:** The packed message containing the plain message and the signature of the message in the form of encrypted digest along with the Public Key of the sender is encrypted using the Symmetric Key calculated in step 3 to form signed and encrypted message.
6	**Encryption:** The Symmetric Key is encrypted to form encrypted Symmetric Key using Public Key of the recipient
7	**Packing:** The encrypted and signed message and encrypted Symmetric Key are packed into a single unit called encrypted and signed message with encrypted symmetric key.
	Process: Signature Verification
Steps	**Operation**
1	**Unpack:** The received encrypted and signed message with encrypted symmetric key is unpacked in this step.
2	**Decryption:** The encrypted symmetric key is decrypted using the Private Key of the recipient to get the Symmetric Key used for encryption in step 5 of signing and encryption.
3	**Decryption:** In this step the received message that is signed and encrypted is decrypted using the Symmetric Key decrypted in step 2 to form a packed message containing plain message, the signature, and the public key of the sender.
4	**Unpack:** This step is same as for Digital Signature detailed in step 2 of decryption and verification of section 4.2.3.
5	**Hashing:** This step is same as for Digital Signature detailed in step 3 of decryption and verification of section 4.2.3.
6	**Decrypt:** This step is same as for Digital Signature detailed in step 4 of decryption and verification of section 4.2.3
7	**Comparison:** This step is same as for Digital Signature detailed in step 5 of decryption and verification of section 4.2.3.

DIGITAL SIGNATURES CERTIFICATES

The simple implementations of encryption and digital signature are not applicable in situations where in the number of communicating parties are very large e.g. e-mail system because it is very difficult to bind public keys with individuals or systems without uncertainty. Further, creation, distribution, and management of keys and interoperability is difficult to achieve. Digital Signature Certificates (hereafter referred as certificates only) a key component of public key infrastructure addresses this problem. Various other elements of public key infrastructure are:

1.   Certification authorities, which act as, trust roots and offer services to authenticate identity of individuals, computers, programs, etc.,
2.   Registration authorities, which are certified by some, root certification authority and issue certificates,
3.   Certificate databases, which store certificate requests, issued and revoked certificates, etc.,
4.   Certificate stores which are on local computers and store certificates, issues, pending or rejected requests, and,
5.   Key Archival Servers, which store encrypted private keys of certificates, issued.

The ITU-T X.509 (Cooper et al, 2008) is the most prominent certification method currently employed. A certificate is a signed (encrypted) data structure that binds a public key to a particular distinguished name (person, computer, code, service, etc.) in the X.500 tradition, or to an alternative name such as a DNS-entry or an e-mail address. Before issuing a certificate, the Certification Authority hashes the contents, signs (encrypts) the hash by using its own private key, and includes the encrypted hash in the issued certificate. The corresponding public key of the CA is distributed in the form of a self-signed CA certificate. X.509 certificates are generally obtained from CA for a subject by submitting a certificate-signing request, which contains the subject's name, the public key, and the algorithm that is used. A chain of multiple certificates comprising a certificate of the public key owner (the end entity) signed by one CA, and none, one or more additional certificates of CAs signed by other CAs may be needed. Such chains, called certification paths, are required because a public key user is only assigned with a limited number of assured CA public keys. A certificate has a limited and fixed valid lifetime indicated in its signed contents, however, in certain special circumstances CA needs to revoke the certificate within the validity period of the certificate. For this purpose, a time-stamped signed data structure called a certificate revocation list is made available in a public repository by a CA or CRL issuer. A certificate among other things contains the CAs identity, the owner's identity, the owner's public key, the certificate expiry date, the CAs signature of that certificate, etc. With the certificate containing the public key, instead of simple public key, a recipient can verify the certificate, its validity, issuer's certificate signature, and trust chain as well. When CA is used to issue X.509 certificates, the encryption and signature procedures are modified. The sender and receiver both obtain their certificates from some trusted CA, keep private key secret and publish their certificate (public key) widely and openly. Further, both sender and receiver have to agree on some CA or have to trust each other's CA. The plain message is hashed to produce a message digest, which is encrypted by the private key of the sender extracted from his private key store to compute message signature. The certificate of the intended recipient is verified to confirm his identity and validity of the certificate. Since the size of the message to be encrypted can be large and asymmetric key encryption/decryption algorithms are slower than their symmetric key counter parts, therefore, a symmetric key is calculated from the plain message, message signature, and the recipient's

Figure 6. Digital signing and encryption with digital signature certificate

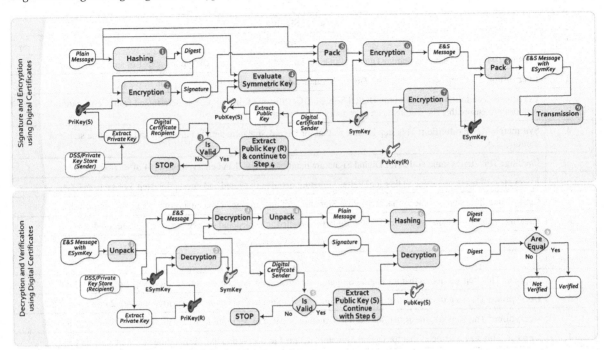

certificate using any private key algorithm. The plain message, message signature and the certificate of the sender are packed together and then encrypted using previously generated symmetric key. The symmetric key is protected by encrypting it using the public key of the intended recipient extracted from his certificate. The encrypted and signed message is packed with the encrypted symmetric key for transmission. The recipient unpacks the packet into individual components and decrypts the encrypted symmetric key using his private key. The encrypted and signed message is decrypted using the symmetric key and unpacked to produce plain message, the message signature, and the certificate of the sender. The certificate is verified and public key contained in it is used to decrypt the signature into message digest. The plain message is hashed to compute the message digest. The two message digests are compared to verify message integrity. With a certificate instead of a public-key, a recipient can verify the identity of senders, validity of certificate and validate signature of CA on the certificate. Figure 6 shows steps involved (Banday, 2011) in digitally signing and encrypting of plain message and subsequent signature verification and decryption employing digital signature certificates.

The operations performed in each step are given in Table 6.

Certificate Structure

The RFC 5280 defines the precise structure and format of a X.509 digital signature certificate. The certificate format in the 1988 standard is called the version 1 format, which was revised in 1993 to version 2 format wherein two more fields were added. The current standard, version 3 format was standardized in 1996, which extends version 2 format, by inclusion of additional extension fields that convey additional information pertaining to subject, key attribute, policy, and certification path constraints. The included extensions also specify whether the subject of a certificate is CA or an end entity. An X.509

Table 6.

colspan="2"	Process: Signing
Steps	**Operation**
1	**Hashing:** This step is same as that for Digital Signature detailed in signing and encryption step 1 of section 4.2.4.
2	**Encryption:** This step is same as that for Digital Signature detailed in signed and encryption step 2 of section 4.2.4.
3	**Certificate Validation:** Validity of the Digital Signature Certificate of the recipient is determined from Certification Authority to ensure that the recipient can later decrypt the message.
4	**Symmetric Key Evaluation:** This step is same as that for Digital Signature detailed in signed and encryption step 3 of section 4.2.4.
5	**Packing:** This step is same as that for Digital Signature detailed in signed and encryption step 4 of section 4.2.4.
6	**Encryption:** This step is same as that for Digital Signature detailed in signed and encryption step 5 of section 4.2.4.
7	**Encryption:** This step is same as that for Digital Signature detailed in signed and encryption step 6 of section 4.2.4.
8	**Packing:** This step is same as that for Digital Signature detailed in signed and encryption step 7 of section 4.2.4.
	Process: Signature Verification
Steps	**Operation**
1	**Unpack:** This step is same as that for Digital Signature detailed in decryption and verification step 1 of section 4.2.4.
2	**Decryption:** This step is same as that for Digital Signature detailed in decryption and verification step 2 of section 4.2.4.
3	**Decryption:** This step is same as that for Digital Signature detailed in decryption and verification step 3 of section 4.2.4.
4	**Unpack:** This step is same as that for Digital Signature detailed in decryption and verification step 4 of section 4.2.4.
5	**Certificate Validation:** Validity of the Digital Signature Certificate of the sender is determined from third party Certification Authority.
6	**Hashing:** This step is same as that for Digital Signature detailed in decryption and verification step 5 of section 4.2.4.
7	**Decrypt:** This step is same as that for Digital Signature detailed in decryption and verification step 6 of section 4.2.4.
8	**Comparison:** This step is same as that for Digital Signature detailed in decryption and verification step 7 of section 4.2.4.

certificate is a sequence of three fields namely TBS certificate (*TBSCertificate*), algorithm identifier (*signatureAlgorithm*) and digital signature (*signatureValue*) formatted according to the (Abstract Syntax Notation One) ASN.1 language to allow the normalization and compression of data among different platforms. The sequence *TBSCertificate* contains information associated with the subject of the certificate and the CA that issued it. The algorithm identifier (*signatureAlgorithm*) sequence is used to identify a cryptographic algorithm used by the CA to sign the certificate. The *TBSCertificate* sequence contains information associated with the subject of the certificate and the CA that issued it. Every *TBSCertificate* contains the names of the subject and issuer, a public key associated with the subject, a validity period, a version number, and a serial number. Some may contain optional subject and issuer unique identifiers. Version 3 certificates also can include standard and private internet extensions. The standard extensions are Authority Key Identifier, Subject Key Identifier, Key Usage, Certificate Policies, Policy Mappings, Subject Alternative Name, Issuer Alternative Name, Subject Directory Attribute, Basic Constraints, Name Constraints, Policy Constraints, Extended Key Usage, CRL Distribution Points, Inhibit any Policy, and Freshest CRL. The Private Internet Extensions are Authority Information Access and Subject Information Access. It is beyond the scope of this chapter to describe the syntax and semantics of each of these fields. RFC 5280 serves as a reference to understanding of each of these fields. The *signature*

Value sequence contains a digital signature computed upon the ASN.1 DER encoded *tbsCertificate*. This signature value is encoded as a BIT STRING and included in the signature sequence. By generating this signature, a CA certifies the validity of the information in the *tbsCertificate* field.

Certificate File Formats

Since the publication of X.509 by ITU in 1988, various file formats for both X.509 digital signature certificates and encryption keys have evolved and required file formats vary from application to application. Binary and PEM encoded digital certificates and RSA's Public Key Cryptography Standards (PKCS) file formats are currently prominent. The data structure of X.509 digital signature certificates in platform independent and it is based on Abstract Syntax Notation (ANS.1) format. They can be either stored in ASCII (PEM) or binary (DER) format based files. CA's mostly use PEM format to issue certificates. PEM format can accommodate server, intermediate and private keys. One PEM file can include several PEM certificate and even the private key. PEM files are ASCII files encoded in Base64 encoding and contain "-----*BEGIN CERTIFICATE*-----" and "-----*END CERTIFICATE*-----" statements. Privacy Enhanced Mail (PEM) certificates usually have extensions such as *.pem*, *.crt*, *.cer*, and *.key*. The Distinguished Encoding Rules (DER) format is a binary form of a certificate and has file extension of *.der* or *.cer*. All types of certificates and private keys can be encoded in DER format. DER is usually used with Java platforms. In PKI, the transport and handling of encryption keys are managed through RSA's Public Key Cryptography Standards (PKCS). The PKCS specifications define syntax for various key related issues and formats. It is beyond the scope of this chapter to discuss all of these specifications in detail. To state examples, the standard PKCS#7 defines a specification for messages that include cryptographic features such as digital signature and encryption. The standard PKCS#8 defines the specifications for encrypting data with a secret key derived from password. Some of the most common file formats include PKCS#1, PKCS#7b, PKCS#8, PKCS#10, and PKCS#12. The encryption keys along with the digital certificates can be manipulated and packaged within various PKCS specifications. Two most common specifications are PKCS#7 and PKCS#12. The PKCS#7 or P7B file format is usually in Base64 ASCII and has .p7b or .p7c file extensions. P7B certificates contain "-----BEGIN PKCS7-----" and "-----END PKCS7-----" statements. A P7B file contains certificates and chain certificates but not the private key. Microsoft Windows, Java Tomcat and various other platforms support P7B files. PKCS #12 defines an archive file format commonly used to store directly a private key along with its X.509 certificate. The PKCS#12 or PFX format is a binary format that stores server certificates, any intermediate certificates, and the private key in one encrypted file. The .pfx files usually have extensions such as .pfx and .p12. Windows machines use .pfx files to import and export certificates and private keys. Various tools are readily available that convert one certificate format to the other, e.g. OpenSSL (http://www.openssl.org/).

Key and Certificate Management

PKI includes software tools and procedures that permit management of keys and certificates. It facilitates the use of Public Key Cryptography efficiently and effectively. By using proper PKI structure, high level of trust management and security can be achieved. Three types of approaches namely stochastic, security policy management, and structured may be used to achieve security on PKI. Different approaches achieve different levels of security for a particular application. Public Key Infrastructure (PKI) has become a ubiquitous feature of cyberspace where organizations choose PKI model of their interest and requirement. PKI structures and models include X.500/X.509, Trust Graph, and PGP. The X.509 originally developed for global directory for Internet access is hierarchically structured lookup table. It is organized under a common root named Root Certification Authority (RCA), which the users are assumed to know it through some Certification Authority (CA). In open networks, directed trust graph models confidence in public keys using certificates. In such a system, either confidence is established by direct trust or indirect trust. Non-cryptographic functions are used to establish confidence in direct trust but cryptographic functions are used in indirect trust to establish authentication of public keys of nodes. PGP offers certification based encryption for e-mail communication under unspecified structure authentication infrastructure. In it, users trust each other at will and a key ring of trust is established as this trust grows. PKI system may be internal or external to organizations. In in-house PKI, organizations deploy trusted in-house PKI deployments that has ability to chain to some third party root certificate that is inherently trusted by all browsers, operating systems, and devices. A managed PKI solution gives access to digital certificates without the need to buy, establish, operate, and protect an in-house certification authority, which results in reduced project costs and a fast time to market. Both offer their advantages and limitations. An external PKI in which key and certificate management is done by some trusted third party may offer advantages such as reduced costs for wide scale use, global trust, high availability, and scale of service, independent auditing, and disaster recovery. The in-house or internal PKI system may be economical to implement for limited use, and offers centralized and local control.

A set of applications is required to create, maintain, and manage keys and certificates in a managed PKI system such as X.509. These include creation of certificates and keys, issuance and revocation of certificates and keys, methods to distribute keys, protection of private keys, backup, and recovery of private keys, updating certificates, and keys, and history of certificates and keys. Several standards such as RFC 5280, RFC 3279, RFC 4055, RFC 4491, and X.502 have been established to guide creation, and management of certificates and keys. These guidelines have made it mandatory to use SHA-256 hash algorithm and 2048 bit RSA key digital signature certificates from 1st January, 2012. A particular implementation of PKI, has well established procedures to generate keys using available algorithms and rules to issue certificates to users. These rules verify credentials of users before issuance of certificate. In some cases, the users may have to present himself before certificate issuing authorities. The private key is often protected with a strong password mechanism and sometimes distributed on a special token to protect it from malicious users. The certificate revocation facility permits, revocation of certificates in case it has been stolen or compromised. The PKI system maintains certificate revocation lists to permit users to reject certificates that have been compromised. Some mechanism to backup private key of users is maintained in the PKI to address the issue of lost keys. This permits genuine users to decrypt encrypted files, which can only be decrypted by the corresponding private key. Since certificates are valid for a particular time span, therefore, PKI includes mechanism to update certificates for users whose certificates are nearing expiry. A mechanism for managing the history of keys and certificates is also included in the PKI system to enable users to choose proper certificate among many of his certificates to decrypt files. Often PKI implementations maintain their PKI repositories using LDAP protocol to archive their certificate databases, revocation lists, and public keys.

Recent Certificate Security Issues

An information security system employing the use of digital signature certificates e.g. to safeguard HTTPS communications with SSL/TLS certificates, determining the source of authenticity of a program, etc. builds a chain of trust among its communicating entities, therefore, the integrity and authenticity of each certificate is crucial to the security of the entire system. A compromise of some higher-level certificate or CA signing key or root keys can be disastrous as fraudulent certificates can be issued to create phishing websites, distribute malware, steal sensitive data, etc., which can result in severe problems and financial losses to users, the impersonated company and the certification authority. In a weakly controlled CA, the signing keys may be misused even if the certificates themselves have not been compromised. Certificates are issued by certification authorities and, therefore, the entire system is only as strong as the weakest certification authority. It is an individual's choice to trust or not to trust a certificate or certification authority; however, it requires technical skills to make correct decisions with respect to trusting a certificate or certification authority. The naïve users believe that necessary security system is in place with applications/web browsers and therefore, entrust them to make appropriate decisions regarding trusting certificates and certificate authorities.

Recently, PKI infrastructure and several digital signature certificates of individuals, enterprises including certification authorities and government organizations have been misused through attacks of different types. In one such type, certificates have been stolen and the associated private keys used to sign malicious software. E.g. in February, 2013, a security breach at Bit9 (2013) allowed a malicious third party to illegally gain temporary access to one of their digital code-signing certificates that was used to illegitimately sign malware apparently a Java applet. In June 2013, a Norwegian browser maker Opera Software discovered that a targeted internal network infrastructure attack had led to the theft of a code-signing certificate that had subsequently been used to sign malware (SecurityWeek, 2013). In September 2012, code-signing certificates were stolen from a compromised Adobe build server with access to the Adobe code-signing infrastructure, which were used to sign malicious utilities (Adobe, 2012). Analysis of some antivirus programs collected by Microsoft has classified them as rogue security programs (Microsoft, n.d.). Such fake antivirus programs are increasingly using stolen code-signing certificates (PCWorls, 2013; TrendMicro, 2014). Attacks have also been launched using weak or improper certificates. E.g. in February 2014, a Brazilian banking/password stealer program was detected. It was signed with a real and valid digital certificate issued by DigiCert to "Buster Paper Commercial Ltd," a non-existent Brazilian company that was registered with bogus data (MalwareBytes, 2013). In November 2011, Entrust discovered that DigiCert Sdn. Bhd. (not US based DigiCert) had issued 22 weak 512-bit RSA certificates with missing certificate extensions to the Malaysian government (Entrust, 2011). Later, it was also reported that two of these were used to sign malware used in a spear phishing attack against another Asian certificate authority (NakedSecuity, 2011). In another incident, fraudulent digital certificate were issued by a root certification authority TURKTRUST Inc. which incorrectly created two subsidiary CAs (*.EGO.GOV.TR and e-islem.kktcmerkezbankasi.org). The *.EGO.GOV. TR subsidiary CA was then used to issue a fraudulent digital certificate to *.google.com (Microsoft-Technet, 2013). It led to the impersonation of Google's servers (NakedSecurity, 2013). Such fraudulent certificates could also be used to spoof content, perform phishing attacks, or perform man-in-the-middle attacks. In March 2011, a Comodo Trusted Partner in Southern Europe was compromised and the attacker obtained its username and password. Nine fraudulent SSL certificates were issued to sites in 7 domains including Google, Yahoo! and Windows Live (Comodo, 2011). Between 17th and 29th of June

2011, an intruder compromised systems in the Office-net network segment of web servers in DMZ-ext-net of Dutch CA DigiNotar owned by VASCO Data Security International and subsequently penetrated into certificate-issuing servers and had complete control of all eight of the company's certificate-issuing servers (ThreatPost, 2015). The intruder used multiple systems as proxies in order to obscure identity. DigiNotar at that time was entrusted for issuance of both commercial as well as government certificates. The attacker had obtained valid wildcard certificate, issued by DigiNotar, for *.google.com, giving the attacker the ability to impersonate Google and valid certificates of other high-value domains, including Yahoo, Mozilla and others. The first public acknowledgement of the attack was with the discovery of a large-scale man-in-the-middle attack launched against around 300,000 Gmail users in Iran. The Dutch government took over operational management of DigiNotar's systems in September 2011 and the company was declared bankrupt in the same month. On June 25, 2014 the certificate issuance process of National Informatics Centre (NIC) of India, which holds several intermediate CA certificates trusted by the Indian Controller of Certifying Authorities (India CCA) was compromised (Google, 2014). These included three for Google domains and one for the Yahoo domain. These certificates could have been used to perform phishing or spoofing attacks or intercept SSL-encrypted connections to support surveillance activity against users of Gmail, Yahoo Mail and other Google and Yahoo services. The certificates were blocked in Google Chrome with a CRLSet push. These certificates were included in the Microsoft Root store and therefore, revoked to guard against any possible surveillance attacks (CRN, 2014). Attackers can launch main-in-the-middle attack (MiTM) by circumventing the trust established by digital certificates and intercepting SSL/TLS traffic in order to gain access to sensitive data. Stolen or compromised certificates are used to redirect traffic to an untrusted site, where the data is stolen, and then send to the original destination. It is difficult for the user applications to detect MiTM attacks. Attacks can also be launched through installations of illegitimate certificates on user systems by first infecting the system with malware and then making the system trust these rouge certificates.

Securing Certificates and Public Key Infrastructure

Several initiative have been taken in recent times to strengthen the process of issuance, validation, and utilization of certificates. These include steps to make software and operating systems more secure, launch of SSL observatory project, launch of certificate transparency project, support for public key pinning, etc. The operating systems and software using certificates are maintaining more up-to-date certificate revocation lists. The vendor support for automatic distribution of updated listing of revoked certificates has been enhanced in recent times. Browsers update CRL's frequently and certificate issues are taken up on priority. SSL observatory project (EFF, n.d.) permits cataloging of SSL/TLS certificates thereby enabling interested researchers to examine certificates for vulnerabilities and future recommendations. Google transparency project CertificateTransparency (n.d.) encourages CAs to publish issued certificates in a publically accessible place to make issuance of certificate by malicious CAs for a particular domain difficult without the knowledge of the respective domain owner. To ensure that certificates are signed by expected CAs, software such as Chrome now store association between certificates and the CAs (ImperialViolet, 2011). Microsoft's Enhanced Mitigation Experience Toolkit (EMET) allows administrators to "pin" certificates for any Windows application (EMET, n.d.). Security is being given top priority and forensic tools such as CAWatch are used by administrators to monitor network activities in real time.

PKI serves as a top-level security layer for organizations who deploy it to secure sensitive data and infrastructure against persistent and determined attackers. Therefore, to gain unauthorized access, attackers launch attacks to breach this PKI security layer for elevation of privilege, persistent access, or impersonation. Some successful attacks may result in obtaining fraudulent certificates that can permit penetration into network without easy detection. A PKI may be compromised by exploiting its weak, insecure, or outdated implementations. These include PKI misconfigurations, inadequately secured certification authority systems, inadequately secured RA systems or through social engineering. An improperly configured PKI may permit an attacker to obtain desired certificates that can allow them to create subordinate certification authorities. An insecure certification authority may have used default passwords, generic configurations, or excessive administrative rights. It may be exploited by an attacker to gain access to accounts having PKI privileges. The credentials of some RA, which is not adequately secured, may be used by attackers to issue certificates. Attackers may use social engineering to obtain certificates from RA. Therefore, PKI must be deployed and implemented with careful planning either as part of the internal IT infrastructure or by using some external commercial certification authority. Irrespective of the type of solution adopted for its implementation, special considerations towards CA hierarchy, physical security control, PKI security process, technical controls, certificate algorithms and usage, protection of CA keys, monitoring of CA infrastructure and compromise response must be taken into account.

A Typical deployment of PKI is hierarchical (one tier, two tier and three tier) arrangement of root CA, sub CAs, RA, etc. In one tier arrangement, a single CA serves as both root CA as well as issuing CA. This arrangement is simple, has lower implementation and managerial costs, but has lowest level of security and flexibility. This arrangement is only suitable for simple implementation such as a single project managed at multiple sites. A larger implementation of single tier PKI is prone to compromise, and difficult to expand. Compromise of the only CA compromises the entire PKI. A three-tier PKI implementation has a root CA that operates offline, intermediate CAs preferably operating offline and issuing CAs operating online. The intermediate CAs are used as policy or administrative CAs, which can validate issuing CAs, and issue or revoke CAs certificates. Having an intermediate tier improves security, flexibility, and scalability of the PKI as compromised CAs can be revoked, different designs can be applied and policies and administrative boundaries can be established. However, it increases costs and manageability and reduces performance. Two-tier implementation is a compromise between the other two implementations. In this, there are geographically isolated multiple issuing CAs under an offline root CA. In comparison to single tier hierarchy, the roles of issuing and root CAs are well-separated permitting improved security control, flexibility, and scalability at slightly increased operational and managerial costs. Such an implementation is recommended for most in-house PKI implementations.

Since unauthorized physical access can lead to complete compromise of PKI, it is highly desired to devise strong physical security mechanism including operational and functional mechanisms to safeguard PKI infrastructure against compromise from unauthorized physical access. Physical security mechanism must track and audit physical access requests to sensitive data so that unapproved access can be detected. Strong authentication mechanisms such as biometrics may be used to grant physical access. Physical access control mechanism may be devised to reject single person entry to safeguard critical data from malicious insiders. Tailgating, a process by which access to unauthorized person is possible through an authorized person may be prohibited through some override procedures. Detective control mechanisms such as alarm and camera systems may be placed to raise an alarm when unplanned access is initiated or to record the physical access. The sensitive data may be backed up regularly on backup sites that are geographically separate from the primary sites. Based on the functions performed by each component of PKI, different policies and levels of physical security may be devised for its individual components. Physical security may also take into consideration various operational aspects such as environment, geographical location, structure hardening, interior climate and safety measures.

PKI is a trusted service and therefore is deployed and operated with clearly defined policies, procedures, and standards to enable its components to validate certificates. A PKI policy defines cryptographic algorithms, certificate usage, constraints, practices, issuance control, etc. It takes into consideration regulatory standard, industrial requirements besides internal requirements of an organization. It includes certificate policy that specifies its applicability and certificate practice statement that specifies the allowable operations. The certificate policy statement translates certificate policy into procedures. Certificate policy specifies procedures for policy management, security policy management, security management, personal security, operations management, development, maintenance, monitoring, compliance, auditing, etc. The PKI policy governance acts as a policy authority and ensures management, formation, applicability, and review of the PKI policy. Trustworthy individuals are assigned different roles and responsibilities in the operation of PKI to prevent unauthorized access and compromise of sensitive operations. The highly trusted roles include administration, certificate management, installation, configuration, and maintenance, backup and recovery, etc. of software and hardware facilities. Often multiple trusted individuals are required to carry out some operations such as administration, physical access to critical infrastructure, and activity log maintenance. Roles are well separated from each other and every role has specific qualifications, experience, and proof of background.

To make the design of PKI secure against exploitation, adequate technical controls are undertaken to secure its hardware and software resources, CAs, roles, backups, certificate templates, and operations. A baseline configuration for all CAs and RAs is created to enable efficient technical management of multiple CAs and RAs. The security of online CAs is hardened by disabling CD-ROM autoplays, renaming of administrator and guest accounts, disabling of local administrator and guest accounts, creating unique and strong passwords for administrator accounts, and disabling DMA devices. Systems functioning as online certificate authorities are secured by separating them from other system such as domain controllers, prohibiting Internet access, limiting remote management to essential services, and by installing only essential applications. To increase the security control, hardware based multi-factor authentication such as use of smart cards is employed (Bernstein et al, 2013). The CAs serving root or at a level close to the root issue limited number of certificates and are generally kept offline. Offline CAs perform their designated roles, software/certificate updation and maintenance through truly offline modes and the required data is not transferred through any online mode. Virtualization of both online and offline CAs whenever necessary is performed through systems that provide security control similar to real CAs. Certificate templates and template store are secured to protect them from any possible misuse. User addition of subject alternate name field in the certificate is controlled through an approval process.

To maintain confidence in PKI, strong cryptographic algorithms, appropriate key lengths, and validity periods are planned, otherwise, algorithms may be susceptible to failure and therefore, potential security threats can get introduce. Proper combinations of signature scheme and hash algorithm such as RSASSA-PKCS-v1.3 with SHA-2, RSASSA-PSS with SHA-2 and ECDSA with SHA-2 are used to create strong and collision resistant cryptographic algorithms. New algorithms and hash functions such as those based on ECC and SHA-3 with adequate key lengths are recommended for fresh PKI implementations. The validity period of certificates and keys are planned adequately so that the underlying algorithms and hash functions remain secure during their validity. The validity period of certificates of issuing authorities are kept longer than that of certificates issued by them. When the validity period of a certificate is checked for expiration, every CA certificate in the chain is checked. Certificate constraints and extensions are planned to disallow its unintended uses and creation of subordinate CA in the PKI hierarchy. Special consideration are given to key usage, extended key usage, and critical extensions.

To prevent external and internal threats to the integrity of PKI systems, private keys are secured through HSMs, and tokens, which are themselves secured against tampering and self-destruction. HSMs permit multi person control, ensure physical access, ensure security of keys though internal cryptographic operations, and provide tamper evidence. HSMs permit import of software keys; however, to ensure secrecy of keys HSM generated keys are generally preferred. For online and offline CAs, networked HSMs are used through private networks. HSMs permit strong multi person access control, however, in absence of HSMs, multiple door locks, and multiple passwords can be used to enforce multi-person access control. Storage of other artifacts of PKI system such as backup files, written communications, inventories, etc. are highly secured to prevent unauthorized access. Monitoring PKI system for unauthorized changes and their timely alert provides a strong detective control, which can limit the extent of damage caused by an attack. CAs are treated as high value systems and are monitored closely for suspicious activity. Events generating security alert are deeply investigated to identify its type, severity and cause so that measures to address loopholes if any may be devised. Often a hierarchy auditing policy is devised to monitor effectively PKI infrastructure. In case of a compromise, necessary measures are required to allow quick recovery and remediation of PKI infrastructure. Therefore, it is vital to have a generalized and comprehensive response plan, which could be tamed to suite to a particular situation.

TIME STAMPING AND TIME STAMPING SERVICES

To prove beyond any doubt, date and time of creation or submission of electronic documents or digital data such as contracts, e-mail messages, files, tenders, logs, etc., it is required to ensure its correctness, accuracy, and reliability. Since it is easier to forge date and time of electronic documents in comparison to paper-based documents, requirement of unique and unforgettable timestamps become compulsory to associate a datum with a particular time. Time stamping services support assertion of proof that a particular datum existed before a particular time. Time stamping a digital document ensures that data and time of its creation or submission can be verified later if required. Digital documents can be time stamped by using a Time Stamping Protocol (TSP) that ensures accurate and reliable time stamping using a Time Stamping Authority (TSA) over PKI. An authority issuing such timestamps called Time Stamping Authority (TSA) may be established within an organization for internal use or may be operated as some Trusted Third Party (TTP) service. Time Stamping Protocol (TSP) is described in RFC 3161 (Adams et al, 2001) which has been updated by RFC 5816 and RFC 5544. TSP ensures accurate and reliable time stamping using a TSA, which creates and sends a time stamp for a requested digital document whose hash is send by the client to the TSA. The time stamp is merged by the client with the document. The time stamp request generated by the requesting entity and the time stamp response generated by the requested TSA are the two types of translations that happen in TSP. TSP defines the format of transactions taking place between the client and the TSA and provides some suggestions for their transport. TSA has many requirements, that include: a) Use of a trustworthy source of time, b) Inclusion of a unique integer for each time stamp token generated, c) Only a hash representation of the datum should be timestamp, d) Production of timestamp token on the reception of a valid request whenever possible, e) Inclusion of an identifier to uniquely indicate the security policy under which the token was generated, f) Examination of OID, g) Non examination of imprint other than length of the imprint being time stamped, h) Non-inclusion of any identification of the requestor, i) Signing of time stamp token using an exclusive key meant for this purpose, and, j) Inclusion of some other information in the token only if requested by the requestor. There are many service providers that provide third party trusted time stamping services for competitive rates which can timestamp diverse range of documents. When a time stamp is added to a signature then there is an external witness. Time stamping becomes a key feature when legal use of electronic documents with a long lifetime is required and as such, several European countries have included time stamping in their legislations. A timestamp on digital data can be used for data authenticity/integrity verification, business process protection, copyrights protection, and intellectual property protection.

The process of adding a time stamp to a signature does not send the document outside one's computer. Time stamping does not compromise the privacy of one's document - only a hash of the signature is sent to Time Stamping Authority to create the timestamp. A hash of the document to be time stamped is generated and signed with the private key of the document owner, which is formatted as RFC 3161 time stamp request. It is submitted to a trusted time stamping authority, which generates a time stamp response containing the time stamp signed by its private key. The time stamp is issued and send to the requestor and is stored in the database of TSA. The time stamp is packed with the document, to form a time stamped document. An online or offline process (Tsutomu, Tadahiro and Keisuke, 2007) is used to check the correctness of data/time of a time stamped document. In online verification process, verification is performed by the TSA and in offline method; it is done on the client itself. In online verification, a time stamped document is unpacked to get the time stamp, which is formatted as RFC 3161 format to produce a request for time stamp verification. This is submitted to the trusted time stamping authority for verification. The time stamping server replies with a time stamping verification response containing the time validation. During time stamping process some other operations, including verification of the digital signature of TSA in the time stamp token before using it is done to determine authenticity of the TSA. Similar process is also used during verification operation.

One of the major uses of time stamping is to time stamp a digital signature. This is used to ensure that the digital signature was created before a given time. It enables to check whether the digital signature was affixed on the electronic record before it was time stamped and whether the digital signature was created before or after the revocation of digital signature certificate. Figure 7 demonstrates the use of time stamping appended to the digital signature for ensuring the correctness of date and time of the signature.

As shown in Figure 7, after computing the message digest and generation of the signature, the signature is formatted as RFC 3161 time stamp request. This request is submitted to a trusted time stamping authority, which generates a time stamp response containing the time stamp. The time stamp is packed with the plain message, signature, and public key to form a packed message, which is encrypted using the public key of the receiver and the resultant encrypted, and signed message containing time stamp is transmitted to the receiver. The above process is reversed by the receiver in order to verify the time stamp and signature and to decrypt the message. The encrypted and signed message along with time stamp is decrypted by the receiver using his private key, which is unpacked into the individual components (time stamp, plain message, signature, public key of sender (PubKey(S)). The signature is verified as discussed earlier. The time stamp and the signature are formatted as RFC 3161 format to produce a request for time stamp verification, which is submitted to the trusted time stamping authority for verification. The time stamping server replies with a time stamping verification response containing the time validation.

Figure 7. Time stamping digital signature

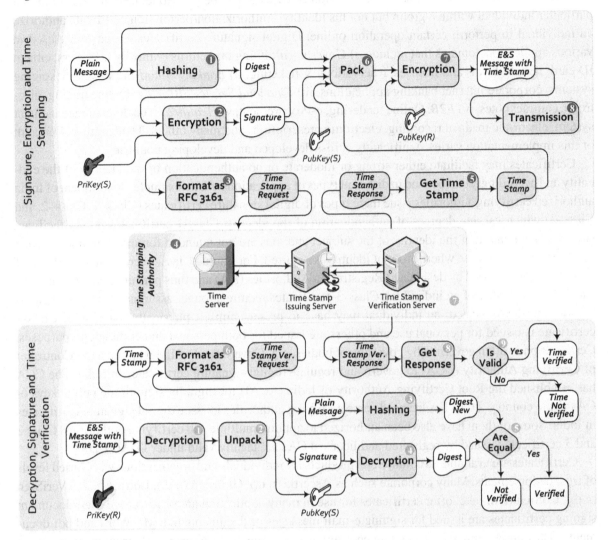

APPLICATIONS OF DIGITAL SIGNATURE CERTIFICATES

Digital signature certificates are used in diverse services, applications, and devices for varied purposes. Accordingly, the certificate providers are providing different types of certificates, which not only vary in the structure and format but also differ in their purpose. A Certificate may be a root-CA, sub-CA, an intermediate-CA, or an end-entity certificate. A root certificate may be either an unsigned public key certificate or a self-signed certificate used to identify the root-CA. The root certificate is the anchor of trust in a digital certificate and is used to validate the entire certification tree. Intermediate-CA and end-entity certificates are endorsed and signed by a root-CA. They can establish different levels and types of trust between individuals, services, devices, programs, etc. Certificates are intended for particular purpose(s), which is indicated by specific values in various fields that include fields like key usage, extended key usage, algorithms used, subject, subject alternative name, certificate policy, etc. A digital certificate may be identity, accreditation, or authorization/permission certificate. Identity certificates can uniquely identify an individual. Accreditation certificates can be used to identify membership of a particular individual within a group but not his identity. Authorization/permission certificate authorize an individual to perform certain operation online. Digital signature certificates are currently used in various application domains that include: i) *Government*: Filing tax returns online by taxpayers, citizen ID card, issuing forms and licenses, reservations & ticketing, ii) *Banking*: Inter/ Intra bank messaging systems, corporate Internet banking applications, iii) *Financial Services/Broking*: Online trading, electronic contract notes, iv) *B2B*: Online tendering, e-Procurement, v) *Healthcare*: healthcare management system, electronic medical recording, electronic prescriptions and many others. The length and breadth of this implementation varies significantly across developed and developing countries.

Certificates may facilitate either strong or moderate or no authentication of the identity of the end-entity and accordingly can be used in different types of applications. As an example Government of India authorized certifying authorities issue three types of digital signature certificates (Class–1, Class–2, and Class–3) which varying degrees of authentication of the identity. Class-1 certificates do not facilitate strong authentication of the identity of the subject and thus are not intended for and shall not be relied upon for commercial use where proof of identity is required. For issuing Class-2 certificates the detail of individuals are verified by designated Registration Authorities (RA) and thus permit moderate authentication of the identity of an individual. Class-3 certificates require stronger assurances of an applicant's identity and for this need; an individual may have to present himself physically before RA. Class-1 certificate is issued for personal use and others are issued for both personal and commercial purposes. Certification is often governed by government bodies, e.g. Government of India has enacted Controller of Certifying Authority (CCA) to govern and regulate digital signature certificates in India. The CCA has established the Root Certifying Authority of India (RCAI) for digitally signing the public keys of CAs in the country. RCAI has licensed some certifying authorities to issue digital signature certificates in India. Some of them have also been authorized to appoint multiple sub certifying authorities. Class 2 and 3 certificates issued by registered and licensed CAs are legally valid under IT ACT 2000.

Certificates are available as commercial products for individuals and organizations with varied levels of trust endorsements. Many corporate such as Ascertia (n.d.), Globsign (n.d.), Entrust (n.d.), VeriSign (n.d.), CoSign (n.d.), etc. offer certificates for use in many application areas. Identity/e-mail/document signing certificates are issued for signing e-mail messages or documents like MS Word and pdf documents. They allow digitally signing and encrypting e-mail messages to protect their integrity in transit allowing only intended recipients to read the same. They also allow authentication of sender and sender non-repudiation. These certificates can also secure document workflows not only between computers over networks but within a computer as well by encrypting or signing them. Such certificates can also be used for backups or document sharing. Some corporate also provide free personal e-mail certificates and personal identity certificates to users. SSL certificates are used to secure fully qualified domain names such as www.banday.info. They are the fastest and most affordable ways to activate strong protection for websites. They activate the browser padlock and https. These include cloud-based SSL, multi-domain SSL, Wild Card SSL, SSL Server, and SSL Client certificates. Mobile and Desktop Code Signing certificates secure applications for mobile phones and desktop and ensure their authenticity and integrity. End users who download digitally signed software stay confident about the source of the downloaded code is authentic and has not changed since it was signed. Code Signing certificates using digital signatures, enable inclusion of information about software developers with the executables such as .exe, .ocx, .dll, .cab, kernel mode software, VBA scripts, Apple Mac OS, Adobe AIR, Java apps, Mozilla apps, etc. using Microsoft Authenticode technology.

Cryptographic algorithms and digital signature certificates are also used in time stamping to prove existence of an electronic document at a given point of time, SSL for securing communication over insecure transmission lines, Kerberos for client authentication, IPsec in TCP/IP version 6 protocol for securing IP connections, Big Data for ensuring its integrity, certified mail, certificate based smart cards and various e-mail protocols such as S/MIME, DKIM, and SPF.

Secure Sockets Layer (SSL) is a cryptographic protocol originally developed by Netscape that governs server authentication, client authentication, and encrypted communication between servers and clients. The use of SSL protocol provides privacy and reliability between two communicating parties by transferring some reliable transport protocol such as TCP into a secure communication channel. Different versions of SSL and its IETF implementation, the Transport Layer Security (TLS) protocol use different cryptographic algorithms to ensure this secure communication between communicating parties. Since the SSL/TLS protocol is layered between the application layer and the transport layer, it supports multiple application layer protocols such as FTP, HTTP, TELNET, SMTP, etc. SSL/TLS comprises of two layers namely handshake layer and record layer. The handshake layer comprises of handshake protocol, change cipher spec protocol and the alert protocol. SSL/TLS uses both symmetric key and asymmetric key encryption. They use public key encryption to authenticate server to the client (and optionally the client to the server). Public key encryption is also used to generate a session key, which is used in symmetric algorithms to encrypt bulk of data, thereby, improving efficiency as well as speed of operation. SSL/TLS employs X.509 certificates to support both client side as well as server side authentications. Though TLS is mostly an updated and standardized version of SSL, however, they are not compatible with each other. SSL uses MD5 and SHA-1 in a straight manner whereas TLS uses a pseudorandom function to compute session key. TLS uses SSL v3.0 (RFC 6101) as basis towards the development of TLS. TLS underwent several revisions namely TLS v1.0 (RFC 2246), TLS v1.1 (RFC 4346), TLS v1.2 (RFC 5246) and DTLS (Datagram TLS) v1.0 (RFC 4347) and DTLS (Datagram TLS) v1.2 (RFC 6347). The drafts for (D)TLS v1.3 is currently under consideration of IETF. It proposes improved flexibility particularly for the negotiation of cryptographic algorithms. The MD5/SHA-1 combination in the pseudorandom function has been replaced with cipher suit specified pseudorandom function. All cipher suits use P-SHA256. The MD5/SHA-1 combination in the digitally signed element has been replaced with a single hash and the signed element includes a field that can explicitly specify the hash algorithm used. Further, support for authenticated encryption with additional data modes has also been added.

Kerberos (Neuman and Ts'o, 2004) (RFC 1510) developed at MIT is another popular authentication protocol based on cryptographic algorithms by which clients and servers are able to authenticate each other. Kerberos is a network authentication protocol that uses secret key cryptography to authenticate a client to a server or to different servers at the same time. Since its version 5, the protocol base of Kerberos has been extended to support asymmetric encryption including public and private keys and digital signature certificates. It authenticates clients and servers through a trusted third party in an open network environment. Trusted Third Party server functions as an authentication server, which share secret keys with all entities. Ticketing system is used for authenticating clients. Kerberos supports use of public key authentication using PKINIT (Public Key Cryptography for Initial Authentication in Kerberos) which permits use of smart cards, soft tokens, and multifactor authentications.

IPsec (Internet Protocol Security) is a set of protocols defined by IETF for IP security at the network or packet processing layer of network communication. IPsec is widely used in VPN (Virtual Private Networks). VPN is made up of two parts namely Internet Key Exchange Protocol (IKE) which is used for connection initiation and management and IPsec protocols which are used for encryption, authentication and data transfer. IKE protocol is used as a method of distributing session keys, provide means for the endpoints to authenticate each other, establish new IPsec connections, and manage existing connections. IPsec protocols are Authentication Header (AH) and Encapsulating Security Payload (ESP), which protects the traffic passing through the VPN. The AH protocol guarantees connectionless integrity and data origin authentication of IP packets and optionally can protect data against replay attacks using sliding window technique. The cryptographic algorithms used with IPsec include HMAC-SHA-1 for integrity and authentication, Triple DES-CBC, and AES-CBC for ensuring confidentiality.

Secure messaging is the ability to provide privacy, sender authentication, data integrity, non-repudiation, and protection against mail forgery (Oppliger, 2004). Various add-on protocols that work on top of SMTP aim to add these secure messaging features to SMTP. Some of them are based on end-to-end symmetric or asymmetric cryptographic schemes. These include Privacy-Enhanced Mail (PEM) (Kent, 1993), Pretty Good Privacy (PGP, n.d.), (Whiten and Tygar, 1999), GNU Privacy Guard (GPG) (Koch, 2003) and Secure Multi-purpose Internet Mail Extensions (S/MIME) (Ramesdell, 2004a; Ramesdell, 2004b). S/MIME is a widely deployed protocol. It uses X.509 identity certificates to provide privacy, authentication, message integrity, and non-repudiation by using digital signatures (Kuhn, 2001; Nielsoen, 2005). Prominent digital signature based anti-spoofing standard, besides PGP and S/MIME, is DomainKeys Identified Mail (DKIM) (Allma, 2007) that adds authentication, authorization and integrity to SMTP at domain level. Secure SMTP over Transport Layer Security (TLS) secures communication channel between the sender and the receiver during SMTP transactions without the efforts of end user. Secure SMTP over TLS secures e-mail path between e-mail clients and mail servers but does not secure it at the endpoints. In addition to these cryptographic e-mail protocols, certified e-mail systems have also been developed. These messaging systems allow messages to be exchanged for an acknowledgement. Like conventional postal system, this system ensures delivery of the message and provides its proof in the form of an electronic receipt, which may also include a time-stamp. Certified e-mail permits secure, reliable messaging while ensuring confidentiality, integrity, and non-repudiation of origin, recipient, submission, and delivery. It uses fair protocols, cryptographic algorithms, and digital signature certificates to prove authenticity of the sender. Certified mail is an e-mail whitelisting technique wherein service providers allow authenticated senders to bypass their e-mail filters. This system has been adopted by many service providers in parallel to the conventional system, however, it is controversial, as it is being feared that e-mail whitelisting will give paying senders a direct route into user's mailboxes.

PKI is feasible for use in the BIG data Security. Big Data refers to large quantum of data sets that exist online in applications such as finance, banking, stock exchange, etc. Big Data management involves management, administration, and organization of large volumes of structured and unstructured data. Big Data is characterized by volume, variety, and velocity. Since Big Data is transmitted to remote computers online for processing, it is essential to protect its integrity during transmission. PKI is used to attain integrity of this large set of data by establishing an encrypted channel between the host computers during the transmission. Be it wired or wireless network, client-server, cloud, or grid computing, desktop or web application, instant or regular messaging, or direct or indirect use of PKI for online information security are enormous and are in continuous growth.

LEGAL VALIDITY AND GOVERNMENT USE OF DIGITAL SIGNATURES

Over the last few decades, the cyberspace has witnessed a massive increase in cybercrime. Subsequent, adoption of constantly evolving technology to ensure security of online transactions has also increased. In addition, legal status of technological measures to their control has initially been uncertain. This has created some confusion about legal validity of technologies especially confusion between electronic and digital signatures. Initially, many laws were technology specific (e.g. the IT Act 2000 of India) which would have not given legal recognition to the use of new and more dependable technologies. An electronic signature as defined by the Electronic Signatures in Global and National Commerce Act, may be an electronic sound, symbol or process attached to or logically associated with a record and executed or adopted by a person with the intend to sign the record (Mir and Banday, 2012). These are no universal standards for electronic signature and they often exist in proprietary format. For some products, they may involve simply typing one's name, entering a personal ID or password, placing scan/digital image of one's hand signature on a document, signing through an electronic pad, etc. Electronic signatures may or may not include additional means to ensure security. Several products such as Adobe EchoSign (EchoSign, n.d.) and Forrester Research's SIGNiX (n.d.) add security features to electronic signatures to secure document integrity. If such additional means are not included with electronic signatures, they cannot maintain integrity and security and are therefore, considered as insecure methods of signing. They are vulnerable to copying and tampering and therefore, may invite forgery. Digital signature is a sub-group of electronic signature, which, provide highest level of security and are universally accepted. Therefore, all electronic signatures are not digital signatures but as of now all digital signatures are electronic signatures (SIGNiX, n.d.; DocuSign, 2015).

With an aim to expand commerce across the Internet, governments of various countries especially developed countries throughout the globe have taken initiatives to make use of electronic and digital signatures in their day-to-day business. They have adopted legislation such as eSIGN Act of United States and Information Technology Act 2000 (and its amendment in 2008) of India for using information technology including electronic and digital signatures in diverse applications such as electronic commerce, citizen services, healthcare, etc. Most of these countries have adopted regulations and legislation that gives legal recognition to secure electronic signatures such as digital signatures and deem them legally binding signatures. Individual approach to meet specific criteria regarding signatures and their implementation are different from country to country. These include: eSIGN (2001), UETA (1999), SEAL (1998), GPEA (2013), and UCC (2010) Acts and Codes of the United States, UECA (2003) of Canada, Chapter 7 of Electronic Communication Act 2000 (ECA, 2000) of the United Kingdom, EU Directive for Electronic Signature (1999/93/EC) (EUDCS, 2000), EU VAT directive (EUVATD, 2006) of the Europe, Electronic Signature Law (ESLPRC, 2007) of the People's Republic of China and Information Technology Act 2000 (IT ACT 2000, 2000) and its amendments in 2008 of India. Most of these laws, acts, and regulations are in harmony with the Model Law (UNCITRA, 2001) of Electronic Signatures adopted by the United Nations in 2001. In addition, several industry regulations and standards have also recognized digital signatures as a binding signature. These include: FDA's 21 CFR Part 11 (FDA, 2003) in Life Sciences, HIPAA (1996) in Healthcare, Public Law 108-390 (EDOCKET, 2006) for Homeland Security, Financial Services Modernization Act of 1999 (FSMA, 1999) in Finance, Cross-Media Reporting Regulation (CROMERR, 2013) in Environment, Sarbanes-Oxley Act 2002 (FRWEBGATE, 2002) in Public Companies, USDA EIA (Coggins) Testing (USDA, 2000) in Veterinary/Equine, FAA's CFR Title 14 (FAA, 2012) in Aviation, European Telecommunications Standards institute and ISO (9001:2000).

Like other countries, the government of India is actively promoting the use of digital signatures through various e-Governance projects. Despite regular use of digital signatures in business, several mission mode projects have been commissioned by the union and state governments to promote paperless government functioning. Examples include: a) The MCA21 a mission mode project under National e-Governance Plan (NeGP), which, is one of the first e-Governance projects under NeGP that successfully implemented digital signatures; b) IRCTC Ticket Booking, Indian Railways Catering, and Tourism Corporation, an Indian Railways subsidiary that uses class 3 individual digital signature certificates to book railway tickets to its express trains such as Shatabdi and Rajdhani expresses, c) Income Tax e-filing facility of the Department of Income tax by offering greater convenience while filing tax returns using digital signature certificates, and, e) Nemmadi Project in the state of Karnataka towards establishing a single window system at the village level to offer all government services as "signature less services" using digital signatures. Currently, in India digital signatures are also used for eProcurement, eOffice, eTendering, eFilling, and many other electronic application filling system in state and union government offices such as Reserve Bank of India, Directorate General of Foreign Trade (DGFT), Railways, Indian Farmers Fertiliser Cooperative (IFFCO), Oil and Natural Gas Corporation Limited (ONGC), Neyveli Lignite, Bharat Heavy Electricals Limited (BHEL), Defense, Steel Authority of India (SAIL), National Rugby League (NRL), Metals and Minerals Trading Corporation of India (MMTC), Oil India, CENTRAL PUBLIC WORKS DEPARTMENT (CPWD), and EMPLOYEES' PROVIDENT FUND ORGANISATION (EPFO). In some states like Uttar Pradesh, they are also used for online counseling, voter list preparation, and Post.

IMPLEMENTING DIGITAL SIGNATURE CERTIFICATES

Students, programmers, and researchers can take advantage of popular Cryptographic learning resources to understand cryptographic procedures and PKI libraries to develop programs or modify existing cryptographic algorithms to investigate future improvements. These include CrypTool (2014), OpenSSL (2014), Network Security Services (NSS) (2014), X Certificate and Key Management (XCA) (2014), OpenCA (2015), Enterprise Java Bean CA (EJBCA) (n.d.), Bouncy Castle Crypto APIs (BCC) (2013), FlexiProvider (2012) and MS DOT NET Library (n.d.). In addition to these, various other state-of-the-art libraries that include Cryptix/Elliptix (2005), GNU Crypto (2006), jBorZoi (2006), Crypto++ (2013), Nettle (n.d.) Libgcrypt (2011), Sodium (2013) have been developed to facilitate application developers to implement cryptographic routines in applications. These libraries are portable, pakagable, installable and are available for diverse programming languages and operating platforms. Some of these libraries implement complete cryptographic libraries while other offer solutions to specific cryptographic algorithms. Use of cryptographic libraries drastically reduce the risk of building insecure constructions as they exposes a very simple, high-level API, with a tiny set of functions to the users for each operation but use high-speed, highly-secure primitives and constructions, implemented with extreme care to avoid side-channel attacks.

CrypTool

CrypTool, through a range of software's namely CrypTool 1, CrypTool 2, JCrypTool and CrypTool online, which are open source and free to use has become a leading e-learning platform for cryptography and cryptanalysis. CrypTool 1 has been coded in C++ programming language and runs on MS Windows machines. It can be used as a teaching tool to learn cryptography or as an awareness tool to create awareness among employees and civil servants. Cryptool 1 can help the students to learn algorithms such as Caesar cipher, the ADFGVX cipher, the double-column transposition (permutation), the Enigma encryption algorithm, etc. which are classical cryptosystems. It also permits better understanding of modern cryptographic algorithms such as RSA and AES algorithms, hybrid encryption, algorithms based on lattice reduction and elliptic curves, etc. It benefits users to understand through visualizations algorithms such as Caesar, Enigma, RSA, Diffie-Hellman, digital signatures, AES, etc. In addition, CrypTool 1 also permits cryptanalysis of Vigenère, RSA, AES, and other algorithms. The Cryptanalytical measurement methods such as entropy, n-grams, autocorrelation, etc. can also be practiced. CrypTool 2, provides visual programming GUI to experiment with cryptographic procedures and to animate their cascades. Its GUI is vector-oriented and is based on Windows Presentation Foundation. JCrypTool, allows building of applications and analysis of cryptographic algorithms through Java programming language on Linux, MAC OS X, and Windows platforms. CryptTool online is a web based interactive cryptography and cryptosystem learning tool which does not require installation of any software on local machine. It is an online version of CrypTool 1.

OpenSSL

OpenSSL is an open source cryptographic library written in C programming language, and can be used from varied programming languages and operating environments. It is available free of cost for both commercial, and non-commercial uses under Apache-style license. It implements various cryptographic functions including SSL, and TLS protocols. It allows creation of X.509 certificates, CSRs and CRLs. RSA, DH and DSA algorithms with different key parameters can be implemented through it. It also allows the calculations of message digests and encryption and decryption of data and S/MIME e-mail.

OpenCA

OpenCA is available under BSD license and provides a framework for studying and development of PKI. Among other, it currently provides OpenCA PKI, which permits implementation of Certification Authority and LibPKI, which provides PKI library for use by applications. The libraries have been coded in CGI and Perl languages. It implements modern cryptographic algorithms including ECDH, AES, various version of DES, RC, MD, and SHA algorithms. It also implements SSL and TLS protocols, different types of PKCS, S/MIME, and X.509 certificates. Different databases including Oracle, MySQL, and PostgreSQL are currently supported by OpenCA.

X Certificate and Key Management

X Certificate and Key Management (XCA) is a GUI application interface for creating and managing certificates, asymmetric keys like RSA, DSA and EC, Smartcards, revocation lists and CRLs. The certificates and keys are stored in the database in the Triple DES encryption. It uses the OpenSSL and Qt4 library for the cryptographic functions and operations. Data structures i.e. Keys, Certificate signing requests, Certificates, and Templates can be imported and exported in many formats like DER (Distinguished Encoding Rules) or PEM (Privacy-Enhanced Mail). The CAs can be used to create CRLs and extend certificates. All keys carry a use counter, which counts the times it has been used. X Certificate is a free to use software under BSD license and is intended as a small CA for creation and signing certificates. XCA supports multiple root and intermediate Certificate authorities and can sign sub-CAs recursively. Certificates and requests can be created and signed and many x.509 v3 extensions can be added. The file-formats supported include PEM, DER, PKCS#7, PKCS#8, PKCS#10, PKCS#12, and SPKAC. X Certificate can be used with operating systems like POSIX, BSD, Free BSD, Mac OSX, Linux and Windows.

Microsoft DOT NET Cryptographic Library

Microsoft DOT NET Framework provides a rich library of cryptographic algorithms available in the form of compiled API. The library is object oriented and highly extensible through inheritance and overloading. The class hierarchy includes abstract algorithm type classes e.g. Symmetric Algorithm, Asymmetric Algorithm and Hash Algorithm classes, abstract algorithm classes e.g. Aes, ECDiffieHellman, and RC2 classes, and algorithm implementation classes e.g. RC2CryptoServiceProvider, AesManaged and ECDiffieHellmanCng classes. The library includes implementation of AES-128/192/256, SHA-1/256/384/512, ECDSA-256/384/521, ECDH-256/384/521 and other cryptographic algorithms published by NSA in its suite B. The Microsoft implementation of PKI also includes Cryptography Next Generation (CNG), PKIView, clustered active and passive CA, version 3 certificate templates, and many other new features to facilitate creation and management of Certification Authorities.

EJBCA PKI CA

Enterprise Java Bean Certification Authority is an enterprise level PKI Certification Authority software built using Java Enterprise Edition (JEE). It is a robust, Platform independent, component based, flexible, and high performance PKI library that can be used to implement a complete PKI infrastructure including certificate authority, validation authority and OCPS responder. Using EJBCA root CAs, SubCAs, Multiple CAs and various levels of CAs can be created. They can issue unlimited certificates, which can also be signed by public CAs such as Comodo. It supports SHA, RSA, DSA, ECDSA, X.509, SSl, TLS, and card verification Certificates, and other NSA Suite B algorithms. It also supports revocation and certificate revocation lists (CRLs), CRL creation and URL-based CRL distribution points, online certificate status protocol, distribution of CA certificates and CRLs over HTTP, key recovery, and varied hardware security modules. It can issue hundreds of certificates per second and store millions of them it its underlying database. It supports varies database management systems including Oracle, MS SQL, My SQL, DB2, and PostgreSQL.

Bouncy Castle Crypto APIs

The Bouncy Castle Crypto APIs are cross platform Java implementations of cryptographic algorithms for both the Java and the C# programming languages and are available under MIT X Consortium license. They are organized into three groups: a) Light-weight API, b) JCA/JCE provider, and, c) APIs for handling of other cryptographic protocols. Lightweight API provides direct access to cryptographic services. JCA/JCE provider built on top of the lightweight API and provides access to services required to use the JCA/JCE. The other APIs included provide handling of protocols such as Cryptographic Message Syntax

(CMS), OpenPGP, S/MIME, Time Stamp Protocol (TSP), and Certificate Management Protocol (CMP). They also include APIs for generating Certification Requests (CRMF, PKCS#10), X.509 certificates, PKCS #12 files, and several other protocol elements.

FlexiProvider

The FlexiProvider is a flexible open source cryptographic service provider (CSP) for the JCA/JCE that provides easy to use cryptographic modules, which can be plugged into applications built on top of the JCA/JCE. It has been developed at the Theoretical Computer Science Research Group at the Department of Computer Science at Technische Universität Darmstadt, Germany. It includes modules for both asymmetric and symmetric ciphers. In addition, it also includes key exchange modules, pseudo-random number generators, signature algorithms, and hash functions. JCrypTool, a leading e-learning cryptography platform makes use of the FlexiProvider cryptographic modules through FlexiAPI. The FlexiAPI extends the interfaces and Service Provider Interface (SPI) classes provided by standard JCA and establishes a top layer within FlexiProvider. It includes plugins that provide various services to extend its offered features.

RECENT DEVELOPMENTS IN CRYPTOGRAPHY

Both classic and modern cryptographic algorithms and protocol form the core of secure information systems. On one hand existing protocols are continuously being revised to coupe up with growing computational power of computers and on another hand, new protocols, and techniques are developed to explore alternatives cryptographic technologies. This section introduces some recent developments in cryptographic research. These include SHA-3, KECCAK, functional encryption, identity based encryption, quantum cryptography, post-quantum cryptography, DNA based cryptography and biological cryptography.

Development of SHA-3 and KECCAK

Work towards the development of SHA-3 hashing algorithm was taken up by the National Institute of Science and Technology (NIST) (http://csrc.nist.gov) to convert a variable length string to much shorter digest, useful for digital signatures, message authentication, and many other security applications. To develop a new, more secure and flexible cryptographic hash algorithm named SHA-3, the NIST opened a public competition in 2007. In the first round out of 64 submissions, NIST selected 51 candidates. In the second round, 14 candidates were shortlisted. The third round selected five candidate algorithms namely BLAKE, Grøstl, JH, KECCAK and Skein which were put to public review for eighteen months. In 2012, NIST announced KECCAK as the winning algorithm of the SHA-3 competition (NIST, 2012). The KECCAK algorithm (Bertoni, 2013) pronounced as (pronounced "catch-ack"), was created by Guido Bertoni, Joan Daemen and Gilles Van Assche of STMicroelectronics and Michaël Peeters of NXP Semiconductors. It has an elegant design and ability to run well on different computing devices. The clarity of KECCAK'S construction lends itself to easy analysis and has higher performance in hardware implementations than SHA-2. KECCAK uses a new "sponge construction" domain extender, with a 1600-bit permutation, which can be readily adjusted to trade generic security strength for throughput, and can generate larger or smaller hash outputs, as required. The KECCAK designers have also defined a modified chaining mode for KECCAK that provides authenticated encryption. The message block size varies according to the output size: KECCAK-512 has a block size of 576 bits, KECCAK-384 has 832 bits, KECCAK-256 has 1088 bits, and KECCAK-224 has 1152 bits. It also defined a number of additional variants. Recently, FIPS announced SHA-3: Permutation-Based Hash and Extendable-Output Functions (FIPS PUB 202) (NIST, 2014) as standard hashing functions on binary data. FIPS also announced KECCAK-p family of mathematical permutations, including the permutation that underlies KECCAK, as the main components of additional cryptographic functions that may be specified in the future. The SHA-3 family consists of four cryptographic hash functions, called SHA3-224, SHA3-256, SHA3-384, and SHA3-512, and two extendable-output functions (XOFs), called SHAKE128 and SHAKE256 each of which is based on an instance of the KECCAK algorithm that NIST selected as the winner of the SHA-3 Cryptographic Hash Algorithm Competition. The functions are designed to provide special properties, such as resistance to collision, preimage, and second preimage attacks. SHA3-224, SHA3-256, SHA3-384, and SHA3-512 are alternatives to the SHA-2 functions, and they are designed to provide resistance against preimage, second preimage, and collision attacks, which equals or exceeds the resistance that the corresponding SHA-2 functions provide. The SHA-3 functions are also designed to resist attacks such as length-extension attacks that would be resisted by a random function of the same output length, providing security strength up to the hash function's output length in bits, when possible. SHAKE128 and SHAKE256 are designed to resist collision, preimage, second preimage attacks, and other attacks that would be resisted by a random function of the requested output length, up to the security strength of 128 bits for SHAKE128, and 256 bits for SHAKE256.

Functional Encryption

Functional Encryption (FE) (Boneh, Sahai and Waters, 2011; Waters, 2013) is seen as an emerging tool for public key encryption especially for cloud security, searchable encryption, secure auditing, and secure data sharing. In this, the decryption ability of a receiver is determined by whether the secret key and the cipher text can be computed by functions or not. The idea of FE was proposed by Boneh, Raghunathan, and Segev in August 2013. They constructed a function private identity-based encryption scheme that guaranteed information security as secret key revealed nothing to malicious adversary with equality functions. Identity-based encryption (IBE) (Boneh and Franklin, 2001; Li, Zhang and Wang, 2006) that supports an equality functionality is a functional encryption scheme. Fuzzy identity-based encryption (Sahai and Waters, 2005) is the first functional encryption that supports nontrivial functionality. Many other functional encryption schemes namely predicate encryption (Katz, Sahai and Waters 2008) and inner product encryption (Lewko et al, 2010) have been proposed to support certain specific functionalities. Searchable Encryption supporting two party model proposed by Song et al. (2000) to meet the demand of applying search on remote encrypted data is a special class of functional encryption. More secure searchable encryption based schemes (Song, Wagner and Perrig, 2000; Chang and Mitzenmacher, 2005; Eu-Jin, 2003) and public key encryption with keyword search (PEKS) (Boneh et al, 2004) belong to functional encryption.

Identity Based Cryptography

The major limitation of PKI is the complex management of certificates, which worsens with the growing number of public keys in its certificate store. To solve this issue, Shamir (Tan, Yau and Lim, 2014) proposed Identity Based Cryptography/Encryption (IBC/IBE). In this form of cryptography, the public key of the user is derived from its unique identity such as e-mail address or IP address. A Trusted Third Parties (TTP) or the Key Generation Center (KGC) generates the corresponding private keys. Thus, IBC does not require a digital certificate to certify the public key. Key escrow is an inherent property in IBC systems, i.e. the TTP can generate each users' private key, because the TTP owns the master key used to generate users' secret keys. This property can be useful for IDS to decrypt network traffic on the fly and perform content scanning on encrypted traffic. It can solve certificate management issues of PKI by employing use of user's unique identity such as e-mail address, phone number, social security number, etc. as public key. However, in these system services of Trusted Third Parties are required to function as Private Key Generators. It is also not backward compatible with the existing PKI. Further, separate sets of key pairs are required to both sign and encrypt digital data. However, its advantages such as reduced costs, eased certificate management, and organizational administrative control have made large corporations such as Microsoft, IBM, TrendMicro, and Cannon to adopt it. Al-Riyami and Paterson recently introduced certificateless public key cryptography based on bilinear maps, which is identical to IBE and in contrast to the traditional public key cryptography does not require the use of certificates. This form of cryptography does not require certificates, does not rely on some trusted third party, generates short private and public keys, and does not suffer from key escrow property of identity-based cryptography (Al-Riyami and Paterson 2013).

Quantum Cryptography

Quantum physicists, Charles Bennett and his colleagues (Bennett, Brassard, Breidbard, and Wiesner, 1982; Bennett and Brassard, 1984) proposed a new type of cryptosystem known today as quantum cryptography (QC) (Gisin et al, 2002) which unlike the conventional cryptography is secure from advancements in computing power, new mathematical algorithms and quantum computers and is based on the quantum phenomena. In comparison to conventional cryptography wherein security depends upon a key pair obtained from factorizing very large integers, QC is based on Heisenberg's uncertainty principle (dual nature of light i.e. wave and particles). It is secure because an intruder cannot replicate a photon to recreate the key. Any eavesdropping attempt causes an irreversible change in the quantum states i.e. the wave function of photons will be collapsed (Hughes et al, 1996). In QC the sender transmits photons randomly in one of the four possible polarized directions (parallel - 00, perpendicular - 900, and diagonals - +450 and -450) which are detected using the corresponding polarizations and detected with the detector by the receiver. A correct polarization is required at the receiver to detect the photon, which will otherwise be destroyed. A well know example of QC is its use for secure distribution of keys in PKI called Quantum Key Distribution (QKD) (DeJesus, 2001) wherein PKI secret keys are distributed through photons. QKD was implemented by BBN for IPSec in 2002. University of Geneva and IdQuantique implemented fully integrated quantum cryptography prototype machine across a telecommunication network using fiber-optics. Over the period of years, many experiments have been carried out to use QKD for various network protocols and many QKD products such as IdQuantique, Clavis, Vectis, Quantis, MagiQ have been developed to use QKD over varied transmission systems. An important aspect of quantum authentication is quantum identity authentication. A quantum authentication protocol based on duality information was proposed in 2001 by Curty and Santos (2001). A quantum identity authentication scheme and quantum message authentication scheme (Mihara, 2002) based on quantum entanglement swapping was proposed in 2002 by Mihara. A quantum identity authentication based on ping-pong technique for photons capable to achieve the update of the authentication key was proposed in 2006 by Zhang (2006). Another key development in QC are the works towards development of quantum digital signatures. A quantum Signature Scheme with Weak Arbitrator was proposed by Luo et al (2012). A quantum digital signature based on quantum one-way functions was proposed in 2005 by Lu et al (2005). Other development include the proposals of arbitrated quantum-signature scheme in 2001 by Zeng et al (2002), quantum signature systems with message recovery relying on the availability of an arbitrator by Lee et al (2004), and arbitrated quantum message signature scheme in 2005 by Lu et al (2005). Recently, Quantum Digital Certificate, an identity certificate based on quantum theory has been proposed by Rigui Zhou (2014). The study has built a model of QDC, which can be issued by some legal Quantum Certification Authority (QCA), stored in quantum computers and use when required to encrypt or decrypt information.

Post-Quantum Cryptography

Post-quantum cryptography refers to the cryptographic algorithms that are secure against cryptanalysis with conventional as well as quantum computers. Post-quantum cryptography is different from quantum cryptography. In former quantum phenomena is used to make the cryptographic algorithms secure and in the later new cryptographic algorithms secure against the enormous computing power of future quantum computers are developed. Since 2005, cryptographic community has shown growing interest towards development of popular public key cryptographic systems that are not based on the conventional integer factorization or discrete logarithm problems. The reason being the fear that due to enormous computing power of the future quantum computers conventional public key algorithms based on integer factorization or discrete logarithm problems shall be easily solvable through Shor's algorithm (Shor, 1995). In contrast to public key cryptographic algorithms, symmetric key algorithms that can be broken through Grover's algorithm (Bernstein, 2009) given enormous computing power can be made secure against quantum computers by increasing the key size. Two hash-based and two code-based families of post-quantum algorithms are currently believed to be secure against attacks (on integer factoring and discrete logarithm) through future quantum computers. Hash-based algorithms for digital signatures such as one time signature scheme based on directed tree graph (Lamport, 1979) and enhanced one time signatures based on binary trees (Merkle, 1989) use some hash function as a base operation. The Merkle Signature Scheme (MSS) was further enhanced (Buchmann et al, 2006) by constructing multiple levels of Merkle hash trees to permit large number of signatures. Code-based public key algorithms such Niederreiter cryptosystem (Niederreiter, 1986) and code-based signature scheme (Courtois, Finiasz, and Sendrier, 2001) as are based on error-correcting codes wherein the core operation is the matrix-vector multiplication. The main decryption operation involves the use of Euclidean algorithm. Multivariate-Quadratic Cryptographic algorithms such Rainbow (Ding, Wolf and Yang 2007; Bernstein, Lange and Page, 2008) is based on problem of solving multivariate quadratic equations (MQ-problem) over finite fields. Both signature and encryption schemes have been proposed, however, only signature schemes have proved to be secure against cryptanalysis (Wolf and Preneel, 2005). Lattice-based cryptographic schemes are based on lattices. As opposite to MQ-problems, lattice based encryption is stronger than

Table 7. Adapted from Bochum (2013)

PQC Scheme	Core Operation	Data Types	Key Size (Approx.)	Encryption	Signature	Maturity
Hash-Based	Hashing	Hash outputs	20	Yes	No	High
Multivariable Quadratic	Matrix Multiplication, Solving LSE	GF(2m)	10k	Yes	No	Low, medium for conservative schemes
Lattice Based NTRU	Convolution	Zq	<0.1k	Maybe	Yes	Medium
Lattic Based General Lattice	Matrix Multiplication	GF(2m)	100k	Maybe	Yes	Medium
Code-Based	Matrix Multiplication, decoding	GF(2m)	100k	Expensive	Yes	High, with precautions to implement

lattice based signature schemes. The lattice based encryption schemes include GHQ (Goldreich, Goldwasser and Halevi, 1997), HNF (Micciancio, 2001), and LDE schemes and its variants (Regev, 2005). NAEP/SVES-3 (Howgrave-Graham, Silverman, Singer and Whyte, 2003), a revised version of NTRU lattice scheme is very efficient, secure and has been standardized by IEEE (IEEE 1363.1 standard). A summary of post-quantum cryptographic schemes is given in Table 7 (Bochum, 2013).

Hash based post-quantum cryptographic algorithms particularly MMS has a very short public key, a relatively long signature length, long private key, expansive computational key generations, and extensive choice of hashing algorithms, however, their performance depends on the underlying hash functions. Code based post-quantum cryptographic algorithms permit fast encryption and decryption and good security; however, they have large key sizes, and computationally expensive signature generation. In Multivariable Quadratic post-quantum cryptographic algorithms, the size of keys can exceed several kilobytes; however, it offers a great choice for selection of data types, and underlying finite field. A vital issue in these algorithms is to compute affine transformations. The encryption and decryption is very fast in Lattice Based NTRU algorithm. Its bit complexity is quadratic in comparison to cubic bit complexity of conventional public key schemes.

Homomorphic Cryptography

In addition to above discussed encryption techniques, encryption algorithms based on homomorphic mathematical structures have been developed. Homomorphic is a Greek word that means "same structure". It is used to describe the transformation of one data set into another while preserving relationships between elements in both sets. Homomorphic encryption techniques (Rivest, Adleman and Dertouzos, 1978) enable mathematical operations on encrypted data producing results equivalent to those that would have been produced if identical mathematical operations had been performed on the original data. Thus, homomorphically-encrypted data can be analyzed and worked as if it were still in its original form. This feature is highly desired in shared data services where different operations on the data are performed at different locations (such as cloud computing) because it lets these operations be performed without exposing the original data (Gahi, Guennoun and El-Khatib, 2011; Gahi, Guennoun, Guennoun and El-Khatib, 2012). Partially homomorphic encryption algorithms such as unpadded RSA, ElGamal,

Goldwasser-Micali, Benaloh and Paillier and fully homomorphic encryption are the two broader classes of homomorphic encryption. With partially homomorphic encryption (also called nearly homomorphic encryption), only selected mathematical operations are possible, however, fully homomorphic encryption supports all required mathematical operations but their implementation require enormous computing resources (Gentry, 2009; Coron, Naccache and Tibouchi, 2012). Aiming at developing algorithms to permit searching within encrypted data major corporations including IBM and Darpa are currently working on fully homomorphic encryption (Gentry and Halevi, 2011). In December 2013, IBM has secured a patent on fully homomorphic encryption technique, which according to IBM will be useful for securing sensitive data in cloud environment.

DNA Cryptography

Adleman's research contribution (Adleman, 1994) in bio-computations lead to solve difficult computational problems using DNA computing. Boneh et al showed that efficient and exponential DNA computing could break conventional DES (Boneh, Dunworth and Lipton, 1995). The features of DNA computing permitted One Time Password (OTP) cryptography and steganography (Gehani, LaBean and Reif, 1999). Ning (2009) introduced pseudo DNA cryptography wherein the original data is transformed into a DNA sequence. This sequence is further transformed into spliced and protein forms of DNA by dividing introns into specific patterns. Mills et al (1999), Soni and Johar (2012), and Wasiewicz et al (2000) performed a few biological and algebraic operations such as addition and subtraction using DNA cryptography. DNA based Java Crypto binary encryption scheme is based on the A, T and G features of DNA (Leier et al, 2000; Tatiana, 2008). A DNA digital coding technique called Polymerase Chain Reaction (PCR) (Cui, Qin, Wang and Zhang, 2008) has been used by Cherian et al for transforming data into DNA template (using forward primer) (Cherian, Raj and Abraham, 2013). Decryption is performed using complimentary process involving reverse primer. A two key-based DNA asymmetric encryption method was proposed recently by Lai et al in 2010 wherein one key is used for encryption and decryption and the other is used for creating DNA structures (Lai et al, 2010). Combination of traditional and DNA cryptographic approaches called hybrid security has recently been proposed to provide improved security (Tripathi, Jaiswal and Singh, 2013). In this approach, public key cryptography is integrated within the traditional DNA security algorithms by applying asymmetric encryption to data represented through DNA sequencing.

Biometric Encryption

Conventional secret and public key cryptographic methods are secure as long as the underlying key, which protects them, is secured. There is also a lack a direct connection between the user and the key, which does not directly permit identification of the legitimate users. Biometric Encryption (BE) overcomes these limitations and offers protection of key by using biometric authentication. It permits secure authentication and ease of operation (Qinghai, 2010). Tomoko et al introduced the concept of BE in 1994 (Tomko, Soutar and Schmidt, 1996). BE is not an encryption algorithm but it may be used in conventional cryptographic algorithms for generating or protecting keys (secret key or private and public key pair) through biometrics. It securely binds a key to a biometric or generates a key (called "secure sketch" or "fuzzy extractor") (Dodis, Reyzin and Smith, 2004) from the biometrics resulting in a key called biometrically encrypted key, which is also called biometric template or helper data. Biometric encryption applies to any physical biometric patters such as fingerprint, hand, eye, face or voice, however, fingerprint based BE has been mostly studied and widely implemented. Regardless of the type of physical biometric patter, the biometric sample is fuzzy in nature, therefore, a major challenge in BE is generation and verification of digital key from fuzzy samples of an individual. Many attempts have suffered excessive false rejection rates, which is unaccepted for practical applications. Two possible biometric encryption approaches are key binding and key generation. In the former, a randomly generated key is securely bound to the biometric data of an individual and in the later, the key itself is derived from the biometric data of an individual. Biometric encryption schemes such as Fuzzy Commitment (Juels, 1999) and Fuzzy Vault (Juels and Sudan, 2002) can be used in either approaches. Development of reliable biometric encryption can overcome the key management issue of PKI systems; however, many challenges such as reliability, cost, interoperability, etc. are associated with it.

CONCLUSION

The need for information security, privacy of individuals, authentication of communicating identities, integrity of content, non-repudiation of communicating parties besides other security requirements have been discussed. Online information security through public key infrastructure particularly digital signature certificates has been explained and illustrated. Asymmetric key encryption, key exchange, its advantages, and disadvantages over conventional symmetric key encryption have been discussed. In addition, public key infrastructure and its working besides various other contemporary development in public key infrastructure have been explained. Distinct steps involved in encryption, signing, digital signatures, and digital signature certificates have been detailed through illustrations. This includes discussion on digital signatures and certificates, the process of signing, encryption, decryption, signature verification through them, current algorithms used, keys, structure, types, standards, etc. Use of time stamping and time stamping services with digital signature certificates have been presented. Current applications of certificates in different domains has been discussed. Legal validity and the current use of digital signature certificates in governments especially government of India are presented. Recent certificate issues and security steps to secure them have been discussed. An introduction to cryptographic tools and PKI libraries for students and developers to use digital signature certificates for securing documents and e-mail messages have been presented. Further, recent developments in cryptography such as quantum, post quantum, monomorphic, DNA, and biometric cryptographic techniques have been introduced.

REFERENCES

Adams, C., Pinkas, D., Cain, P., & Zuccherato, R. (2001). *Internet X.509 Public Key Infrastructure Time Stamp Protocols (TSP)*. IETF RFC 3161, Retrieved from http://www.ietf.org/rfc/rfc3161.txt

Adleman, L. M. (1994). Molecular computation of solutions to combinatorial problems. *Science, 266*(5187), 1021–1024. doi:10.1126/science.7973651 PMID:7973651

Adobe. (2012). Retrieved from http://blogs.adobe.com/security/2012/09/inappropriate-use-of-adobe-code-signing-certificate.html

Al-Riyami, S. S. Paterson, K. G. (2013). *Certificateless Public Key Cryptography*. Academic Press.

Allma, E. Callas, J. Delan, M. Libbey, M. Fenton J. Thomas, M. (2007). *DomainKeys Identified Mail (DKIM)*. Internet Engineering Task Force (IETF), RFC 4871.

Anderson, R., & Biham, E. (1996). Tiger: A Fast New Hash Function. *Fast Software Encryption, Third International Workshop Proceedings*. Springer-Verlag.

ANSI X9.62. (1999). *Public Key Cryptography for the Financial Services Industry: The Elliptic Curve Digital Signature Algorithm* (ECDSA). Author.

Ascertia. (n.d.). Retrieved from http://www.ascertia.com

Banday, M. T. (2011). Easing PAIN with Digital Signatures. *International Journal of Computer Applications*. Retrieved from http://research.ijcaonline.org/ volume29/number2/pxc3874822.pdf

BCC. (2013). *Bouncy Castle Crypto APIs*. Retrieved from https://www.bouncycastle.org/

Bennett, C. H., & Brassard, G. (1984). Quantum cryptography: Public key distribution and coin tossing. In *Proc. of IEEE International Conference on Computers, Systems and Signal Processing*. Bangalore, India: IEEE.

Bennett, C. H., Brassard, G., Breidbard, S., & Wiesner, S. (1982). Quantum Cryptography, or Unforgivable Subway Tokens. In Proceedings of Crypto 1982. Santa Barbara, CA: Academic Press.

Bernstein, D. J. (2009). *Introduction to post-quantum cryptography*. Post-Quantum Cryptography.

Bernstein, D. J., Chang, Y., Cheng, C., Chou, L. P., Heninger, N., Lange, T., & Someren, N. (2013). Factoring RSA Keys from Certified Smart Cards: Coppersmith in the Wild. Advances in Cryptology - ASIACRYPT 2013. *Lecture Notes in Computer Science, 8270*, 341–360. doi:10.1007/978-3-642-42045-0_18

Bernstein, D. J., Lange, T., & Page, D. (2008). *eBATS. ECRYPT Benchmarking of Asymmetric Systems Performing Benchmarks (report)*. Retrieved from http://www.ecrypt.eu.org/ebats/

Bertoni, G., Daemen, J., Peeters, M., & Van Assche, G. (2013). Keccak. In Advances in Cryptology–EUROCRYPT 2013 (pp. 313-314). Springer Berlin Heidelberg.

Bit9. (2013). Retrieved from https://blog.bit9.com/2013/02/08/bit9-and-our-customers-security/

Bochum, S. H. (2013). *Post Quantum Cryptography: Implementing Alternative Public Key Schemes on Embedded Devices*. Germany: Faculty of Electrical Engineering and Information Technology at the Ruhr-University Bochum.

Boneh, D., Dunworth, C., & Lipton, R. J. (1995). Breaking DES using a molecular computer. In *Proceedings of DIMACS Workshop on DNA Based Computers*. Princeton, NJ: DIMACS.

Boneh, D., & Franklin, M. (2001). Identity-based encryption from theWeil pairing. In Advances in Cryptology-CRYPTO 2001 (pp. 213–229). Springer.

Boneh, D., Sahai, A., & Waters, B. (2011). Functional encryption: definitions and challenges. In Theory of Cryptography (pp. 253–273). Springer.

Boneh, K. D., Crescenzo, G. D., Ostrovsky, R., & Persiano, G. (2004). Public key encryption with keyword search. In Advances in Cryptology-Eurocrypt 2004 (pp. 506–522). Springer.

Buchmann, J., Coronado, C., Dahmen, E., D"oring, M., & Klintsevich, E. (2006). CMSS - an improved merkle signature scheme. In INDOCRYPT 2006 (pp. 349–363). Academic Press.

Canava, J. E. (2001). *Fundamentals of Network Security*. London: Artech House.

Certificate Transparency. (n.d.). Retrieved from http://www.certificate-transparency.org/

CGI Group Inc. (2004). *Public Key Encryption and Digital Signature: How do they work?* CGI Group Inc. Retrieved from http://www.cgi.com/files/white-papers/cgi_whpr_35_pkie.pdf

Chang, Y. C., & Mitzenmacher, M. (2005). Privacy preserving keyword searches on remote encrypted data. In *Proceedings of the 3rd International Conference on Applied Cryptography and Network Security (ACNS '05)* (pp. 442–455). ACNS. doi:10.1007/11496137_30

Cherian, A., Raj, S. R., & Abraham, A. (2013). A Survey on different DNA cryptographic methods. *International Journal of Science and Research, 2*(4), 167–169.

Code, U. S. (2012). *US Code, 44 U.S.C. § 3542(b)(1)*. Title 44-public printing and documents, chapter 35-coordination of federal information policy, subchapter iii-information security. Retrieved from http://www.gpo.gov/fdsys/pkg/USCODE-2011-title44/pdf/USCODE-2011-title44-chap35-subchapIII-sec3542.pdf

Comodo. (2011). Retrieved from https://blogs.comodo.com/uncategorized/the-recent-ra-compromise/

Cooper. (2008). *Internet X.509 Public Key Infrastructure Certificate and Certificate Revocation List (CRL) Profile*. RFC 5280. Retrieved from http://www.ietf.org/rfc/rfc5280.txt

Coron, J. S., Naccache, D., & Tibouchi, M. (2012). Public Key Compression and Modulus Switching for Fully Homomorphic Encryption over the Integers. *Lecture Notes in Computer Science, 7237*, 446–464. doi:10.1007/978-3-642-29011-4_27

CoSign. (n.d.). Retrieved from http://www.arx.com

Courtois, N., Finiasz, M., & Sendrier, N. (2001). How to achieve a McEliece-based digital signature scheme. In ASIACRYPT 2001 (LNCS), (vol. 2248, pp. 157–174). Springer. doi:10.1007/3-540-45682-1_10

CRN. (2014). Retrieved from http://www.crn.com/news/security/300073396/microsoft-revokes-digital-certs-to-guard-against-possible-attacks-surveillance.htm

CROMERR. (2013). *Cross-Media Electronic Reporting Regulation (CROMERR)*. Retrieved from http://epa.gov/cromerr/about.html

Cryptix/Elliptix. (2005). *Cryptix/Elliptix*. Retrieved from www.cryptix.org

Crypto. (2006). *GNU Crypto*. Retrieved from www.gnu.org/software/gnu-crypto

Crypto++. (2013). *Crypto++*. Retrieved from www.cryptopp.com

Cryptool. (2014). *Cryptool*. Retrieved from www.cryptool.org/en/

Cui, G. Z., Qin, L., Wang, Y., & Zhang, X. (2008). An encryption scheme using DNA technology. In *Proceedings of IEEE 3rd International Conference on Bio-Inspired Computing: Theories and Applications*. Adelaide, Australia: IEEE. doi:10.1109/BICTA.2008.4656701

Curty, M., & Santos, D. J. (2001). Quantum authentication of classical messages. *Physical Review A.*, *64*(6), 062309. doi:10.1103/PhysRevA.64.062309

DeJesus, E. (2001). *Cryptography: Quantum Leap*. Information Security.

Ding, J., Wolf, C., & Yang, B. J. (2007). l-invertible cycles for multivariate quadratic (MQ) public key cryptography. In PKC 2007 (LNCS), (vol. 4450, pp. 266–281). Springer.

DocuSign. (2015). *Digital Signatures FAQ*. Retrieved from http://www.arx.com/learn/about-digital-signature/digital-signature-faq/

Dodis, Y., Reyzin, L., & Smith, A. (2004). Fuzzy Extractors: How to Generate Strong Keys from Biometrics and other Noisy Data. In *Proceedings of Eurocrypt* (pp. 523–540). Springer-Verlag. doi:10.1007/978-3-540-24676-3_31

DOTNET. (n.d.). *Microsoft Dot Net*. Retrieved from http://www.microsoft.com/

ECA. (2000). *Electronic Communications Act 2000*. Retrieved from http://www.opsi.gov.uk/acts/acts2000/ukpga_20000007_en_1

EchoSign. (n.d.). Retrieved from https://www.echosign.adobe.com/

EDOCKET. (2006). *Public Law*. Retrieved from http://edocket.access.gpo.gov/2006/E6-9283.htm

EFF. (n.d.). Retrieved from https://www.eff.org/observatory

EJBCA. (2015). *Open Java Development Kit*. Oracle Inc. Retrieved from http://openjdk.java.net/

EMET. (2014). *Microsoft's Enhanced Mitigation Experience Toolkit (EMET)*. Retrieved form http://support.microsoft.com/kb/2458544

Entrust. (2011) Retrieved from http://www.entrust.net/advisories/malaysia.htm

Entrust. (n.d.). Retrieved from http://www.entrust.com

eSIGN. (2001). Retrieved from http://www.ftc.gov/os/2001/06/esign7.htm

ESLPRC. (2007). *Electronic Signature Law of the People's Republic of China*. Retrieved from http://tradeinservices.mofcom.gov.cn/en/b/2007-11-29/13694.shtml

Eu-Jin, G. (2003). *Secure Indexes*. Cryptology ePrint Archive, Report 2003/216. Retrieved from http://eprint.iacr.org/2003/216/

EUDCS. (2000). *EU Directive for Electronic Signatures (1999/93/EC)*. Retrieved from http://eurlex.europa.eu/LexUriServ/LexUriServ.do?uri=CELEX:31999L0093:EN:HTML

EUVATD. (2006). *EU VAT directive*. Retrieved from http://www.vatlive.com/eu-vat-rules/eu-vat-directive/

FAA. (2012). *FAA's CFR Title 14*. Retrieved from http://www.airweb.faa.gov/Regulatory_and_Guidance_Library/rgAdvisoryCircular.nsf/0/c2c91cc068e0dd7b86256c7100609d5f/$FILE/AC%20120-78%20final.pdf

FDA. (2003). *FDA's 21 CFR Part 11*. Retrieved from http://www.fda.gov/RegulatoryInformation/Guidances/ucm125067.htm

FIPS. (1996). Digital Signature Standard (DSS). *FIPS PUB 186-3*. Information Technology Laboratory, National Institute of Standards and Technology. Retrieved from http://csrc.nist.gov/publications/fips/fips186-3/fips_186-3.pdf

FlexiProvider. (2012). *FlexiProvider*. Retrieved from http://www.flexiprovider.de

FRWEBGATE. (2002). *Sarbanes-Oxley Act of 2002*. Retrieved from http://frwebgate.access.gpo.gov/cgi-bin/getdoc.cgi?dbname=107_cong_bills&docid=f:h3763enr.tst.pdf

FSMA. (1999). *Financial Services Modernization Act of 1999 (Gramm-Leach-Bliley)*. Retrieved from http://www.ftc.gov/privacy/glbact/glbsub1.htm

Gahi, Y., Guennoun, M., & El-Khatib, K. (2011). A Secure Database System using Homomorphic Encryption Schemes. In *Proceedings of the Third International Conference on Advances in Databases, Knowledge, and Data Applications* (pp. 54–58). Academic Press.

Gahi, Y. Guennoun, M. Guennoun, Z. El-Khatib, K. (2012). Privacy Preserving Scheme for Location-Based Services. *The Journal of Information Security*, 105–112.

Gehani, A., LaBean, T. H., & Reif, J. H. (1999). DNA-based cryptography. In *Proceedings of 5th Annual DIMACS Meeting on DNA Based Computers*. Cambridge, MA: DIMACS.

Gentry, C. (2009). Fully Homomorphic Encryption Using Ideal Lattices. In *Proceedings of 41st ACM Symposium on Theory of Computing (STOC)*. doi:10.1145/1536414.1536440

Gentry, C., & Halevi, S. (2011). Implementing Gentry's fully-homomorphic encryption scheme. In Proceedings of Advances in Cryptology--EUROCRYPT 2011 (pp. 129-148). Springer.

Gisin, N., Ribordy, G., Tittel, W., & Zbinden, H. (2002). Quantum cryptography. *Reviews of Modern Physics*, *74*(1), 145–195. doi:10.1103/RevModPhys.74.145

Globsign. (n.d.). Retrieved from https://www.globalsign.com

Goldreich, O., Goldwasser, S., & Halevi, S. (1997). Public-key cryptosystems from lattice reduction problems. In CRYPTO'97 (LNCS), (vol. 1294, pp. 112–131). Springer. doi:10.1007/BFb0052231

Google. (2014). Retrieved from http://googleonlinesecurity.blogspot.in/2014/07/maintaining-digital-certificate-security.html

GPEA. (2013). *Government Paperwork Elimination Act*. Retrieved from http://www.whitehouse.gov/omb/fedreg/gpea2.html

HIPAA. (1996). *Health Insurance Portability and Accountability Act (HIPAA)*. Retrieved from http://aspe.hhs.gov/admnsimp/pL104191.htm

Howgrave-Graham, N., Silverman, J. H., Singer, A., & Whyte, W. (2003). *NAEP: Provable Security in the Presence of Decryption Failures*. In IACR ePrint Archive, Report 2003-172. Retrieved from http://eprint.iacr.org/2003/172/

Hughes, R. J. (1996). Quantum cryptography over underground optical fibers. In *Crypto96-Proc. of the 16th Annual International Cryptology Conference on Advances in Cryptology*. Springer-Verlag.

ImperialViolet. (2011). Retrieved from https://www.imperialviolet.org/2011/05/04/pinning.html

IT ACT 2000. (2000). *The Information Technology Act, 2000*. Government of India. Retrieved from http://www.mit.gov.in/sites/upload_files/dit/files/downloads/itact2000/itbill2000.pdf

jBorZoi. (2006). *jBorZoi*. Retrieved from http://nixbit.com/cat/programming/libraries/borzoi

Juels, A. (1999). *A fuzzy commitment scheme*. In *Proceedings of Sixth ACM Conference on Computer and Communications Security* (pp. 28–36). ACM Press. doi:10.1145/319709.319714

Juels, A., & Sudan, M. (2002). A fuzzy vault scheme. In *Proceedings of IEEE International Symposium on Information Theory*. IEEE. doi:10.1109/ISIT.2002.1023680

Katz, J., Sahai, A., & Waters, B. (2008). Predicate encryption supporting disjunctions, polynomial equations, and inner products. In Advances in Cryptology—EUROCRYPT 2008 (pp. 146–162). Springer. doi:10.1007/978-3-540-78967-3_9

Kent, S. T. (1993). Internet Privacy Enhanced Mail. *Communications of the ACM, 36*(8), 48–60. doi:10.1145/163381.163390

Koch, W. (2003). *The GNU privacy guard*. Retrieved from http://www.gnupg.org

Kuhn, D. R., Hu, V. C., Polk, W. T., & Chang, S. J. (2001). *Introduction to Public Key Technology and federal PKI Infrastructure*. NIST Gaithersburg. Retrieved form http://www.csrc.nist.gov/publications/nistpubs/ 80032/ sp80032.pdf

Lai, X. J., Lu, M. X., Qin, L., Han, J. S., & Fang, X. W. (2010). Asymmetric encryption and signature method with DNA technology. *Science China Information Sciences, 53*(3), 506–514. doi:10.1007/s11432-010-0063-3

Lamport, L. (1979). *Constructing digital signatures from a one-way function*. Technical Report SRI-CSL-98. SRI International Computer Science Laboratory.

Lee, H., Hong, C., Kim, H., Lim, J., & Yang, H. J. (2004). Arbitrated quantum signature scheme with message recovery. *Physics Letters. [Part A], 321*(5-6), 295–300. doi:10.1016/j.physleta.2003.12.036

Leier, A., Richter, C., Banzhaf, W., & Rauhe, H. (2000). Cryptography with DNA binary strands. *Bio Systems, 57*(1), 13–22. doi:10.1016/S0303-2647(00)00083-6 PMID:10963862

Lewko, A., Okamoto, T., Sahai, A., Takashima, K., & Waters, B. (2010). Fully secure functional encryption: attribute-based encryption and (hierarchical) inner product encryption. In Advances in Cryptology—EUROCRYPT 2010 (pp. 62–91). Springer.

Li, J., Zhang, F., & Wang, Y. (2006). A new hierarchical ID-based cryptosystem and CCA-secure PKE. In *Embedded and Ubiquitous Computing, International Conference (EUC)* (LNCS), (pp. 362–371). Springer.

Libgcrypt. (2011). *Libgcrypt*. Retrieved from www.gnu.org/software/libgcrypt

Lu, X., & Feng, D. (2005). Quantum digital signature based on quantum one-way functions. In *Proceedings of Advanced Communication Technology*. IEEE.

Lu X, Feng D G. (2005). An arbitrated quantum message signature scheme. In *Computational and Information Science*. Springer Berlin Heidelberg.

Luo, M. X., Chen, X. B., Yun, D., & Yang, Y.-X. (2012). Quantum Signature Scheme with Weak Arbitrator. *International Journal of Theoretical Physics, 51*(7), 2135–2142. doi:10.1007/s10773-012-1093-y

MalwareBytes. (2013) Retrieved from https://blog.malwarebytes.org/intelligence/2013/02/digital-certificates-and-malware-a-dangerous-mix/

Merkle, R. C. (1989). A certified digital signature. In CRYPTO (pp. 218–238). Academic Press.

Micciancio, D. (2001). Improving Lattice Based Cryptosystems Using the Hermite Normal Form. *Lecture Notes in Computer Science, 2146*, 126–145. doi:10.1007/3-540-44670-2_11

Microsoft. (n.d.). Retrieved from http://www.microsoft.com/security/portal/mmpc/shared/glossary.aspx#rogue_security_software

MicrosoftTechnet. (2013). Retrieved from https://technet.microsoft.com/library/security/2798897

Mihara, T. (2002). Quantum identification schemes with entanglements. *Physical Review A., 65*(5), 052326. doi:10.1103/PhysRevA.65.052326

Mills, A. P. Jr, Yurke, B., & Platzman, P. M. (1999). Article for analog vector algebra computation. *Bio Systems, 52*(1-3), 175–180. doi:10.1016/S0303-2647(99)00044-1 PMID:10636042

Mir, F. A., & Banday, M. T. (2012). Authentication of Electronic Records: Limitations of Indian Legal Approach. *Journal of International Commercial Law and Technology, 7*(3), 223–232.

NakedSecuity. (2011). Retrieved from http://nakedsecurity.sophos.com/2011/11/03/another-certificate-authority-issues-dangerous-certficates/

NakedSecurity. (2013). Retrieved from http://nakedsecurity.sophos.com/2013/01/04/turkish-certificate-authority-screwup-leads-to-attempted-google-impersonation/

Nettle. (2015). *Nettle*. Retrieved from www.lysator.liu.se/~nisse/nettle

Neuman, B. C. & Ts'o, T. (2004). Kerberos: an authentication service for computer networks. *IEEE Communication Magazine, 32*(9).

Niederreiter, H. (1986). Knapsack-type cryptosystems and algebraic coding theory. *Problems Control Inform. Theory/Problemy Upravlen. Teor. Inform (Silver Spring, Md.), 15*(2), 159–166.

Nielsoen, R. (2005). Observations from the development of large scale PKI. In *Proceedings 4th Annual PKI R&D Workshop*. NIST.

Ning, K. (2009). *A pseudo DNA cryptography method.* Retrieved from http://arxiv.org/abs/0903.2693

NIST. (2012). *Third-Round Report of the SHA-3 Cryptographic Hash Algorithm Competition.* doi:10.6028/NIST.IR.7896

NIST. (2014). *FIPS SHA-3 Standard: Permutation-Based Hash and Extendable-Output Functions.* DRAFT FIPS PUB 202. Retrieved from http://csrc.nist.gov/publications/drafts/fips-202/fips_202_draft.pdf

NSS. (2014). *Network Security Services.* Retrieved from https://developer.mozilla.org/en/docs/NSS

Open, C. A. (2015). *OpenCA.* Retrieved from http://www.openca.org/

OpenSSL. (2014). *Open Source Secure Socket Layer Project.* Retrieved from https://www.openssl.org/

Oppliger, R. (2004). Certified Mail: The next challenge for secure messaging. *Communications of the ACM, 47*(8), 75–79. doi:10.1145/1012037.1012039

PCWorld. (2013). Retrieved from http://www.pcworld.com/article/2080620/bogus-antivirus-program-uses-a-dozen-stolen-signing-certificates.html

PGP. (2015). *Pretty Good privacy (PGP).* Retrieved from http://www.pgp.com

Qinghai, G. (2010). Recent Developments on Applying Biometrics in Cryptography. *Journal of Applied Security Research, 5*(1), 107–137. doi:10.1080/19361610903176328

Ramesdell, B. (2004a). *Secure/Multipurpose Internet Mail Extensions (S/MIME) Version 3.1 message specification.* Internet Engineering Task Force (IETF), RFC 3851.

Ramesdell, B. (2004b). *Secure/Multipurpose Internet Mail Extensions (S/MIME) Version 3.1 Certificate Handling.* Internet Engineering Task Force (IETF), RFC 3850.

Regev, O. (2005). On lattices, learning with errors, random linear codes, and cryptography. In *Proceedings of STOC* (pp. 84–93). STOC.

RIPE. (1995). *Integrity Primitives for Secure Information Systems. Final Report of RACE Integrity Primitives Evaluation (RIPE-RACE 1040), LNCS, 1007.* Springer-Verlag.

Rivest, R. (1992). *The MD5 Message-Digest Algorithm.* IETF RFC 1321, Retrieved from http://www.ietf.org/rfc/rfc1321.txt

Rivest, R. L., Adleman, L., & Dertouzos, M. L. (1978). On data banks and privacy homomorphisms. In Foundations of Secure Computation.

RSA. (2002). *RSA Cryptography Standard.* RSA Security Inc. Retrieved from ftp://ftp.rsasecurity.com/pub/pkcs/pkcs-1/pkcs-1v2-1.pdf

Sahai, A., & Waters, B. (2005). Fuzzy identity-based encryption. In Advances in Cryptology—EUROCRYPT 2005 (pp. 457–473). Springer. doi:10.1007/11426639_27

Schneier, B. (1996). Applied Cryptography: Protocols, Algorithms, and Source Code in C (2nd ed.). John Wiley & Sons, Inc.

SEAL. (1998). *Digital Signature And Electronic Authentication Law*. Retrieved from http://thomas.loc. gov/cgi-bin/query/z?c105:H.R.3472.IH

SecurityWeek. (2013). Retrieved from http://www.securityweek.com/opera-software-hit-infrastructure-attack-malware-signed-stolen-cert

SHA. (1995). *Federal Information Processing Standards Publication 180-1*. Retrieved from http://www. itl.nist.gov/fipspubs/fip180-1.htm

Shor, P. W. (1995). *Polynomial-Time Algorithms for Prime Factorization and Discrete Logarithms on a Quantum Computer*. arXiv:quant-ph/9508027, Retrieved from http://arxiv.org/abs/quant-ph/9508027

SIGNiX. (2014). Retrieved from http://www.signix.com/

Sodium (2013). *Sodium*. Retrieved from http://labs.opendns.com/2013/03/06/announcing-sodium-a-new-cryptographic-library

Song, D. X., Wagner, D., & Perrig, A. (2000). Practical techniques for searches on encrypted data. In *Proceedings of the IEEE Symposium on Security and Privacy* (pp. 44–55). IEEE.

Soni, R., & Johar, A. (2012). An encryption algorithm for image based on DNA sequence addition operation. *World Journal of Science and Technology*, 2(3), 67–69.

Tan, S. Y., Yau, W. C., & Lim, B. H. (2014). An implementation of enhanced public key infrastructure. *Multimedia Tools and Applications*. doi:10.1007/s11042-014-2119-7

Tatiana, H., Mircea-Florin, V., Monica, B., & Cosmin, S. (2008). A java crypto implementation of DNAProvider featuring complexity in theory and practice. In *Proceedings of 30th International Conference on Information Technology Interfaces*. Dubrovnik, Croatia. doi:10.1109/ITI.2008.4588479

ThreatPost. (2015). Retrieved from http://threatpost.com/final-report-diginotar-hack-shows-total-compromise-ca-servers-103112/77170

Tomko, G. J., Soutar, C., & Schmidt, G. J. (1996). *Fingerprint controlled public key cryptographic system*. U.S. Patent 5541994, July 30, 1996 (Filing date: Sept. 7, 1994).

TrendMicro. (2014). Retrieved from http://blog.trendmicro.com/fake-antivirus-solutions-increasingly-stolen-code-signing-certificates/

Tripathi, S. P. N., Jaiswal, M., & Singh, V. (2013). Securing DNA Information through Public Key Cryptography. *MIS Review*, 19(1), 45–59.

Tsutomu, M., Tadahiro, S., & Keisuke, I. (2007). *Time stamping system for electronic documents and program medium for the same*. US Patent No. 7266698, Retrieved from http://www.patentgenius.com/patent/7266698.html

UCC. (2010). *The Uniform Commercial Code*. Retrieved from http://www.law.cornell.edu/ucc

UECA. (2003). *Uniform Electronic Commerce Act*. Retrieved from http://gcis.nat.gov.tw/eclaw/english/PDF/UniformElectronicCommerceAct.pdf

UETA. (1999). *Uniform Electronic Transactions Act.* Retrieved from http://euro.ecom.cmu.edu/program/law/08-732/Transactions/ueta.pdf

UNCITRA. (2001). *UNCITRAL Model Law on Electronic Signatures with Guide to Enactment.* United Nations Publication, Sales No. E.02.V.8. Retrieved from http://www.uncitral.org/pdf/english/texts/electcom/ml-elecsig-e.pdf

USDA. (2000). *USDA EIA (Coggins) Testing.* Retrieved from http://207.57.99.197/legislation/paeia.htm

VeriSign. (2015). Retrieved from http://www.verisigninc.com

Wasiewicz, P., Mulawka, J. J., Rudnichi, W. R., & Lesyng, B. (2000). Adding numbers with DNA. In *Proceedings of 2000 IEEE International Conference on Systems, Man and Cybernetics.* Nashville, TN: IEEE. doi:10.1109/ICSMC.2000.885000

Waters, B. (2013). Functional encryption: origins and recent developments. In Public-Key Cryptography—PKC 2013 (pp. 51–54). Springer. doi:10.1007/978-3-642-36362-7_4

Whiten, A., & Tygar, J. (1999). Why Jonny can't Encrypt: A usability evaluation of PGP 5.0. In *Proceedings of 8th USENIX Security System.* Retrieved from http://www.ieee-security.org/Cipher/PastIssues/1999/issue9911/issue9911.txt

Wolf, C., & Preneel, B. (2005). *Taxonomy of public key schemes based on the problem of multivariate quadratic equations.* Retrieved from http://eprint.iacr.org/2005/077/

XCA. (2014). *X Certificate and Key Management.* Retrieved from http://xca.sourceforge.net/

Zeng, G., & Keitel, C. H. (2002). Arbitrated quantum-signature scheme. *Physical Review A., 65*(4), 042312. doi:10.1103/PhysRevA.65.042312

Zhang, Z., Zeng, G., Zhou, N., & Xiong, J. (2006). Quantum identity authentication based on ping-pong technique for photons. *Physics Letters. [Part A], 356*(3), 199–205. doi:10.1016/j.physleta.2006.03.048

Zheng, Y., Imai, H., & Imai, H. (Eds.). (2007). Public Key Cryptography. Springer.

Zhou, R. L. I. W., & Huan, T. (2014). Quantum Identity Authentication and Digital Signature through Quantum Digital Certificate. *Journal of Computer Information Systems, 10*(10), 4425–4432.

KEY TERMS AND DEFINITIONS

Cryptosystem: A computing system that implements one or more specific encryption algorithms.

Digital Signature Certificate: Digital Signature Certificates are Digital Signatures that have themselves been signed using the Digital Signature of some trusted authority, thus creating a chain of authentications.

Digital Signature: An electronic, encrypted, stamp of authentication on digital information such as e-mail messages, macros, or electronic documents. A signature confirms that the information has originated from the signer and it has not been altered.

Encryption: The process of encoding a plain text message so that it cannot be understood by intermediate parties who do not know the key to decrypt it.

Hashing: The process to compute a small and fixed length message digest also called fingerprint, hash, or message abstract from a bit string of arbitrary length to ensure faster signing.

Public Key Infrastructure: The facilitation comprising of certification authorities, registration authorities, certificate databases, certificate stores and key archival servers that implement Public Key Encryption using Asymmetric Key Pair (Public Key and Private Key) from which one key is used for encryption and the other is used for decryption.

Time Stamping: A process of associating date and time with a digital document in a cryptographically strong way to support assertions of proof that a datum existed before a particular time.

Chapter 8
Cryptomodules in Wireless Networks Using Biometric Authentication:
Securing Nodes in Wireless Networks

Martin Drahanský
Brno University of Technology, Czech Republic

Martin Henzl
Brno University of Technology, Czech Republic

Petr Hanáček
Brno University of Technology, Czech Republic

František V. Zbořil
Brno University of Technology, Czech Republic

František Zbořil
Brno University of Technology, Czech Republic

Jaegeol Yim
Dongguk University at Gyeongju Gyeongbuk, South Korea

Kyubark Shim
Dongguk University at Gyeongju Gyeongbuk, South Korea

ABSTRACT

This chapter shows how cryptomodules can increase security of wireless sensor network and possibilities of biometric authentication against a node or the whole network. For secure operation of a wireless sensor network, security objectives such as confidentiality, integrity, and authentication must be implemented. These security objectives typically employ cryptography, therefore sensor nodes should be able to compute cryptographic algorithms and provide secure tamper-resistant storage for cryptographic keys. Use of dedicated secure hardware for this purpose and security threats are discussed. Two scenarios where the biometric authentication would be appreciated are introduced – smart home and storehouse with medicaments. Biometric generation of cryptographic keys, biometric authentication in wireless network and possible attacks on biometrics are presented. When designing and verifying communication protocols using informal techniques, some security errors may remain undetected. Formal verification methods that provide a systematic way of finding protocol flaws are discussed.

DOI: 10.4018/978-1-4666-9426-2.ch008

INTRODUCTION

The wireless networks are well known conception for various solutions, not only in academic (research) area, but are very often used in industrial solutions. However, their use in industrial solutions opens two very important questions – how we can secure the communication within the wireless network and how we can determine whether there is any possibility of authentication against a node or the whole wireless sensor network (WSN). The answers to these questions might be found in this chapter.

As an example we can take two different industrial solutions that can be used for wireless networks could be installed – see the following two subsections. In both cases, the above mentioned questions can be addressed, because they play a very important role in the whole process.

Smart Home Example

The first case could be a smart home (household) – the sensors collect information about various parts of the house and send it into the main central unit, where this data is processed and the commands are sent to actuators, which influence the actual situation of the house. Anyway the communication among wireless nodes has to be enciphered, because an attacker could corrupt the data exchanged among the units and this could influence the behavior of the whole system, e.g. the attacker can evoke a false fire alarm, which could lead to the lower security of the house in the expectation of arrival of firefighter, who has to get the access to the burning zone. This security change could be misused by the attacker to get into the house without big troubles. Another part of this topic is authentication of the house residents to the system that they will get the access into the house and the selected parts of the household will be adjusted to the settings of the concrete user. Therefore a (preferably) biometric authentication to a wireless network node is requested.

As a good example, we can take the RF Touch product from the company ELKO EP[1]. This company provides intelligent electronic systems and solutions for a comfortable household control. RF Touch is the main control unit of the new wireless system generation called RF Control. How this unit and the entire system work and what are its capabilities will be described in this chapter, based on Kubát (2011).

This RF control system (Wang 2009) allows the user to control and maintain the entire building - from lights and sun-blinds, through heating system, to garage door and garden swimming pool. Every RF unit connected to some specific device like light switch or heating thermo regulator is communicating with the RF Touch control unit by a wireless protocol, so there is no need to damage the walls and strain new wires when installing the system. The RF units are mounted between the original switch and the device, so the function of the primary switch is preserved.

The heart of the system is the RF Touch control unit, which identifies all connected peripheries (based on their name and physical address) and keeps a list of them sorted in various categories based on the theme of their role in the system (e.g. lights or heating). This main unit (ELKO EP 2010) communicates with the peripheries (sometimes called actuators) and is responsible for all the actions taken in the system. These actions may be invoked either by the user himself (sending real-time commands from any control device connected) or triggered automatically depending on any behavior scheme programmed in the device.

The unit itself is manufactured in two versions (RF Control and RF Touch 2010). The first is a stand-alone type designed to be hung on a wall or laid on a table. It is powered by a 12V DC adapter (2,1mm jack) or by 85-230V AC supply voltage (push-in terminal on the back side). The second type should

Figure 1. Visualization of iNELS RF control

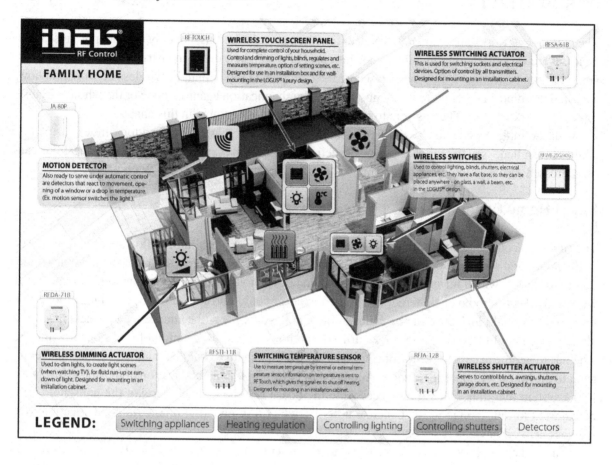

be installed to the wall electric box with a 230V AC supply voltage. The color of the unit can also be customized as well as the color and material of the outside frame. Communication between the main control unit and the other units (as was mentioned before) is realized via a wireless protocol. This is running on the frequency of 868.5 MHz and has a maximum active range of 200 meters – depending on the construction materials used in the building (the worst in this case is steel/metal, followed by rein-forced concrete). The graphical user interface is represented by a 3,5" touch screen with a resolution of 320×240 pixels and 262.144 colors, with an active white LED backlight. It is possible to check the state of all the connected units (sorted by their function or location) from this screen and send direct com-mands and control them by only a few taps. The interface also allows the user to update the connected device list, to rename the items and the main thing – to program their function and behavior (more in the next chapter). In the standby mode, the screen shows a big clock along with actual date and some more predefined information fields like inside/outside temperature, running heating program etc. In ad-dition, some more common tools like calendar, calculator or message-board can be displayed and used. Last interface included is a micro SD card reader, so the user can back up his programs, update the unit firmware or load some more GUI skins.

As it is mentioned above, there are various types of connected units in the RF Control system. These RF units can be thematically divided into five groups (ELKO EP 2010): heating, switching, lights, sun-blinds and detectors. Each of these categories has a little bit different control interface and also can be programmed in a different way. The heating group contains various thermal sensor and heat regulator units logically divided into rooms, so the system can keep the desired temperature in every room included. In the "initial" mode there are three schemes predefined – economic, common and party – each of them adjusted to a different temperature, which can be changed. Second mode is called "heating program", and allows the user to set different temperatures to every room, hour and day of the week. The third - "holiday" mode allows exceptions from the previous one for the case of uncommon situations.

Switching and lights groups are used to control lights and any other devices, which can be switched remotely (e.g. garden watering system). From the menu, the user can check the status of every switch and manually turn it on or off. There is also an option to set a time offset to specify the moment of the command execution. In addition, the programmable week calendar is also available.

When using light units with a dark fall effect, it is also possible to specify the desired brightness level and even the duration of the brightening / darkening effect. This can imitate the feeling of a sunrise or nightfall. Sun-blinds group contains all devices with the end position sensor like marquise or garage door. When initializing such devices, the correct time needed to move from one end position to the opposite one is measured. After that, the user is able to fully open / close the device or stop in any position between. The programmable week calendar is included as well. The last group of units are the detectors. These simple devices can be installed to the door or window frames, so the user can simply check whether it is closed or not. Another type of this sensor is a motion detector. All these units are supposed to be used together with other devices. For example such detector can turn on the alarm in case of an unauthorized intrusion.

There is one last programmable function in the RF Control system, which is called "the fast control" (Perrig et al. 2002). This feature unites various units from all the categories listed above in order to execute several commands by only one touch. For example in the "movie" scenario the sun-blinds are closed, the lights are darkened to some low level brightness level and the room temperature is slightly increased.

Last pieces of hardware in the RF Control system are additional remote controllers – there are two types of them (RF Control and RF Touch 2014). The first one is small and often paired with a single RF unit. This is called RF Key and for instance can be carried with the car key to open and close the garage door.

The second one is called RF Pilot. It is much bigger, has its own OLED display and a 4-way control button. This device partly doubles the main RF Touch control unit, so it can be placed in any room in the house to ensure even more comfortable control from any place the user needs.

Storehouse with Medicaments Example

The second industrial scenario is connected to the storehouse with medicaments. Some of the medicaments are liable to a special status, because they are only for recipes from medical doctors. It is not possible that any person working in the company is allowed to enter this restricted area. The access control to this area could be based on authentication of the user against the wireless network node. Only authorized employees of the company will get an access into this restricted area. Another problem connected to this restricted area arises – the wireless data transfer from this area has to be enciphered, because the attacker could detect and read the data about the stock state, i.e. how many medicament packages are stored there, what could be crucial information for burglars, who are interested in a concrete group of medicaments.

Figure 2. Example of a storehouse with medicaments, incl. restricted area

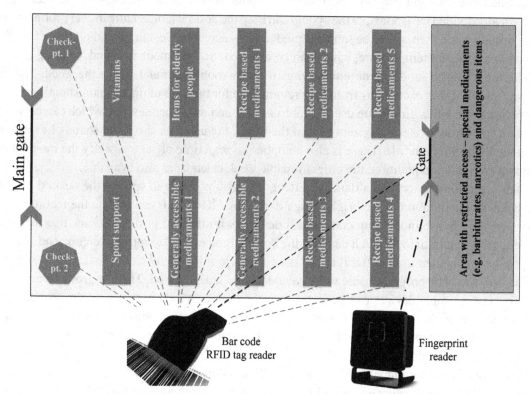

One example is shown in Figure 2. There is a store with medical material. The access is through the main gate. Two check points are in the corners – these are used for checking of incoming and outgoing medical material. The checking is done by the use of bar codes and/or RFID tags, as well as the reading of separate items in the racks. At the end of the storehouse there is an area with the restricted access. This access control is done by a biometric system (e.g. based on fingerprint recognition). All the data are transferred using wireless network to the main server. The security is necessary – the whole communication has to be enciphered, incl. the fingerprint reader.

COMMUNICATION IN SENSOR NETWORK

Sensor network systems are usually based on technologies that have been developed for ad-hoc network with nodes of critically limited sources of energy. Structure of such system is divided into cluster where a cluster head node for each cluster is responsible to collect data from cluster nodes and to manipulate with them. It means that they make data aggregation, pass forward to the base station and manage the cluster structure. The communication in these systems is usually based on protocols from the ZigBee protocol family that includes 802.15.4 protocol on its physical and mac layers and ZigBee protocol on the network layer. At the link layer, level communication within WSN is performed by sending short messages among nodes. Specification of these protocols omits transport layers and a way how to transport messages from one point to another is left to the application developers. It is important to understand that WSN systems are focused onto data centric instead of address centric which means that it is not important to address one concrete station by its address but to find correct data in the system. At the present time there exist several ways how to manage communication at higher levels. Usually there is the possibility to forward messages from base stations toward final nodes, as it is done in XMesh (XMesh User's Manual 2007) system for CrossBow family of wireless sensor nodes.

In some systems with hybrid structure, it is needed to transport data between concrete nodes that may be (but do not need to be) a part of sensor system. A way how to create such communication is to adopt sensors as a part of Internet of Things, where each node in the system is understood as a device with its own IP address that may be addressed within the system. Systems, where are present systems having significant energy constraint and are also of unstable structure, are also referred as Low-Power and Lossy (LL) systems. The recent popular tool for implementation of Internet of things is Contiki (Dunkels et al. 2004). Contiki is a system that enables to implement parallel and event driven tasks called Protothreads that may share data and communicate among themselves by signal passing.

Data Transfer in WSN

To enable the communication inside the WSN, Contiki provides either ZigBee stack implementation for pure WSN systems or also IP protocols for realization of communication in the Internet manner. There has been implemented TCP/IP stack in its lighted version, which is named µIP (micro IP) as well as stack for IPv6 protocols as 6LoWPAN (De Couto et al. 2003) stack. With these protocol stacks there are new layers upon 802.15.4 physical and link layers that enable data transmission between a pair of nodes.

The network layer of the µIP stack uses RPL routing algorithm (Vasseur et al. 2011). With this algorithm data may be routed from a device that is registered in the system to a destination or root node. Because of limited resources and loss network structure, routing is done toward a station with referred address on the bases of Destination Oriented Directed Acyclic Graph (DODAG) with one DAG root node. Each node holds a rank number which represents a heuristic to the root node. It may be based on the expected Transmission (ETX) (De Couto et al. 2003) which represents supposed distance from the node to the DODAG root node, but there could be more metrics that take into account, e.g., communication links, remaining energy on the nodes and so on. In WSN systems it is useful to alter routing paths because nodes which are closer to root nodes may be exhausted sooner than others. More DODAG for one destination node may exist in the system.

When a node tries to joins the system it obtains the information about distance to root from its parent node and then it may compute its own rank number. The RPN protocol is constructed in such a way that it may react to changes in network structures via control messages.

For the purposes of this text we consider a system where a pair of devices provides some services and needs to deliver messages point to point. Then there exist two DODAG's which have the first or the second device as their roots. Upon this µIP is able to establish TCP or UDP connection in the system and to transfer data from one node to another. In our case we will study the possibility to send commands as messages from one point to another. We may be satisfied with UDP transport for a system where commands from smart cards are sent to or from another node in the system. If we are happy with UDP we may take CoAP (Constraint Application Protocol) (Colitti et al. 2011) and use it as a protocol on the application layer of the protocol stack. CoAP addresses individual entities in the system by their URL (Unifier Resource Locator) and allows sending messages in HTTP manner, i.e. that it is possible to use commands like GET, PUT or POST.

Security in ZigBee and µIP Based Communication

The ZigBee and Contiki (Colitti et al. 2011) architectures also include a security module. Their main task is to maintain and distribute keys for secure communication and also to authorize a new device onto the network. The stack architecture is shown in Figure 3. In general, the main secure objective is to avoid threads to WSN systems. Countermeasures do authentication of new nodes and securing communication within the system. Identification and authentication of a node that wants to join the system prevents the network from malicious nodes that may have harmful intentions to one or more parts of this one. The recent systems offer some security solutions. TinyOS system has itself TinySEC system (Shelby & Bormann 2009), Contiky has ContikySEC (Lowe & Casper 1998) inspired by the TinySEC system and offers a security of networking in. The CoAP protocols use similar security mechanism like HTTP, to be concrete datagram security at the transport layer called DTLS.

SECURE HARDWARE IN WIRELESS NETWORK NODES

There are many applications of wireless sensor networks with various security requirements, from simple measurements with no impact on safety or assets, to very security sensitive applications, where health and safety of people are exposed. Sensor nodes are usually scattered in a hostile environment, so the adversary can gain access to them. To ensure secure operation of a wireless sensor network, security

Figure 3. The stack architecture

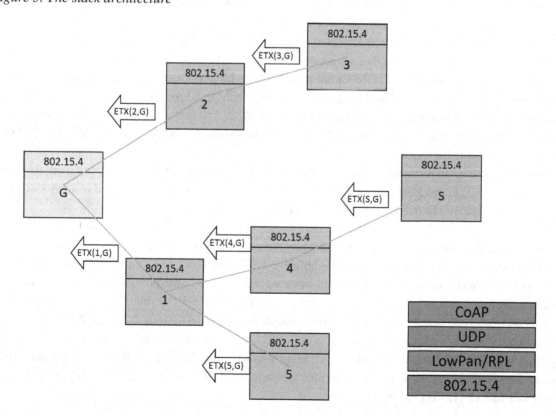

objectives such as confidentiality, integrity, and authentication must be implemented. These security objectives typically employ cryptography, therefore sensor nodes should be able to compute cryptographic algorithms and provide secure tamper-resistant storage for cryptographic keys.

Current most widely used sensor node platforms are not equipped with any specialized hardware dedicated to cryptographic operations. Conventional hardware with general purpose CPU is usually used, restricting the cryptography only to software implementations. There are libraries providing cryptographic algorithms and secure protocols, which can be used. This approach is the least expensive; however, the computation is slow and the data storage is not tamper-resistant.

More secure approach is using a secure hardware in the sensor node. The secure hardware implements cryptographic algorithms, so the execution of computationally intensive cryptography can be delegated to this chip from the general purpose CPU. Sensitive data such as cryptographic keys can be stored in secure hardware, which is a tamper-resistant device. Secure hardware properties are specified in the U.S. government computer security standard FIPS 140-2 named Security Requirements for Cryptographic Modules, which defines four levels of physical security and three types of secure hardware realizations, each of them fulfilling different security requirements: a single-chip cryptographic module, multiple-chip embedded cryptographic module, and multiple-chip standalone cryptographic module.

Cryptography in Sensor Nodes

Cryptographic algorithms are usually computationally intensive; however, sensor nodes do not provide much computational power because they are designed to be as energy efficient as possible. New more efficient cipher algorithms are therefore implemented in order to save energy, but these algorithms are usually not as secure as standard algorithms. It is a tradeoff between security and efficiency. Sensor nodes usually use symmetric cryptography rather than asymmetric, because symmetric algorithms are less computationally intensive and use shorter keys. Shorter signatures used in symmetric cryptography are also more efficient to be transmitted between nodes. The most efficient algorithms seem to be Elliptic curve cryptography (ECC) algorithms; however, patents are limiting the massive spread of these algorithms in devices.

Agent platforms are usually based on a conventional hardware with no hardware or software cryptographic support. Cryptographic abilities of such platforms could be improved in several ways:

- Cryptography algorithms could be implemented into the firmware of sensor node. This least expensive solution provides usually only the private key cryptography at low speed. Performance of this cryptography could be sufficient for simple applications. Security of stored cryptographic keys is usually very low.
- Sensor nodes could be extended with an auxiliary microprocessor(s) implemented parallel computing of the cryptographic algorithms. Performance and security of this solution depends on auxiliary microprocessor(s).
- Sensor nodes could be improved by an add-on secure microcontroller with secure memory and hardware crypto engine sup-porting AES and 3DES encryption standards. The encryption engine increase encrypted communication speed up to several Mbps. Regrettably, the current crypto-accelerators, suitable for sensor networks, usually have no support for public key cryptography.

Figure 4. Smart-card structure (Tiresias 2011); Typical smart-card contacts (SmartCardsBasis 2011)

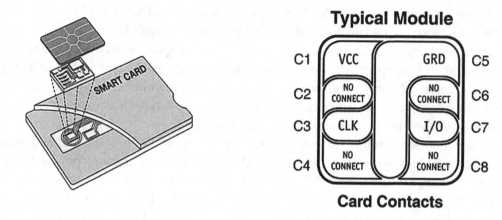

- Sensor node could be extended with an FPGA module implementing fast symmetric and asymmetric cryptography algorithms. This solution offers high speed encryption and key generation at a highest price and power consumption (depends on FPGA module).
- Smart cards (Figure 4), as the tamper resistant devices, could be used as crypto accelerators and also as a secure storage for cryptographic keys. These crypto-accelerators ordinarily support symmetric and asymmetric cryptography together with low power consumption. Smart card consumption can be also decreased powering them up only for cryptographic operations. Furthermore, cost of high-end smart cards is lower than cost of the same feature crypto-processors and FPGAs.

Hardware for Cryptography Acceleration

Sensor nodes may use the following hardware extensions to improve functionality and performance (Oracle Corporation 2014):

- Additional microcontroller can be dedicated to cryptographic algorithms computation. Performance depends on the particular microcontroller. Standard microcontrollers are not tamper-resistant and do not provide secure memory.
- Additional secure microcontroller with secure memory can be used for cryptography acceleration. Current crypto accelerators suitable for sensor nodes support only symmetric cryptography algorithms such as AES or 3DES and lack support for asymmetric cryptography.
- FPGA can be used to implement fast symmetric and asymmetric cryptography algorithms. The high speed of computation is, however, compensated with high price and high power consumption.
- Smart cards can be used for cryptography acceleration and also as a secure storage, because smart cards are tamper-resistant hardware. Smart Cards usually support symmetric and asymmetric cryptography. The other advantage of smart cards is the low power consumption.
- Smart Cards provide good performance and security for the same or lower price than other low-power microcontrollers. Some cryptographic microcontrollers have security vulnerabilities, while smart cards, as a tamper-resistant hardware, are proved to be highly secure by using in applications where high security is necessary for many years. Smart cards are used in banking, as SIM cards,

ID cards, electronic passports, etc. Because of the large number of smart cards being produced for various applications, the cost is quite low.

Smart Card

Smart card is a plastic card equipped with a chip. Some smart cards are simple memory cards, other are microprocessor cards offering general computational capabilities. From the security perspective, the most interesting type of smart cards is the cryptographic smart card, providing cryptographic algorithms and secure data storage. Such smart cards can be used for identification, authentication, data storage and application processing. The provided functionality may be used in a non-typical way to accelerate cryptographic operations in low-power devices.

Java Card technology (Oracle Corporation 2014) is a good candidate for implementation in sensor nodes. These cards allow executing Java applications called Java Card applets, and provide secure separation between multiple applets on the card. Java Cards support symmetric cryptography algorithms DES and AES, asymmetric cryptography algorithms RSA, DSA, ECC, and hash functions such as MD5 and SHA1. This functionality makes these cards good candidates for using in highly secured applications to perform hardware acceleration of cryptography.

Hardware Realization and Power Consumption Analysis

The sensor node can be realized using common sensor node hardware and a smart card (Pecho 2009). Connection between the sensor node and the smart card in this solution is performed via serial interface. Some modifications to the source code of UART interface in TinyOS were made in order to enable the communication with the smart card, no hardware modifications were needed. The experiments were made on MICAz platform, equipped with the ATMega128 processor, connected with Java card GemX-presso Pro R3 and GemXpresso R4. Figure 5 shows the scheme of the sensor node with smart card as the tamper-resistant module.

Figure 5. Scheme of connection between sensor node and smart card (Tobarra 2009)

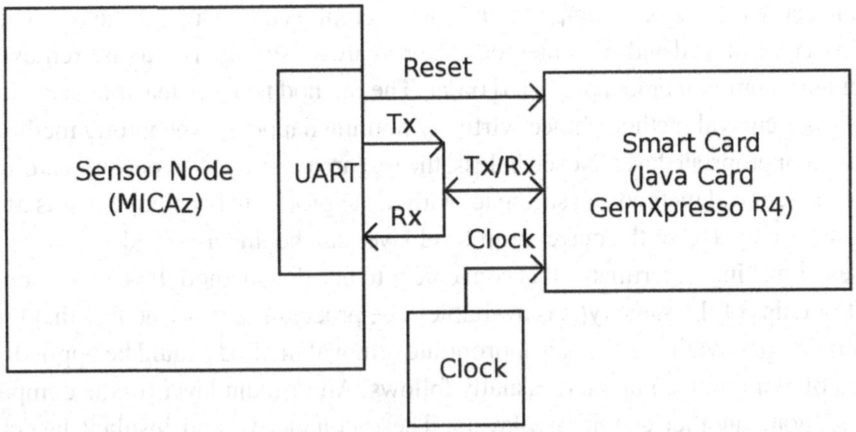

Power consumption measurements were made on RSA algorithm with four standard key lengths. The efficiency of RSA signature and encryption performed on smart card connected to the sensor node is much better compared to the software implementation executed in the node's processor. In case of RSA with 1,024-bit keys, the complexity and power consumption can be reduced up to 30 times. For 2,048-bit keys, the execution time can be reduced up to 88 times and power consumption up to 70 times (Pecho et al. 2009). The UART interface has significant impact on power consumption if large data are transferred.

Attack on the Chip in a Smart Card

Our previous work focused on the first phase of the whole analysis process (Malčík & Drahanský 2012) – the decapsulation process. The decapsulation process has been described in detail. In the case of interest to obtain chips from PCBs (*Printed Circuit Board*) or in the main decapsulation process, we recommend to read the paper (Malčík & Drahanský 2011 + Malčík & Drahanský 2012).

Currently, we are able to obtain bare chips from different types of plastic packages. Moreover, this chapter presents further steps in chips deprocessing and gaining of desired pictures of bare transistor layers. With such an ability we will go on working on the main analysis of the transistor layers.

Each modern chip is a composition of different layers with different functions. Layers are made of particular compounds with respect to the desired functionality. Using an ordinary grinder can result in a destruction of a processed specimen, because the layers are very thin and so it is sometimes very difficult to determine the correct time frame of grinding. In addition, it is also very difficult (and sometimes almost impossible with an ordinary lab grinder) to keep the whole chip surface in an absolutely same level to polish exactly the same amount of compound in each point of the surface to achieve the precise result.

Apart from using a grinder to remove the layers, there is a chemical way of removing particular layers. We would like to introduce two methods based on one chemical approach in the following text. Let us name the processes as a reduced process and a complete process. As the processes' names reveal, the reduced process can be understood as some kind of subset of the complete process.

Reduced Process

The reduced process jumps directly to the decomposition of the chip without any knowledge of its composition. This may seem to be inconvenient, however, for our purposes, it is mainly sufficient to apply this approach, because of a typical composition scheme employed by chip producers. This method can be considered as a type of trial and error method. The researcher simply tries to use removal methods for particular layers in a common or in a predicted order. The method is really feasible due to the fact that in the case of a wrong removal method choice, virtually nothing happens – the wrong method simply does not react with an inappropriate layer. Nevertheless, the researcher still has to be very careful, because the incorrectly chosen removal method can still react with the appropriate layer edge that is usually exposed on the border of the chip and so the current top level layer can be under-etched.

For purposes of making experiments it is convenient to use this method. It is also assumed that a sufficient amount of chips of the same type is available. The process relies on the fact that the first layer is usually some kind of passivation and so an appropriate removal method should be applied. A conductive layer composed of aluminum compounds usually follows. An insulant layer (oxide compounds) should be present to separate another conductive layers. These conductive and insulant layers then usually alternate down to the silicon layer. The mentioned approach can be used for many of the contemporary chips (we have successfully applied this reduced method to different RFID chips). For some chips it is necessary to experiment also with incorporating plasmatic etching or even with an absolutely different removal method at some point of the decomposition process because of the presence of a different layer type. It is strongly recommended to investigate the deprocessing results after each particular procedure to avoid any unwanted damage of the chip.

Complete Process

The complete process is recommended in the case of us not having a sufficient amount of the same type of chips, because it incorporates an analysis regarding the layers' composition. For this analysis it is necessary to have at least one specimen of the chip. At least another one piece is needed for the main deprocessing.

The complete process is usually recommended for situations when a precise decomposition is necessary in the first attempt of the deprocessing. As mentioned earlier in this chapter, it is needed to have at least two specimens – the first one has to be sacrificed for the material composition analysis (cross-section analysis) of particular layers and the second one can be then deprocessed according to the information gained from the first step.

- **Cross-Section Analysis:** Let us assume that a bare chip is available for further steps. A suitable grinder is needed for making a specimen cross-section. It is not necessary to have a specific type of a grinder, but it is rather important to be able to obtain the chip cross-section.

After the cross-section has been made, the next step is to employ one of the spectrometric techniques to acquire the elements' composition. For example an electron microscope equipped with an X-ray detector can provide such information. Afterwards, a precise deprocessing procedure can be prepared according to the composition and thickness of each layer. This can obviously result in a very precise scheme of the main decomposition.

- **The Main Deprocessing:** With the outcome of the cross-section analysis, an exact sequence of particular steps can be performed in order to get the coveted deprocessed chip. The form of the whole process naturally depends on our objectives. Usually, a picture of bare transistors is desired, however, it is not a rule. Therefore, the process can be sometimes completely different, e.g. just to get rid of the first passivation layer or to obtain pictures of all conductive layers, etc.

Common Layers Deprocessing

The decomposition process usually consists of a specific sequence of particular steps. The most common layers and matching chemical procedure are described below. The correct combination of actions is naturally dependent on the chip type.

- **Passivation:** The very first layer is mostly a passivation. To remove this layer type, it is recommended to use plasmatic etching. The whole process takes about 45 minutes with our old plasmatic etcher TESLA 214 VT, but the actual plasmatic etching lasts only 4 minutes out of the mentioned time period (the length of plasmatic etching process depends on the type of plasmatic etcher and should be adjusted according to the particular machine performance). The rest of time is devoted to prepare conditions necessary for performing this procedure.

Figure 6. Two images of MIFARE class 1kB. The decapsulated chip without any application of decomposition (left). The same chip after several steps of deprocessing (right).

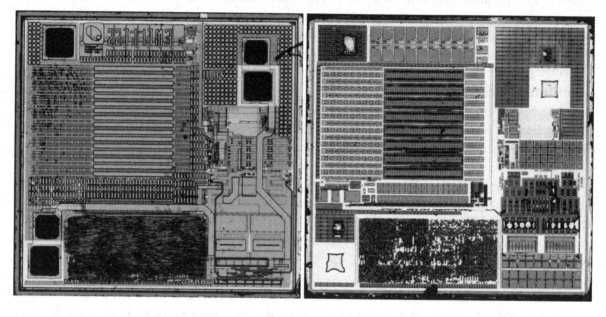

- **Aluminum Compounds:** Conductive layers made of aluminum compounds can be taken away by application of phosphoric acid etching mixture, PEWS 765-140-57-36 3. The recommended working temperature is 50°C, the common time of bath should be from 2 to 6 minutes.
- **Oxide Compounds:** A special chemical mixture is available also for removing oxide compounds. Precisely, the mixture consists of ammonium fluoride and hydrofluoric acid in ratio 7:1. The working temperature is 30°C, the common time of bath should be from 2 to 6 minutes.

Summarization of Attack Possibilities on Smart Card Chip

Just to illustrate our research, let us introduce two figures. The first one depicts differences between decapsulated chip with a preserved passivation layer (see the left part of Figure 3) and the same specimen after five steps of decomposition process (see the right part of Figure 6) – 4 minutes of plasmatic etching (passivation); 4 minutes of etching – use of PEWS (aluminum compounds); 4 + 2 minutes of etching – use of ammonium fluoride and hydrofluoric acid in ratio 7:1 (oxide compounds); 5 minutes of etching – use of PEWS (aluminum compounds); 3 minutes of plasmatic etching (removing the last layer above transistors).

The second picture shows the final result of our effort – bare transistors prepared for the analysis (see Figure 7). It is obvious that the image quality is not ideal, because of limitations of optical microscopy. We intend to use an electron microscope for the future work. This will assure sufficient image quality.

Figure 7. The detail of an RFID tag – bare transistors can be recognised. This image was acquired by optical microscope Olympus BX61 with insufficient magnification abilities; our intention is to use an electron microscope to obtain better quality images for analysis.

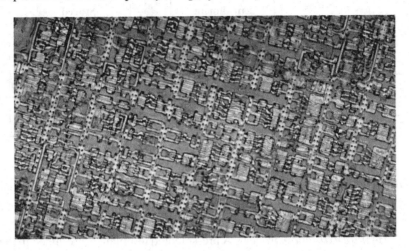

BIOMETRIC GENERATION OF CRYPTOGRAPHIC KEYS

The functionality of biometric systems based on fingerprint recognition is influenced not only by the used technology, but also by the surrounding environment (including skin or other diseases). Biased or damaged biometric samples could be rejected after revealing their poor quality, or may be enhanced, what leads to the situation that samples, which would be normally rejected, are accepted after the enhancement process. But this process could present also a risk, because the poor quality of a sample could be caused not only by the sensor technology or the environment, but also by using an artificial biometric attribute (imitation of a finger(print)). Such risk is not limited just to the deceptional technique, but if we are not able to recognize whether an acquired biometric sample originates from a genuine living user or an impostor, we would then scan an artificial fake and try to enhance its quality using an enhancement algorithm. After a successful completion of such enhancement, such fake fingerprint would be compared with a template and if a match is found, the user is accepted, notwithstanding the fact that he can be an impostor! Therefore the need of careful liveness detection, i.e. the recognition whether an acquired biometric sample comes from a genuine living user or not, is crucial.

Attack on Biometric Systems

Each component of a biometric system presents a potentially vulnerable part of such system. The typical ways of deceiving a biometric system are as follows (Figure 8) (Dessimoz et al. 2006, Jain 2005, Ambalakat 2005, Galbally et al. 2007):

Placing fake biometrics on the sensor. A real biometric representation is placed on the device with the aim to achieve the authentication, but if such representation has been obtained in an unauthorized manner, such as making a fake gummy finger, an iris printout or a face mask, then it is considered as a deceiving activity.

Figure 8. Basic components of a biometric system

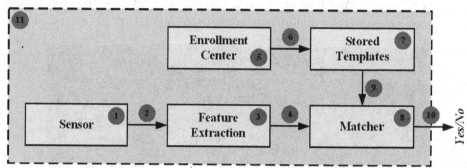

1. *Resubmitting previously stored digitized biometric signals (replay attack).* A digitized biometric signal, which has been previously enrolled and stored in the database, is replayed to the system, thus circumventing the acquisition device.

2. *Overriding the feature extraction process.* A pre-selected template is produced in the feature extraction module using a Trojan horse.

3. *Tampering with the biometric feature representation.* During the transmission between the feature extraction and matching modules, a fraudulent feature set replaces the template acquired and processed by the device.

4. *Attacking the enrollment center.* The enrollment module is also vulnerable to spoof attacks such as those described in the previous points 1 to 4.

5. *Attacking the channel between the enrollment center and the database.* During the transmission, a fraudulent template replaces the template produced during the enrollment.

6. *Tampering with stored templates.* A template, previously stored in the database (distributed or not), can be modified and used afterward as corrupted template.

7. *Corrupting the matcher.* A pre-selected score is produced in the matching extraction module using a Trojan horse.

8. *Attacking the channel between the stored templates and the matcher.* During the transmission between the database and the matching module, a fraudulent template replaces the template previously stored.

9. *Overriding the final decision.* The result of the decision module can be modified and then used for the replacement of the output obtained previously.

10. *Attacking the application.* The software application can also be a point of attack and all possible security systems should be used to reduce the vulnerability at this level.

From the above list of possible attacks we can deduce that most security risks or threats are quite common and could be therefore resolved by traditional cryptographic tools (i.e. encryption, digital signatures, PKI (Public Key Infrastructure) authentication of communicating devices, access control, hash functions etc.) or by having vulnerable parts at a secure location, in tamper-resistant enclosure or under constant human supervision (Kluz 2005).

When a legitimate user has already registered his finger in a fingerprint system, there are still several ways how to deceive the system. In order to deceive the fingerprint system, an attacker may put the following objects on the fingerprint scanner (Matsumoto et al. 2005, Ambalakat 2005, Roberts 2006):

- *Registered (enrolled) finger.* The highest risk is that a legitimate user is forced, e.g. by an armed criminal, to put his/her live finger on the scanner under duress. Another risk is that a legitimate user is compelled to fall asleep with a sleeping drug in order to make free use of his/her live finger. There are some deterrent techniques against similar crimes, e.g. to combine the standard fingerprint authentication with another method such as a synchronized use of PINs or identification cards; this can be helpful to deter such crimes.

- *Unregistered finger (an impostor's finger).* An attack against authentication systems by an impostor with his/her own biometrics is referred to as a non-effort forgery. Commonly, the accuracy of authentication of fingerprint systems is evaluated by the false rejection rate (FRR) and false acceptance rate (FAR) as mentioned in the previous chapters. FAR is an important indicator for the security against such method (because a not enrolled finger is used for authentication). Moreover, fingerprints are usually categorized into specific classes (Collins, 2001). If an attacker knows what class the enrolled finger is, then a not enrolled finger with the same class (i.e. similar pattern) can be used for the authentication at the scanner. In this case, however, the probability of acceptance may be different when compared with the ordinary FAR.

- *Severed fingertip of enrolled finger.* A horrible attack may be performed with the finger severed from the hand of a legitimate user. Even if it is the finger severed from the user's half-decomposed corpse, the attacker may use, for criminal purposes, a scientific crime detection technique to clarify (and/or enhance) its fingerprint.

- *Genetic clone of enrolled finger.* In general, it can be stated that identical twins do not have the same fingerprint, and the same would be true for clones (Matsumoto et al., 2005). The reason is that fingerprints are not entirely determined genetically but rather by the pattern of nerve growth in the skin. As a result, such pattern is not exactly the same even for identical twins. However, it can be also stated that fingerprints are different in identical twins, but only slightly different. If the genetic clone's fingerprint is similar to the enrolled finger, an attacker may try to deceive fingerprint systems by using it.

- *Artificial clone of enrolled finger.* More likely attacks against fingerprint systems may use an artificial finger. An artificial finger can be produced from a printed fingerprint made by a copy machine or a DTP technique in the same way as forged documents. If an attacker can make then a mold of the enrolled finger by directly modeling it, he can finally also make an artificial finger from a suitable material. He may also make a mold of the enrolled finger by making a 3D model based on its residual fingerprint. However, if an attacker can make an artificial finger which can deceive a fingerprint system, one of the countermeasures against such attack is obviously based on the detection of liveness.

- *Others.* In some fingerprint systems, an error in authentication may be caused by making noise or flashing a light against the fingerprint scanner, or by heating up, cooling down, humidifying, impacting on, or vibrating the scanner outside its environmental tolerances. Some attackers may use such error to deceive the system. This method is well known as a "fault based attack" (e.g. denial of service), and may be carried out by using one of the above mentioned techniques. Furthermore, a fingerprint image may be made protruding as an embossment on the scanner surface, if we spray some special material on such surface.

It is clear from (Matsumoto 2005) that the production of a fake finger(print) is very simple (Drahanský 2010b). Our own experiments have shown that to acquire some images (e.g. from glass, CD, film or even paper) is not very difficult and, in addition, such image could be enhanced and post-processed, what leads to a high-quality fingerprint. The following production process of a fake finger(print) is simple and can be accomplished in several hours. After that, it is possible to claim the identity as an impostor user and common (nearly all) fingerprint recognition systems confirm this false identity supported by such fake finger.

Therefore, the application of liveness detection methods is a very important task, and should be implemented (not only) in all systems with higher security requirements, such as border passport control systems, bank systems etc. The biometric systems without the liveness detection could be fooled very easily and the consequences might be fatal.

The security of a biometric system should never be based on the fact that biometric measurements are secret, because biometric data can be easily disclosed. Unlike typical cryptographic measures where a standard challenge–response protocol can be used, the security of a biometric system relies on the difficulty of replicating biometric samples (Kluz 2005). This quality known as the liveness ensures that the measured characteristics come from a live human being and are captured at the time of verification. We should realize that any testing of liveness is worthless unless the capture device and communication links are secure. Due to the fact that a biometric system uses physiological or behavioral biometric information, it is impossible to prove formally that a capture device provides only genuine measurements. Consequently, it cannot be proven that a biometric system as a whole is fool-proof (Kluz 2005). Each solution of this problem has its own advantages and disadvantages; it is more suitable for a certain particular type of the biometric system and environment than for other. Some solutions are software-based; other require a hardware support. Methods which combine both approaches can also be used.

Generation of a Cryptographic Key Using Biometrics

Like many other technologies, the biometric systems have some advantages and disadvantages. It is usual and it is necessary to ask some important questions before a biometric system is applied. The questions can be as follows:

- Which object is to be protected?
- How valuable is the protected object?
- Where should be the biometric system installed?
- How strong should be the protection?
- Will the biometric system pay off?

Of course, another problem is the biometric data security. The questions relating to data security can be e.g. as follows (Jain 2005):

- Whom I give my biometric information to? (for driving license, passport, registration for e-voting or bank transactions, for access to a company area or runway)
- Could my biometric data be released freely from the database to all ranges of usage?
- How can I protect the templates in my smart card or in my passport?

Figure 9. Three main phases of the biometric security system (key generation) (Drahanský 2010b)

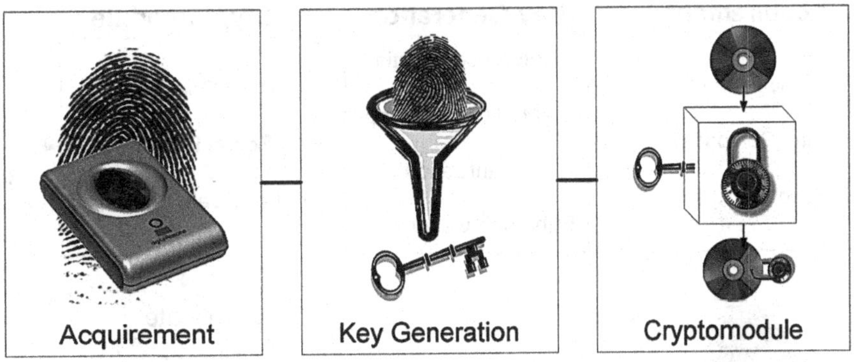

| Acquirement | Key Generation | Cryptomodule |

The above mentioned aspects (pros and cons + data security) have to be considered when designing a biometric system.

The biometric security system consists of a general biometric system (based on fingerprints in our case) and a general cryptographic system. A new special step, an art of pipe through both systems, has been developed and tested. This connecting step corresponds to the key generation from the fingerprint. The biometric system ac-quires and processes biometric data (fingerprint images). Then a key is generated in an intermediate step and such key is delivered to the cryptographic module at the end. These three main steps are schematically shown in Figure 9.

Any biometric attribute can be used as the input biometric information, as it has been said in the general introduction of the Biometric Security System. The only requirement is the entropy power in the selected biometric attribute. If there is not enough entropy information, it is impossible to generate strong cryptographic keys, even if the process of key generation is realizable.

Besides, the individual phases shown in the Figure 9 can be described in a more detailed way (Drahanský 2010b). In the first phase, called *Acquirement*, not only fingerprint scanning, but also all image processing algorithms are applied with the aim to extract the minutiae from the fingerprint. The output of the first phase is the set of minutiae points with their characteristic information data (position, gradient and type). The second phase called *Key Generation* is dedicated to biometric key generation. The minutiae from the previous phase are taken as an input and some mathematical operations are done with them. These mathematical operations generate sub-vectors from the set of minutiae points and these sub-vectors can be considered as keys. Although it is not absolutely necessary to generate more sub-vectors, as a single vector representing the whole minutiae set would be theoretically sufficient, it is not recommendable to limit ourselves to such single vector. As the output of the second phase, the set of sub-vectors is processed by a cryptographic module. Well-tried cryptographic modules exist and therefore is not necessary to develop an own crypto-module. That is why some common cryptographic algorithm can be used, such as DES or 3DES (only symmetric cryptography is considered further).

In order to make it more complicated, the whole biometric security system must be divided into two separate concepts. The first one is the *Certificate Creation* concept, and the second one is the *Certificate Usage* concept. Both concepts have some common steps, but there are some differences in these two main parts of the biometric security system. Both concepts consist of the same phases as discussed above (i.e. Acquirement, Key Generation and Crypto-module). But the difference is visible in each phase, and indeed, the execution and handling modes are not identical. Let us describe both concepts of the biometric security system in a more detailed way.

Figure 10. Concept of certificate creation in the biometric security system (Drahanský 2010b)

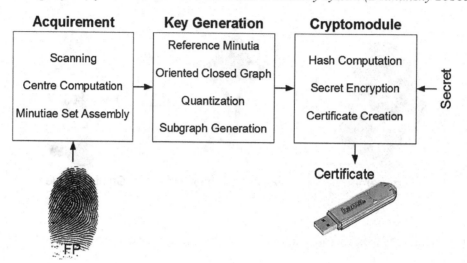

Certificate Creation Concept

In this concept, the certificate is generated, including appropriate biometric information – see Figure 10. The certificate could be based on the X.509 standard (Straub 2004, Santesson et al. 2004), but an own format of the certificate structure can also be used. The main idea is that the certificate should be generated only by that administrator who possesses the key pair of the certification authority. This guarantees that the whole process of key generation and storage of relevant information to the certificate will be successful and trustful. If the whole process is completed without problem and all steps of certificate generation are under control, then the content of the certificate can be signed first. The signed certificate guarantees the correctness of all items (name, organization, department, personal number, biometric data, etc.) and the fact that these items were saved under control by a trustworthy person. Such certificates can be used also in other areas and not only for private data protection, but this will be discussed later. It is important that this Certificate Creation is done only once. Since this creation is done by an administrator, the certificate does not need to be reloaded and naturally, there is no reason to generate the certificate several times, only if some part of the certificate is to be modified or when the certificate is no more valid. In such cases, a new certificate has to be created. The same biometric attribute can be used in other applications, as the biometric data are not saved (not even as a template) in the certificate and therefore cannot be compromised.

BIOMETRIC AUTHENTICATION IN WIRELESS NETWORK

The first question in authentication of the user against a wireless node is the selection of a suitable biometric characteristic, which is reliable, the acquirement and processing do not take a long time, the generated biometric template is not big etc. These all conditions/properties have to be considered, because some biometric characteristics generate a big template, which has to be sent via wireless connection, what can cause troubles. The template size plays an important role in storage of data in wireless nodes, because they have a limited data capacity due to decreased production costs. The best suitable biometric characteristics will be, e.g., fingerprint, eye iris, eye retina, 2D hand shape. 3D face, gait etc. have larger templates, i.e. they are not suitable for data exchange within the wireless network.

The best possibility how to distribute the biometric templates for verification (1:1 comparison) or identification (1:N comparison) could be either stored directly in the concrete authentication wireless node or could be sent via wireless transfer to this node from the central unit. The first case is suitable for small amount of registered users of the system, because the capacity of the node's memory is limited – e.g. this is the case of a flat or house, where only 1 family lives (incl. close relatives). On the other hand, a pharmaceutics company has generally many hundreds or thousands of employees, i.e. the storage of the whole database wouldn't be possible. If the database is stored in one concrete wireless node, it is done after the registration of the users. At the beginning the selected biometric characteristic of all accepted family members is acquired and registered into the biometric system. When all biometric characteristics from all expected users (after test verification that their biometric profile is without a failure) are stored in the database, this database is copied into the node (either using a cable connection or wireless connection (this is slower)), i.e. there does exist a duplicate of the biometric database from the central unit. Anyway the database in the authentication node is not updated in this case, this will be kept in that same status in which this was built at the beginning. If you want to add a new user, you have to repeat the upload of the whole database into the wireless node from the beginning. And there is another biometric risk in such solution – some biometrics need template averaging (if the user is successfully recognized and the access is granted to her/him, the biometric template will be updated (mixed) with new biometric data. The reason for it is altering of biometric data stored in biometric templates, therefore this step is very important (e.g. for keystroke dynamics, 2D/3D hand geometry). In such cases you can only update the local biometric template, but if there will be done any other change in the future, where the data will be copied from the central control unit, all the updated templates will be rewritten by new data, which could be altered. From these reasons, it is better to use the second principle of biometric data storage. The best way is to store only the mostly used data for, e.g., 5 till 10 users, who use the authentication to the concrete wireless node the most frequently. The chance that these users come to this concrete wireless node is very high, i.e. they do not need to wait till their biometric template will be sent from the central control unit and they could be authenticated immediately. All other users, who do not use this node so often, their biometric template has to be downloaded from the central control unit, i.e. it can take some time. After a successful data transfer, the comparison can start. The advantage by this solution is the adaptability to actual status of the authentication requirements and the averaged biometric template could be sent directly back to the central control unit, where this new data will be stored. Furthermore, this solution is the only one suitable for big companies, because it is not possible to store all the workers of the company and/or co-workers from other co-operation companies. On the other hand, in the case of authentication trial of a user, who does not use this concrete authentication wireless module very often, there is some delay in processing and the power consumption increases. It is appreciable that the whole data transfer in a wireless network has to be enciphered, because if the attacker can get access to the biometric template, it is generally not difficult to generate a synthetic biometric characteristic, which is based on minutiae or relevant features from such biometric characteristic, stolen during data transfer. The attack could be realized either by sending a synthetic data instead of actually acquired data, i.e. the biometric system would process a synthetic data. Very comparable situation could be achieved if this synthetic biometric characteristic will be produced in a form of a biometric fake. In such cases, there is not needed any access to the

Figure 11. Examples of biometric fakes (fingerprints)

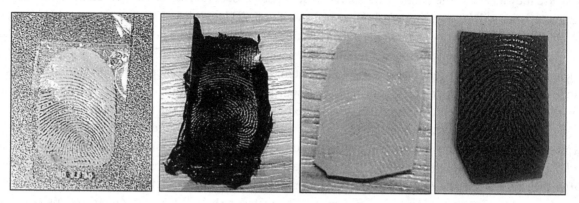

hardware that you input the synthetic data, but you can use the synthetic biometric fake for presenting at the sensor. In such cases the liveness detection for a biometric system is necessarily needed, because otherwise you cannot recognize the real biometric characteristic from a fake one. Some examples of biometric fakes (fingerprints are shown in Figure 11). Anyway the liveness detection has to deal with human diseases, because sometimes people suffer from some diseases (eye diseases for eye recognition, skin diseases for fingerprint recognition etc.), what is very difficult task.

FORMAL VERIFICATION

When designing and verifying security protocols using informal techniques, some security errors may remain undetected. Formal verification methods provide a systematic way of finding protocol flaws. The protocol is specified in a formal way and the correctness of security properties is proved or disproved using formal methods and mathematics. The most suitable formal verification technique for determining security properties of protocols is model checking. Model checking is used for verifying finite-state-concurrent systems by exploring all states and transitions in the model. It is fully automatic and provides trace that leads to the source of the error. Temporal logics such as linear temporal logic (LTL) or computational tree logic (CTL) are used to define properties which should be verified. The great downside of model checking is that it is only usable for models with relatively small number of states. The state explosion problem has to be addressed in most real-world problems.

Formal Verification Methods

Formal methods have been used in the security protocol analysis since the 1980s. Formal verification methods are used for proving security properties of protocols such as authentication, integrity, confidentiality and anonymity. Not only they tell us whether the protocol meets these properties but they can also find the counterexample. These counterexamples can be considered as possible attacks. Formal methods therefore provide us with the automated way of finding attacks and can also be used for proving that some attacks are not possible. Formal methods can be classified into three main categories:

- Theorem proving
- Model checking
- Formal logic

Theorem proving is a method using higher-order logic to reason about possible protocol executions by creating a convincing proof that a particular property always holds. These logics can be used in automated tools and proof checking and are not restricted by finite bounds. The theorem proving methods are based on various proof search strategies. Some inductive theorem provers are very time-consuming because they involve interactive theorem proving by experts.

Model checking is a method to formally verify a finite-state concurrent system. The verification is performed by checking if the formal specification can be satisfied by the model, represented by temporal logic formulas. Model checking uses usually either CTL (Computation Tree Logic) or LTL (Linear Temporal Logic) for temporal logic formulas. Model checking provides an automated way of proving formulas or finding counterexamples, but faces the state explosion problem. This problem can be reduced by symbolic algorithms, partial order reduction, abstraction or by on the fly model checking. There are many tools used for security protocol analysis, using a general-purpose or a special-purpose model checker.

Formal logic focuses on the study of inference with a set of rules for making deductions that are made explicit. Formal logic includes many logical systems, such as predicate logic or modal logic. The important logic from the security protocol analysis point of view is the BAN (Burrows, Abadi and Needham) logic. This logic is able to represent belief, freshness and some other properties that are fundamental for analyzing security protocols. The BAN logic was used to analyze common protocols and successfully detected some minor bugs.

Model Checking

Model checking is an automatic, model-based, property-verification technique, intended to be used for concurrent and reactive systems. Model checking has the following three steps:

1. Modeling;
2. Specification;
3. Verification.

The system is represented by a model M, which is a transition system. To model the transition system the Kripke structure is used, which is a node-labeled graph. The labeled nodes of the graph represent system states; the edges of the graph represent system transitions.

Specification, which is a property of the system to be verified, is defined by formula φ in temporal logic. There are two types of temporal logics that are used for system specification, linear time logics (LTL), where the time is a set of paths, and branching time logics (CTL), where time is represented as a tree.

The verification method is computing whether a model M satisfies φ: $M \models \varphi$.

It is an automatic process for finite models. The model checker uses an exhaustive search of the finite state space of the system to determine whether the specification is true or not. When the system does not satisfy the specification, the model checker produces a counterexample that shows the wrong behavior. This trace provides insight to understand and fix the problem. An error trace can also be a false negative, which could be result of incorrect modeling of the system or incorrect or inconsistent specification. Given sufficient resources the model checker will always terminate with a result. However, theory of computability shows that some mathematical tasks cannot be computed by an algorithm, which also limits the model checking. There are therefore some restrictions on systems and properties to be verified.

General purpose model checking tools can be used for protocol verification, but there are also model checking tools devoted to verification of security protocols, such as Casper/FDR2 toolbox (Lowe 1998) or AVISPA (Armando et al. 2005). We have chosen the popular AVISPA tool to demonstrate protocol modeling and security verification.

AVISPA (Armando et al. 2005) is a tool funded by the European Union developed for the analysis of security-sensitive protocols and applications. High level of abstraction enables fast model definition and easy demonstration. AVISPA utilizes four backend model checkers for validation of security protocols: On-the-fly Model-Checker (OFMC), Constraint-Logic-based Attack Searcher (CL-AtSe), SAT-based Model-Checker (SATMC), and Tree Automata based on Automatic Approximations for the Analysis of Security Protocols (TA4SP). A protocol model in AVISPA is defined by roles; each role can be played either by legitimate party or by an intruder. All roles are played concurrently. Protocols in AVISPA can be defined using one of the following formats: the High-Level Protocol Specification Language (HLPSL), or on a lower level using an Intermediate Format (IF). When the protocol is defined in HLPSL, AVISPA makes translation from this high-level language to the corresponding low-level IF, which is a common input format for all backend model checkers used by AVISPA.

The semantics of the HLPSL is based on Lamport's Temporal Logic of Actions (TLA (Lamport 1994)). The protocol is defined by states and transitions between these states. States are determined by an assignment of concrete values to all variables. Transitions are described by relations between the values of two subsequent states. A state predicate or state formula is a first-order formula on a role's state variables and constants. A transition predicate or formula is similar and includes variables of the current state together with variables of the next state, represented by primed variables. An event in the protocol is a conjunction of transition predicates, changing at least one state variable.

HLPSL offers several data types, such as natural numbers, symmetric keys, simple messages, or hash functions. Hash functions are one-way functions with properties of perfect cryptographic hash functions. There is also a possibility to create sets of variables. HLPSL does not support arithmetic operations.

In the wireless networks an intruder can eavesdrop on the communication, intercept and modify messages, and inject new arbitrary messages. HLPSL supports this intruder model, which is called Dolev-Yao intruder model. All communication is synchronous with the intruder, the intruder intercepts the messages from the legitimate user and each legitimate user receives messages only from the intruder.

HLPSL has some predefined security goals, such as secrecy and weak and strong authentication, additional security goals can be specified using temporal formulae. Goal formulae are defined over goal events, which are predicates that become true when they appear on the right hand side of a transition. HLSPL lacks goal for integrity of messages, which can be created.

Integrity is a security goal which assures that the data were not modified by the intruder and that the recipient received the data he requested. In this situation we use this term for ensuring that the recipient gets the same data as the sender sent. The fact that the data are encrypted and authenticated does not automatically mean that the data are the same as requested or that they were not changed.

We have established the variable Integrity to represent this security goal. The meaning of this variable is that when the integrity of message is violated, the intruder gets this variable into his knowledge. At the beginning of the protocol run, this variable is not in the intruder's knowledge. Each role that receives data contains the condition comparing the received data with the expected data. The data in the model is not represented by the actual value, it is rather represented by name, therefore it is possible to distinguish between data that was expected and counterfeit data.

Finding Vulnerabilities

This section is to present two examples of vulnerability finding using formal verification. To demonstrate how we implemented integrity as the security goal in protocol model, we provide an example of a protocol in which at one point one entity requests some data from the other entity (Henzl et al. 2013). This example is based on formal verification of the communication with Mifare DESFire smart card. The request contains the file name, offset, and length of the data. The response contains the data represented by the name. The name is constructed as a hash of file name concatenated with offset and length. This representation allows the recipient to determine whether the received data was the data it expected or not. The intruder cannot modify the internal values of the hash and cannot create the hash himself, so it can be considered suitable representation.

1. $A \rightarrow B$: select Application(AppNumber)
2. $A \rightarrow B$: authenticate (KeyNumber)
3. $B \rightarrow A$: $\{Nonce_B\}_{ekAB}$
4. $A \rightarrow B$: $\{Nonce_A + Nonce_B\}_{dkAB}$
5. $B \rightarrow A$: $\{Nonce_A\}_{ekAB}$
6. $A \rightarrow B$: readData (FileNumber, Offset, Length)
7. $B \rightarrow A$: $\{MAC(FileNumber, Offset, Length)\}_{ekAB}$

The following attacks were found using AVISPA:
Attack trace 1:

1a. $A \rightarrow I$: select Application(AppNumber)
1b. $I \rightarrow B$: select Application(AppNumber')

The intruder I can change the AppNumber in the first command, which is not authenticated. Recipient A will therefore receive data from sender B from another application than requested.
Attack trace 2:

6a. $A \rightarrow I$: readData(FileNumber, Offset, Length)
6b. $I \rightarrow B$: readData(FileNumber', Offset, Length)
7a. $B \rightarrow I$: $\{MAC(FileNumber', Offset, Length)\}_{ekAB}$
7b. $I \rightarrow A$: $\{MAC(FileNumber', Offset, Length)\}_{ekAB}$

The intruder I can change the FileNumber, which is not encrypted nor protected using MAC. This change will result in recipient A receiving data from another file than requested.

Attack trace 3:

6a. A → I: readData(FileNumber, Offset, Length)

6b. I → B: readData(FileNumber, Offset', Length)

7a. B → I: {MAC(FileNumber, Offset', Length)}$_{ekAB}$

7b. I → A: {MAC(FileNumber, Offset', Length)}$_{ekAB}$

The intruder I can change the Offset of data in the file. The application and file will remain same; therefore the file will exist in the system, which increases the chance of successful attack. The recipient A will get data from desired file, but from different offset.

We assumed that the adversary does not change the length of the data, which would be easily recognized. If we omit this assumption, changing the Length on the row 6 will lead to another attack.

Formal verification methods helped to find vulnerabilities in existing wireless sensor network architectures. These vulnerabilities include replay attacks, man-in-the-middle attacks, or type flaw attacks. For example, the following man-in-the-middle attack was found (Tobarra et al. 2009) using AVISPA tool in TinySec authenticated encryption.

Node A shares a pairwise key with all its neighbors. Node B is one of the neighbors of A.

1. $A \rightarrow B$: A,Nonce$_A$

2. $B \rightarrow A$: B.{MAC(Nonce$_A$.B)}$_{H(Km.B)}$

3. $A \rightarrow B$: B.AM$_1$.Size$_1$.Data$_A$.
   {MAC(B.AM$_1$.Size$_1$.Data$_A$)}$_{K'AB}$
   where K'_{AB} = H(H(Km.B).A)

4. $B \rightarrow A$: IV$_2$.{(IV$_2 \oplus$ Data$_B$)}K$_{AB}$.
   {MAC(IV$_2$.Data$_B$)}K$'_{AB}$
   where IV$_2$ = A.AM$_2$.Size$_2$.B.Counter
   and K$_{AB}$ = F(F(Km.N$_2$).N$_1$)

AVISPA found the following attack trace:

1. $I_A \rightarrow B_1$: A,Nonce$_I$

2. $B_1 \rightarrow I_A$: B.{MAC(Nonce$_I$.B)}$_{H(Km.B)}$

1. $A \rightarrow I_{B2}$: A,Nonce$_A$

2. $I_A \rightarrow B_2$: N$_x$.Nonce$_A$

2. $B_2 \rightarrow A$: B.{MAC(Nonce$_A$.B)}$_{H(Km.B)}$

3. $A \rightarrow I_{B2}$: B.AM$_1$.Size$_1$.Data$_A$. {MAC(B.AM$_1$.Size$_1$.Data$_A$)}$_{K'AB}$

3. $I_A \rightarrow B_1$: B.AM$_1$.Size$_1$.Data$_A$. {MAC(B.AM$_1$.Size$_1$.Data$_A$)}$_{K'AB}$

4. $B_1 \rightarrow I_A$: A.AM$_2$.Size$_2$.B.Counter. {(IV$_2 \oplus$ Data$_B$)}$_{KAB}$. {MAC(IV$_2$.Data$_B$)}$_{K'AB}$

The protocol is started by the intruder I$_A$ (playing role A) by sending a false nonce to B$_1$. Node A starts a session with B$_2$ and intruder I$_{B2}$ intercepts this message, modifies it, and sends to B$_2$ the identity of a false node N$_x$ together with the nonce of A. Then B sends the answer to A, and A requests the data from B. The request is intercepted by the intruder and redirected to B$_1$. Now B$_1$ thinks that it has received correct request from A and sends data to A. The result is that B$_1$ sent data to the intruder and B$_2$ thinks that it has communicated with node N$_x$, which does not exist.

CONCLUSION

This chapter started with an introduction to general wireless sensor networks. Two important cases of wireless sensor network installation were mentioned – concretely WSN for intelligent household and for store with restricted medicaments. In both cases the securing of data transfer in WSN is necessary and simultaneously an authentication of a user against the WSN. The second part of the chapter summarizes the possibilities for securing the WSN that the data couldn't be read/modified by an unauthorized user. The question of user authentication against the WSN is opened in the third part, where some possibilities of template storage are discussed. The last part of this chapter is devoted to a formal verification of WSN for ensuring the proper functionality and resistance against various kinds of attacks.

The future research could be oriented on implementation of data encryption and biometric authentication on low-performance and low-power devices. The formal verification could be prepared in correspondence with validation requests from the industry, i.e. for explosive environments due to SIL.

ACKNOWLEDGMENT

This research has been supported by the projects *"The IT4Innovations Centre of Excellence"* – MŠMT ED1.1.00/02.0070 (Czech Republic) and *"Reliability and Security in IT"* – FIT-S-14-2486 (Czech Republic), the fellowship research activity at the Tokyo Institute of Technology supported by the Matsumae International Foundation (Japan) and the National Research Foundation of Korea (NRF-2011-0006942) and the project *"Development of Global Culture and Tourism IPTV Broadcasting Station"* (10037393).

REFERENCES

Ambalakat, P. (2005). *Security of Biometric Authentication Systems.* 21st Computer Science Seminar, SA1-T1-1.

Armando, A., Basin, D., Boichut, Y., Chevalier, Y., Compagna, L., Cuellar, J., & Vigneron, L. et al. (2005). The AVISPA tool for the automated validation of internet security protocols and applications. In *Proceedings of the 17th international conference on Computer Aided Verification* (CAV'05). Springer-Verlag. doi:10.1007/11513988_27

Casado, L., & Philippas, T. (2009). ContikiSec: A Secure Network Layer for Wireless Sensor Networks under the Contiki Operating System, Distributed Computing and Systems. In Identity and Privacy in the Internet Age (pp. 133-147). Academic Press.

Casido, L., & Tsigas, P. (2009). ContikySec: A Secure Network Layer for Wireless Sensor Networks under the Contiki Operating System. *LNCS, 5383*, 133-147.

Ching-Ling, C., & Chent-Ta, L. (2008). Dynamic Session-Key Generation for Wireless Sensor Networks. *EURASIP Journal on Wireless Communications and Networking, 2008.* doi: 10.1155/2008/691571

Colitti, W., Steenhaut, K., & de Caro, N. (2011). Integrating Wireless Sensor Networks with the Web. In Extending the Internet to Low Power and Lossy Networks (IP+SN 2011). Academic Press.

De Couto, D., Aguayo, S. J., Bicket, J., & Morris, R. (2003). A high-throughput path metric for multi-hop wireless routing. In *Proceedings of the 9th annual international conference on Mobile computing and networking*. San Diego, CA: Academic Press. doi:10.1145/938985.939000

Dessimoz, D., Richiardi, J., Champod, C., & Drygajlo, A. (2006). Multimodal Biometrics for Identity Documents, Research Report, PFS 341-08.05, Version 2.0. *Université de Lausanne & École Polytechnique Fédérale de Lausanne, 2006*, 161.

Drahanský, M. (2010). *Biometric Cryptography Based on Fingerprints*. Saarbrücken: LAP.

Drahanský, M. (2010a). *Fingerprint Recognition Technology: Liveness Detection, Image Quality and Skin Diseases*. (Habilitation thesis). Brno, Czech Republic.

Drahanský, M. (2010b). *Biometric Cryptography Based on Fingerprints*. Saarbrücken: Lambert Academic Publishing.

Dunkels, A., Gronvall, R., & Voigt, T. (2004). Contiki - A Lightweight and Flexible Operating System for Tiny Networked Sensors. In *Proceedings of the 29th Annual IEEE International Conference on Local Computer Networks* (pp. 455-462). doi:10.1109/LCN.2004.38

ELKO EP s.r.o. (2010). *RF Touch control unit user manual*. Holešov.

Galbally, J., Fierrez, J., & Ortega-Garcia, J. (2007). Vulnerabilities in Biometric Systems. *Attacks and Recent Advances in Liveness Detection, Biometrics Recognition Group, Madrid, Spain, 2007*, 8.

Henzl, M., & Hanáček, P. (2013). Modeling of Contactless Smart Card Protocols and Automated Vulnerability Finding, (ISBAST). In *Proceedings of 2013 International Symposium on Biometrics and Security Technologies* (pp. 141-148). Academic Press. doi:10.1109/ISBAST.2013.26

Jain, A. K. (2005). *Biometric System Security, Presentation*. Michigan State University.

Kantof, C., Sastry, N., & Wagner, D. (2004). TinySec: A Link Layer Security Architecture for Wireless Sensor Networks. In *Proceedings of Second International Conference on Embedded Networked Sensor Systems* (SenSys '04) (pp. 162-175). Academic Press.

Kluz, M. (2005). *Liveness Testing in Biometric Systems*. (Master Thesis). Faculty of Informatics, Masaryk University Brno, Czech Republic.

Kubát, D., & Drahanský, M. (2011). RF Touch for Wireless Control of Intelligent Houses. In *Proceedings of Ubiquitous Computing and Multimedia Applications: Second International Conference*. Berlin: Springer Verlag.

Lamport, L. (1994). The temporal logic of actions. *ACM Transactions on Programming Languages and Systems, 16*(3), 872–923. doi:10.1145/177492.177726

Lowe, G. (1998). Casper: A compiler for the analysis of security protocols, *Journal of Computer Security, 6*(1-2), 53-84.

Malčík, D., & Drahanský, M. (2011). *Microscopic analysis of Chips, Security Technology 2011*. Jeju Island, KR: Springer.

Malčík, D., & Drahanský, M. (2012). Microscopic Analysis of The Chips: Chips deprocessing. *Advanced Science and Technology Letters*, (7), 80-85.

Matsumoto, T., Matsumoto, H., Yamada, K., & Hoshino, S. (2005). Impact of Artificial "Gummy" Fingers on Fingerprint Systems, In *Proceedings of SPIE* (Vol. 4677, p. 11). SPIE.

Oracle Corporation. (2014). *Java Card Classic Platform Specification 3.0.4*. Available at: http://www.oracle.com/technetwork/java/javame/javacard

Pecho, P. (2009). *Security of Tamper-Resistant Nodes in Wireless Sensor Networks*. (Dissertation Thesis). FIT BUT 2009.

Pecho, P., Nagy, J., & Hanáček, P. (2009). Power Consumption of Hardware Cryptography Platform for Wireless Sensor. In *Proceedings of 2009 International Conference on Parallel and Distributed Computing, Applications and Technologies* (pp. 318-323). Academic Press. doi:10.1109/PDCAT.2009.39

Pecho, P., Zbořil, F., Jr., Drahanský, M., & Hanáček, P. (2009). Agent Platform for Wireless Sensor Network with Support for Cryptographic Protocols. In *Proceedings of J. UCS* (pp. 992-1006). Academic Press.

Perrig, A., Szewczyk, R., Tygar, J., Wen, V., & Culler, D. (2002). SPINS: Security Protocols for Sensor Networks. *Wireless Networks*, 8(5), 521–534. doi:10.1023/A:1016598314198

RF Control and RF Touch product pages. (2014). Retrieved from http://www.elkoep.cz/produkty/inels-rf-control/

Roberts, C. (2006). Biometric Attack – Vectors and Defences. Academic Press.

Santesson, S., Nystrom, M., & Polk, T. (2004). *Internet X.509 Public Key Infrastructure – Qualified Certificates Profile*. Microsoft & RSA Security & NIST.

Shaheen, J., Ostry, D., Sivarman, V., & Jha, S. (2007). *Confidential and Secure Broadcasting in Wireless Sensor Networks, Personal, Indoor and Mobile Radio Communications, 2007*. IEEE.

Shelby, I., & Bormann, C. (2009). *6LoPAN: The Wireless Embedded Internet*. Wiley.

SmartCardsBasis. (2011). Retrieved from http://www.smartcardbasics.com/smart-card-types.html

Straub, T. (2004). *Spezifikation von X.509-Zertifikatsprofilen unter dem Gesichtspunkt Benutzbarkeit*. Technical University Darmstadt.

Tiresias. (2011). Retrieved from http://www.tiresias.org/research/guidelines/cards_and_smart_media.htm

Tobarra, L., Cazorla, D., Cuartero, F., Díaz, G., & Cambronero, E. (2009, April). Model checking wireless sensor network security protocols: TinySec + LEAP + TinyPK. *Telecommunication Systems*, 40(3-4), 91–99. doi:10.1007/s11235-008-9131-z

Vasseur, J.P., Agarwal, N., Hui, J., et al. (2011). *RPL: The IP routing protocol designed for low power and lossy networks*. IPSO Alliance.

Wang, S. (2009). *Intelligent Buildings and Building Automation*. London: Spon Press.

KEY TERMS AND DEFINITIONS

Authentication: Confirmation of user's identity.

Biometrics: Automated recognition of persons based on their physiological or behavioral characteristics.

Cryptography: Science of protecting information by encryption.

Cryptomodule: Hardware unit (node) enabling cryptographic operations.

Information Security: Practice of defending information from unauthorized access.

Network Node: Connection or redistribution point in a network.

Smart Home: Intelligent household automation.

Wireless Network: Digital network where data are transferred using wireless connection.

ENDNOTE

[1]   http://www.elkoep.cz

Section 5
Multimedia Security

This section deals with methods for improving information security of multimedia and implementation on graphical processing unit.

Chapter 9
Improving the Security of Digital Images in Hadamard Transform Domain Using Digital Watermarking

V. Santhi
VIT University, India

D. P. Acharjya
VIT University, India

ABSTRACT

In recent days, due to the advancement in technology there are increasing numbers of threats to multi-media data which are floating around in the Internet especially in the form of image data. Many methods exist to provide security for digital images but transform domain based digital watermarking could be considered as a promising method. Many transformation techniques are used to insert watermark in cover data, but this chapter deals with watermarking approaches in Hadamard transform domain. In traditional watermarking approaches the scaling parameter is empirically considered for inserting watermark but to maintain the quality of underlying cover images it needs to be calculated based on the content of the cover images. In order to make the watermarking algorithm completely automated the embedding and scaling parameters are calculated using the content of cover images. Many methods are existing for calculating scaling parameter adaptively but this chapter discusses various approaches using computational intelligence to arrive at optimum value of scaling and embedding parameters.

INTRODUCTION

With the advent of the Internet, the proliferation of images is creating a pressing need for copyright en-hancement schemes that protect copyright ownership. The development in technologies make information processing relatively simple and quick but at the same time the rate of exposure to various attacks is very high due to the availability of tools and software as stated in Hartung and Kutter (1999) and Potdar et al

DOI: 10.4018/978-1-4666-9426-2.ch009

(2005)'s work. Protecting copyrights of digital images or any other multimedia data becomes challenging and to accomplish the same various security mechanisms have been developed including cryptography, steganography and digital watermarking. Cryprographic techniques could be used to protect digital data during transmission between sender to the receiver as described in Langelaar et al (2000)'s and Macq and Quisquater (1995)'s work. Steganography could be used for secret communication between trusted parties with the limitation of payload stated in Anderson and Petitcolas (1998)'s work. Thus digital watermarking is the elegant and most promising method to protect copyrights of image data. Based on human perception the existing watermarking schemes could be classified into visible and invisible watermarking schemes. Based on working domain digital image watermarking techniques could be classified as spatial domain and frequency domain techniques. Many works are existing in both working domains, out of which watermarking in spatial domain includes works of van Schyndel et al (1994), Langelaar et al (1997), Iftekharuddin and Frigui (2009) and Luo et al (2010). In general these spatial domain methods are fragile to image/signal processing operations or other attacks.

The other kind of watermarking techniques are transform domain technique in which watermark is embedded by modulating the magnitude of transform coefficients and provide robust watermarking schemes against common attacks. Different transformation techniques are used to transform an image intensity samples into frequency components include, Discrete Cosine Transformation (DCT), Discrete Wavelet Transform (DWT), Discrete/Fast Fourier Transform (DFT/FFT), Hadamard Transform (HT). Similarly, singular value decomposition (SVD) could also be used in digital watermarking field and its basics could be found in description of Andrews and Patterson (1976). Hadamard transform coefficients have components equivalent to many DCT low frequency AC coefficients in middle and high frequency bands. Out of all the transformation techniques, Hadamard transformation is considered as suitable for watermarking in high noise environment. Thus Hadamard transform based watermarking schemes are discussed in this chapter elaborately due to its simplicity. In the subsequent sections, literature review for both visible and invisible watermarking is presented.

REVIEW OF VISIBLE WATERMARKING SCHEMES

According to human perception watermarking fall into two categories: visible and invisible. Visible watermarking is predominantly used to identify the ownership and protect copyrights of digital images. It also prevents unauthorized use of copyrighted images as stated in Yeung et al (1997)'s work. Visible watermarking could be classified into two types namely reversible and irreversible watermarking. In reversible watermarking (Yang et al., 2009), the original signal is recovered after the removal of watermark but in irreversible watermark (Braudaway et al. 1996) the original signal could not be recovered after the removal of watermark.

Initially, the IBM digital library section has used a visible watermarking technique to watermark the digitized pages of manuscripts from the Vatican archive by Braudaway et al (1996). The watermarking method embeds watermark by modifying pixel luminance values and hence considered as spatial domain visible watermarking scheme. In this work, a bright pixel is darkened / brightened or a dark pixel is darkened / brightened by perceptually equal amount. Rao et al (1998) proposed automatic visible watermarking of images using the measurement of image texture to automate the adjustment of watermark intensity through a linear regression model. Lin and Chen (2000) have proposed a visible watermarking mechanism to embed a gray level watermark into the cover image based on a statistic approach. First, the cover image is divided into equal blocks and the standard deviation in each block is calculated. The standard deviation value will determine the amount of gray value of the pixel in the watermark to be embedded into the corresponding cover image. Based on image features, they first classified the details of both cover image and watermark images into different perceptual classes and it is used by the pixel-wise watermark embedding. In the low pass sub band, they use the truncated Gaussian function to approximate the effect of luminance masking in the embedding rule.

In Xianghonget al (2005)'s watermarking scheme, SVD technique is combined with Hadamardtransfomation technique to achieve robustness. Huang and Tang (2006) have proposed visible watermarking technique in wavelet domain using contrast sensitive function and block classification method in DWT domain. The intensity of the watermark in different regions of the image is changed depending on the underlying content of the image and humans' sensitivity to spatial frequencies. This is achieved by computing the composite coefficients using global and local characteristics of the cover and watermark images. The strength of the watermark is changed to ensure that it is perceptually uniform over different regions of the image.

Hu and Jeon (2006) proposed visible watermarking for lossless recovery of original images. This approach is based on data compression and uses a payload adaptive scheme. Yang et al (2009) proposed a lossless visible watermarking scheme that adaptively varies the watermark strength to be embedded in different areas of the cover image, depending on the underlying image content and HVS characteristics. In this work, the size of the watermark is smaller than the size of the cover image. In cover image the region to be watermarked is divided into non-overlapping blocks of size 8 and each block is DCT transformed. Based on the underlying content either DC coefficients alone or both DC and AC coefficients are used for calculating the scaling and embedding factors. Tsai et al (2011a) has proposed a visible watermarking system based on the game-theoretic architecture that provides an optimum solution for the decision maker by studying the intensity and perceptual efficiency.

The insertion of a visible watermark should satisfy two conflicting conditions: the watermark should be strong enough to be perceptible and it should be light enough to leave the underlying content to be visible. In order to bring about the above said requirements, the intensity or luminance value of a cover image need to be adjusted. If intensity adjustment is carried out manually then it may not be suitable for all type of images. Thus, it is desirable to have a technique to adjust or select the strength of the watermark automatically based on the content of each image (Mohanty et al., 2000).

REVIEW OF INVISIBLE WATERMARKING SCHEMES

The other type of watermarking scheme based on human perception is called imperceptible watermarking. In order to protect copyrights of the digital images imperceptible watermarking is employed to greater extent. The early watermarking scheme which hides undetectable electronic watermark using Least Significant Bit (LSB) manipulation in gray scale image is proposed by van Schyndel et al (1994). In this, pseudo random sequence is used as electronic watermark which is generated randomly through linear shift register. Zhao and Koch (1995) proposed a scheme to embed robust label into digital monochrome, color and binary images for copyright protection. In their approach, certain features are extracted from the content of cover image and key is used to insert watermark through bit modification method.

Kankanhalli and Ramakrishnan (1998) proposed content based watermarking scheme based on noise sensitivity of every pixel based on edges, texture and luminance information. An early attempt to integrate image coding and watermarking using wavelets has been made by Su et al (1999). Podilchuk and Zeng (1998) describe perceptual based digital watermarking techniques for images and video signal that are designed to exploit human visual system in order to provide a transparent invisible but robust watermark. Their approach could be classified as image adaptive watermarks, that is, watermarks which depend not only on the frequency response of the human eye but also the properties of the image itself. The scaling factor is empirically selected to insert watermark.

In Falkowski and Lim (2000)'s work, multi resolution Hadamard transformation is used to decompose the image into many frequency bands. Lowest frequency band is selected for embedding watermark using complex Hadamard transform technique. The proposed algorithm is tested for JPEG compression and dithering distortion attacks and proved to be robust. Ho et al (2002) Fast Hadamard based robust digital image in image watermarking algorithm. In their approach image is used as watermark and inserted in Hadamard coefficients of cover image. To increase the invisibility of the watermark, a visual model based on original image characteristics, such as edges and textures are incorporated to determine the watermarking strength factor. The watermark strength factor can be controlled according to the texture areas. High textured areas are watermarked with higher strength and outstanding edge areas and smooth areas are watermarked with less strength. In this way, the invisibility of watermarked image can be improved.

Tsui et al (2008) have proposed color image watermarking in Multidimensional Fourier domain. Watermark casting is performed by estimating the just-noticeable distortion of the images, to ensure watermark invisibility. Similarly, robust phase watermarking scheme for still digital images based on the sequency-ordered complex Hadamard transform (SCHT) is presented in Aung et al (2011)'s work. Fourier Mellin Transform is used on the extracted features for watermark insertion and showed that the method is robust to geometric attacks. Yang et al (2012) have proposed digital watermarking algorithm in undecimated wavelet domain which is claimed as robust schemes. In Manoharan and Vijila (2013)'work, an enhancement procedure is proposed over the watermarking results on medical images using Singular Value Decomposition, contourlet transform and Discrete Cosine Transform. The enhanced watermarked image is subjected to various attacks and proved that the enhanced image does not disturb the watermark content embedded in the cover data.

Based on the literature survey, it is observed that to insert watermark the value of scaling and embedding parameter could be considered either empirically or it could be calculated adaptively from the content of the cover images. Moreover, in adaptive watermarking schemes cited in literature demonstrates that the automatism in inserting watermark is not complete and it implies that the dependency of user is required. Thus, to make the watermarking algorithm completely automated the calculation of scaling and embedding parameter need to be carried out using computational intelligence. In this chapter, adaptive digital watermarking algorithms using computational intelligence in particular, usage of activation functions of artificial neural networks and PSO are discussed. In the subsequent section the basics of Discrete Hadamard Transformation technique, artificial neural networks and PSO are presented.

BACKGROUND

Digital watermarking in general uses many functions such as Discrete Hadamard Transform (DHT), activation functions in neural networks like threshold function, signum function, sigmoid function, hyperbolic tangent function, and bipolar sigmoid function. In addition, it also uses particle swarm optimization. This section discusses these functions in brief so as to provide a clear idea on digital watermarking.

Discrete Hadamard Transformation

In general, to make watermarking algorithm more robust the cover image is transformed from spatial domain to frequency domain. To accomplish it Hadmard transformation technique could be used. It is a non-sinusoidal, orthogonal transformation that decomposes a signal into a set of orthogonal, rectangular waveforms called Walsh functions [30]. The two-dimensional Hadamard transform has been extensively used in image processing and image compression applications. Now, we state two-dimensional Hadamard function more formally.

Let H be a Hadamard matrix. According to the principle of identity, the product of H and its transpose H^T is an identity matrix I. Mathematically, we write as

$$HH^T = I \tag{1}$$

We define the (1×1) Hadamard transform H_1 by the identity 1. Thus, we have $H_1 = 1$ and then define H_2 recursively with the help of H_1 as follows:

$$H_2 = \frac{1}{\sqrt{2}} \begin{bmatrix} H_1 & H_1 \\ H_1 & -H_1 \end{bmatrix} = \frac{1}{\sqrt{2}} \begin{bmatrix} 1 & 1 \\ 1 & -1 \end{bmatrix} \tag{2}$$

Let I_m represents the original image and I'_m is the transformed image then the two dimensional Hadamard transform of I_m and its inverse I'_m are given as:

$$I'_m = \frac{H_n I_m H_n}{n} \tag{3}$$

and

$$I_m = \frac{H_n^{-1} I'_m H_n^*}{n} = \frac{H_n I'_m H_n}{n} \tag{4}$$

where H_n represents Hadamard matrix of order $(n \times n)$ and n is apower of two. In addition, H_n^* is the conjugate of the matrix H_n. Also, in Hadamard matrix, the rows are orthogonal to each other. Similarly, the columns of it are also orthogonal to each other. Therefore, we have

$$H = H^* = H^T = H^{-1} \tag{5}$$

Activation Functions in Artificial Neural Networks

In artificial neural networks (ANN), every neuron model consists of a processing element with synaptic input connections and a single output. It could be called as a mapping network if it is able to compute some functional relationship between its input and output. In neural network, input is given to the non-linear filter called activation function which is also called transfer function or squash function at the last layer to produce the output. A very commonly used activation functions are thresholding, signum function, sigmoidal function, bipolar sigmoidal function and hyperbolic tangent function or continuous Tan-Sigmoid Function. The general representation of simple neural network with activation function is shown in the following Figure 1.

Threshold Function

A threshold function is a function that takes value 1 if the argument of the function exceeds a given threshold T and 0 otherwise. The pictorial representation of simple thresholding function used in artificial neural network is shown below in Figure 2. Mathematically

$$f(x) = \begin{cases} 1 \text{ if } x \geq T \\ 0 \text{ if } x < T \end{cases} \tag{6}$$

Signum Function

This is another activation function which is an odd mathematical function that extracts the sign of a real number. It produces either 1 or 0 or -1 as output based on threshold value T. Mathematically, we define the signum function ($\text{sgn}(x)$) as below. The pictorial representation of signum function is shown in Figure 3.

Figure 1. General representation of neural networks

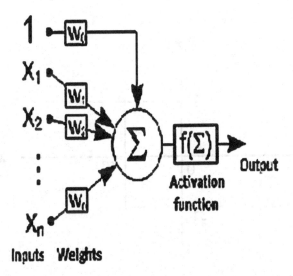

Figure 2. Threshold function

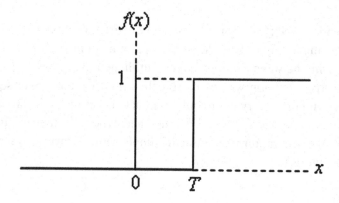

$$\text{sgn}(x) = \begin{cases} -1 \text{ if } x < T \\ 0 \text{ if } x = T \\ 1 \text{ if } x > T \end{cases} \tag{7}$$

Sigmoid Function

Sigmoid function has been used as an activation function in computing the output at different layers in the artificial neural network. It is a"S" shaped curve. Mathematically it is defined as below, where x represents the slope parameter which adjusts the abruptness of the function.

$$f(x) = \frac{1}{1 + e^{-x}} \tag{8}$$

Figure 3. Signum function

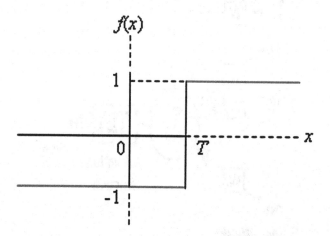

The main advantage of sigmoid function is that it is real valued function and differentiable. Since, it is differentiable, it is continuous also. The power of sigmoid function lies in the exponential term e^{-x} which is unique, non-trivial and is its own derivative. The value of the function is 0 (zero) if $x \rightarrow -\infty$; the value of the function is 1 if $x \rightarrow \infty$ and the value is 0.5 if $x = 0$.

Hyperbolic Tangent Function

Hyperbolic tangent function has also been used as an activation function in computing the output at different layers in the artificial neural network. In order to calculate adaptive scaling factor, the hyperbolic tangent function could also be used. The statistical analysis cover images are carried out given as input to the Tanh function and it calculates scaling factor. The scaling factor is calculated as below.

$$f(x) = \frac{e^x - e^{-x}}{e^x + e^{-x}}$$
(9)

Bipolar Sigmoid Function

Bipolar Sigmoid function is another activation function used predominantly in computing the output at different layers in the artificial neural network and it is a S shaped curve which is defined by Simpson (1991). The power of bipolar sigmoid function lies in the exponential term e^x which is unique, non-trivial and is its own derivative. In general, this activation function is used in digital watermarking to calculate scaling and embedding parameter. Digital watermarking carried using activation function is presented mathematically as below.

$$f(x) = \frac{1 - e^{-\lambda x}}{1 + e^{-\lambda x}}$$
(10)

Digital Watermarking

Digital Watermarking is defined as a process of embedding a piece of digital information into digital images which could be extracted later for intended purposes. Digital Watermarking, as opposed to steganography, must possess additional characteristic called robustness against attacks. Even if the existence of the hidden information is known it is difficult for an attacker to destroy the embedded watermark. The watermark to be inserted can be of logo, text data, numbers or any other type of images. In the following section the basic principle of digital image watermarking and its requirements, applications and common attacks to be incorporated for robustness test of watermarking schemes are presented. The general image watermarking system consists of a watermark embedding algorithm and a watermark extraction algorithm. The embedding algorithm takes cover image and watermark as input and produce watermarked image as output. Similarly the watermark extraction algorithm takes watermarked image as input and extract watermark from it. During the extraction process if the watermarking algorithm require original image then it is called non-blind scheme otherwise it is called blind watermarking scheme. The general watermarking scheme is shown in Figure 4.

Figure 4. (a) General non-blind watermarking scheme (b) General blind watermarking scheme

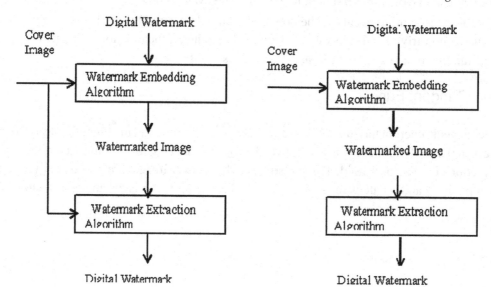

Common Attacks

In order to make use of both visible and invisible watermarking schemes for copyright protection, the inserted watermark should be robust to image processing operations, transmission noise, cropping operation and geometric manipulations. These image processing operations and other manipulations such as cropping and geometric manipulations are called attacks. A watermarked image is likely to be subjected to all the above said attacks to test its robustness as given in works of Lin and Chen (2000), Langelaar et al (1997) and Xin et al (2004) and Gonzalez and Woods (2005).

- **Noise Addition:** Additive noise introduced by communication channel during the transmission of digital images could be considered as noise addition attacks.
- **Low Pass Filtering:** In low pass filtering attack, the watermarked image is subjected to low pass filtering i.e., attenuating the high frequency components by passing lower frequency components.
- **Median Filtering:** Median filtering introduces less amount of blur in the image.
- **Histogram Equalization:** Histogram equalization enhances the gray level distribution of the watermarked image and hence the quality of an image is also increased.
- **Lossy Compression:** Joint Photographic Expert Group (JPEG) compression is considered as attack as it removes high frequency components of an image. Apart from these above said attacks the robustness of watermarking algorithm could also be tested against cropping and geometric distortions attack. The rotation scaling and translation operations are considered as geometric attacks as stated in Acharya and Kundu (2008). In addition to implementing geometric distortion independently, it could be applied together in the form of affine transform.

DISCRETE HADAMARD TRANSFORM BASED WATERMARKING SCHEMES

Hadamard transformation technique is considered as one of the orthogonal transformation technique. Hadamard transformation matrix generation process could be implemented using fast implementation approach like fast Fourier transforms. As Hadamard transformation matrix consists of +1 or -1 as its elements it is very simple to transform any image into frequency components. Because of its properties, digital watermarking techniques using both conventional approaches and computational intelligence are presented in the following sections. In addition to conventional watermarking approaches, techniques using neural networks activation functions are elaborated.

Image Watermarking using the Complex Hadamard Transform (2000)

In this paper, Falkowski and Lim(2000) have proposed a novel method based on the multi-resolution and complex Hadamard transforms. The experimental results show that the proposed scheme is robust to JPEG compression, image resizing, cropping, dithering distortion. The original image and watermarked image is shown in Figure 5.

The algorithm proposed by Falkowski and Lim(2000) is shown in Figure 6. Authors have exploited multi resolution Hadamard transform concept and utilized low frequency band to insert watermark. In particular, watermark insertion is carried out in complex Hadamard transform domain. The procedure adopted to do the same is shown as flowchart in Figure 6.

In this work, similar to the discrete Fourier Transform (DFT) based watermarking technique, the phase components of the selected transform coefficients are altered to convey the watermark information. Because of inserting watermark by modulating the phase angle of the Complex Hadamard Transform (CHT), the inserted watermark is more robust to tampering and from communications theory, it is well known that phase modulation possesses superior noise immunity when compared to amplitude modulation. The authors have tested and exhibits robustness to JPEG compression up to 10% quality

Figure 5. (a) Original image (b) Watermarked image

(a)　　　　(b)

Figure 6. Insertion of watermark

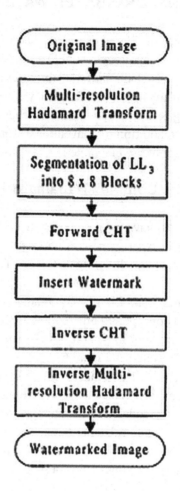

factor, successive watermarking, dithering distortion (25%), cropping and scaling up to 56.25% of the original image. The scheme proposed only allows the watermark to be extracted by the copyright owner since the original image is required in the extraction process. Hence it could be classified as non-blind watermarking scheme.

Robust Digital Image-in-Image Watermarking Algorithm using the Fast Hadamard Transform (2003)

Digital watermarking algorithm using the Fast Hadamard Transform (FHT) is proposed for the copyright protection of digital images by Ho and Shen (2003). This algorithm can embed or hide an entire image or pattern as a watermark such as a company's logo or trademark directly into the original image. The performance of the proposed algorithm is tested using attacks given by Stirmark benchmark.

The proposed watermarking algorithm pseudo randomly selects the sub-blocks for watermark insertion using an m-sequence random number generator. The seed of m-sequence and initial state are stored in the key file. The determination of the watermark strength factor is based on the original image textures and edges characteristic. It is found that edge information of an image is the most important

Figure 7. (a) Original image (b) Watermarked image

(a)   (b)

factor for human perception of the image, so it is essential to maintain edge integrity to preserve the image quality. In this proposal, scaling parameter is calculated adaptively using above said parameters. The authors Ho and Shen (2003) proved that this algorithm is very robust and can survive most of the Stirmark attacks. The simplicity of the Fast Hadamard Transform (FHT) also offers a significant advantage in shorter processing time and ease of hardware implementation than other orthogonal transforms, such as the discrete cosine transform and wavelet transform. The original image and watermarked image obtained based on algorithm proposed by Ho and Shen (2003) is shown in Figure 7 and obtained results are shown in Table 1.

The experimental results showed that the proposed method was robust against 60-70% of Stirmark. As per Ho and Shen (2003), the Hadamard transform has more useful middle and high frequency hands than several high gain transforms, such as DCT. It also offers a significant advantage in shorter processing time and ease of hardware implementation than commonly used transform techniques.

A Watermarking Algorithm Based on the SVD and Hadamard Transform (2005)

Xianghong et al (2005) have proposed a novel technique for copyright of protection of digital products. The general block diagram used to insert watermark using SVD technique is shown in Figure 8.

Table 1. Implemented attacks and obtained results

Sl.No.	Image Operation	Obtained Correlation
1.	Sharpening 3x3	0.9573
2.	1 Row and 1 column Removal	0.9866
3.	Frequency Mode Laplacian Removal	0.9580
4.	JPEG Compression of Factor 30	0.8688
5.	Changing aspect ratio	0.8199

Figure 8. The Block diagram of the Hadamard-SVD algorithm

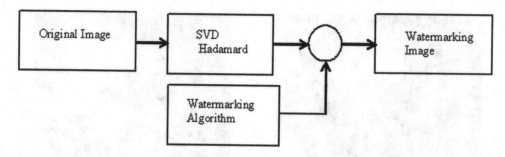

Authors have implemented various attacks including rotation, clipping, translation and zoom. From the obtained results it is proved that the proposed algorithm is robust to above mentioned attacks. The obtained results after zooming attack are shown in Table 2. Based on the properties of the Hadamard transform and the singular value decomposition (SVD), the experimental results show that the watermarking algorithm possess good transparency and robust, especially against the geometrical operations and JPEG lossy compression. The graphical representation of rotation attacks is shown in Figure 9. It is evident that the obtained NC values are above 80 percent for different angle of rotation.

Figure 9. Robust to rotation attacks

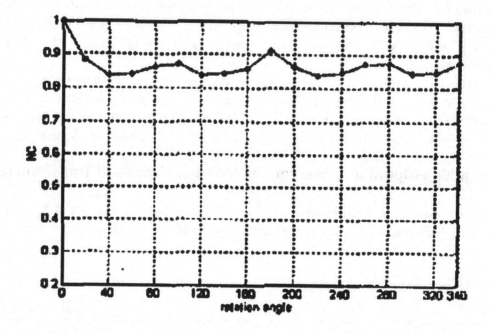

Table 2. Obtained NC value of the zoomed image

Times	2.2	2.0	1.8	1.6	1.2	0.8	0.7
NC	0.883	0.888	0.892	0.902	0.930	0.810	0.746

Figure 10. (a) Original image (b) Watermark (c) Watermarked image

(a)   (b)   (c)

In this proposal, watermark is encrypted before insertion into a cover image. As most of the energy is concentrated on first term of the transform coefficients, the change of which affects the quality of the image mostly, thus first coefficient is left unaltered. Thus, authors have proposed algorithm to embed watermark bits not in the first term but others. In this way, not only the embedded watermarking affect small on the quality of the image, but also can against all kinds of attacks efficiently. Xianghong et al (2005)'s scheme presents a good robust especially against image geometry manipulation, lossy compression, and filtering etc.

A Robust Block-Based Image Watermarking Scheme using Fast Hadamard Transform and Singular Value Decomposition (2006)

Abdallah et al (2006) have presented a new approach for transparent and high rate embedding of watermarks into digital images using FHT and singular value decomposition (SVD). The proposed algorithm consists of three main steps: dividing the cover image into small blocks, applying the FHT to each block, and distributing the singular values of the visual watermark image over the transformed cover blocks. The main attractive features of this approach are simplicity, flexibility in data embedding capacity, and real-time implementation. The experimental results show the much improved performance of the proposed method in comparison with existing techniques, and also its robustness against the most common attacks. The original image, watermark and watermarked images are shown in Figure 10 in Abdallah et al (2006)'s work. Similarly the obtained NCC value after each attack is shown in Figure 11.

An Image Watermarking Scheme Based on FWHT-DCT (2010)

Digital image watermarking is frequently used for many purposes, such as image authentication, fingerprinting, copyright protection, and tamper proofing. Imperceptibility and robustness are the watermark requirements of good watermarks. In this work, Marjuniet al (2010) have proposed the Fast Walsh Hadamard transform (FWHT) combined with the Discrete Cosine Transform (DCT) as a new image watermarking scheme. The FWHT reorders the high-to-low sequence components contained in the signal. This scheme produces high perceptual transparency of the embedded watermark. Experimental results

Figure 11. Obtained correlation coefficient after each attacks

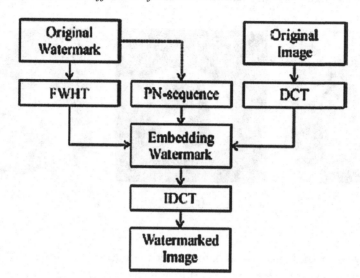

show that the proposed scheme has good visual perception and is robust against attacks. The architectural diagram proposed by Marjuniet al (2010) is shown in Figure 12. Similarly the original image, watermark and watermarked images are shown in Figure 13.

Marjuniet al (2010) have presented the evaluation of the watermarking performances in imperceptibility and robustness as the watermarking requirements. The experimental results show that the proposed scheme has a good perceptual invisibility and is also robust against attacks.

Discrete Walsh Hadamard Transform Based Visible Watermarking Technique for Digital Color Images (2010)

Santhi and Arunkumar Thangavelu(2010) have proposed visible watermarking scheme to protect digital images from unauthorized access. In this proposal, watermarking is carried in Hadamard transform domain to make the system robust to many signal processing attacks. Initially watermark is embedded in particular band of frequency but to make it robust to compression and cropping attack, watermark is

Figure 12. Watermark embedding process

Figure 13. (a) Original image (b) Watermark (c,d) Watermarked image

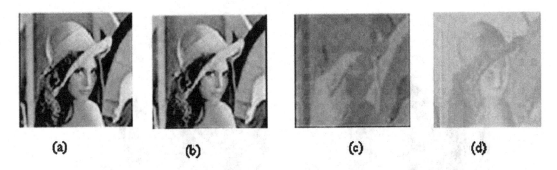

embedded in tiling manner in all the range of frequencies. The robustness of the algorithm is tested against noise addition, cropping, compression, Histogram equalization and resizing attacks. The experimental results show that the algorithm is robust to common signal processing attacks and the observed peak signal to noise ratio (PSNR) of watermarked image is varying from 20 to 30 db depends on the size of the watermark. This proposal is implemented for color images and obtained YUV channels are shown in Figure 14. The original and watermarked image is shown in Figure 15. In Figure 16 the watermarked image using tiling method is shown.

Figure 14. (a) Original image (b) Y-Channel

Figure 15. (a) Original image (b) Watermarked image

Figure 16. (a) Watermarked image tiling method (b) Logo - watermarked image

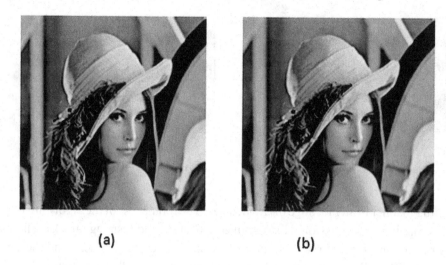

(a)   (b)

Santhi and Arunkumar Thangavelu (2010) have implemented Hadamard based watermarking algorithm for digital color images in YUV domain. The color Image in RGB color space is transformed into YUV color channel to decorrelate the pixels relations. Y channel is Hadamard transformed and watermark is embedded in Y channel. The proposed method is tested with few attacks and extracted watermark is compared with original watermark to measure the similarity. It is observed that the quality of the extracted watermark is good. The quality of the watermarked image is measured through the peak signal to noise ratio and it is observed that the calculated value ranging from 20 dB to 30 dB.

Resistant Image Watermarking in the Phases of the Complex Hadamard Transform Coefficients (2010)

Kountchev et al (2010) proposed a new watermarking method for digital content protection in transform domain. In order to carry out this, the digital image is transformed using Complex Hadamard Transform (CHT), and the watermark data is then inserted in the imaginary part of the transform coefficients. The selection of the suitable for watermarking transform coefficients is done in accordance with pre-defined rules. The so inserted watermark is perceptually invisible. The method permits the insertion of relatively large amount of data, retaining the high quality of the protected image. The main advantages of the algorithm for digital watermarking, based on the CHT are that it is resistant against attacks, based on high-frequency filtration (JPEG compression); it permits the insertion of significant amount of data, and the watermark detection could be done without using the original image. Kountchev et al (2010)'s results are shown in Figure 17.

The main advantages of the algorithm are:

- The algorithm is highly resistant against attacks, based on high-frequency filtration (JPEG compression), which is confirmed by the almost constant value of MSE for the extracted watermark.
- The high quality of the watermarked image ensures the transparency of the inserted watermark data.

Figure 17. (a) Original Image (b) Watermarked Image

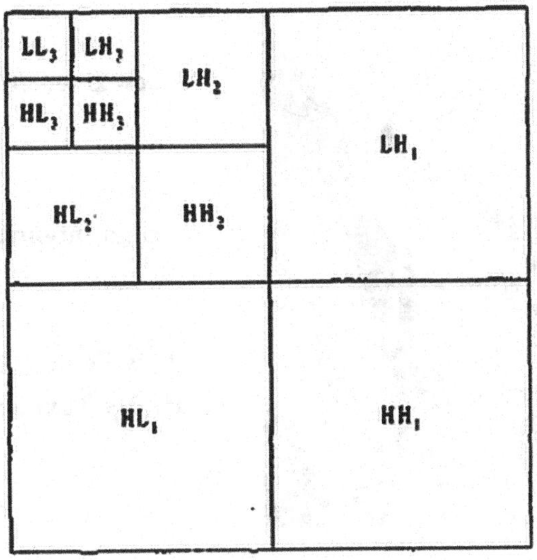

- The algorithm permits the insertion of significant amounts of data (the number of bits is approximately equal to ¾ of the total number of pixels).
- The watermark detection check could be done without the original image (i.e., it offers "blind" watermark detection)

Image Watermarking Using the Complex Hadamard Transform (2010)

In this paper, a new method for watermarking digital images based on the multi-resolution Hadamard and the complex Hadamard transforms is proposed and developed. The multi-resolution integer valued Hadamard transform is applied to decompose the image into a pyramid structure with various bands such as the low-low frequency band, low-high frequency band, high-high frequency band etc. as shown in Figure 18. The lowest frequency band (LL3) is then segmented into 8 x 8 blocks. The two-dimensional CHT is applied next. The above approach ensures that the watermark is robust and secure as it is placed in the most significant components of the data. Hence, an attacker must target the fundamental structural components of the data, thereby increasing the chances of fidelity degradation.

Similar to the DFT-based watermarking technique the phase components of the selected transform coefficients are altered to convey the watermark information. The reasons for selecting the phase components are as follows:

1. A watermark that is embedded in the phase of the CHT coefficients is more robust to tampering.
2. From communications theory, it is well known that phase modulation possesses superior noise immunity when compared to amplitude modulation.

The current scheme only allows the watermark to be extracted by the copyright owner since the original image is required in the extraction process. With further efforts, it is expected that the proposed scheme will be able to extract the embedded watermark without referring to the original image.

Figure 18. Multiresolution representation of image

Low Intensity Smooth Block

High Intensity Smooth Block

Low Textured Region
Highly Textured Region

Robust Optical Watermarking Technique by Optimizing the Size of Pixel Blocks of Orthogonal Transform

We previously proposed a novel technology with which the images of real objects with no copyright protection could contain invisible digital watermarking, using spatially modulated illumination. In this "optical watermarking" technology we used orthogonal transforms such as a Discrete Cosine Transform (DCT) or a Walsh-Hadamard Transform (WHT) to produce watermarking images, where I-bit binary information was embedded into each pixel block. Here, we propose a new robust technique of optical watermarking that varies the size of pixel blocks by a trade-off in the efficiency of embedded watermarking. We conducted experiments where 4x4, 8x8, and 16x16 pixels were used in one block. A detection accuracy of 100% was obtained by using a block with 16x16 pixels when embedded watermarking was extremely weak, although the accuracy did not reach 100% by using blocks with 4x4 or 8x8 pixels under the same embedding conditions. The results from experiments revealed the effectiveness of our proposed technique.

Adaptive Visible Watermarking in Hadamard Domain for Digital Images (2013)

Santhi et al have proposed a novel approach for adaptive visible watermarking algorithm using Hadamard transformation technique for copyright protection of digital images. In this work, watermark is inserted into luminance component of a cover image and hence the proposed scheme could be used for both color and monochrome images. In order to maintain quality of the given cover image as well as the visibility of inserted watermark, calculation of scaling and embedding factors is automated using the content of cover image. The performance of the proposed watermarking algorithm is tested with different types of grayscale / color images and the results show the efficiency of the pro- posed work. The visibility of embossed watermark is evident from the results obtained without much degradation in quality of the underlying cover image. The statistical observations further strengthen the claim. The method adapted for inserting watermark would be based on the textural properties would be based on the textural quality of the image. Texture based classification is shown in Figure 19.

Figure 19. Classification of image blocks based on textural properties image in spatial domain process

In order to retain the quality of a cover image as well as to make the imprinted watermark more visible the scaling and embedding factors are adaptively determined from the content of a cover image itself. The content of the image is classified based on the textural properties of the cover image. The performance of proposed watermarking algorithm is tested with different types of grayscale / color images. The parameters used to measure the quality of watermarked image include normalized correlation, entropy content, energy content, contrast value and peak signal to noise ratio.

The obtained results are given below. - The calculated normalized correlation shows that the similarity of original and watermarked image is above 99% for gray scale images and above 97% for color images. - The difference in entropy value of cover image and watermarked image is varying from 1% to the maximum of 3%. - The contrast difference between the original cover image and the watermarked image is varying from 1% to 3% which is considerably very less. - Similarly the difference in energy content between original image and watermarked image is varying from 1% to 4%. - The obtained peak signal to noise ratio is ranging from 21.2903 dB to 34.8195 based on the unique property of each image. In future the visible image adaptive watermarking algorithm could be implemented based on the selected region of an image.

Hadamard Transform Based Adaptive Visible/Invisible Watermarking Scheme for Digital Images (2013)

In this work, Santhi and Arulmozhivarman (2013) proposed a method which uses an adaptive procedure for calculating scaling factor using sigmoid function in Hadamard transform domain. The value of scaling factor is adjusted by a control parameter to make the watermarking scheme as either visible or invisible. The calculation of scaling factor is carried using sigmoid activation function from neural networks. The mean value of image I_m in Hadamard domain is carried out and given as input to sigmoid function as shown below.

$$\mu(I_m') = \frac{1}{P \times Q} \sum_{a=1}^{P} \sum_{b=1}^{Q} I_m'(a,b) \qquad (10)$$

$$\alpha_1 = \frac{1}{\left(1 + e^{-\mu(I')}\right)} \qquad (11)$$

The scaling factor obtained from (11) is adjusted by multiplying it with inverse multiples of 10 as given in Eq. (12). Here m is used to control strength of scaling factor α to get the desired watermarking scheme.

$$\alpha = \alpha_1 \times \frac{1}{10^m} \qquad (12)$$

Based on the value of m, the watermarking scheme is classified as either visible or invisible. If the control parameter $m=1$ the visibility of the watermark is good without destroying the underlying content and it is shown in Figure 20.

For $m=2$ the watermark become invisible without degrading the quality of underlying digital image. Thus the value of controlling parameter $m=1$ provides visible watermarking scheme and provides invisible watermarking scheme and it is shown in Figure 21.

The authors tested watermarked images for robustness against various attacks and shown as graph in Figure 22.

Figure 20. Original image, watermark, watermarked image

Figure 21. Original image, watermark, watermarked image

Figure 22. Obtained NCC values after various attacks

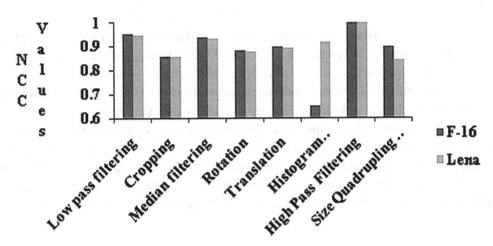

The major contribution of the proposed method is that it uses adaptive mathematical model using sigmoid function that inserts watermark either visibly or invisibly based on users' requirements by adjusting the controlling parameter. The visible watermarking results show the superiority of the proposed method when compared with results of Yang et al.'s method. The statistical results show that the normalized correlation coefficient is better than the value obtained in Yang et al.'s method. Similarly, the proposed invisible watermarking results are compared with the results of Mohanty et al.'s method and Tian et al.'s method. It is proved that the performance of proposed adaptive invisible watermarking scheme is better than the results of both Mohanty et al.'s method and Tian et al.'s method. Thus the performance of proposed adaptive watermarking model for both visible and invisible watermarking scheme confirmed its efficiency through experimental analysis.

FUTURE RESEARCH DIRECTIONS

In this chapter, digital watermarking works carried out in Hadamard transform technique are presented. Initially in Hadamard transform domain, watermarking works are carried out by using empirically selected value as scaling factor and is tested using sample cover images. But it is found that the proposed watermarking scheme could not be extended for other images as the scaling factor is chosen empirically which introduces visual degradation in the quality of cover images. In literature review, digital watermarking schemes carried out in both perceptible and imperceptible category are presented elaborately. In both kind of watermarking schemes, to retain the quality of a cover image as well as to make the imprinted watermark more visible/invisible the scaling and embedding factors need to be determined adaptively from the content of the cover images itself. Recently, researchers have started incorporating intelligence concepts in calculating scaling and embedding parameters which will help to fulfill the requirements of any watermarking schemes. Further, analysis of cover images could be carried out for deriving required parameters using intelligence techniques. Similarly the proposed watermarking schemes could also be extended to video signal.

CONCLUSION

In this chapter, basics of watermarking schemes, computational intelligence such as activation functions and Hadamard transformation technique are presented. Digital Watermarking is the most promising method to protect copyrights of digital images. Based on the literature survey, it is observed that works contributed in Hadamard Transformation domain, towards adaptive visible and invisible watermarking schemes are few. In this chapter, watermarking schemes implemented have been proposed using constant scaling factor in both visible and invisible mode. Moreover, in adaptive watermarking schemes cited in literature demonstrates that the automatism in inserting watermark is not complete and it implies that the dependency of user is required. Thus it is required to calculate scaling and embedding parameter using the content of cover image to make watermarking useful to the intended purpose. Based on the results analysis it is found that the parameters derivation using computational intelligence has fulfilled the purpose.

REFERENCES

Abdallah, E. E., Hamza, A. B., & Bhattacharya, P. (2006).A robust block-based image watermarking scheme using fast Hadamard transform and singular value decomposition. In *Proc. 18th International Conference on Pattern Recognition* (*Vol. 3*, pp. 673–676). Academic Press. doi:10.1109/ICPR.2006.167

Acharyya, M., & Kundu, M. K. (2008). Extraction of noise tolerant, gray-scale transform and rotation invariant features for texture segmentation using wavelet frames. *International Journal of Wavelets, Multresolution, and Information Processing, 6*(3), 391–417. doi:10.1142/S0219691308002252

Ahmed, N., Rao, K., & Abdussattar, A. L. (1971). BIFORE or Hadamard transform. *IEEE Transactions on Audio and Electroacoustics, 19*(3), 225–234. doi:10.1109/TAU.1971.1162193

Anderson, R. J., & Petitcolas, F. A. (1998). On the limits of steganography. *IEEE Journal on Selected Areas in Communications, 16*(4), 474–481. doi:10.1109/49.668971

Andrews, H., & Patterson, C. (1976). Singular value decompositions and digital image processing. *IEEE Transactions on Acoustics, Speech, and Signal Processing, 24*(1), 26–53. doi:10.1109/TASSP.1976.1162766

Aung, A., Ng, B. P., & Rahardja, S. (2011). A robust watermarking scheme using sequency-ordered complex Hadamard transform. *J. Signal Process. Syst., 64*(3), 319–333. doi:10.1007/s11265-010-0492-7

Bao, P., & Ma, X. (2005). Image adaptive watermarking using wavelet domain singular value decomposition. *IEEE Transactions on Circuits and Systems for Video Technology, 15*(1), 96–102. doi:10.1109/TCSVT.2004.836745

Braudaway, G. W. (1997). Protecting publicly-available images with an invisible image watermark. In *Proc. International Conference on Image Processing* (Vol. 1, pp. 524–527). Academic Press. doi:10.1109/ICIP.1997.647965

Braudaway, G. W., Magerlein, K. A., & Mintzer, F. C. (1996). Protecting publicly available images with a visible image watermark. In *Electronic Imaging: Science & Technology* (pp. 126–133). International Society for Optics and Photonics.

Eggers, J., & Girod, B. (2002). *Informed watermarking* (Vol. 685, pp. 1–5). Norwell, MA: Kluwer Academic. doi:10.1007/978-1-4615-0951-6_1

Falkowski, B. J., & Lim, L. S. (2000). Image watermarking using Hadamard transforms. *Electronics Letters*, *36*(3), 211–213. doi:10.1049/el:20000257

Gonzalez, R. C., & Woods, R. E. (2005). Digital Image Processing, Pearson Education. *South Asia*, 142–172.

Hartung, F., & Kutter, M. (1999). Multimedia watermarking techniques. *Proceedings of the IEEE, 87*(7), 1079–1107. doi:10.1109/5.771066

Ho, A. T., Shen, J., & Tan, S. H. (2003a). Character-embedded watermarking algorithm using the fast Hadamard transform for satellite images. In *Proc. International Symposium on Optical Science and Technology*. International Society for Optics and Photonics. doi:10.1117/12.451249

Ho, A. T., Shen, J., & Tan, S. H. (2003b). *Robust digital image-in-image watermarking algorithm using the fast Hadamard transform*. Seattle, WA: Proc. InternationalSymposium on Optical Science and Technology. doi:10.1109/ISCAS.2003.1205147

Ho, A. T., Shen, J., Tan, S. H., & Kot, A. C. (2002). Digital image-in-image watermarking for copyright protection of satellite images using the fast Hadamard transform. In *Proc. IEEE International Symposium on Geoscience and Remote Sensing* (Vol. 6, pp. 3311–3313). IEEE. doi:10.1109/IGARSS.2002.1027166

Hu, Y., & Jeon, B. (2006). Reversible visible watermarking and lossless recovery of original images. *IEEE Transactions on Circuits and Systems for Video Technology, 16*(11), 1423–1429. doi:10.1109/TCSVT.2006.884011

Hu, Y., & Kwong, S. (2001). Wavelet domain adaptive visible watermarking. *Electronics Letters, 37*(20), 1219–1220. doi:10.1049/el:20010838

Hu, Y., & Kwong, S. (2003). An image fusion based visible watermarking algorithm. In *Proc. International Symposium on Circuits and Systems* (Vol. 3, pp. 794–797). Academic Press.

Hu, Y., Kwong, S., & Huang, J. (2006). An algorithm for removable visible watermarking. *IEEE Transactions on Circuits and Systems for Video Technology, 16*(1), 129–133. doi:10.1109/TCSVT.2005.858742

Iftekharuddin, K. M., & Frigui, N. (2009). A Robust Spatial Domain Binary Signature Watermarking Technique. *Int. J. Tomography Simulation, 11*(W09), 76–85.

Kankanhalli, M. S., & Ramakrishnan, K. R. (1998). Content based watermarking of images. In *Proc. Sixth ACM international conference on Multimedia* (pp. 61-70). ACM. doi:10.1145/290747.290756

Kutter, M., Bhattacharjee, S. K., & Ebrahimi, T. (1999).Towards second generation watermarking schemes. In *Proc. International Conference on Image Processing* (Vol. 1, pp. 320–323). Academic Press.

Langelaar, G. C., Lagendijk, R. L., & Biemond, J. (1998). Real-time labeling of MPEG-2 compressed video. *Journal of Visual Communication and Image Representation, 9*(4), 256–270. doi:10.1006/jvci.1998.0397

Langelaar, G. C., Setyawan, I., & Lagendijk, R. L. (2000). Watermarking digital image and video data.A state-of-the-art overview. *IEEE Signal Processing Magazine, 17*(5), 20–46. doi:10.1109/79.879337

Langelaar, G. C., van der Lubbe, J. C., & Lagendijk, R. L. (1997). Robust labeling methods for copy protection of images. In Proc. Electronic Imaging, International Society for Optics and Photonics (pp. 298–309). Academic Press.

Lee, Y., Kim, H., & Park, Y. (2009). A new data hiding scheme for binary image authentication with small image distortion. *Information Sciences, 179*(22), 3866–3884. doi:10.1016/j.ins.2009.07.014

Lin, S. D., & Chen, C. F. (2000). A robust DCT-based watermarking for copyright protection. *IEEE Transactions on Consumer Electronics, 46*(3), 415–421. doi:10.1109/30.883387

Luo, L., Chen, Z., Chen, M., Zeng, X., & Xiong, Z. (2010). Reversible image watermarking using interpolation technique. *IEEE Trans. Inf. Forensics Secur., 5*(1), 187–193. doi:10.1109/TIFS.2009.2035975

Ma, L., & Song, S. (2009).Improved image watermarking scheme using nonnegative matrix factorization and wavelet transform. In *Proc. International Conference on Wireless Communications & Signal Processing* (pp. 1–5). Academic Press. doi:10.1109/WCSP.2009.5371664

Macq, B. M., & Quisquater, J. J. (1995). Cryptology for digital TV broadcasting. *Proceedings of the IEEE, 83*(6), 944–957. doi:10.1109/5.387094

Manoharan, J. S., & Vijila, K. S. (2013). A Hybrid Transform for Robustness Enhancement of Watermarking of Medical Images. *Int. J. Imaging & Robotics, 9*(1), 73–83.

Marjuni, A., Logeswaran, R., & Ahmad Fauzi, M. F. (2010). *An image watermarking scheme based on FWHT-DCT. Proc. Networking and Information Technology.* Manila: ICNIT.

Mohanty, S. P., & Bhargava, B. K. (2008). Invisible watermarking based on creation and robust insertion-extraction of image adaptive watermarks. *ACM Trans. Multimedia Comput. Commun. Appl., 5*(2), 12:1–12:22.

Mohanty, S. P., Ramakrishnan, K. R., & Kankanhalli, M. S. (2000).A DCT domain visible watermarking technique for images. In *Proc. IEEE International Conference on Multimedia and Expo (ICME)* (Vol. 2, pp. 1029–1032). IEEE. doi:10.1109/ICME.2000.871535

Podilchuk, C. I., & Zeng, W. (1998). Image-adaptive watermarking using visual models. *IEEE Journal on Selected Areas in Communications, 16*(4), 525–539. doi:10.1109/49.668975

Potdar, V. M., Han, S., & Chang, E. (2005).A survey of digital image watermarking techniques. In *Proc. IEEE International Conference on Industrial Informatics (INDIN 2005)* (pp. 709–716). IEEE. doi:10.1109/INDIN.2005.1560462

Pratt, W. K., Kane, J., & Andrews, H. C. (1969). Hadamard transform image coding. *Proceedings of the IEEE, 57*(1), 58–68. doi:10.1109/PROC.1969.6869

Rao, A. R., Braudaway, G. W., & Mintzer, F. C. (1998). *Automatic visible water- marking of images. In Proc. Photonics West'98 Electronic Imaging* (pp. 110–121). International Society for Optics and Photonics.

Santhi, V., & Thangavelu, A. (2009). DWT-SVD combined full band robust watermarking technique for color images in YUV color space. *Int. J. Comput. Theory Eng.*, *1*(4), 424–429. doi:10.7763/IJCTE.2009. V1.68

Simpson, P. K. (1991). *Artificial neural systems: foundations, paradigms, applications, and implementations.* Windcrest/McGraw-Hill.

Tian, J. (2003). Reversible data embedding using a difference expansion. *IEEE Transactions on Circuits and Systems for Video Technology*, *13*(8), 890–896. doi:10.1109/TCSVT.2003.815962

Tian, L., Zheng, N., Xue, J., Li, C., & Wang, X. (2011). An integrated visual saliency based watermarking approach for synchronous image authentication and copyright protection. *Signal Processing Image Communication*, *26*(8), 427–437. doi:10.1016/j.image.2011.06.001

Tsai, J. S., Huang, W. B., & Kuo, Y. H. (2011b). On the selection of optimal feature region set for robust digital image watermarking. *IEEE Transactions on Image Processing*, *20*(3), 735–743. doi:10.1109/ TIP.2010.2073475 PMID:20833602

Tsui, T. K., Zhang, X. P., & Androutsos, D. (2008). Color image watermarking using multidimensional Fourier transforms. *IEEE Trans. Inf. Forensics Secur.*, *3*(1), 16–28. doi:10.1109/TIFS.2007.916275

Van Schyndel, R. G., Tirkel, A. Z., & Osborne, C. F. (1994). A digital watermark. In *Proc. IEEE International Conference on Image Processing* (Vol. 2, pp. 86–90). IEEE. doi:10.1109/ICIP.1994.413536

Xianghong, T., Lianjie, Y., Hengli, Y., & Zhongke, Y. (2005). A watermarking algorithm based on the SVD and Hadamard transform. In *Proc. International Conference on Communications, Circuits and Systems* (Vol. 2, pp. 874–877). Academic Press. doi:10.1109/ICCCAS.2005.1495248

Xin, Y., Liao, S., & Pawlak, M. (2004).Geometrically robust image watermarking via pseudo-Zernike moments. In *Proc. Canadian Conference on Electrical and Computer Engineering* (Vol. 2, pp. 939–942). Academic Press.

Yang, H. Y., Wang, X. Y., & Wang, C. P. (2012). *A robust digital watermarking algorithm in undecimated discrete wavelet transform domain.* Comput.Electri.Eng.

Yang, Y., Sun, X., Yang, H., Li, C. T., & Xiao, R. (2009). A contrast-sensitive reversible visible image watermarking technique. *IEEE Transactions on Circuits and Systems for Video Technology*, *19*(5), 656–667. doi:10.1109/TCSVT.2009.2017401

Yeung, M. M., Mintzer, F. C., Braudaway, G. W., & Rao, A. R. (1997).Digital watermarking for high-quality imaging. In *Proc. IEEE First Workshop on Multimedia Signal Processing* (pp. 357–362). IEEE. doi:10.1109/MMSP.1997.602661

Zhao, J., & Koch, E. (1995).Embedding robust labels into images for copyright protection. In *Proc. International Congress on Intellectual Property Rights for Specialised Information, Knowledge and New Technologies* (pp. 21-25). Academic Press.

KEY TERMS AND DEFINITIONS

Activation Functions: Functions which are used in neural networks to obtain the results.

Adaptive Watermarking: Process of calculating scaling and embedding factor using the content of cover image is called adaptive watermarking.

Computational Intelligence: Process of incorporating intelligence through the application of optimization technique, fuzzy logic and neural networks.

Digital Watermarking: Process of inserting a piece of digital information in a cover data is called digital watermarking.

Image Security: Process of providing security to images.

Sigmoid Function: One of the activation function which is used at output layer in artificial neural networks.

Transform Domain: In order to decorrelate the signal transformation technique is used. Domain in which signal gets decorrelated.

Chapter 10
Computational Aspects of Lattice–Based Cryptography on Graphical Processing Unit

Sedat Akleylek
Ondokuz Mayis University, Turkey

Zaliha Yuce Tok
Middle East Technical University, Turkey

ABSTRACT

In this chapter, the aim is to discuss computational aspects of lattice-based cryptographic schemes focused on NTRU in view of the time complexity on a graphical processing unit (GPU). Polynomial multiplication algorithms, having a very important role in lattice-based cryptographic schemes, are implemented on the GPU using the compute unified device architecture (CUDA) platform. They are implemented in both serial and parallel way. Compact and efficient implementation architectures of polynomial multiplication for lattice-based cryptographic schemes are presented for the quotient ring both $Z_p [x]/(x^n-1)$ and $Z_p [x]/(x^n+1)$, where p is a prime number. Then, by using these implementations the NTRUEncrypt and signature scheme working over $Z_p [x]/(x^n+1)$ are implemented on the GPU using CUDA platform. Implementation details are also discussed.

INTRODUCTION

Immediately after Shor proposed a polynomial time algorithm to solve integer factorization and discrete logarithm problem on a quantum computer (Shor, 1997), the demand to post-quantum cryptographic schemes started to increase. After this proposal, RSA, El-Gamal cryptosystem, elliptic curve based schemes became unreliable which causes a high demand for secure cryptographic protocols. These advancements also raise the importance of the studies on finding alternative systems that have efficient implementations on software/hardware platforms which are resistant to quantum attacks.

DOI: 10.4018/978-1-4666-9426-2.ch010

Post-quantum cryptographic schemes refer to the algorithms that are resistant to quantum attacks. These are the alternatives of public key cryptographic schemes such as RSA, DLP-based and elliptic curve based schemes. These schemes have been proposed for public key encryption, signature schemes and hash functions. Post-quantum cryptographic schemes can be classified as: code-based, hash-based, multivariate and lattice-based cryptography (Bernstein et al., 2009). The main problem in most of the post-quantum cryptographic schemes (code-based, multivariate and lattice-based cryptography) is the large key sizes. In hash-based schemes key sizes are relatively small such as 368-bit for 80-bit security. Due to large key sizes, in some cases they are not suitable for embedded devices such as smart cards, FPGAs. Another concern is the multiplication operation must be efficiently implemented in lattice-based cryptographic schemes since it is the most frequently used arithmetic operation.

Lattice-based cryptographic schemes are one of the most widely studied post-quantum cryptographic protocols. The security of these schemes depends on the hardness of lattice problems under some parameters (Bernstein et al., 2009). For several years lattice-based cryptographic schemes have only been considered secure for large system parameters causing inefficient implementations. Therefore, it's thought that they were not practical. In 1998, NTRU cryptosystem was proposed as a public key cryptographic scheme over polynomial rings using the computational properties of hard problems over lattices as an alternative to factorization or discrete logarithm problem based schemes (Hoffstein et al., 1998). Standardization of the NTRU is drafted in IEEE P1363 (IEEE, 2008) still in progress and commercialized by Security Innovation (Security Innovation, 2014). After this draft was published, the progress has shown that the design has robustness against different kind of attacks. Its encryption process is almost 10 times faster and decryption processes is almost 100 times faster than RSA for the 1024-bit security level. Furthermore, there is no evidence that it's vulnerable to practical or quantum attacks (Steinfeld, 2014). In this chapter, we focus on the arithmetic over the quotient ring $\mathbb{Z}_p[x]/(x^n - 1)$ used in NTRU schemes and also $\mathbb{Z}_p[x]/(x^n + 1)$ used in a signature scheme (Güneysu et al., 2012). The quotient ring $\mathbb{Z}_p[x]/(x^n + 1)$ can work with Fast Fourier Transform-based multiplications resulting in a more efficient scheme. This is why this quotient ring is preferred in most of the recent ring-based cryptographic schemes (Banerjee et al. 2012; Lyubashevsky et al., 2008; Lyubashevsky et al., 2013).

Graphical processing units (GPU) have attracted attention due to having high performance computing abilities. The main application area of GPUs is to execute commands in parallel with the computer graphics; hence they have been produced for gaming community. A general purpose GPU, having many cores (for example NVIDIA Quadro 600 has 96 cores), has a place on high performance computing applications. Due to processing unit having multiple processors, there is a need to implement such protocols on these platforms. There are several studies on parallel implementations of cryptographic protocols since they are useful for operations requiring lots of processing units (Cook et al., 2006). In this study, we give some ideas to combine advances of lattice-based cryptographic schemes and GPU implementations of them.

Arithmetic operations on the GPU have been widely studied for public key cryptographic schemes such as RSA and elliptic curve based protocols. Now, we give a brief information on how GPUs are utilized for various applications and academic studies. In (Szerwinski et al., 2008) efficient implementations of computationally expensive operations in RSA-1024 and 2048 and curve-based cryptographic schemes on NVIDIA 880GTS graphic card were presented. Standard radix form and residue number system approaches were used. This was the first study using the CUDA framework for general purpose GPU in public key cryptography. Shortly after (Szerwinski et al., 2008), (Gutierrez et al., 2008) proposed a radix-two decimation-in-time FFT implementation using the advantages of the GPU memory architecture. This FFT implementation can be used in multiplication operation. One year later, (Harrison et al., 2009) introduced an efficient GPU implementation of RSA. High performance modular exponentiation implementation both in standard form and residue number system form was presented. According to the experimental results GPU implementation of RSA was at least 4 times faster than CPU implementation for 1024-bit security level. Same year, (Giorgi et al., 2009) explained arithmetic operations over finite fields of large prime characteristic and elliptic curve scalar multiplication operations on the GPU. They also presented both serial and parallel version of these operations for large integers. Later on (Emeliyanenko, 2009) performed the parallelization of NTT algorithm on NVIDIA GTX280 using Chinese Remainder Theorem. (Wu, 2010) analyzed GPU implementations using CUDA platform of modular multiplication and exponentiation algorithms. A comparison of RSA implementation both on the CPU and GPU was given. In (Hinitt et al., 2010) the implementation of FFT algorithm on the GPU using the CUDA platform was demonstrated by exploiting the computational capability available to achieve high throughput. With this implementation interprocessor communication was reduced. In (Maza et al., 2010) CUDA implementation of polynomial multiplication with Fast Fourier Transform (FFT) over finite fields was presented. In (Neves et al., 2011) the required arithmetic operations for RSA-1024 such as modular multiplication, exponentiation were implemented on NVIDIA GT200 GPU. Interleaved Montgomery modular multiplication and exponentiation algorithm were used. Dense polynomial arithmetic techniques over finite fields were implemented on NVIDIA GTX285 running CUDA and discussed the efficiency of these in (Haque et al., 2012). Speeding up techniques for integer multiplication using FFT on GPU was given in (Bantikyan, 2013) with the help of cuFFT library. Recall that cuFFT is optimized version of FFT on the GPU for the parallel processing.

The first implementation of NTRU on a GPU was given in (Hermans et al., 2010). They implemented schoolbook multiplication in a circular cyclic manner with $O\left(n^2\right)$ complexity on NVIDIA GTX280. The required data was generated on the CPU and then sent to the GPU for the other computations. They also showed that although the schoolbook multiplication method was used, for the same security level NTRU had a better performance than RSA and elliptic curve based cryptographic schemes.

There has been an interest for the implementation of lattice-based cryptography in FPGA. The main reason is to run the arithmetic operations in a parallel way. Multiplication algorithms which are the core part of the lattice-based cryptographic schemes for FPGAs were discussed in (Pöppelmann et al., 2012). They gave the implementation details of how to parallelize NTT algorithm for the precomputed values. Due to the memory requirements of finding the values, the precomputation step was not performed on the FPGA but these values were given to the system directly. In (Aysu et al., 2013) low-cost and area efficient hardware architecture for polynomial multiplication with NTT applications in lattice-based cryptographic schemes was presented. They computed all values on the FPGA. In (Guneysu et al., 2014) a provably secure lattice-based signature scheme and its implementation on different reconfigurable hardware devices were presented. This study can be considered as an extended version of (Güneysu et al., 2012). In (Chen et al., 2014) hardware architecture of FFT-based polynomial multiplication algorithm with $O\left(n \log n\right)$ complexity was performed. They also provided an efficient modular reduction design.

In (Akleylek et al., 2014-3) modified version of interleaved Montgomery modular multiplication method for lattice-based cryptography was given. With the proposed algorithms, the multiplication complexity was significantly improved and GPU implementation was provided.

In this chapter our aim is to give a different point of view for implementation of lattice-based cryptographic schemes on the GPU. To do this, we firstly discuss the well-known polynomial multiplication algorithms and then present modified versions of them to improve the performance of the scheme. The goal is to parallelize the algorithms efficiently. We also provide the implementation details on the GPU using the CUDA platform. Then, we compare the results with compute unified Fast Fourier Transform (cuFFT) library optimized to provide high performance on the GPUs. We show that in some cases, using modified algorithms increases the performance of the NTRUEncrypt and signature schemes.

This chapter is organized as follows: In Section 2 we give the details of NTRUEncrypt and signature scheme working over $\mathbb{Z}_p[x]/(x^n+1)$. We also summarize the GPU technologies and CUDA platform used to implement the algorithms. In Section 3 we discuss the polynomial multiplication techniques and their modification to the lattice-based cryptographic schemes. In Section 4 we compare the implementations of multiplication algorithm described in Section 3. Then, we give the implementation details for the selected lattice-based cryptographic schemes such as NTRUEncrypt and signature scheme working over $\mathbb{Z}_p[x]/(x^n+1)$. We also compare our results with the previous ones. We conclude and give future research ideas in Section 5.

BACKGROUND

In this section, the details of Number Theory Research Unit (NTRU) cryptosystems are briefly explained. Parameter selection, key generation, encryption, decryption, signature generation and verification processes are discussed. Then, an overview is presented about of how the GPU and CUDA platform are utilized in implementations.

NTRU was firstly introduced as an encryption scheme in (Hoffstein et al., 1998). Then, in 2003, digital signature scheme using the NTRU lattices was proposed in (Hoffstein et al., 2003). Since NTRU encryption scheme has homomorphic properties under addition and multiplication, fully homomorphic schemes based on NTRU have been received much attention (Lopez-Alt et al., 2012). NTRU has a practical key size compared to other lattice-based cryptographic schemes. However, it still needs improvement on computational intelligence issues. The main operation in NTRU cryptosystems is the polynomial multiplication over a polynomial ring. The efficiency of NTRU encryption scheme depends on the arithmetic in (x^n-1) where the modular reduction is almost free. This section consists of three parts: NTRUEncrypt over $\mathbb{Z}_p[x]/(x^n-1)$, signature scheme working over $\mathbb{Z}_p[x]/(x^n+1)$ and an overview of GPU CUDA.

NTRUEncrypt

In this section we give the basic encryption and decryption phases for NTRU described in (Hoffstein et al., 1998).

Let $\mathbb{Z}_q$ be the ring of integers modulo q. The system parameters of NTRU are (n,p,q) with $\gcd(p,q)=1$ and $n/2<q<n$ is always larger than p. For example, in (IEEE, 2008) it is recommended that $n=251, q=128$ and $p=3$. In general p is chosen from the set $\{2,3,2+x\}$ which allows

very efficient arithmetic. Note that reduction with 3 gives one of the following elements $\{-1,0,1\}$. NTRUEncrypt is a cryptosystem working on the polynomial ring $\mathbb{Z}_p[x]/(x^n-1)$. The main operation in NTRUEncrypt is the multiplication of two polynomials over the quotient ring.

One needs to define four polynomial sets called $f \in \mathcal{L}_f, g \in \mathcal{L}_g, r \in \mathcal{L}_r$ and $m \in \mathcal{L}_m$ to choose private keys f and g, random polynomial r and the message m. New integer parameters (d_1, d_2) are required to obtain the desired sets. Let $\mathcal{L}(d_1, d_2)$ be the set of polynomials in $\mathbb{Z}_p[x]/(x^n-1)$ having d_1 coefficients equal to 1, d_2 coefficients equal to -1 and all other coefficients set to 0. There are several choices to define the sets of polynomials $\mathcal{L}_f, \mathcal{L}_g, \mathcal{L}_r$. Since our goal is to obtain an effective scheme, we should consider in which cases we have easy arithmetic operations such as multiplication with 1, almost free inversion computation. Thanks to (Geissler et al., 2005) for the selected parameters d_f, d_g and d_r, we have:

$$\mathcal{L}_f = \left\{1 + p * f : f \in \mathcal{L}(d_f, 0)\right\}, \; \mathcal{L}_g = \mathcal{L}(d_g, 0), \; \mathcal{L}_r = \mathcal{L}(d_r, 0)$$

By using these sets, it's guaranteed that computing f_p^{-1} is particularly easy and $f_p^{-1} \equiv 1 \bmod p$. Now, we are ready to summarize the key generation, encryption and decryption phases for NTRUEncrypt.

Key Generation

Input: NTRU domain parameters(n, p, q)
Output: private key $f \in \mathbb{Z}_q[x]/(x^n-1)$, public key h

1.   Choose random polynomial $f \in \mathcal{L}_f$
2.   Choose random polynomial $g \in \mathcal{L}_g$
3.   Compute f_q^{-1} such that $ff_q^{-1} \equiv 1 \bmod q$
4. $h \equiv \left(p * f_q^{-1} * g\right) \bmod q$

Encryption

Input: Message m, public key h
Output: Ciphertext e

1.   Choose random polynomial $r \in \mathcal{L}_r$ as a masking (blinding) factor
2. $e \equiv \left(r * h + m\right) \bmod q$

Decryption

Input: Private key f, f_p^{-1}, f_q^{-1}, ciphertext e
Output: Message m

1. $a \equiv \left(e * f \right) mod \ q$
2. $a \equiv \left(r * p * f_q^{-1} * g * f + m * f \right) mod \ q$
3. $a \equiv \left(p * r * g + m * f \right) mod \ q$
4. $a * f_p^{-1} \equiv \left(p * r * g * f_p^{-1} + m * f * f_p^{-1} \right) mod \ p$
5. $a * f_p^{-1} \equiv \left(m * f * f_p^{-1} \right) mod \ p$
6. $m \equiv a \ mod \ p$ since $f_p^{-1} \equiv 1 \ mod \ p$

Signature Scheme

In this section we recall the lattice-based signature scheme implemented on the FPGA (Güneysu et al., 2012). The main reason to choose this signature scheme is the higher efficiency compared to other proposed schemes.

Let n be a power of 2 and $\mathbb{Z}_p$ be the ring of integers modulo p, where p is a prime number and $p \equiv 1 \ mod \ 2n$. The signature scheme is defined over the polynomial ring $\mathbb{Z}_p[x] / (x^n + 1)$. The polynomials are in the quotient ring of degree at most *(n-1)* with coefficients in $\left[-\dfrac{(p-1)}{2}, \dfrac{(p-1)}{2} \right]$.

The proposed scheme works on the ring $\mathbb{Z}_p[x] / (x^n + 1)$. Key generation, signature generation and signature verification processes are given below. Hash, compression and transform algorithms are in (Güneysu et al., 2012).

Key Generation

Input: Prime p, polynomial degree n
Output: Public key t, private key (s_1, s_2)

1. Choose random polynomials s_1, s_2 from the polynomial ring $\mathbb{Z}_p[x] / (x^n + 1)$ where all integer coefficients are from the set {-1, 0, 1}
2. $t = as_1 + s_2$

Signature Generation

Input: Private key (s_1, s_2), message $m = \{0,1\}^*$

Output: Signature (z_1, z_2') with integer coefficients in the range $[-(k\text{-}32), k\text{-}32]$ and 160-bit hash output c.

1. Choose random polynomials (y_1, y_2), from the polynomial ring $\mathbb{Z}_p[x] / (x^n + 1)$ with integer coefficients from the set $\{-k, \ldots, -1, 0, 1, \ldots, k\}$ where k is the predefined security parameter
2. $c =$ Hash(Transform( ), m) // 160-bit hash value of the higher order bits of $(ay_1 + y_2)$
3. $z_1 = s_1 c + y_1$
4. $z_2 = s_2 c + y_2$
5. If the coefficients of z_1 or z_2 are not in the range $[-(k\text{-}32), k\text{-}32]$ then go to Step 1.
6. $z_2' = Compress(ay_1 + y_2, p, k - 32)$ // compression of the polynomial z_2 into z_2'
7. If compression fails, go to Step 1

Signature Verification

Input: Signature (z_1, z_2') with integer coefficients in the range $[-(k\text{-}32), k\text{-}32]$, public key t, 160-bit hash output c, message $m = \{0,1\}^*$

Output: "Verified" or "not verified"

1. if the coefficients of z_1 or z_2' are not in the range $[-(k\text{-}32), k\text{-}32]$
2.   return "not verified"
3.   if $c = Hash\left(Transform\left(az_1 + z_2' - tc\right), m\right)$
4.   return "verified"
5. else
6.   return "not verified"

GPU Technologies

In this section we give a short introduction to GPU technologies and CUDA platform. 2000s manufacturers' main goal is to speed up the clock cycle of the processors. However limitations on manufacturing integration circuits made infeasible to get big performance gains on central processors. This causes the huge usage of parallel environments in multicore computers, notebooks and even mobile phones.

With these developments parallel environments have shifted from super computers to tools we use daily. In the meantime, graphic processing underwent a dramatic revolution. Revolutions started with 2D display accelerators used in personal computers and continued with 3Ds used in many applications like graphics and gaming. NVIDIA and ATI technologies evolved the graphic accelerators and made affordable to users on many applications (NVIDIA Graphics, 2014; ATI Graphics, 2014).

Figure 1. Simple CPU/GPU hardware configuration

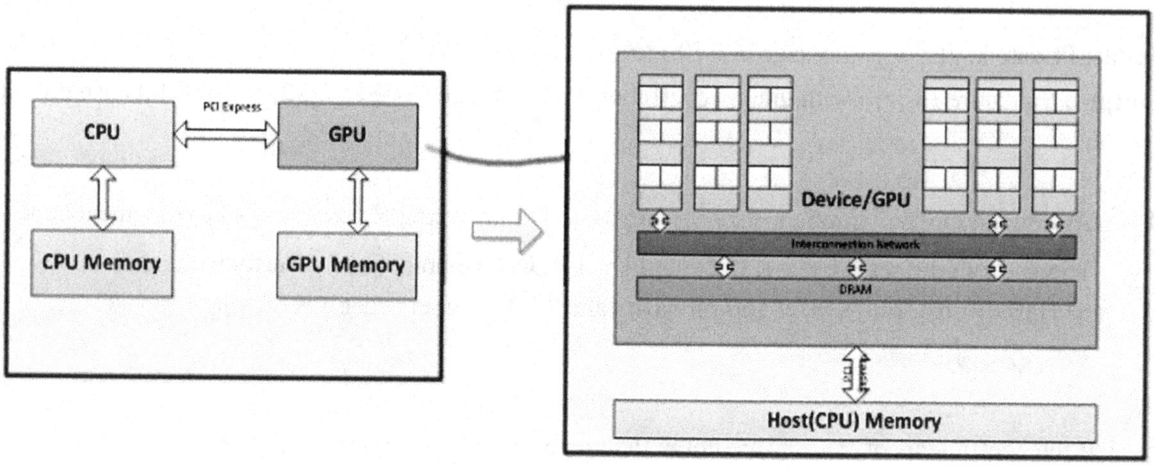

Early release of NVIDIA GPUs used Microsoft's DirectX standard. Then NVIDIA announced the first GPU cards GeForce 8800 GTX that is built with NVIDIA's CUDA. This new architecture has brought new components designed for strictly GPU computing and new alternatives for usage of graphic processors on general-purpose applications. In this study we prefer to use NVIDIA (Quadro 600) GPU, because it has more implementation alternatives compared to ATI technologies. Now we give a brief survey on hardware and software configuration of NVIDIA CUDA.

NVIDIA GPU Hardware Configurations

The main functionality of the "chipset" or "core logic" is connecting the CPU to outside world. Every input/output from network controllers, disk, keyboards, GPUs goes through this chipset (Wilt, 2013). GPUs were connected through this chipsets called PCI Express bus. Theoretically PCI Express designed to deliver about 500 MB/s of bandwidths which was not appropriate for GPUs. With new hardware configurations GPUs are designed up to 8G/s of bandwidths which is appropriate for parallel applications. Figure 1 shows the basic GPU architecture.

Multiple CPUs, CPU with integrated memory controller and integrated GPUs have different architectures that are widely used in GPU hardware for different needs. For interested readers, we recommend The CUDA Handbook (Wilt, 2013).

NVIDIA GPU Software Configurations

CUDA software designed in layer basis, at the deepest level starts with driver and continues with some tools such as driver APIs, runtime environment, libraries. In Figure 2 layered structure of CUDA software is given.

CUDA software, designed to operate on Windows, Linux and MacOS, is a parallel computing programming model maintained by NVIDIA. Since CUDA is an extension of the C programming language, applications are developed in C/C++ programming language by directly using CUDA driver API or special libraries for linear algebra operation, matrix operations etc.

Figure 2. Layered structure of CUDA software

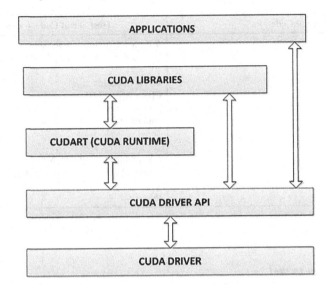

CUDA Program Structure

A CUDA program consists of two parts which are run on either the host (CPU) or a device such as a GPU. The parts that have rich amount of data parallelism are implemented in the device code. The program has a single source code for both host and device code. The NVIDIA C Compiler (NVCC) compiles the host code on standard C compiler and runs it as an ordinary process. The device code is written using CUDA API including parallel functions, compiled by NVCC and then executed on a GPU device. Figure 3 shows the CUDA execution model. Each GPU kernel call launches CUDA grids and device code run on the GPU.

CUDA parallel functions (kernel functions) use special thread structure that is composed of grids and blocks. At the basic level grids map to GPUs, blocks map to MultiProcessors (MP) and threads map to Stream Processors (SP). All threads have unique coordinates to handle which portion of the data to be processed. 2D hierarchy exists called blockId and threadId in CUDA runtime system for thread. Figure 3 shows the CUDA grid structure. CUDA grids have two dimensions which defines the size of the grid in x and y dimension. Each block consists of 2D or 3D thread structure in x, y or x,y,z dimensions. Both block and thread dimensions defines which thread will perform the required process.

A sample code for parallel CUDA implementation with the serial version is as follows (Table 1).

The function to be parallelized called with kernel launch according to given block-thread structure. In the sample code VectorAdd function uses 1 block with N threads. Since only one block is called and 1D thread is used CUDA defined threadIdx parameter is sufficient. For multiple blocks and 2D, 3D threads CUDA predefines parameters block dimension y and thread dimension z.

CUDA in Cryptographic Applications

Unlike previous parallel programming languages, CUDA gives an alternative way to easy development of parallel application on different fields such as cryptographic protocols. Several works are done for lots of cryptosystems on CUDA. The performance results are shared especially for block ciphers such

Table 1. Sample code

Host – Serial Code	Host Serial Code + Device Parallel Code
```void MatAdd(float* A, float* B, float* C]) { for(int i=0; i<N; i++) C[i] = A[i] + B[i]; } void serial_sample() { … VectorAdd(A, B, C); } (a)```	```// Kernel definition, device side ____global__ void VecAdd(float* A, float* B, float* C) { int i = threadIdx.x; C[i] = A[i] + B[i]; } void parallelSample //host side { … // Kernel invocation with N threads VectorAdd<<<1, N>>>(A, B, C);... } (b)```

Figure 3. CUDA execution model

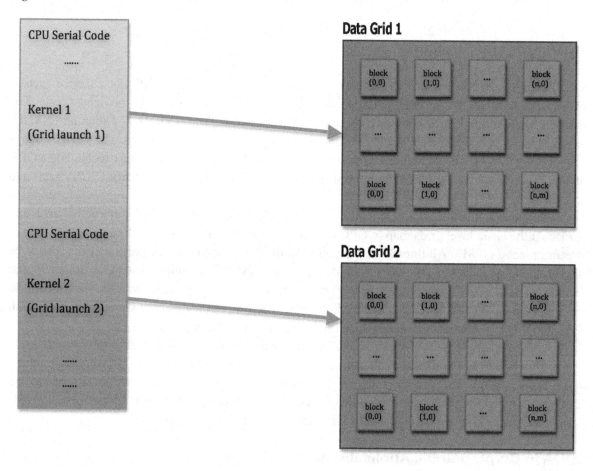

Figure 4. CUDA grid structure

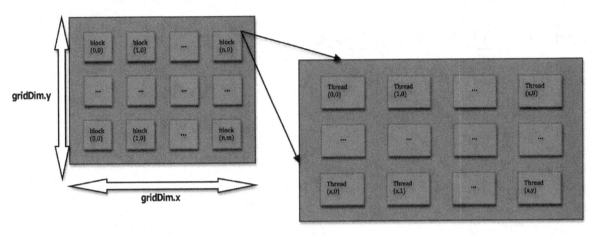

as AES and DES (Manavski, 2007). Also public key cryptographic protocols such as RSA, ECDSA and NTRU were implemented (Harrison et al., 2009; Hermans et al., 2010; Neves et al., 2011; Szerwinski et al., 2008; Wu, 2010).

In this paper, we use CUDA API for polynomial multiplication operations. Note that CUDA has several libraries such as cuFFT and cuBLAS that are efficiently designed for specific operations. We also use the cuFFT library for polynomial multiplication operations which gives us a big performance gain on large bit sizes. cuFFT is the NVIDIA's Fast Fourier Transform product (NVIDIA CUDA, 2014). It consists of two separate libraries cuFFT and cuFFTW. The cuFFT library is designed to provide high performance on NVIDIA GPUs. The cuFFTW library is provided as a porting tool to enable users of FFTW to start using NVIDIA GPUs with a minimum amount of effort. We use the cuFFT library for comparison.

MULTIPLICATION TECHNIQUES

In this section, we discuss the polynomial multiplication techniques modified to be used in lattice-based cryptographic schemes. The selected methods are schoolbook method (serial and parallel versions), number theoretic transform (NTT – parallel, iterative and parallel iterative versions), CUDA fast Fourier transform (FFT), fast convolution and its sliding window version. We also explain faster arithmetic for NTT. We divide this section into two parts:

- Multiplication over the quotient ring $\mathbb{Z}_p[x]/(x^n - 1)$
- Multiplication over the quotient ring $\mathbb{Z}_p[x]/(x^n + 1)$

Algorithm 1. Schoolbook method

Input: $a(x) = \sum_{i=0}^{n-1} a_i x^i$ and $b(x) = \sum_{i=0}^{n-1} b_i x^i \in \mathbb{Z}_p[x] / (x^n - 1)$

Output: $c(x) = a(x)b(x) = \sum_{i=0}^{n-1} c_i x^i$

```
1. Set all coefficients of c(x) to 0
2.     for k=0 to n
3.         for i=0 to n
4.             c_k = c_k +b_i a_{n+k-i} mod p
5.         end for
6.     end for
7.     return c(x)
```

Multiplication over the Quotient Ring $\mathbb{Z}_p[x] / (x^n - 1)$

We now give the modular multiplication techniques: (parallelized) schoolbook method, fast convolution method and its sliding window version. Let $a(x) = \sum_{i=0}^{n-1} a_i x^i$ and $b(x) = \sum_{i=0}^{n-1} b_i x^i$ be polynomials in $\mathbb{Z}_p[x] / (x^n - 1)$ and $c(x) = a(x)b(x)$ with $c_j = \sum_{i=0}^{j} a_i b_{j-i} + \sum_{i=j+1}^{n-1} a_i b_{n+j-i}$ by using $x^n \equiv 1 \mod(x^n - 1)$.

Schoolbook Method

In Algorithm 1, the naïve multiplication method called schoolbook is given. In this method, each coefficient of the first polynomial is multiplied with the other polynomial and then modular reduction operation according to p is performed. The classical schoolbook algorithm has a quadratic complexity $O(n^2)$ with n^2 multiplications and $(n-1)^2$ additions.

In Algorithm 2 parallelized version of schoolbook method is given. Algorithm 2 consists of two parts: CPU and GPU sides. In CPU side, there is a need to create GPU grids and blocks with respect to the degree of the polynomial. Then, from Step 2 to Step 4 allocating memory operation is performed on CUDA platform. By calling GPU schoolbook procedure, parallel multiplication is performed in Step 5. In Step 6 the results are turned back to the host. In GPU side, each coefficients of $a(x)$ is multiplied by $b(x)$ and then added to $c(x)$ in threads.

Fast Convolution Method

Fast convolution algorithm (Lee et al., 2007; Lee et al., 2013) uses the following modular reduction fact: $x^n \equiv 1 \mod(x^n - 1)$, $x^{n+1} \equiv x \mod(x^n - 1)$, ..., $x^{2n-2} \equiv x^{n-2} \mod(x^n - 1)$. With the help of these equations the modular multiplication of two elements $a(x) = \sum_{i=0}^{n-1} a_i x^i$ and $b(x) = \sum_{i=0}^{n-1} b_i x^i$ can be written in a matrix-vector product form as follows:

Algorithm 2. Parallelized Schoolbook Method (CPU and GPU side)

Input: $a(x) = \sum_{i=0}^{n-1} a_i x^i$ and $b(x) = \sum_{i=0}^{n-1} b_i x^i \in \mathbb{Z}_p[x] / (x^n - 1) \, \mathbb{Z}_p[x] / \langle x^n \pm 1 \rangle$

Output: $c(x) = a(x)b(x) = \sum_{i=0}^{n-1} c_i x^i$

```
CPU side
1. grids, blocks = create gpu grids and blocks according to n
2. allocate_cuda_memory(cuda_a);
3. allocate_cuda_memory(cuda_b);
4. allocate_cuda_memory(cuda_c);
5. call gpu_schoolbook_procedure <<grids, blocks>(cuda_a,cuda_b,cuda_c)
6. cuda_copy(cuda_c,c);
7. return c
GPU side (gpu_schoolbook_procedure)
1. thread_idx = block_id.x * block_dimension.x+ threadIdx.x
2. if thread_idx > n
4. return;
5. end if
6. for i=0 to n
```
7. $c_{thread\_idx} = c_{thread\_idx} + b_{thread\_idx-i} a_i \; mod \; p$
```
8. end for
9. return c(x)
```

$$c(x) = \begin{pmatrix} a_0 & a_{n-1} & \cdots & a_2 & a_1 \\ a_1 & a_0 & \cdots & a_3 & a_2 \\ \vdots & \vdots & \ddots & \vdots & \vdots \\ a_{n-2} & a_{n-3} & \cdots & a_0 & a_{n-1} \\ a_{n-1} & a_{n-2} & \cdots & a_1 & a_0 \end{pmatrix} \begin{bmatrix} b_0 \\ b_1 \\ \vdots \\ b_{n-2} \\ b_{n-1} \end{bmatrix}$$

Notice that $c_j = \sum_{i+k \equiv j \bmod n} a_i b_k$ each row of this A matrix is the one cyclic shift of the previous row. In Algorithm 3 we give the fast convolution algorithm step by step. Note that the complexity of fast convolution algorithm depends on the Hamming of $a(x)$. Assume that Hamming weight of $a(x)$ is e. Then, the required number of operations is $(e+1)n$ (Step 4 and Step 8) and n (Step 8), additions and modular reductions, respectively.

Fast Convolution with Sliding Window Method

One can speed up the fast convolution method by using some patterns in the polynomials, which is called sliding window method for NTRU (Lee et al., 2007; Lee et al., 2013). This method needs some memory to store the results for the corresponding pattern. In order to apply multiplication with sliding

Algorithm 3. Fast convolution algorithm

Input: $a\left(x\right)=\sum_{i=0}^{n-1}a_i x^i$ and $b\left(x\right)=\sum_{i=0}^{n-1}b_i x^i$ are the elements of $\mathbb{Z}_p\left[x\right]/\left(x^n-1\right)$. d is an array showing the index of 1's in a(x) and e is the number of 1's.

Output: $c\left(x\right)=a\left(x\right)b\left(x\right)=\sum_{i=0}^{n-1}c_i x^i$

```
1. Set all coefficients of c(x) to 0
2.      for i=0 to e-1
3.           for j=0 to n-1
4.                     c_{j+d[i]} = c_{j+d[i]} +b_j
5.           end for
6.      end for
7.      for i=0 to n-1
8.                c_i = (c_i +c_{i+n}) mod p
9.      end for
10.    return c(x)
```

window method, one needs to convert the coefficients to binary form. By searching for simple patterns like 1,11,101,1001, etc. the same coefficients are calculated only once and stored in the look-up table. The main idea is to find patterns that have many 1's and repeat many times in the coefficients for an efficient implementation. Note that the selected patterns do not share the same 1's. Lemma 1 gives the improvement in the required number of additions.

Lemma 1: Let u be the number of 1's in the pattern and v be the number of occurrences for the selected pattern. Then, the required number of additions is $n(v+u-1)$ over $\mathbb{Z}_p\left[x\right]/\left(x^n-1\right)$.

By Lemma 1 patterns in different forms help to reduce the required number of additions. We have the following steps to use multiplication with sliding window method:

- **Finding Patterns:** We partition the binary string into short blocks of a fixed length, w, except for the parts containing consecutive zeroes. This is equivalent to a sliding window method with window size w in the context of modular exponentiation in RSA. Pattern search technique is given in Algorithm 4. In this study we focus on finding the patterns having only two 1's with the first and last position of the string for example 11, 101, 1001 and so on.
- **Recoding:** After using Algorithm 4, we make a list to show where the pattern ends in the binary representation. For example, let $a=(1001011101)$ and $w=3$. Then, $d_0=\left\{0,6\right\}$ shows the positions of 1's not in the any pattern. $d_2=\left\{5,9\right\}$ gives the positions where the pattern (101) finishes (numbering is left to right). Note that since we use the 1's only once, there is no (11) pattern; so d_1 is an empty set.

Algorithm 4. Pattern search algorithm

Input: y is a binary string having n elements and w is the window size.
Output: d_0, is an integer array representing the positions of '1's not included in any pattern. d_1, d_2, and d_{w-1} is also an array giving the positions of 1's in y for 11, 101, . .., 100...1 of length w, respectively..

```
1.i = n - 1
2.while i≥0
3.        while i≥0 and y[i] !=1
4.                i=i-1
5.        end while
6.         for j=1 to w-1
7.                if y[i-j] == 1
8.                     append i to d_j
9.                     i =i - j -1
10.                else
11.                    append i to d_o
12.                    i=i-w
13.                end if
14.            end for
15.  end while
16.return all d_i's
```

- **Precomputation:** By using the selected patterns, a look-up table is computed.
- **Multiplication:** The coefficients of the *c(x)* are computed as in fast convolution manner.

In Algorithm 5, fast convolution with sliding window method is given. In this method the operations are done for the related pattern obtained by using Algorithm 4. Note that the number of stored integers is *n(w-1)*. Precomputation is done from Step 2 to Step 10. Multiplication is performed between Step 11 and Step 21.

Multiplication over the Quotient Ring $Z_p[x]/(x^n + 1)$

In this section, we give some of the selected algorithms: modified fast convolution, number theoretic transform in serial and parallel type and CUDA-based FFT (cuFFT). We focus on the arithmetic over the quotient ring $\mathbb{Z}_p[x]/(x^n + 1)$ having important applications in lattice-based cryptographic schemes due to the applicability of FFT-based polynomial multiplication enabling efficient modular multiplication (Banerjee et al. 2012; Chen et al., 2014; Güneysu et al., 2012; Lyubashevsky et al., 2008; Lyubashevsky et al., 2013). Note that we also implement the schoolbook method over the quotient ring $\mathbb{Z}_p[x]/(x^n + 1)$. Since the idea is very similar to Algorithm 1 and Algorithm 2, we omit it.

Algorithm 5. Fast convolution with sliding window method

Input: For $0 \leq i \leq (w - 1)$ d_i is an array having the positions e_i of the pattern p_i in the binary polynomial a(x). b(x) is a polynomial of degree (n-1) and w is the window size.

Output:: $c\left(x\right) = a\left(x\right)b\left(x\right) = \sum_{i=0}^{n-1} c_i x^i$

1. Set all coefficients of c(x) to 0
2. for j=0 to w-1
3. $b_{j+n} = b_j$
4. end for
5. *for $i = 1\, to\, w - 1$*
6. *for $0 \leq j \leq n$*
7. $C_i\left[j\right] = b_j + b_{j+1}$
8. end for
9. end for
10. *Let $C_0 = b$ i.e. $C_0\left[k\right] = b_k\, for\, 0 \leq k \leq n$*
11. *for $i = 0\, to\, w - 1$*
12. *for $j = 0\, to\, e_i$*
13. *for $k = 0\, to\, n$*
14. $c_{k + d_i[j]} = c_{k + d_i[j]} + C_i\left[k\right]$
15. end for
16. end for
17. end for
18. *for $j = 0\, to\, n$*
19. $c_j = c_j + c_{j+n}\, mod\, p$
20. end for
21. return c(x)

Number Theoretic Transform

Number Theoretic Transform (NTT) algorithm was proposed in (Pollard, 1974) to avoid rounding errors in Fast Fourier Transform (FFT). NTT, a Discrete Fourier Transform defined over a ring or a finite field, is used to multiply two integers and does not require arithmetic operations in complex numbers. The multiplication complexity is quasi-linear $\left(O\left(nlogn\right)\right)$. The main idea is to transform polynomials to NTT form. Algorithm 6 describes the iterative NTT which is the modified version of (Akleylek et al., 2014; Akleylek et al., 2014-2; Arndt, 2011).

There are some restrictions on applying NTT algorithm:

- The degree of the quotient ring $\left(\mathbb{Z}_p[x] / (x^n + 1) \right)$ n should divide $(p\text{-}1)$
- $\omega^n \equiv 1 \bmod p$ and for each $i < n$, $\omega^i \neq 1 \bmod p$

Let w be the primitive n-th root of unity. For $a(x) = \sum_{i=0}^{n-1} a_i x^i \in \mathbb{Z}_p[x]$ by using w, NTT $\left(NTT_w(a) \right)$ is defined as follows:

$$A_i = \sum_{j=0}^{n-1} a_j \omega^{ij} \bmod p, i = 0, 1, \ldots n - 1$$

where $A = \{A_0, A_1, \ldots, A_{n-1}\}$ is the NTT form. The inverse transform $NTT_w^{-1}(A)$ is given as:

$$a_i = n^{-1} \sum_{j=0}^{n-1} A_j \omega^{-ij} \bmod p, i = 0, 1, \ldots n - 1$$

By using Convolution Theorem (Winkler, 1996) arbitrary polynomials can be multiplied and then reduce according to chosen reduction polynomial. However appending n 0's to the inputs doubles the transform size. To use NTT to multiply two elements in $\mathbb{Z}_p[x] / (x^n + 1)$ the condition is $p \equiv 1 \bmod 2n$ due to wrapped convolution approach (Lyubashevsky et al., 2008). This idea is given in lattice-based hash function SWIFFT which needs modular reduction operations in $(x^n + 1)$.

After computing NTT of two polynomials, the multiplication operation can be performed. Algorithm 7 gives polynomial multiplication with iterative NTT (Akleylek et al., 2014; Akleylek et al., 2014-2;).

In Algorithm 8 the parallel version of iterative NTT method is given. To make it efficient, we focus on "for" loops. Parallelization is achieved by determining the required number of threads. This algorithm needs data transfer between CPU and GPU. Thus, there is a delay and this causes inefficiency.

CUDA Fast Fourier Transform (cuFFT) Based Multiplication

The NVIDIA cuFFT library enables the users to have very fast FFT computations with an interface on the GPU by using CUDA platform (NVIDIA CUDA, 2014). cuFFT is optimized for a wide range application area from computational physics to signal processing. In this study we use cuFFT to obtain an efficient polynomial multiplication over the quotient ring. In Algorithm 9 we give the parallel version of polynomial multiplication method using CUDA. In Step 5 the schedule is planned to have FFT value on GPU and then in Step 6 and Step 7 the computed values are stored. The component wise multiplication is performed in a parallel way in Step 8. Forward FFT is achieved in Step 9. The result is sent to host in Step 11. From Step 13 to Step 15 normalization of the computed values is performed by simply dividing the result to the polynomial degree n.

Algorithm 6. Iterative NTT algorithm

Input: $a \in \mathbb{Z}_p[x]/(x^n+1)$ and $\omega \in \mathbb{Z}_p[x]/(x^n+1)$ is the primitive n-th root of unity.

Output: NIT$_w$(a)

```
1.   f = BitReverseCopy(a)
2.   f = SumDiff(f)
3.   n = 2ldn //length of the sequence
4.   rn = element_of_order(n)
5.   if reverse NTT  then rn = rn(-1)
6.   end if
7.   for ldm=1 to ldn
8.       m  = 2^ldm
9.       mh = m/2
10.      dw = rn^2^{ldn-ldm}
11.      w  = 1
12.      for j=0 to mh-1
13.          for r=0 to n-m step m
14.              t1 = r + j
15.              t2=t1+mh
16.              v = f[t2]*w
17.              u = f[t1]
18.              f[t1] = u+v
19.              f[t2] = u-v
20.          end for
21.      end for
22.      w = w * dw  // trig recursion
23. end for
24. return f
```

Algorithm 7. Polynomial multiplication with iterative NTT

Input: $a(x)b(x) \in \mathbb{Z}_p[x]/(x^n+1)$

Output: $c(x) = a(x)b(x)$

```
1. ntta[]=iterative_NTT(a[], ldn, forward)
2. nttb[]=iterative_NTT(b[], ldn, forward)
3. for i=0 to n-1
4.      c[i]= ntta[i]nttb[i] mod p
5. end for
6. c=iterative_NTT(c[], ldn, inverse)
7. for i=0 to n-1
8.      c[i]=c[i]/(ldn-1)
9. end for
10. return c
```

Algorithm 8. Parallelized Iterative NTT Method (CPU and GPU side)

Input: $b(x) = \sum_{i=0}^{n-1} b_i x^i \in$ and $\mathbb{Z}_p[x]/<x^n+1>$

Output: $c(x) = a(x)b(x) = \sum_{i=0}^{n-1} c_i x^i$

```
1.   f = BitReverseCopy(a)
2.   f = SumDiff(f)
3.   ldn base 2 logarithm of n
4.   rn = element_of_order(n)
5.   if reverse NTT  then rn = rn⁻¹ modp
6.   end if
7.   for   ldm=2 to ldn
8.      m  = 2^ldm
9.      mh = m/2
10.     dw = rn^2^ldn-ldm
11.     create blocks and grids
12.     call gpu_ntt_procedure  <<<grids, blocks>> (f,dw)
13. end for
14. return f
gpu_procedure_1 (f, dw)
1. thread_idx = block_id.x * block_dimension.x+ threadIdx.x
2. thread_idy = block_id.y * block_dimension.y+ threadIdx.y
3. if (thread_idx>0 or thread_idy== 0
4.      return
5. end if
6. for i = 0 to thread_idy
7.     w=w.dw modp
8. end for
9. t1 = thread_idx *mh + thread_idy
10.  t2= t1*mh
11. v= at2*w modp
12. u = at1
13. at1 = u +v modp
14. at1 = u -v modp
```

Algorithm 9. cuFFT-based multiplication

Input: $a(x) = \sum_{i=0}^{n-1} a_i x^i$ and $b(x) = \sum_{i=0}^{n-1} b_i x^i \in \mathbb{Z}_p[x] / \langle x^n + 1 \rangle \mathbb{Z}_p[x] / \langle x^n \pm 1 \rangle$

Output: $c(x) = a(x) b(x) = \sum_{i=0}^{n-1} c_i x^i$

```
1.  allocate_cuda_memory(cuda_a)
2.  allocate_cuda_memory(cuda_b)
3.  cuda_copy(a, cuda_a)
4.  cuda_copy(b, cuda_b)
5.  cufftPlan1d(planForward, n, CUFFT_D2Z, 1)
6.  cufftExecD2Z(planForward, cuda_a, cuda_a);
7.  cufftExecD2Z(planForward, cuda_b, cuda_b);
8.  multiply_complex(cuda_a, cuda_b, cuda_a)
9.  cufftPlan1d(planInverse, n, CUFFT_Z2D, 1)
10. cufftExecD2Z(planInverse, cuda_a, cuda_a);
11. copy the result from gpu to host
12. cuda_copy(cuda_a, c);
13. for i=0 to n
```
14. $c_i = c_i / n$
```
15. end for16.
16. return c
```

RESULTS AND COMPARISON

In this section, we give timing results of the multiplication algorithms, NTRUEncrypt, signature generation and verification processes. To obtain more consistent results the algorithms are run 1000 times for the uniformly random polynomials in the multiplication operation. To compare the multiplication operation on the GPU using CUDA platform we fix $p = 49201153$ satisfying $p \equiv 1 \bmod 2n$. In Table 2, we list the properties of experiment platform.

Table 2. The configuration of our experiment platform

CPU	Intel(R) Xeon E3-1230 3.30GHz
Memory	8 GB
Operating System	Windows 7 (64-bit)
GPU Accelerator	NVIDIA Quadro 600
GPU Memory	1 GB

Table 3. Timing results of multiplication of two elements in $\mathbb{Z}_p[x]/(x^n-1)$ (n/second)

n	1024	2048	4096	8192
Schoolbook Method	14,856	58,918	238,165	967,287
Fast Convolution Method	1,768	6,999	28,109	109,441
Fast Convolution with Sliding Window Method	0,994	3,892	15,307	59,486
Parallelized Schoolbook Method	2,964	5,298	19,745	80,319

Experimental Results for Multiplication Algorithms over $Z_p[x]/(x^n$ - $1)$

Table 3 shows the performance results of multiplication algorithms to multiply two elements in $\mathbb{Z}_p[x]/(x^n-1)$ for $n=1024, 2048, 4096$ and 8192. Recall that in Background section, we give the algorithms of schoolbook method, parallelized school method, fast convolution method and fast convolution method with sliding window for multiplication operation over the quotient ring $\mathbb{Z}_p[x]/(x^n-1)$. For $n=1024$ fast convolution method is better than parallelized schoolbook method. However, $n>1024$ parallelized schoolbook method is much more efficient than fast convolution method.

In Figure 5 timing comparison of the selected multiplication algorithms is demonstrated. Note that since schoolbook method has the worst timing results, we omit it in the figure. According to the timing results, for every parameter of n fast convolution with sliding window method is the best method to multiply two elements over $\mathbb{Z}_p[x]/(x^n-1)$. Recall that in fast convolution with sliding window method the required number of additions is drastically reduced when we compare this with the fast convolution method.

Figure 5. Timing comparison of multiplication methods over $\mathbb{Z}_p[x]/(x^n-1)$ (second/n)

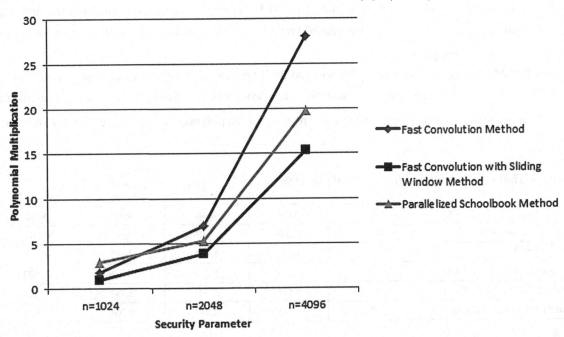

Figure 6. Timing comparison of multiplication methods over $\mathbb{Z}_p[x]/(x^n+1)$ (second/n)

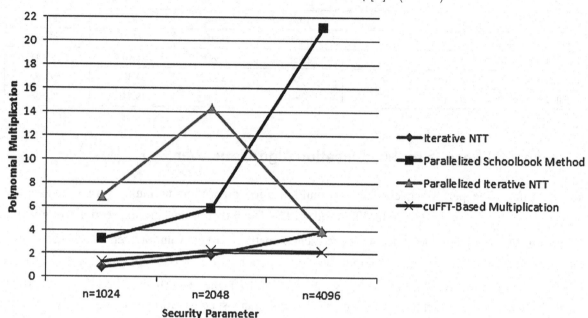

Experimental Results for Multiplication Algorithms over $Z_p[x]/(x^n+1)$

The performance results of multiplication algorithms to multiply two elements in $\mathbb{Z}_p[x]/(x^n+1)$ for $n=1024, 2048, 4096$ and 8192 is given in Table 4. The polynomials are generated randomly whose coefficients are $\{-1, 0, 1\}$. Recall that we give the algorithms of schoolbook method, parallelized schoolbook method, iterative NTT, parallelized iterative NTT and cuFFT-based multiplication method over the quotient ring $\mathbb{Z}_p[x]/(x^n+1)$. By embedding the sliding window idea to the fast convolution method we improve the performance.

In Figure 6 timing comparison of the selected multiplication algorithms to multiply two elements over $\mathbb{Z}_p[x]/(x^n+1)$ is demonstrated. Note that since schoolbook method has the worst timing results, we omit it in the figure. According to the timing results, for the polynomials of degree *n=1024* and *2048*,

Table 4. Timing results of multiplication of two elements in $\mathbb{Z}_p[x]/(x^n+1)$ (n/second)

n	1024	2048	4096	8192
Schoolbook Method	15,148	60,419	242,856	973,655
Iterative NTT	0,860	1,884	3,882	8,383
Parallelized Schoolbook Method	3,254	5,821	21,129	82,627
Parallelized Iterative NTT	6,851	14,343	3,983	118,326
cuFFT-Based Multiplication	1,318	2,240	2,204	3,512

Table 5. Recommended parameter sets for NTRUEncrypt in IEEEp1363.1

	n	p	q	d_f	d_g	d_m	d_r	Security Level
ees401ep1	401	3	2048	113	133	113	113	112
ees541ep1	541	3	2048	49	180	49	49	112
ees659ep1	659	3	2048	38	219	38	38	112
ees449ep1	449	3	2048	134	149	134	134	128
ees613ep1	613	3	2048	55	204	55	55	128
ees761ep1	761	3	2048	42	253	42	42	128
ees653ep1	653	3	2048	194	217	194	134	192
ees887ep1	887	3	2048	81	295	81	81	192
ees1087ep1	1087	3	2048	63	362	63	63	192
ees853ep1	853	3	2048	268	289	268	268	256
ees1171ep1	1171	3	2048	106	390	106	106	256
ees1499ep1	1499	3	2048	79	499	79	79	256

iterative NTT method is the most efficient one. For $n>2048$ cuFFT-based multiplication has the best timing results since the library is designed to work with large data sets. The parallelization of cuFFT library is very effective when working with large data sets. Note that other parallelized methods such as iterative NTT do not give the expected improvement since the data transfer between CPU and GPU multiple times increases the execution time and affects the efficiency. cuFFT-based multiplication has a better performance since data transfer is performed once. This decreases the latency according to the other methods. Recall that cuFFT is an optimized library for the GPU.

Experimental Results for NTRUEncrypt

For NTRUEncrypt cryptosystem IEEEp1363.1 "Standard Specifications for Public-Key Cryptographic Techniques Based on Hard Problems over Lattices" (IEEE, 2008) recommends a set of parameters for different security levels. In Table 5 the parameters for NTRUEncypt with different security levels are summarized. NTRUEncrypt cryptosystem is implemented according to each of these parameters.

Table 6 reports the performance results of NTRUEncrypt cryptosystem with various multiplication algorithms for the different security levels shown in Table 5. Encryption operation is performed 1000 times to obtain consistent results. For each encryption process the required elements are randomly chosen. The experimental results show that the performance of NTRUEncrypt does not directly depend on the polynomial degree. In other words, for the same security level (for example 128-bit security level one can choose one of ees449ep1, ees613ep1, ees761ep1) the choice of domain parameter set does not affect the performance. The timing results are very close to each other for quotient ring with different degrees. Other domain parameters have an important role on the timing. According to the timing results, using fast convolution with sliding window method in NTRUEncrypt improves the performance of the scheme. Recall that in Table 3 we use modulo $p = 49201153$. In NTRUEncrypt the reduction is done modulo $q = 2048$. This is almost free since this reduction equals to taking the least significant 11-bit of the result. This explains why the results in Table 3 and Table 6 are very close.

Table 6. Timing results of NTRUEncrypt for the IEEEp1363.1 parameter set (parameter set/second)

Parameter Set	Schoolbook Method	Fast Convolution with Sliding Window Method	Fast Convolution Method	Security Level
ees401ep1	2,863	0,177	0,274	112
ees541ep1	5,140	0,162	0,217	112
ees659ep1	7,614	0,181	0,196	112
ees449ep1	3,587	0,215	0,373	128
ees613ep1	6,612	0,197	0,253	128
ees761ep1	10,158	0,221	0,246	128
ees653ep1	7,467	0,316	0,584	192
ees887ep1	13,845	0,353	0,506	192
ees1087ep1	20,776	0,418	0,475	192
ees853ep1	12,679	0,648	1,199	256
ees1171ep1	24,149	0,573	0,787	256
ees1499ep1	39,739	0,645	0,794	256

In Figure 7 a comparison for NTRUEncrypt encryption process with different multiplication techniques is demonstrated. Recall that in Figure 5 fast convolution with sliding window gives better performance. Since the main operation in NTRUEncrypt is the polynomial multiplication, the implementation with this method NTRUEncrypt gives better performance.

Figure 7. Timing results of NTRUEncrypt for the IEEEp1363.1 parameter set (second/parameter set)

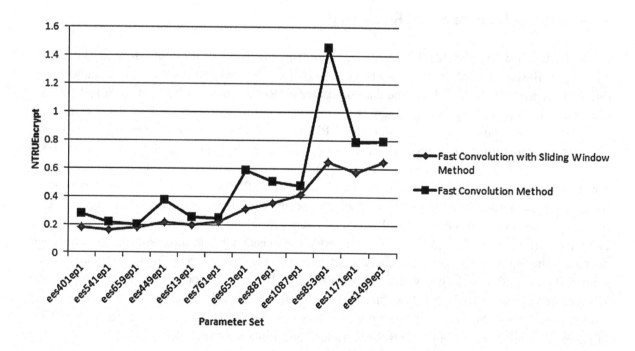

Table 7. Timing results of signature generation (n/second)

n	1024	2048	4096	8192
Schoolbook Method	65,82	273,466	1191,049	5949,218
Iterative NTT	4,285	9,263	20,057	55,036
Parallelized Schoolbook Method	12,571	24,564	104,152	482,399
Parallelized Iterative NTT	29,016	65,104	166,621	485,218
cuFFT-Based Multiplication	5,846	9,919	18,258	25,685

Experimental Results for Signature Scheme

In this section we give the implementation results of the signature scheme defined over the polynomial ring $\mathbb{Z}_p[x]/(x^n+1)$. Recall that we choose $p = 49201153$ satisfying $p \equiv 1 \bmod 2n$. To obtain more accurate results, we run the signature generation and verification processes 1000 times.

Table 7 shows the timing results of signature generation process with various multiplication algorithms. According to the timing results, iterative NTT method has more efficient results than others for $n<4096$. For $n \geq 4096$ signature generation with cuFFT-based multiplication is the fastest one. In signature generation process the most time consuming part is the polynomial multiplication. Serial implementation of the algorithms gives better results up to polynomial degree 8192.

In Figure 8 a timing comparison of signature generation phase with various multiplication algorithms defined in Multiplication Techniques section. The signature c is composed of 32 1's and -1's. Since the number of the coefficients different than 0 is very small, modified fast convolution method has better results. Recall that the efficiency of modified fast convolution method depends on Hamming weight of the input.

Table 7 shows the timing results of signature verification process with various multiplication algorithms. According to the timing results, as in signature generation phase iterative NTT method is more efficient than others for $n<4096$. For $n \geq 4096$ signature verification with cuFFT-based multiplication is the most efficient one. These results show that parallelized algorithms have better performance for the higher security levels.

In Figure 9 a timing comparison of signature generation phase with various multiplication algorithms defined in Multiplication Techniques section is demonstrated.

Table 8. Timing results of signature verification (n/second)

n/Second	1024	2048	4096	8192
Schoolbook Method	31,048	126,125	504,425	2000,192
Iterative NTT	1,978	4,245	8,688	18,265
Parallelized Schoolbook Method	5,870	14,413	39,295	168,217
Parallelized Iterative NTT	14,831	28,021	13,381	38,976
cuFFT-Based Multiplication	2,914	4,290	6,539	8,892

Figure 8. Timing comparison of signature generation phase with multiplication algorithms (second vs. n)

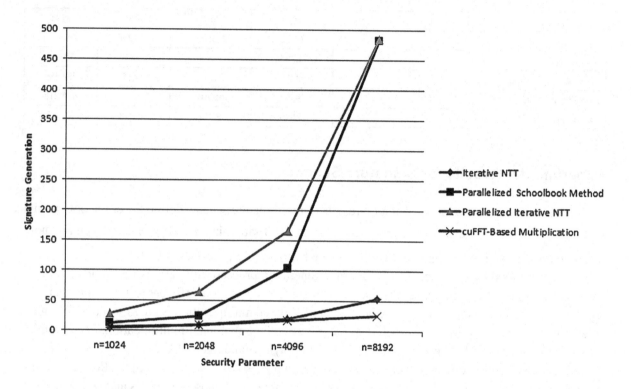

Figure 9. Timing comparison of signature verification phase with multiplication algorithms (second vs. n)

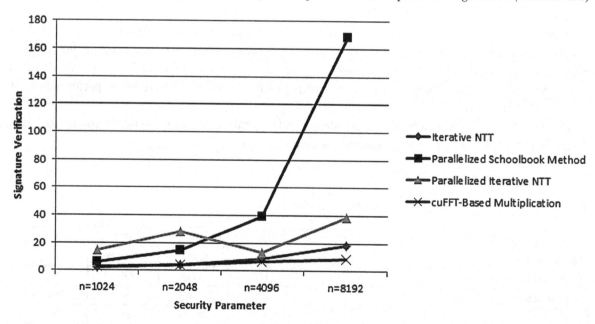

CONCLUSION

In this chapter we discuss the computational aspects of lattice-based cryptographic schemes focused on NTRUEncrypt and signature scheme. We give the details of the selected modular multiplication algorithms. We also explain the improvements of the multiplication algorithms for GPU-based implementations. We also modify the polynomial multiplication methods considering the needs of the selected cryptosystems. We show that in some cases they give better performance results than iterative NTT method. Some of the multiplication methods running efficiently in CPU platform do not give the expected performance on the GPU. Data latency between CPU and GPU causes inefficient implementations especially for the small data sets since CUDA platform is designed to work with large data sets. Every kernel call causes latency since kernel initialization is done for each call specific to CUDA platform. We obtain the highest efficiency of cuFFT-based multiplication method for the polynomial degree larger than 4096. It's concluded that for efficient GPU implementation using CUDA platform of cryptographic schemes, more effort is required for modular arithmetic operations.

ACKNOWLEDGMENT

Sedat Akleylek is partially supported by TÜBITAK under 2219-Postdoctoral Research Program Grant. Sedat Akleylek performed this study while he was a postdoctoral researcher at Cryptography and Computer Algebra Group, TU Darmstadt.

REFERENCES

Akleylek, S., Dağdelen, Ö., & Tok, Z. Y. (2014). *On the Efficiency of Polynomial Multiplication for Lattice-Based Cryptography on GPUs using CUDA*. Unpublished manuscript.

Akleylek, S., & Tok, Z. Y. (2014). Efficient Arithmetic for Lattice-Based Cryptography on GPU Using the CUDA Platform. In *Proceedings of the IEEE 22nd Signal Processing and Communications Applications Conference* (pp.854-857). New York, NY: IEEE. doi:10.1109/SIU.2014.6830364

Akleylek, S. and Tok, Z.Y., (2014). Efficient Interleaved Montgomery Modular Multiplication for Lattice-Based Cryptography. *IEICE Electronics Express, 11-22*, 1-6. DOI: .10.1587/elex.11.20140960

Arndt, J. (2011). *Matters Computational: Ideas, Algorithms, Source Code*. New York, NY: Springer-Verlag. doi:10.1007/978-3-642-14764-7

Aysu, A., Patterson, C., & Schaumont, P. (2013). Low-cost and Area Efficient FPGA Implementations of Lattice-based cryptography. In Proceedings of IEEE HOST (pp. 81–86). IEEE. doi:10.1109/HST.2013.6581570

Banerjee, A., Peikert, C., & Rosen, A. (2012). Pseudorandom Functions and Lattices. In *EUROCRYPT 2012 (LNCS), (vol. 7237*, pp. 719–737). New York, NY: Springer-Verlag.

Bantikyan, H. (2013). Speed up Large Integer Multiplication Using Fourier Transforms and CUDA Technology. In *Proceedings of International Conference Parallel and Distributed Computing Systems* (pp.19-22). Kharkiv.

Berstein, D. J., Buchmann, J., & Dahmen, E. (2009). *Post-Quantum Cryptography*. New York, NY: Springer-Verlag. doi:10.1007/978-3-540-88702-7

Chen, D. D., Mentens, N., Vercauteren, F., Roy, S. S., Cheung, R. C. C., Pao, D., & Verbauwhede, I. (2014). High-Speed Polynomial Multiplication Architecture for Ring-LWE and SHE Cryptosystems. *IEEE Transactions on Circuits and Systems-I: Regular Papers*. Doi: 10.1109/TCSI.2014.2350431

Cook, D., & Keromytis, A. D. (2006). *CryptoGraphics: Exploiting Graphics Cards for Security. Advances in Information Security*. New York, NY: Springer Verlag.

Emeliyanenko, P. (2009). Efficient Multiplication of Polynomials on Graphics Hardware. In *Advanced Parallel Processing Technologies (LNCS), (pp. 5737,* pp. 134–149). New York, NY: Springer-Verlag. doi:10.1007/978-3-642-03644-6_11

Geissler, K., & Smart, N. P. (2005). *D.AZTEC.2 Lightweight Asymmetric Cryptography and Alternatives to RSA: The NTRU Public-Key Cryptosystem*. ECRYPT European Network of Excellence in Cryptology.

Giorgi, P., Izard, T., & Tisserand, A. (2009). Comparison of Modular Arithmetic Algorithms on GPUs. In *Proceedings of ParCo'09, Advances in Parallel Computing* (vol. 19, pp. 315-322). IOS Press.

ATI Graphics. (2014). Retrieved from http://www.amd.com/en-us/products/graphics

Nvidia Graphics. (2014). Retrieved from https://research.nvidia.com/

Güneysu, T., Lyubashevsky, V., & Pöppelmann, T. (2012). Practical Lattice-Based Cryptography: A Signature Scheme for Embedded Systems. In *CHES 2012 (LNCS), (vol. 7428,* pp. 530–547). New York, NY: Springer-Verlag. doi:10.1007/978-3-642-33027-8_31

Güneysu, T., Lyubashevsky, V., & Pöppelmann, T. (2014). Lattice-Based Signatures: Optimization and Implementation on Reconfigurable Hardware. *IEEE Transactions on Computers*. doi: 10.1109/TC.2014.2346177

Gutierrez, E., Romero, S., Trenas, M. A., & Zapata, E. L. (2008). Memory Locality Exploitation Strategies for FFT on the CUDA Architecture. In *High Performance Computing for Computational Science – VECPAR 2008 (LNCS), (vol. 5336,* pp. 430–443). New York, NY: Springer-Verlag. doi:10.1007/978-3-540-92859-1_39

Haque, S. A., & Maza, M. M. (2012). Plain Polynomial Arithmetic on GPU. In *High Performance Computing Symposium* (vol. 385, pp. 1-10). IOP Publishing.

Harrison, O., & Waldron, J. (2009). Efficient Acceleration of Asymmetric Cryptography in Graphics Hardware. In *AFRICACRYPT (LNCS), (vol. 5580,* pp. 350–367). New York, NY: Springer-Verlag. doi:10.1007/978-3-642-02384-2_22

Hermans, J., Vercauteren, F., & Preneel, B. (2010). Speed Records for NTRU. In *CT-RSA (LNCS), (vol. 5985,* pp. 73–88). New York, NY: Springer-Verlag.

Hinitt, N., & Koçak, T. (2010). GPU-Based FFT Computation for Multi-Gigabit WirelessHD Baseband Processing. *EURASIP Journal on Wireless Communications and Networking, 2010*(1), 359081. doi:10.1155/2010/359081

Hoffstein, J., Howgrave-Graham, N., Pipher, J., Silverman, J. H., & Whyte, W. (2003). NTRUSIGN: Digital Signatures Using the NTRU Lattice. In *CT-RSA (LNCS), (vol. 2612*, pp. 122–140). New York, NY: Springer-Verlag. doi:10.1007/3-540-36563-X_9

Hoffstein, J., & Silverman, J. H. (1998). NTRU: A Ring-based Public Key Cryptosystem. In *ANTS-III (LNCS), (vol. 1423*, pp. 267–288). New York, NY: Springer-Verlag.

IEEE, (2008). *P1363.1: Standard Specifications for Public-Key Cryptographic Techniques Based on Hard Problems over Lattices*. IEEE P1363.1 Draft.

Lee, M. K., Kim, J. W., Song, J. E., & Park, K. (2007). Sliding Window Method for NTRU. In *ACNS (LNCS), (vol. 4521*, pp. 432–442). New York, NY: Springer-Verlag.

Lee, M. K., Kim, J. W., Song, J. E., & Park, K. (2013). *Efficient Implementation of NTRU Cryptosystem Using Sliding Window Methods. IEICE Trans. Fundamentals, E96-A*(1), 206–213.

Lopez-Alt, A., Tromer, E., & Vaikuntanathan, V. (2012). On-the-fly Multiparty Computation on the Cloud via Multikey Fully Homomorphic Encryption. In *Proceedings of the 44th ACM Symposium on Theory of Computing* (pp.1219-1234). New York, NY: ACM. doi:10.1145/2213977.2214086

Lyubashevsky, V., Micciancio, D., Peikert, C., & Rosen, A. (2008). SWIFFT: A Modest Proposal for FFT Hashing. In *FSE (LNCS), (vol. 5086*, pp. 54–72). New York, NY: Springer-Verlag. doi:10.1007/978-3-540-71039-4_4

Lyubashevsky, V., Peikert, C. and Regev, O., (2013). On Ideal Lattices and Learning with Errors over Rings. *Journal of the ACM, 60*(6), 43:1-43:35.

Manavski, A. S. (2007). CUDA Compatible GPU as an Efficient Hardware Accelerator for AES. In *Proceedings of IEEE International Conference on Signal Processing and Communications* (pp.65-68). Dubai, UAE: IEEE. doi:10.1109/ICSPC.2007.4728256

Maza, M. M., & Pan, W. (2010). Fast Polynomial Multiplication on a GPU. In *High Performance Computing Symposium* (vol. 256, pp. 1-13). IOP Publishing.

Neves, S., & Araujo, F. (2011). *On the Performance of GPU Public Key Cryptography. In Proceedings of IEEE Application-Specific Systems, Architectures and Processors (ASAP)* (pp. 133–140). Santa Monica, CA: IEEE.

NVIDIA CUDA. (2014). *CUDA Toolkit Documentation*. Retrieved from http://docs.nvidia.com/cuda/eula/index.html

Pollard, J. M. (1971). The Fast Fourier Transform in a Finite Field. *Mathematics of Computation, 25*(114), 365–374. doi:10.1090/S0025-5718-1971-0301966-0

Pöppelmann, T., & Güneysu, T. (2012). Towards Efficient Arithmetic for Lattice-based Cryptography on Reconfigurable Hardware. In *LATINCRYPT (LNCS), (vol. 7533*, (=pp. 139–158). New York, NY: Springer-Verlag. doi:10.1007/978-3-642-33481-8_8

Security Innovation the Application Security Company. (2014). Retrieved from https://www.securityinnovation.com/

Shor, P. W. (1997). Polynomial-time Algorithms for Prime Factorization and Discrete Logarithms on a Quantum Computer. *SIAM Journal on Computing, 26*(5), 1484–1509. doi:10.1137/S0097539795293172

Steinfeld, R. (2014). NTRU Cryptosystem: Recent Developments and Emerging Mathematical Problems in Finite Polynomial Rings. In H. Niederreiter, A. Ostafe, D. Panario, & A. Winterhof (Eds.), *Algebraic Curves and Finite Fields: Cryptography and Other Applications: 16* (pp. 1–33). De Gruyter. doi:10.1515/9783110317916.179

Szerwinski, R., & Güneysu, T. (2008). Exploiting the Power of GPUs for Asymmetric Cryptography. In *CHES 2008 (LNCS), (vol. 5154*, pp. 79–99). New York, NY: Springer-Verlag. doi:10.1007/978-3-540-85053-3_6

Wilt, N. (2013). *The CUDA Handbook: A Comprehensive Guide to GPU Programming.* Addison-Wesley.

Winkler, F. (1996). *Polynomial Algorithms in Computer Algebra.* New York, NY: Springer-Verlag. doi:10.1007/978-3-7091-6571-3

Wu, H. (2010). *Implementation of Public Key Algorithms in CUDA.* (M.Sc. Thesis). Gjovik University, Norway.

KEY TERMS AND DEFINITIONS

Compute Unified Device Architecture (CUDA): CUDA, more than a programming model, is specially organized for parallel computing applications on the GPUs.

Fast Convolution Method: Fast convolution method is a modular multiplication algorithm running very fast modulo $(x^n - 1)$.

Graphical Processing Unit (GPU): GPU is a special processor with the capability of executing more works in parallel.

Lattice-Based Cryptography: Lattice-based cryptography defines a set of cryptographic schemes whose security depends on the hard problems in lattices such as the closest vector problem, the shortest vector problem.

Number Theoretic Transform: NTT is a Discrete Fourier Transform defined over a ring or a finite field and is used to multiply two integers over the defined group.

Number Theory Research Unit (NTRU): NTRU is a public key cryptosystem based on the hardness of lattice problems and is resistant against known quantum attacks.

Post-Quantum Cryptography: Post-quantum cryptography is the cryptography secure and resistant against quantum attacks for a reasonable time.

Compilation of References

Abbas, S. A. (1998). *Use of GA in the cryptanalysis of a class of stream cipher systems.* (Ph.D. thesis). University of Technology, Baghdad, Iraq.

Abdallah, E. E., Hamza, A. B., & Bhattacharya, P. (2006).A robust block-based image watermarking scheme using fast Hadamard transform and singular value decomposition. In *Proc. 18th International Conference on Pattern Recognition* (*Vol. 3*, pp. 673–676). Academic Press. doi:10.1109/ICPR.2006.167

Abd-Elmonim, W. G., Ghali, N. I., & Abraham, A. (2011, October). Known-plaintext attack of DES-16 using particle swarm optimization. In *Proceedings ofThird World Congress on Nature and Biologically Inspired Computing* (NaBIC), (pp. 12-16). doi:10.1109/NaBIC.2011.6089410

Abdullah, A. H., Enayatifar, R., & Lee, M. (2012). A hybrid genetic algorithm and chaotic function model for image encryption. *International Journal of Electronics and Communications, 66*(10), 806–816. doi:10.1016/j.aeue.2012.01.015

Abdulsalam, A. A. (2011). Keystream generator based on simulated annealing. *Journal of Applied Computer Science & Mathematics, 10*(5).

Abraham, A. (2001). Neuro fuzzy systems: State-of-the-art modeling techniques. In Connectionist Models of Neurons, Learning Processes, and Artificial Intelligence (pp. 269-276). Springer Berlin Heidelberg.

Abraham, S., & Sanglikar, M. (2001). *A Diophantine equation solver-a genetic algorithm application* (Vol. 15). Mathematical Colloquium Journal.

Abraham, S., Sanyal, S., & Sanglikar, M. (2010). Particle swarm optimization based Diophantine equation solver. *International Journal of Bio-inspired Computation, 2*(2), 100–114. doi:10.1504/IJBIC.2010.032126

Abraham, S., Sanyal, S., & Sanglikar, M. (2013). Finding numerical solutions of Diophantine equations using ant colony optimization. *Applied Mathematics and Computation, 219*(24), 11376–11387. doi:10.1016/j.amc.2013.05.051

Abuhaiba, I. S. & Hassan, M. A. (2011). Image encryption using differential evolution approach in frequency domain. *Signal and Image Processing: An International Journal, 2*(1).

Acharyya, M., & Kundu, M. K. (2008). Extraction of noise tolerant, gray-scale transform and rotation invariant features for texture segmentation using wavelet frames. *International Journal of Wavelets, Multresolution, and Information Processing, 6*(3), 391–417. doi:10.1142/S0219691308002252

Adams, C., Pinkas, D., Cain, P., & Zuccherato, R. (2001). *Internet X.509 Public Key Infrastructure Time Stamp Protocols (TSP).* IETF RFC 3161, Retrieved from http://www.ietf.org/rfc/rfc3161.txt

Adleman, L. M. (1994). Molecular computation of solutions to combinatorial problems. *Science, 266*(5187), 1021–1024. doi:10.1126/science.7973651 PMID:7973651

Adobe. (2012). Retrieved from http://blogs.adobe.com/security/2012/09/inappropriate-use-of-adobe-code-signing-certificate.html

Afarin, R., & Mozaffari, S. (2013). Image encryption using genetic algorithm. In *8th Iranian Conference on Machine Vision and Image Processing (MVIP)*.

Agarwal, A. (2012). Secret key encryption algorithm using genetic algorithm. *International Journal of Advanced Research in Computer Science and Software Engineering, 2*(4), 216–218.

Aguiar, H. Jr. (2014). *Diophantine Equations and Fuzzy Adaptive Simulated Annealing* (Vol. 13). WSEAS Transactions on Mathematics.

Aguilar, J., & Molina, C. (2013). The multilayer random neural network. *Neural Processing Letters, 37*(2), 111–133. doi:10.1007/s11063-012-9237-x

Ahmed, N., Rao, K., & Abdussattar, A. L. (1971). BIFORE or Hadamard transform. *IEEE Transactions on Audio and Electroacoustics, 19*(3), 225–234. doi:10.1109/TAU.1971.1162193

Akleylek, S. and Tok, Z.Y., (2014). Efficient Interleaved Montgomery Modular Multiplication for Lattice-Based Cryptography. *IEICE Electronics Express, 11-22*, 1-6. DOI: .10.1587/elex.11.20140960

Akleylek, S., Dağdelen, Ö., & Tok, Z. Y. (2014). *On the Efficiency of Polynomial Multiplication for Lattice-Based Cryptography on GPUs using CUDA*. Unpublished manuscript.

Akleylek, S., & Tok, Z. Y. (2014). Efficient Arithmetic for Lattice-Based Cryptography on GPU Using the CUDA Platform. In *Proceedings of the IEEE 22nd Signal Processing and Communications Applications Conference* (pp.854-857). New York, NY: IEEE. doi:10.1109/SIU.2014.6830364

Al Jadaan, O., Lakishmi, R., & Rao, C. R. (2005). Improved selection operator for genetic algorithm. *Journal of Theoretical and Applied Information Technology, 4*(4), 269–277.

Alander, J. T. (1992). On optimal population size of genetic algorithms. In *Proceedings of the IEEE Computer Systems and Software Engineering* (pp. 65–69). IEEE. doi:10.1109/CMPEUR.1992.218485

Alani, M. M. (2012b). *Neuro-Cryptanalysis of DES and Triple-DES. In Neural Information Processing* (pp. 637–646). Springer Berlin Heidelberg. doi:10.1007/978-3-642-34500-5_75

Albassal, E. M. B., & Wahdan, A. (2004). Neural network based cryptanalysis of a feistel type block cipher. In *Proceedings ofInternational Conference on Electrical, Electronic and Computer Engineering, ICEEC'04*. (pp. 231-237). Academic Press. doi:10.1109/ICEEC.2004.1374430

Al-Bastaki, Y., & Awad, W. S. (2004, March). Attacking stream ciphers using genetic algorithm. *Asian Journal of Information Technology*, 206-211.

Al-Husainy, M. A. (2006). Image encryption using genetic algorithm. *Information Technology Journal, 5*(3), 516–519. doi:10.3923/itj.2006.516.519

Al-khalid, A. S., Omran, D. S. S., & Hammood, A. (2013). Using genetic algorithms to break a simple transposition cipher. In *Proceedings of the 6th International Conference on Information Technology (ICIT)*. Academic Press.

Alligood, K. T., Sauer, T. D., & Yorke, J. A. (1997). *Chaos: An Introduction to Dynamical Systems*. Springer. doi:10.1007/978-3-642-59281-2

Allma, E. Callas, J. Delan, M. Libbey, M. Fenton J. Thomas, M. (2007). *DomainKeys Identified Mail (DKIM)*. Internet Engineering Task Force (IETF), RFC 4871.

Al-Riyami, S. S. Paterson, K. G. (2013). *Certificateless Public Key Cryptography*. Academic Press.

Altwaijry, H. & Algarny, S. (2012). Bayesian based intrusion detection system. *Journal of King Saud University – Computer and Information Sciences, 24*, 1–6.

Al-Utaibi, K., & El-Alfy, E.-S. (2010). A bio-inspired image encryption algorithm based on chaotic maps. In *IEEE Congress on Evolutionary Computation*. doi:10.1109/CEC.2010.5586463

Ambalakat, P. (2005). *Security of Biometric Authentication Systems*. 21st Computer Science Seminar, SA1-T1-1.

Amini, M., Jalili, R., & Shahriari, H. R. (2006). RT-UNNID: A practical solution to real-time network-based intrusion detection using unsupervised neural networks. *Computer & Security Elsevier, 25*(6), 459–468. doi:10.1016/j.cose.2006.05.003

Amin, M., Faragallah, O. S., & Abd El-Latif, A. A. (2010). A chaotic block cipher algorithm for image cryptosystems. *Communications in Nonlinear Science and Numerical Simulation, 15*(11), 3484–3497. doi:10.1016/j.cnsns.2009.12.025

Anam, B., Sakib, K., Hossain, M., & Dahal, K. (2010). Review on the Advancements of DNA Cryptography. *arXiv preprint arXiv:1010.0186*.

Anderson, R., & Biham, E. (1996). Tiger: A Fast New Hash Function. *Fast Software Encryption,Third International Workshop Proceedings*. Springer-Verlag.

Anderson, R. J., & Petitcolas, F. A. (1998). On the limits of steganography. *IEEE Journal on Selected Areas in Communications, 16*(4), 474–481. doi:10.1109/49.668971

Andrews, H., & Patterson, C. (1976). Singular value decompositions and digital image processing. *IEEE Transactions on Acoustics, Speech, and Signal Processing, 24*(1), 26–53. doi:10.1109/TASSP.1976.1162766

Andries, P. E. (2006). *Fundamentals of Computational Swarm Intelligence*. John Willey & Sons.

ANSI X9.62. (1999). *Public Key Cryptography for the Financial Services Industry: The Elliptic Curve Digital Signature Algorithm* (ECDSA). Author.

Armando, A., Basin, D., Boichut, Y., Chevalier, Y., Compagna, L., Cuellar, J., & Vigneron, L. et al. (2005). The AVISPA tool for the automated validation of internet security protocols and applications. In *Proceedings of the 17th international conference on Computer Aided Verification* (CAV'05). Springer-Verlag. doi:10.1007/11513988_27

Arndt, J. (2011). *Matters Computational: Ideas, Algorithms, Source Code*. New York, NY: Springer-Verlag. doi:10.1007/978-3-642-14764-7

Arvandi, M., & Sadeghian, A. (2007, August). Chosen plaintext attack against neural network-based symmetric cipher. In *Proceedings of the International Joint Conference on Neural Networks*. IJCNN. doi:10.1109/IJCNN.2007.4371068

Arvandi, M., Wu, S., & Sadeghian, A. (2008). On the use of recurrent neural networks to design symmetric ciphers. *IEEE Computational Intelligence Magazine, 3*(2), 42–53. doi:10.1109/MCI.2008.919075

Arvandi, M., Wu, S., Sadeghian, A., Melek, W. W., & Woungang, I. (2006). Symmetric cipher design using recurrent neural networks. In *Proceedings of the International Joint Conference on Neural Networks*. IJCNN.

Ascertia. (n.d.). Retrieved from http://www.ascertia.com

ATI Graphics. (2014). Retrieved from http://www.amd.com/en-us/products/graphics

Aung, A., Ng, B. P., & Rahardja, S. (2011). A robust watermarking scheme using sequency-ordered complex Hadamard transform. *J. Signal Process. Syst., 64*(3), 319–333. doi:10.1007/s11265-010-0492-7

Awad, W. S. (1998). *Ciphertext-only attack using genetic programming.* (Ph.D. thesis). University of Technology, Baghdad, Iraq.

Awad, W. S. (2011b). Designing stream cipher systems using genetic programming. In Learning and optimization (LNCS), (vol. 6683, pp. 308-320). Berlin: Springer.

Awad, W. S. (2013). The effect of mutation operation on GP- based stream ciphers design algorithm. In *Proceedings of 5th International Conference on Agents and Artificial Intelligence.* Academic Press.

Awad, W. S. (2013). The effect of mutation operation on GP-based stream ciphers design algorithm. In *Proceedings of 5th International Conference on Agents and Artificial Intelligence* (pp. 455-450). Academic Press.

Awad, W. S., (2008). Finding the linear equivalence of keystream generators using genetic simulated annealing. *Information Technology Journal, 7*(3), 541-544.

Awad, W. S. (2011a). On the application of evolutionary computation techniques in designing stream cipher systems. *International Journal of Computational Intelligence Systems, 4*(5), 921–928. doi:10.1080/18756891.2011.9727842

Aysu, A., Patterson, C., & Schaumont, P. (2013). Low-cost and Area Efficient FPGA Implementations of Lattice-based cryptography. In Proceedings of IEEE HOST (pp. 81–86). IEEE. doi:10.1109/HST.2013.6581570

Banday, M. T. (2011). Easing PAIN with Digital Signatures. *International Journal of Computer Applications.* Retrieved from http://research.ijcaonline.org/ volume29/number2/pxc3874822.pdf

Banerjee, A., Peikert, C., & Rosen, A. (2012). Pseudorandom Functions and Lattices. In *EUROCRYPT 2012 (LNCS), (vol. 7237,* pp. 719–737). New York, NY: Springer-Verlag.

Bantikyan, H. (2013). Speed up Large Integer Multiplication Using Fourier Transforms and CUDA Technology. In *Proceedings of International Conference Parallel and Distributed Computing Systems* (pp.19-22). Kharkiv.

Bao, P., & Ma, X. (2005). Image adaptive watermarking using wavelet domain singular value decomposition. *IEEE Transactions on Circuits and Systems for Video Technology, 15*(1), 96–102. doi:10.1109/TCSVT.2004.836745

Bashir, A., Hasan, A. S. B., & Almangush, H. (2012). A new image encryption approach using the integration of a shifting technique and the AES algorithm. *International Journal of Computers and Applications, 42*(9).

BCC. (2013). *Bouncy Castle Crypto APIs.* Retrieved from https://www.bouncycastle.org/

Beasley, J. E., & Chu, P. C. (1996). A genetic algorithm for the set covering problem. *European Journal of Operational Research, 94*(2), 392–404. doi:10.1016/0377-2217(95)00159-X

Beker, H., & Piper, F. (1982). *Cipher systems: The protection of communications.* Northwood Publications.

Bengio, Y. (2009). Learning deep architectures for AI. *Foundations and Trends in Machine Learning, 2*(1), 1–127. doi:10.1561/2200000006

Bennett, C. H., Brassard, G., Breidbard, S., & Wiesner, S. (1982). Quantum Cryptography, or Unforgivable Subway Tokens. In Proceedings of Crypto 1982. Santa Barbara, CA: Academic Press.

Bennett, C. H., & Brassard, G. (1984). Quantum cryptography: Public key distribution and coin tossing. In *Proc. of IEEE International Conference on Computers, Systems and Signal Processing.* Bangalore, India: IEEE.

Bergmann, K. P. (2007). *Cryptanalysis using nature-inspired optimization algorithms.* (Doctoral dissertation). University of Calgary.

Bernstein, D. J. (2009). *Introduction to post-quantum cryptography.* Post-Quantum Cryptography.

Bernstein, D. J., Lange, T., & Page, D. (2008). *eBATS. ECRYPT Benchmarking of Asymmetric Systems Performing Benchmarks (report)*. Retrieved from http://www.ecrypt.eu.org/ebats/

Bernstein, D. J., Chang, Y., Cheng, C., Chou, L. P., Heninger, N., Lange, T., & Someren, N. (2013). Factoring RSA Keys from Certified Smart Cards: Coppersmith in the Wild. Advances in Cryptology - ASIACRYPT 2013. *Lecture Notes in Computer Science, 8270*, 341–360. doi:10.1007/978-3-642-42045-0_18

Berstein, D. J., Buchmann, J., & Dahmen, E. (2009). *Post-Quantum Cryptography*. New York, NY: Springer-Verlag. doi:10.1007/978-3-540-88702-7

Bertoni, G., Daemen, J., Peeters, M., & Van Assche, G. (2013). Keccak. In Advances in Cryptology–EUROCRYPT 2013 (pp. 313-314). Springer Berlin Heidelberg.

Bertsimas, D., & Tsitsiklis, J. (1993). Simulated Annealing. *Statistical Science, 8*(1), 10–15. doi:10.1214/ss/1177011077

Bezdek, J. C. (1994). Chapter. In J. Zurada, B. Marks, & C. Robinson (Eds.), What is computational intelligence? Computational Intelligence Imitating Life (pp. 1–12). Piscataway, NJ: IEEE Press.

Bhateja, A. K., & Din, M. (2013). ANN Based Distinguishing Attack on RC4 Stream Cipher. In *Proceedings of Seventh International Conference on Bio-Inspired Computing: Theories and Applications (BIC-TA 2012)* (pp. 101-109). Academic Press. doi:10.1007/978-81-322-1041-2_9

Bhowmik, S., & Acharyya, S. (2011). Image cryptography: the Genetic algorithm approach. In *IEEE International Conference on Computer Science and Automation Engineering (CSAE)*, (Vol. 2, pp. 223-227). IEEE.

Bigdeli, N., Farid, Y., & Afshar, K. (2012a). A novel image encryption/decryption scheme based on chaotic neural networks. *Engineering Applications of Artificial Intelligence, 25*(4), 753–765. doi:10.1016/j.engappai.2012.01.007

Bigdeli, N., Farid, Y., & Afshar, K. (2012b). A robust hybrid method for image encryption based on Hopfield neural network. *Computers & Electrical Engineering, 38*(2), 356–369. doi:10.1016/j.compeleceng.2011.11.019

Bit9. (2013). Retrieved from https://blog.bit9.com/2013/02/08/bit9-and-our-customers-security/

Blum, C. (2005). Ant colony optimization: Introduction and recent trends. *Physics of Life Reviews, 2*(4), 353–373. doi:10.1016/j.plrev.2005.10.001

Bochum, S. H. (2013). *Post Quantum Cryptography: Implementing Alternative Public Key Schemes on Embedded Devices*. Germany: Faculty of Electrical Engineering and Information Technology at the Ruhr-University Bochum.

Bonabeau, E., Dorigo, M., & Theraulaz, G. (1999). *Swarm Intelligence: From Natural to Artificial Systems*. New York: Oxford University Press.

Boneh, D., & Franklin, M. (2001). Identity-based encryption from the Weil pairing. In Advances in Cryptology-CRYPTO 2001 (pp. 213–229). Springer.

Boneh, D., Dunworth, C., & Lipton, R. J. (1995). Breaking DES using a molecular computer. In *Proceedings of DIMACS Workshop on DNA Based Computers*. Princeton, NJ: DIMACS.

Boneh, D., Sahai, A., & Waters, B. (2011). Functional encryption: definitions and challenges. In Theory of Cryptography (pp. 253–273). Springer.

Boneh, K. D., Crescenzo, G. D., Ostrovsky, R., & Persiano, G. (2004). Public key encryption with keyword search. In Advances in Cryptology-Eurocrypt 2004 (pp. 506–522). Springer.

Boukerche, A., Jucá, K. R. L., Sobral, J. B., & Notare, M. S. M. A. (2004). An artificial immune based intrusion detection model for computer and telecommunication systems. *Parallel Computing Elsevier, 30*(5-6), 629–646. doi:10.1016/j.parco.2003.12.008

Bourbakis, N. G. (1997). Image data compression-encryption using g-scan patterns. In *Proc. IEEE International Conference on Systems, Man, and Cybernetics: Computational Cybernetics and Simulation* (vol. 2, pp. 1117–1120). IEEE.

Bourkache, G., & Mezghiche, M., & Tamine, k. (2011). A Distributed Intrusion Detection Model Based on a Society of Intelligent Mobile Agents for Ad Hoc Network. In *Proceedings of the IEEE 2011 Sixth International Conference on Availability, Reliability and Security (ARES)* (pp. 569-572). Vienna: IEEE. doi:10.1109/ARES.2011.131

Braudaway, G. W., Magerlein, K. A., & Mintzer, F. C. (1996). Protecting publicly available images with a visible image watermark. In *Electronic Imaging: Science & Technology* (pp. 126–133). International Society for Optics and Photonics.

Buchmann, J., Coronado, C., Dahmen, E., D"oring, M., & Klintsevich, E. (2006). CMSS - an improved merkle signature scheme. In INDOCRYPT 2006 (pp. 349–363). Academic Press.

Busin, L., Vandenbroucke, N., & Macaire, L. (2008). Color spaces and image segmentation. *Advances in Imaging and Electron Physics, 151*, 66.

Byrski, A., & Carvalho, M. (2008). Agent-Based Immunological Intrusion Detection System for Mobile Ad-Hoc Networks. In *Proceedings of the International Conference on Computational Science* (584-593). Kraków, Poland: LNCS. doi:10.1007/978-3-540-69389-5_66

Caballero-Gil, P. (2000). New upper bounds on the linear complexity. *Computers and Mathematics with Applications, 39*(3), 31-38.

Canava, J. E. (2001). *Fundamentals of Network Security*. London: Artech House.

Carvalho, A. M., Oliveira, A. L., & Sagot, M. (2007). Efficient learning of Bayesian network classifiers: An extension to the TAN classifier. In *Proceedings of Advances in Artificial Intelligence* (pp. 16–25). Springer.

Casido, L., & Tsigas, P. (2009). ContikySec: A Secure Network Layer for Wireless Sensor Networks under the Contiki Operating System. *LNCS, 5383*, 133-147.

Castiglione, A., De Prisco, R., De Santis, A., Fiore, U., & Palmieri, F. (2014). A botnet-based command and control approach relying on swarm intelligence. *Journal of Network and Computer Applications, 38*, 22–33. doi:10.1016/j.jnca.2013.05.002

Certificate Transparency. (n.d.). Retrieved from http://www.certificate-transparency.org/

CGI Group Inc. (2004). *Public Key Encryption and Digital Signature: How do they work?* CGI Group Inc. Retrieved from http://www.cgi.com/files/white-papers/cgi_whpr_35_pkie.pdf

Chadha, K., & Jain, S. (2015). Hybrid genetic fuzzy rule based inference engine to detect intrusion in networks. *Advances in Intelligent Systems and Computing, 321*, 185–198. doi:10.1007/978-3-319-11227-5_17

Chang, K., & Shin, K. G. (2010). Application-Layer Intrusion Detection in MANETs. In *Proceedings of the 43rd Hawaii International Conference on System Sciences* (1-10). Honolulu, HI: IEEE.

Chang, Y. C., & Mitzenmacher, M. (2005). Privacy preserving keyword searches on remote encrypted data. In *Proceedings of the 3rd International Conference on Applied Cryptography and Network Security (ACNS '05)* (pp. 442–455). ACNS. doi:10.1007/11496137_30

Chen, D. D., Mentens, N., Vercauteren, F., Roy, S. S., Cheung, R. C. C., Pao, D., & Verbauwhede, I. (2014). High-Speed Polynomial Multiplication Architecture for Ring-LWE and SHE Cryptosystems. *IEEE Transactions on Circuits and Systems-I: Regular Papers*. Doi: 10.1109/TCSI.2014.2350431

Chen, C. P., Zhang, T., & Zhou, Y. (2012). Image encryption algorithm based on a new combined chaotic system. In *IEEE International Conference on Systems, Man, and Cybernetics (SMC)*. doi:10.1109/ICSMC.2012.6378120

Chen, D., & Chang, Y. (2011). A novel image encryption algorithm based on Logistic maps. *Advances in Information Science and Service Sciences, 3*(7), 364–372. doi:10.4156/aiss.vol3.issue7.43

Chen, G., Mao, Y., & Chui, C. K. (2004). A symmetric image encryption scheme based on 3D chaotic cat maps. *Chaos, Solitons, and Fractals, 21*(3), 749–761. doi:10.1016/j.chaos.2003.12.022

Chen, R. J., Lu, W. K., & Lai, J. L. (2005). Image encryption using progressive cellular automata substitution and SCAN. In *IEEE International Symposium on Circuits and Systems, ISCAS*. doi:10.1109/ISCAS.2005.1464931

Chen, Z., Fanelli, A. M., Castellano, G., & Jain, L. C. (2001). Introduction to computational intelligence paradigms. In *Computational Intelligence in Games* (pp. 1–38). Physica-Verlag HD. doi:10.1007/978-3-7908-1833-8_1

Cherian, A., Raj, S. R., & Abraham, A. (2013). A Survey on Different DNA Cryptographic Methods. *International Journal of Science and Research*.

Cherian, A., Raj, S. R., & Abraham, A. (2013). A Survey on different DNA cryptographic methods. *International Journal of Science and Research, 2*(4), 167–169.

Ching-Ling, C., & Chent-Ta, L. (2008). Dynamic Session-Key Generation for Wireless Sensor Networks. *EURASIP Journal on Wireless Communications and Networking, 2008*. doi: 10.1155/2008/691571

Chung, Y. Y., & Wahid, N. (2012). A hybrid network intrusion detection system using simplified swarm optimization (SSO). *Applied Soft Computing, 12*(9), 3014–3022. doi:10.1016/j.asoc.2012.04.020

Clark, A. J. (1998). *Optimisation Heuristics for Cryptology*. (Ph.D. thesis). Queensland University of Technology.

Clark, A., & Dawson, E. (1997). A parallel genetic algorithm for cryptanalysis of polyalphabetic substitution cipher. *Cryptologia, 21*(2), 129–138. doi:10.1080/0161-119791885850

Clark, A., Jacob, L., Maitra, S., & Stanica, P. (2004). Almost Boolean functions: The design of Boolean functions by spectral inversion. *Computational Intelligence, 20*(3), 450–462. doi:10.1111/j.0824-7935.2004.00245.x

Code, U. S. (2012). *US Code, 44 U.S.C. § 3542(b)(1)*. Title 44-public printing and documents, chapter 35-coordination of federal information policy, subchapter iii-information security. Retrieved from http://www.gpo.gov/fdsys/pkg/USCODE-2011-title44/pdf/USCODE-2011-title44-chap35-subchapIII-sec3542.pdf

Coiteux, K., & Coskey, S. (2014). *An Introductory Look at Deterministic Chaos*. (Senior Thesis). Boise State University.

Colitti, W., Steenhaut, K., & de Caro, N. (2011). Integrating Wireless Sensor Networks with the Web. In Extending the Internet to Low Power and Lossy Networks (IP+SN 2011). Academic Press.

Comodo. (2011). Retrieved from https://blogs.comodo.com/uncategorized/the-recent-ra-compromise/

Cook, D., & Keromytis, A. D. (2006). *CryptoGraphics: Exploiting Graphics Cards for Security. Advances in Information Security*. New York, NY: Springer Verlag.

Cooper. (2008). *Internet X.509 Public Key Infrastructure Certificate and Certificate Revocation List (CRL) Profile*. RFC 5280. Retrieved from http://www.ietf.org/rfc/rfc5280.txt

Coron, J. S., Naccache, D., & Tibouchi, M. (2012). Public Key Compression and Modulus Switching for Fully Homomorphic Encryption over the Integers. *Lecture Notes in Computer Science*, *7237*, 446–464. doi:10.1007/978-3-642-29011-4_27

CoSign. (n.d.). Retrieved from http://www.arx.com

Courtois, N., Finiasz, M., & Sendrier, N. (2001). How to achieve a McEliece-based digital signature scheme. In ASIACRYPT 2001 (LNCS), (vol. 2248, pp. 157–174). Springer. doi:10.1007/3-540-45682-1_10

CRN. (2014). Retrieved from http://www.crn.com/news/security/300073396/microsoft-revokes-digital-certs-to-guard-against-possible-attacks-surveillance.htm

CROMERR. (2013). *Cross-Media Electronic Reporting Regulation (CROMERR)*. Retrieved from http://epa.gov/cromerr/about.html

Cryptix/Elliptix. (2005). *Cryptix/Elliptix*. Retrieved from www.cryptix.org

Crypto. (2006). *GNU Crypto*. Retrieved from www.gnu.org/software/gnu-crypto

Crypto++. (2013). *Crypto++*. Retrieved from www.cryptopp.com

Cryptool. (2014). *Cryptool*. Retrieved from www.cryptool.org/en/

Cui, G. Z., Qin, L., Wang, Y., & Zhang, X. (2008). An encryption scheme using DNA technology. In *Proceedings of IEEE 3rd International Conference on Bio-Inspired Computing: Theories and Applications*. Adelaide, Australia: IEEE. doi:10.1109/BICTA.2008.4656701

Cui, G., Qin, L., Wang, Y., & Zhang, X. (2008). An encryption scheme using DNA technology. In *Proceedings of 3rd International Conference on Bio-Inspired Computing: Theories and Applications, BICTA*. Academic Press.

Curty, M., & Santos, D. J. (2001). Quantum authentication of classical messages. *Physical Review A.*, *64*(6), 062309. doi:10.1103/PhysRevA.64.062309

da Cunha Neto, R. P., Zair, A., Fernandes, V. P. M., & Froz, B. R. (2013). Intrusion Detection System for Botnet Attacks in Wireless Networks Using Hybrid Detection Method Based on DNS. In T. Sobh & K. Elleithy (Eds.), Emerging Trends in Computing, Informatics, Systems Sciences, and Engineering, Lecture Notes in Electrical Engineering 151 (pp. 689-702). Springer. doi:10.1007/978-1-4614-3558-7_59

Dadhich, A., & Yadav, S. K. (2014). Evolutionary Algorithms, Fuzzy Logic and Artificial Immune Systems applied to Cryptography and Cryptanalysis: State-of-the-art review. *Optimization*, *3*(6).

Danziger, M., & Henriques, M. A. A. (2011). Computational intelligence applied on cryptology: A Brief Review. Paper presented at CIBSI 2011, Bucaramanga, Colombia.

De Couto, D., Aguayo, S. J., Bicket, J., & Morris, R. (2003). A high-throughput path metric for multi-hop wireless routing. In *Proceedings of the 9th annual international conference on Mobile computing and networking*. San Diego, CA: Academic Press. doi:10.1145/938985.939000

Debar, H., Becker, M., & Siboni, D. (1992). A Neural Component for an Intrusion Detection System. *InProceedings of Symposium on Research in Security and Privacy* (pp. 240-250). IEEE. doi:10.1109/RISP.1992.213257

Dehuri, S., Jagadev, A. K., & Panda, M. (Eds.). (2015). *Multi-objective Swarm Intelligence: Theoretical Advances and Applications* (Vol. 592). Springer. doi:10.1007/978-3-662-46309-3

DeJesus, E. (2001). *Cryptography: Quantum Leap*. Information Security.

Deng, L., & Yu, D. (2014). Deep learning: Methods and applications. *Foundations and Trends in Signal Processing, 7*(3–4), 197–387. doi:10.1561/2000000039

Denning, D. E. (1983). An Intrusion-Detection Model. In *Proceedings of the Seventh IEEE Symposium on Security and Privacy* (pp. 119–131). IEEE.

Dessimoz, D., Richiardi, J., Champod, C., & Drygajlo, A. (2006). Multimodal Biometrics for Identity Documents, Research Report, PFS 341-08.05, Version 2.0. *Université de Lausanne & École Polytechnique Fédérale de Lausanne, 2006*, 161.

Devi, V. A., & Bhuvaneswaran, R. S. (2011). Agent Based Cross Layer Intrusion Detection System for MANET. In D. C. Wyld et al. (Eds.), *CNSA 2011, CCIS 196* (pp. 427–440). Springer Verlag-Berlin.

Dhakar, M., & Tiwari, A. (2013). Analysis of K2 based Intrusion Detection System. *Current Research in Engineering, Science and Technology (CREST) Journals, 1*(5), 129–134.

Ding, J., Wolf, C., & Yang, B. J. (2007). l-invertible cycles for multivariate quadratic (MQ) public key cryptography. In PKC 2007 (LNCS), (vol. 4450, pp. 266–281). Springer.

Ditto, W., & Munakata, T. (1995). Principles and applications of chaotic systems. *Communications of the ACM, 38*(11), 96–102. doi:10.1145/219717.219797

DocuSign. (2015). *Digital Signatures FAQ*. Retrieved from http://www.arx.com/learn/about-digital-signature/digital-signature-faq/

Dodis, Y., Reyzin, L., & Smith, A. (2004). Fuzzy Extractors: How to Generate Strong Keys from Biometrics and other Noisy Data. In *Proceedings of Eurocrypt* (pp. 523–540). Springer-Verlag. doi:10.1007/978-3-540-24676-3_31

Dorigo, M. (1992). *Optimization, Learning and Natural Algorithms* (Doctoral Dissertation in Italian). Dipartimento di Elettronica, Politecnico di Milano, Milan, Italy.

Dorigo, M., Birattari, M., & Stützle, T. (2006). Ant colony optimization. *IEEE Computational Intelligence Magazine, 1*(4), 28–39. doi:10.1109/CI-M.2006.248054

Dorigo, M., Maniezzo, V., & Colorni, A. (1996). Ant system: Optimization by a colony of cooperating agents. *IEEE Trans. Systems, Man, and Cybernetics -- Part B, 26*(1), 29–41. doi:10.1109/3477.484436

Dote, Y., & Ovaska, S. J. (2001). Industrial applications of soft computing: A review. *Proceedings of the IEEE, 89*(9), 1243–1265. doi:10.1109/5.949483

DOTNET. (n.d.). *Microsoft Dot Net*. Retrieved from http://www.microsoft.com/

Drahanský, M. (2010a). *Fingerprint Recognition Technology: Liveness Detection, Image Quality and Skin Diseases*. (Habilitation thesis). Brno, Czech Republic.

Drahanský, M. (2010). *Biometric Cryptography Based on Fingerprints*. Saarbrücken: LAP.

Dunkels, A., Gronvall, R., & Voigt, T. (2004). Contiki - A Lightweight and Flexible Operating System for Tiny Networked Sensors. In *Proceedings of the 29th Annual IEEE International Conference on Local Computer Networks* (pp. 455-462). doi:10.1109/LCN.2004.38

Eberhart, R. C., Shi, Y., & Kennedy, J. (2001). *Swarm intelligence*. Elsevier.

Eberhart, R., & Shi, Y. (2008). *Computational Intelligence: Concepts to Implementation*. Morgan Kaufmann.

ECA. (2000). *Electronic Communications Act 2000*. Retrieved from http://www.opsi.gov.uk/acts/acts2000/uk-pga_20000007_en_1

EchoSign. (n.d.). Retrieved from https://www.echosign.adobe.com/

EDOCKET. (2006). *Public Law*. Retrieved from http://edocket.access.gpo.gov/2006/E6-9283.htm

EFF. (n.d.). Retrieved from https://www.eff.org/observatory

Eggers, J., & Girod, B. (2002). *Informed watermarking* (Vol. 685, pp. 1–5). Norwell, MA: Kluwer Academic. doi:10.1007/978-1-4615-0951-6_1

Eiben, A. E., Hinterding, R., & Michalewic, Z. (1999). Parameters control in evolutionary algorithms. *IEEE Transactions on Systems, Man, and Cybernetics*, *16*(1), 122–128.

EJBCA. (2015). *Open Java Development Kit*. Oracle Inc. Retrieved from http://openjdk.java.net/

El-Alfy, E. S., & Al-Utaibi, K. (2011). An Encryption Scheme for Color Images Based on Chaotic Maps and Genetic Operators. In *The Seventh International Conference on Networking and Services, ICNS*.

Elbasiony, R. M., Sallam, E. A., Eltobely, T. E., & Fahmy, M. M. (2013). A hybrid network intrusion detection framework based on random forests and weighted k-means. *Ain Shams Engineering Journal*, *4*(4), 753–762. doi:10.1016/j.asej.2013.01.003

ELKO EP s.r.o. (2010). *RF Touch control unit user manual*. Holešov.

Elomaa, T., & Kääriäinen, M. (2001). An analysis of Reduced Error Pruning. *Journal of Artificial Intelligence Research*, *15*, 163–187.

Emeliyanenko, P. (2009). Efficient Multiplication of Polynomials on Graphics Hardware. In *Advanced Parallel Processing Technologies (LNCS)*, *(pp. 5737*, pp. 134–149). New York, NY: Springer-Verlag. doi:10.1007/978-3-642-03644-6_11

EMET. (2014). *Microsoft's Enhanced Mitigation Experience Toolkit (EMET)*. Retrieved form http://support.microsoft.com/kb/2458544

Enayatifar, R., Abdullah, A. H., & Isnin, I. F. (2014). Chaos-based image encryption using a hybrid genetic algorithm and a DNA sequence. *Optics and Lasers in Engineering*, *56*, 83–93. doi:10.1016/j.optlaseng.2013.12.003

Entrust. (2011) Retrieved from http://www.entrust.net/advisories/malaysia.htm

Entrust. (n.d.). Retrieved from http://www.entrust.com

eSIGN. (2001). Retrieved from http://www.ftc.gov/os/2001/06/esign7.htm

ESLPRC. (2007). *Electronic Signature Law of the People's Republic of China*. Retrieved from http://tradeinservices.mofcom.gov.cn/en/b/2007-11-29/13694.shtml

EUDCS. (2000). *EU Directive for Electronic Signatures (1999/93/EC)*. Retrieved from http://eurlex.europa.eu/LexUriServ/LexUriServ.do?uri=CELEX:31999L0093:EN:HTML

Eu-Jin, G. (2003). *Secure Indexes*. Cryptology ePrint Archive, Report 2003/216. Retrieved from http://eprint.iacr.org/2003/216/

EUVATD. (2006). *EU VAT directive*. Retrieved from http://www.vatlive.com/eu-vat-rules/eu-vat-directive/

FAA. (2012). *FAA's CFR Title 14*. Retrieved from http://www.airweb.faa.gov/Regulatory_and_Guidance_Library/rgAdvisoryCircular.nsf/0/c2c91cc068e0dd7b86256c7100609d5f/$FILE/AC%20120-78%20final.pdf

Falkowski, B. J., & Lim, L. S. (2000). Image watermarking using Hadamard transforms. *Electronics Letters, 36*(3), 211–213. doi:10.1049/el:20000257

Faragallah, O. S. (2012). An enhanced chaotic key-based RC5 block cipher adapted to image encryption. *International Journal of Electronics, 99*(7), 925–943. doi:10.1080/00207217.2011.651689

Farhan, A. F., Zulkhairi, D., & Hatim, M. T. (2008). Mobile Agent Intrusion Detection System for Mobile Ad Hoc Networks: A Non-overlapping Zone Approach. In *Proceedings of the 4th IEEE/IFIP International Conference on Internet* (pp. 1-5). Tashkent: IEEE. doi:10.1109/CANET.2008.4655310

FDA. (2003). *FDA's 21 CFR Part 11.* Retrieved from http://www.fda.gov/RegulatoryInformation/Guidances/ucm125067.htm

Feistel, H. (1973). *Cryptography and computer privacy.* Scientific American.

Feng, W., Zhang, Q., Hu, G., & Huang, J. X. (2014). Mining network data for intrusion detection through combining SVMs with ant colony networks. *Future Generation Computer Systems Elsevier, 37*, 127–140. doi:10.1016/j.future.2013.06.027

Ferreira, C. (2002). Gene Expression Programming: Mathematical Modeling by an Artificial Intelligence. Portugal: Angra do Heroismo.

Feruza, S. & Yusufovna (2008). Integrating Intrusion Detection System and Data Mining. In *Proceedings of International Symposium on Ubiquitous Multimedia Computing* (pp. 256-259). IEEE.

FIPS. (1996). Digital Signature Standard (DSS). *FIPS PUB 186-3.* Information Technology Laboratory, National Institute of Standards and Technology. Retrieved from http://csrc.nist.gov/publications/fips/fips186-3/fips_186-3.pdf

FlexiProvider. (2012). *FlexiProvider.* Retrieved from http://www.flexiprovider.de

Forouzan, B. A. (2007). *Cryptography & Network Security.* McGraw-Hill, Inc.

Fortuna, L., Rizzotto, D. G., Lavorgna, D. M., Nunnari, G., Xibilia, M. G., & Caponetto, D. R. (2001). Neuro-fuzzy networks. In *Soft Computing* (pp. 169–178). Springer London. doi:10.1007/978-1-4471-0357-8_9

Fridrich, J. (1998). Symmetric ciphers based on two-dimensional chaotic maps. *International Journal of Bifurcation and Chaos in Applied Sciences and Engineering, 8*(06), 1259–1284. doi:10.1142/S021812749800098X

Friedman, N., Giegar, D., & Goldszmidt, M. (1997). Bayesian Network Classifiers. *Machine Learning, 29*(2/3), 131–163. doi:10.1023/A:1007465528199

FRWEBGATE. (2002). *Sarbanes-Oxley Act of 2002.* Retrieved from http://frwebgate.access.gpo.gov/cgi-bin/getdoc.cgi?dbname=107_cong_bills&docid=f:h3763enr.tst.pdf

FSMA. (1999). *Financial Services Modernization Act of 1999 (Gramm-Leach-Bliley).* Retrieved from http://www.ftc.gov/privacy/glbact/glbsub1.htm

Fu, C., & Zhu, Z. (2008). A chaotic image encryption scheme based on circular bit shift method. In *The 9th International Conference for Young Computer Scientists, ICYCS* (pp. 3057-3061). doi:10.1109/ICYCS.2008.522

Fu, C., Chen, J. J., Zou, H., Meng, W. H., Zhan, Y. F., & Yu, Y. W. (2012). A chaos-based digital image encryption scheme with an improved diffusion strategy. *Optics Express, 20*(3), 2363–2378. doi:10.1364/OE.20.002363 PMID:22330475

Fu, C., Lin, B. B., Miao, Y. S., Liu, X., & Chen, J. J. (2011). A novel chaos-based bit-level permutation scheme for digital image encryption. *Optics Communications, 284*(23), 5415–5423. doi:10.1016/j.optcom.2011.08.013

Fu, C., Meng, W. H., Zhan, Y. F., Zhu, Z. L., Lau, F., Tse, C. K., & Ma, H. F. (2013). An efficient and secure medical image protection scheme based on chaotic maps. *Computers in Biology and Medicine, 43*(8), 1000–1010. doi:10.1016/j.compbiomed.2013.05.005 PMID:23816172

Fürnkranz, J. (1997). Pruning Algorithms for Rule Learning. *Machine Learning, Kluwer Academic Publishers, 27*(2), 139–172. doi:10.1023/A:1007329424533

Gahi, Y. Guennoun, M. Guennoun, Z. El-Khatib, K. (2012). Privacy Preserving Scheme for Location-Based Services. *The Journal of Information Security*, 105–112.

Gahi, Y., Guennoun, M., & El-Khatib, K. (2011). A Secure Database System using Homomorphic Encryption Schemes. In *Proceedings of the Third International Conference on Advances in Databases, Knowledge, and Data Applications* (pp. 54–58). Academic Press.

Galbally, J., Fierrez, J., & Ortega-Garcia, J. (2007). Vulnerabilities in Biometric Systems. *Attacks and Recent Advances in Liveness Detection, Biometrics Recognition Group, Madrid, Spain, 2007*, 8.

Gambardella, L. M., & Dorigo, M. (1996, May). Solving symmetric and asymmetric TSPs by ant colonies. In *Proceedings ofInternational Conference on Evolutionary Computation* (pp. 622-627). Academic Press. doi:10.1109/ICEC.1996.542672

Garcia, L. J., & Fuster-Sabater, A. (2000). On the linear complexity of the sequences generated by nonlinear filtering. *Information Processing Letters, 76*(1-2), 67–73. doi:10.1016/S0020-0190(00)00117-4

Garey, M. R., & Johnson, D. S. (1979). *Computers and Intractability; A guide to the theory of NP Completeness*. New York: WH Freeman.

Garg, P. (2006). Genetic algorithm attack on simplified data encryption standard algorithm. *Special Issue: Advances in Computer Science and Engineering, 23*, 139–174.

Garg, P. (2009a). Cryptanalysis of SDES via evolutionary computation techniques. *International Journal of Computer Science and Information Security, 1*(1).

Garg, P. (2009b). A Comparison between Memetic algorithm and Genetic algorithm for the cryptanalysis of Simplified Data Encryption Standard algorithm. *International Journal of Network Security & Its Applications, 1*(1), 34–42.

Garg, P. (2010). Cryptanalysis of polyalphabetic substitution cipher using parallel memetic algorithm. *International Journal of Computational Intelligence and Information Security, 1*(4), 31–41.

Gehani, A., LaBean, T. H., & Reif, J. H. (1999). DNA-based cryptography. In *Proceedings of 5th Annual DIMACS Meeting on DNA Based Computers*. Cambridge, MA: DIMACS.

Geissler, K., & Smart, N. P. (2005). *D.AZTEC.2 Lightweight Asymmetric Cryptography and Alternatives to RSA: The NTRU Public-Key Cryptosystem*. ECRYPT European Network of Excellence in Cryptology.

Gelenbe, E. (1989). Random neural networks with negative and positive signals and product form solution. *Neural Computation, 1*(4), 502–510. doi:10.1162/neco.1989.1.4.502

Gelenbe, E. (1990). *Theory of the random neural network*. Technical Report. University of Maryland at College Park College Park.

Gentry, C., & Halevi, S. (2011). Implementing Gentry's fully-homomorphic encryption scheme. In Proceedings of Advances in Cryptology--EUROCRYPT 2011 (pp. 129-148). Springer.

Gentry, C. (2009). Fully Homomorphic Encryption Using Ideal Lattices. In *Proceedings of 41st ACM Symposium on Theory of Computing (STOC)*. doi:10.1145/1536414.1536440

Gilmore, R., & Lefranc, M. (2008). *The topology of chaos: Alice in stretch and squeezeland.* John Wiley & Sons.

Giorgi, P., Izard, T., & Tisserand, A. (2009). Comparison of Modular Arithmetic Algorithms on GPUs. In *Proceedings of ParCo'09, Advances in Parallel Computing* (vol. 19, pp. 315-322). IOS Press.

Gisin, N., Ribordy, G., Tittel, W., & Zbinden, H. (2002). Quantum cryptography. *Reviews of Modern Physics, 74*(1), 145–195. doi:10.1103/RevModPhys.74.145

Globsign. (n.d.). Retrieved from https://www.globalsign.com

Godhavari, T., Alamelu, N. R., & Soundararajan, R. (2005, December). Cryptography using neural network. In Proceedings of IEEE Annual INDICON (pp. 258-261). IEEE. doi:10.1109/INDCON.2005.1590168

Goldberg, D. E. (1989). *Genetic Algorithms in Search, Optimization, and Machine Learning.* Addison-Wesley.

Goldreich, O., Goldwasser, S., & Halevi, S. (1997). Public-key cryptosystems from lattice reduction problems. In CRYPTO'97 (LNCS), (vol. 1294, pp. 112–131). Springer. doi:10.1007/BFb0052231

Gonzalez, R. C., & Woods, R. E. (2005). Digital Image Processing, Pearson Education. *South Asia,* 142–172.

Google. (2014). Retrieved from http://googleonlinesecurity.blogspot.in/2014/07/maintaining-digital-certificate-security. html

Goresky, M., & Klapper, A. (2006). Pseudonoise sequence based on algebraic feedback shift registers. *IEEE Transactions on Information Theory, 52*(4), 1649–1662. doi:10.1109/TIT.2006.871045

GPEA. (2013). *Government Paperwork Elimination Act.* Retrieved from http://www.whitehouse.gov/omb/fedreg/gpea2.html

Grossberg, S. (1988). Nonlinear neural networks: Principles, mechanisms, and architectures. *Neural Networks, 1*(1), 17–61. doi:10.1016/0893-6080(88)90021-4

Gründlingh, W. R., & Vuuren, J. (2007). *Using genetic algorithms to break a simple cryptographic cipher.* Retrieved from http://dip.sun.ac.za/~vuuren/papers/genetic.ps

Grüning, A., & Bohte, S. M. (2014). Spiking neural networks: Principles and challenges. In *Proceedings of European Symposium on Artificial Neural Networks, Computational Intelligence and Machine Learning.* Bruges, Belgium: Academic Press.

Guan, Z.-H., Huang, F., & Guan, W. (2005). Chaos-based image encryption algorithm. *Physics Letters. [Part A], 346*(1), 153–157. doi:10.1016/j.physleta.2005.08.006

Güneysu, T., Lyubashevsky, V., & Pöppelmann, T. (2012). Practical Lattice-Based Cryptography: A Signature Scheme for Embedded Systems. In *CHES 2012 (LNCS), (vol. 7428,* pp. 530–547). New York, NY: Springer-Verlag. doi:10.1007/978-3-642-33027-8_31

Güneysu, T., Lyubashevsky, V., & Pöppelmann, T. (2014). Lattice-Based Signatures: Optimization and Implementation on Reconfigurable Hardware. *IEEE Transactions on Computers.* doi: 10.1109/TC.2014.2346177

Guo, J. I. (2000). A new chaotic key-based design for image encryption and decryption. In *Proceedings of the 2000 IEEE International Symposium on Circuits and Systems.* IEEE.

Gustafson, H., Dawson, E., Nielsen, L., & Caelli, W. (1994). A computer package for measuring the strength of encryption algorithm. *Computers & Security, 14*(8), 687–697. doi:10.1016/0167-4048(94)90051-5

Gutierrez, E., Romero, S., Trenas, M. A., & Zapata, E. L. (2008). Memory Locality Exploitation Strategies for FFT on the CUDA Architecture. In *High Performance Computing for Computational Science – VECPAR 2008 (LNCS), (vol. 5336,* pp. 430–443). New York, NY: Springer-Verlag. doi:10.1007/978-3-540-92859-1_39

Hall, M., Frank, E., Holmes, G., Pfahringer, B., Reutemann, P., & Witten, I. H. (2009). The WEKA Data Mining Software: An Update. *SIGKDD Explorations, 11*(1), 10–18. doi:10.1145/1656274.1656278

Hammood, D. N. (2010). Particles swarm optimization for the cryptanalysis of transposition cipher. *Journal of Al-Nahrain University, 13*(4), 211–215.

Han, J., Kamber, M., & Pei, J. (2006). *Data Mining: Concepts and Techniques.* San Francisco, CA: Morgan Kaufmann Publishers.

Han, S., & Cho, S. (2003). Detecting Intrusion with Rule-Based Integration of Multiple Models. *Computers & Security Elsevier, 22*(7), 613–623. doi:10.1016/S0167-4048(03)00711-9

Haque, S. A., & Maza, M. M. (2012). Plain Polynomial Arithmetic on GPU. In *High Performance Computing Symposium* (vol. 385, pp. 1-10). IOP Publishing.

Harrison, O., & Waldron, J. (2009). Efficient Acceleration of Asymmetric Cryptography in Graphics Hardware. In *AFRICACRYPT (LNCS), (vol. 5580,* pp. 350–367). New York, NY: Springer-Verlag. doi:10.1007/978-3-642-02384-2_22

Hartung, F., & Kutter, M. (1999). Multimedia watermarking techniques. *Proceedings of the IEEE, 87*(7), 1079–1107. doi:10.1109/5.771066

Haykin, S. (2009). *Neural Networks and Learning Machines* (3rd ed.). Upper Saddle River, NJ: Pearson Education.

Haynes, T., Wainwright, R., Sen, S., Sen, I., & Schoenefeld, D. (1995). Strongly typed GP in evolving cooperation strategies. In *Proceedings of the Sixth International Conference on Genetic Algorithms.* Morgan Kaufmann.

Heberlein, L. T., Dias, G. V., Levitt, K. N., Mukherjee, B., Wood, J., & Wolber, D. (1990). A network security monitor. In *Proceedings of Computer Society Symposium on Research in Security and Privacy* (pp. 296-304). IEEE.

Henzl, M., & Hanáček, P. (2013). Modeling of Contactless Smart Card Protocols and Automated Vulnerability Finding, (ISBAST). In *Proceedings of 2013 International Symposium on Biometrics and Security Technologies* (pp. 141-148). Academic Press. doi:10.1109/ISBAST.2013.26

Hermans, J., Vercauteren, F., & Preneel, B. (2010). Speed Records for NTRU. In *CT-RSA (LNCS), (vol. 5985,* pp. 73–88). New York, NY: Springer-Verlag.

Hernández Encinas, L., Martín del Rey, Á., & Hernández Encinas, A. (2002). *Encryption of images with 2-dimensional cellular automata.* Academic Press.

Hernández, J. C., Isasi, P., & Arco-Calderón, C. L. (2003). Finding efficient nonlinear functions by means of genetic programming. In Knowledge-Based Intelligent Information and Engineering Systems (LCNS), (vol. 2773, pp. 1192-1198). Berlin: Springer.

Hinitt, N., & Koçak, T. (2010). GPU-Based FFT Computation for Multi-Gigabit WirelessHD Baseband Processing. *EURASIP Journal on Wireless Communications and Networking, 2010*(1), 359081. doi:10.1155/2010/359081

HIPAA. (1996). *Health Insurance Portability and Accountability Act (HIPAA).* Retrieved from http://aspe.hhs.gov/admnsimp/pL104191.htm

Ho, A. T., Shen, J., & Tan, S. H. (2003a). Character-embedded watermarking algorithm using the fast Hadamard transform for satellite images. In *Proc. International Symposium on Optical Science and Technology*. International Society for Optics and Photonics. doi:10.1117/12.451249

Ho, A. T., Shen, J., & Tan, S. H. (2003b). *Robust digital image-in-image watermarking algorithm using the fast Hadamard transform*. Seattle, WA: Proc. InternationalSymposium on Optical Science and Technology. doi:10.1109/ISCAS.2003.1205147

Ho, A. T., Shen, J., Tan, S. H., & Kot, A. C. (2002). Digital image-in-image watermarking for copyright protection of satellite images using the fast Hadamard transform. In *Proc. IEEE International Symposium on Geoscience and Remote Sensing* (Vol. 6, pp. 3311–3313). IEEE. doi:10.1109/IGARSS.2002.1027166

Hoffstein, J., Howgrave-Graham, N., Pipher, J., Silverman, J. H., & Whyte, W. (2003). NTRUSIGN: Digital Signatures Using the NTRU Lattice. In *CT-RSA (LNCS), (vol. 2612*, pp. 122–140). New York, NY: Springer-Verlag. doi:10.1007/3-540-36563-X_9

Hoffstein, J., & Silverman, J. H. (1998). NTRU: A Ring-based Public Key Cryptosystem. In *ANTS-III (LNCS), (vol. 1423*, pp. 267–288). New York, NY: Springer-Verlag.

Holland, J. H. (1975). *Adaptive in Natural and Artificial Systems*. University of Michigan.

Hong-Song, C., Jianyu, Z., & Lee, H. W. J. (2008). A novel NP-based security scheme for AODV routing protocol. *Journal of Discrete Mathematical Sciences and Cryptography*, *11*(2), 131–145. doi:10.1080/09720529.2008.10698172

Hong-song, C., Zhenzhou, J., Mingzeng, H., Zhongchuan, F., & Ruixiang, J. (2007). Design and performance evaluation of a multi-agent-based dynamic lifetime security scheme for AODV routing protocol. *Elsevier Journal of Network and Computer Applications*, *30*(1), 145–166. doi:10.1016/j.jnca.2005.09.006

Hornik, K., Stinchcombe, M., & White, H. (1989). Multilayer feedforward networks are universal approximators. *Neural Networks*, *2*(5), 359–366. doi:10.1016/0893-6080(89)90020-8

Howgrave-Graham, N., Silverman, J. H., Singer, A., & Whyte, W. (2003). *NAEP: Provable Security in the Presence of Decryption Failures*. In IACR ePrint Archive, Report 2003-172. Retrieved from http://eprint.iacr.org/2003/172/

Huang, C. K., & Nien, H. H. (2009). Multi chaotic systems based pixel shuffle for image encryption. *Optics Communications*, *282*(11), 2123–2127. doi:10.1016/j.optcom.2009.02.044

Huang, X. (2012). Image encryption algorithm using chaotic Chebyshev generator. *Nonlinear Dynamics*, *67*(4), 2411–2417. doi:10.1007/s11071-011-0155-7

Hughes, R. J. (1996). Quantum cryptography over underground optical fibers. In *Crypto96-Proc. of the 16th Annual International Cryptology Conference on Advances in Cryptology*. Springer-Verlag.

Hung-Jen, L., Chun-Hung, R. L., Ying-Chih, L., & Kuang-Yuan, T. (2013). Intrusion detection system: A comprehensive review. *Elsevier Journal of Network and Computer Applications*, *36*(1), 16–24. doi:10.1016/j.jnca.2012.09.004

Hussain, I., Shah, T., & Gondal, M. A. (2013). Application of S-box and chaotic map for image encryption. *Mathematical and Computer Modelling*, *57*(9), 2576–2579. doi:10.1016/j.mcm.2013.01.009

Hu, Y., & Jeon, B. (2006). Reversible visible watermarking and lossless recovery of original images. *IEEE Transactions on Circuits and Systems for Video Technology*, *16*(11), 1423–1429. doi:10.1109/TCSVT.2006.884011

Hu, Y., & Kwong, S. (2001). Wavelet domain adaptive visible watermarking. *Electronics Letters*, *37*(20), 1219–1220. doi:10.1049/el:20010838

Hu, Y., & Kwong, S. (2003). An image fusion based visible watermarking algorithm. In *Proc. International Symposium on Circuits and Systems* (Vol. 3, pp. 794–797). Academic Press.

Hu, Y., Kwong, S., & Huang, J. (2006). An algorithm for removable visible watermarking. *IEEE Transactions on Circuits and Systems for Video Technology*, *16*(1), 129–133. doi:10.1109/TCSVT.2005.858742

IEEE, (2008). *P1363.1: Standard Specifications for Public-Key Cryptographic Techniques Based on Hard Problems over Lattices*. IEEE P1363.1 Draft.

Iftekharuddin, K. M., & Frigui, N. (2009). A Robust Spatial Domain Binary Signature Watermarking Technique. *Int. J. Tomography Simulation*, *11*(W09), 76–85.

Ilgun, K., Kemmerer, R. A., & Porras, P. A. (1995). State transition analysis: A rule-based intrusion detection approach. *IEEE Transactions on Software Engineering*, *21*(3), 181–199. doi:10.1109/32.372146

ImperialViolet. (2011). Retrieved from https://www.imperialviolet.org/2011/05/04/pinning.html

Information and Computer Science, University of California, Irvine. (1999). *KDD Cup 1999 Dataset* [Data file]. Available from http://kdd.ics.uci.edddatabases/kddcup99/kddcup99.html

International, S. R. I. (1992). *A Real-Time Intrusion Detection Expert System (IDES) - Final Technical Report*. Washington, DC: Author.

Isasi, P. (2005). Evolutionary Computation in Computer Security and Cryptography. *Generation Computing*, *23*(3), 193–199. doi:10.1007/BF03037654

Isasi, P., & Julio, C. H. (2004). Introduction to the applications of evolutionary computation in computer security and cryptography. *Computational Intelligence*, *20*(3), 445–449. doi:10.1111/j.0824-7935.2004.00244.x

IT ACT 2000. (2000). *The Information Technology Act, 2000*. Government of India. Retrieved from http://www.mit.gov.in/sites/upload_files/dit/files/downloads/itact2000/itbill2000.pdf

Jacob, G., & Murugan, A. (2013). DNA Based Cryptography: An Overview and Analysis. *International Journal of Emerging Sciences*, *3*(1), 36–27.

Jain, A., & Chaudhari, N. S. (2014, January). Cryptanalytic results on knapsack cryptosystem using binary particle swarm optimization. In *Proceedings ofInternational Joint Conference SOCO'14-CISIS'14-ICEUTE'14* (pp. 375-384). Springer International Publishing.

Jain, A. K. (2005). *Biometric System Security, Presentation*. Michigan State University.

Jain, Y. K. & Upendra. (2012). An Efficient Intrusion Detection based on Decision Tree Classifier Using Feature Reduction. *International Journal of Scientific and Research Publication*, *2*(1), 1–6.

Jang, J. S. (1993). ANFIS: Adaptive-network-based fuzzy inference system. *IEEE Transactions on Systems, Man, and Cybernetics*, *23*(3), 665–685. doi:10.1109/21.256541

Jang, J. S. R., Sun, C. T., & Mizutani, E. (1997). *Neuro-Fuzzy and Soft Computing: A Computational Approach to Learning and Machine Intelligence*. Prentice-Hall, Inc.

Jang, J. S., & Sun, C. T. (1995). Neuro-fuzzy modeling and control. *Proceedings of the IEEE*, *83*(3), 378–406. doi:10.1109/5.364486

Jawad, L. M., & Sulong, G. B. (2013). A review of color image encryption techniques.[IJCSI]. *International Journal of Computer Science Issues*, *10*(6).

jBorZoi. (2006). *jBorZoi*. Retrieved from http://nixbit.com/cat/programming/libraries/borzoi

Jiang, S. Y., Song, X., Wang, H., Han, J., & Li, Q. (2006). A Clustering-based Method for Unsupervised Intrusion Detection. *Pattern Recognition Letters Elsevier, 27*(7), 802–810. doi:10.1016/j.patrec.2005.11.007

Jiang, W., Song, H., & Dai, Y. (2005). Real-time intrusion detection for high-speed networks. *Computers & Security Elsevier, 24*(4), 287–294. doi:10.1016/j.cose.2004.07.005

Jin, J. (2012). An image encryption based on elementary cellular automata. *Optics and Lasers in Engineering, 50*(12), 1836–1843. doi:10.1016/j.optlaseng.2012.06.002

Joo, D., Hong, T., & Han, I. (2003). The neural network models for IDS based on the asymmetric costs of false negative errors and false positive errors. *Expert Systems with Applications Elsevier, 25*(1), 69–75. doi:10.1016/S0957-4174(03)00007-1

Juels, A. (1999). *A fuzzy commitment scheme*. In *Proceedings of Sixth ACM Conference on Computer and Communications Security* (pp. 28–36). ACM Press. doi:10.1145/319709.319714

Juels, A., & Sudan, M. (2002). A fuzzy vault scheme. In *Proceedings of IEEE International Symposium on Information Theory*. IEEE. doi:10.1109/ISIT.2002.1023680

Kankanhalli, M. S., & Ramakrishnan, K. R. (1998). Content based watermarking of images. In *Proc. Sixth ACM international conference on Multimedia* (pp. 61-70). ACM. doi:10.1145/290747.290756

Kanter, I., Kinzel, W., & Kanter, E. (2002). Secure exchange of information by synchronization of neural networks. *Europhysics Letters, 57*(1), 141–147. doi:10.1209/epl/i2002-00552-9

Kantof, C., Sastry, N., & Wagner, D. (2004). TinySec: A Link Layer Security Architecture for Wireless Sensor Networks. In *Proceedings of Second International Conference on Embedded Networked Sensor Systems* (SenSys '04) (pp. 162-175). Academic Press.

Karras, D. A., & Zorkadis, V. (2003). On neural network techniques in the secure management of communication systems through improving and quality assessing pseudorandom stream generators. *Neural Networks, 16*(5-6), 899–905. doi:10.1016/S0893-6080(03)00124-2 PMID:12850049

Kar, S., Das, S., & Ghosh, P. K. (2014). Applications of neuro fuzzy systems: A brief review and future outline. *Applied Soft Computing, 15*, 243–259. doi:10.1016/j.asoc.2013.10.014

Katz, J., Sahai, A., & Waters, B. (2008). Predicate encryption supporting disjunctions, polynomial equations, and inner products. In Advances in Cryptology—EUROCRYPT 2008 (pp. 146–162). Springer. doi:10.1007/978-3-540-78967-3_9

Kellegoz, T., Toklu, B., & Wilson, J. (2008). Comparing efficiencies of genetic crossover operators for one machine total weighted tardiness problem. *Applied Mathematics and Computation, 199*(2), 590–598. doi:10.1016/j.amc.2007.10.013

Kenndy, J., & Eberhart, R. C. (1995). Particle swarm optimization. In *Proceedings of IEEE International Conference on Neural Networks* (Vol. 4, pp. 1942-1948). IEEE. doi:10.1109/ICNN.1995.488968

Kent, S. T. (1993). Internet Privacy Enhanced Mail. *Communications of the ACM, 36*(8), 48–60. doi:10.1145/163381.163390

Khan, L., Awad, M., & Thuraisingham, M. (2007). A New Intrusion Detection System using Support Vector and Hierarchical Clustering. *The VLDB Journal, 16*(4), 507–521. doi:10.1007/s00778-006-0002-5

Kinzel, W., & Kanter, I. (2002). Neural cryptography. In *Proc. of the 9th International Conference on Neural Information Processing*. Academic Press. doi:10.1109/ICONIP.2002.1202841

Kirkpatrick, S., Gelatt, C. D., & Vecchi, M. P. (1983). Optimization by Simulated Annealing. *Science New Series, 220*(4598), 671–680. PMID:17813860

Kluz, M. (2005). *Liveness Testing in Biometric Systems.* (Master Thesis). Faculty of Informatics, Masaryk University Brno, Czech Republic.

Ko, C. (2000). Logic Induction of Valid Behavior Specifications for Intrusion Detection. In *Proceedings of the Symposium on Security and Privacy* (pp. 142-153). IEEE. doi:10.1109/SECPRI.2000.848452

Kocarev, L., & Jakimoski, G. (2001). Logistic map as a block encryption algorithm. *Physics Letters. [Part A], 289*(4), 199–206. doi:10.1016/S0375-9601(01)00609-0

Kocarev, L., & Lian, S. (Eds.). (2011). *Chaos-based Cryptography: Theory, Algorithms and Applications* (Vol. 354). Springer. doi:10.1007/978-3-642-20542-2

Koch, W. (2003). *The GNU privacy guard.* Retrieved from http://www.gnupg.org

Koc, L., Mazzuchi, T. A., & Sarkani, S. (2012). A network intrusion detection system based on a Hidden Naïve Bayes multiclass classifier. *Expert Systems with Applications Elsevier, 39*(18), 13492–13500. doi:10.1016/j.eswa.2012.07.009

Konar, A. (2005). *Computational Intelligence: Principles, Techniques and Applications.* Springer. doi:10.1007/b138935

Koza, J. R. (1992). *Genetic Programming: On the Programming of Computers by Means of Natural Selection.* MIT Press.

Koza, J. R. (1994). *Automatic discovery of reusable programs.* MIT Press.

Koza, J. R. (1994). *GP II: Automatic discovery of reusable programs.* Cambridge, MA: MIT press.

Koza, J. R., & Rice, J. P. (1994). *Genetic Programming II: Automatic Discovery of Reusable Programs.* Cambridge, MA: MIT Press.

Kubát, D., & Drahanský, M. (2011). RF Touch for Wireless Control of Intelligent Houses. In *Proceedings of Ubiquitous Computing and Multimedia Applications: Second International Conference.* Berlin: Springer Verlag.

Kuhn, D. R., Hu, V. C., Polk, W. T., & Chang, S. J. (2001). *Introduction to Public Key Technology and federal PKI Infrastructure.* NIST Gaithersburg. Retrieved form http://www.csrc.nist.gov/publications/nistpubs/ 80032/ sp80032.pdf

Kumar, A. & Ghose, M. (2009). Overview of information security using genetic algorithm and chaos. *Information Security Journal: A Global Perspective, 18*(6), 306–315.

Kumar, A., & Ghose, M. K. (2011). Extended substitution–diffusion based image cipher using chaotic standard map. *Communications in Nonlinear Science and Numerical Simulation, 16*(1), 372–382. doi:10.1016/j.cnsns.2010.04.010

Kumar, P., & Reddy, K. (2014). An Agent based Intrusion detection system for wireless network with Artificial Immune System (AIS) and Negative Clone Selection. In *Proceedings of the International Conference on Electronic Systems, Signal Processing and Computing Technologies* (pp. 429-433). India: IEEE. doi:10.1109/ICESC.2014.73

Kumar, S., & Spafford, E. H. (1995). A software architecture to support misuse intrusion detection. In *Proceedings of the 18th National Conference on Information Security* (pp. 194–204).

Kuppusamy, K., & Thamodaran, K. (2012). Optimized partial image encryption scheme using PSO. In *International Conference on Pattern Recognition, Informatics and Medical Engineering (PRIME).* doi:10.1109/ICPRIME.2012.6208350

Kutter, M., Bhattacharjee, S. K., & Ebrahimi, T. (1999).Towards second generation watermarking schemes. In *Proc. International Conference on Image Processing* (Vol. 1, pp. 320–323). Academic Press.

L'ecuyer, P., & Simard, R. (2007). TestU01: A C library for empirical testing of random number generators. *ACM Transactions on Mathematical Software*, *33*(4), 22–40, es. doi:10.1145/1268776.1268777

Lai, X., Lu, M., Qin, L., Han, J., & Fang, X. (2010). Asymmetric encryption and signature method with DNA technology. *Science China Information Sciences*, *53*(3), 506–514. doi:10.1007/s11432-010-0063-3

Lamport, L. (1979). *Constructing digital signatures from a one-way function*. Technical Report SRI-CSL-98. SRI International Computer Science Laboratory.

Lamport, L. (1994). The temporal logic of actions. *ACM Transactions on Programming Languages and Systems*, *16*(3), 872–923. doi:10.1145/177492.177726

Langelaar, G. C., van der Lubbe, J. C., & Lagendijk, R. L. (1997). Robust labeling methods for copy protection of images. InProc. Electronic Imaging, International Society for Optics and Photonics (pp. 298–309). Academic Press.

Langelaar, G. C., Lagendijk, R. L., & Biemond, J. (1998). Real-time labeling of MPEG-2 compressed video. *Journal of Visual Communication and Image Representation*, *9*(4), 256–270. doi:10.1006/jvci.1998.0397

Langelaar, G. C., Setyawan, I., & Lagendijk, R. L. (2000). Watermarking digital image and video data.A state-of-the-art overview. *IEEE Signal Processing Magazine*, *17*(5), 20–46. doi:10.1109/79.879337

Lappas, T., & Pelechrinis, K. (n.d.). *Data Mining Techniques for (Network) intrusion Detection Systems*. Retrieved from http://www.academia.edu/5016171/Data_Mining_Techniques_for_Network_Intrusion_Detection_Systems

Lari, K., & Young, S. J. (1990). The estimation of stochastic context-free grammars using the Inside-Outside algorithm. *Computer Speech & Language*, *4*(1), 34–56. doi:10.1016/0885-2308(90)90022-X

Laskari, E. C., Meletiou, G. C., Stamatiou, Y. C., & Vrahatis, M. N. (2005). Evolutionary computation based cryptanalysis: A first study. *Nonlinear Analysis: Theory, Methods & Applications, 63*(5).

Laskari, E. C., Meletiou, G. C., Stamatiou, Y. C., & Vrahatis, M. N. (2007). Cryptography and Cryptanalysis through Computational Intelligence. In *Computational Intelligence in Information Assurance and Security* (pp. 1–49). Springer Berlin Heidelberg. doi:10.1007/978-3-540-71078-3_1

Laskari, E. C., Meletiou, G. C., & Vrahatis, M. N. (2005). Problems of cryptography as discrete optimization tasks. *Nonlinear Analysis: Theory, Methods & Applications*, *63*(5), e831–e837.

Lee, J.-G., Sang-Hyun, L. & Kyung-Il, M. (2013). Smart Home Security System Based on ANFIS. In *Proceedings of the 7th International Conference on Information Security and Assurance*. Academic Press.

Lee, H., Hong, C., Kim, H., Lim, J., & Yang, H. J. (2004). Arbitrated quantum signature scheme with message recovery. *Physics Letters. [Part A]*, *321*(5-6), 295–300. doi:10.1016/j.physleta.2003.12.036

Lee, M. K., Kim, J. W., Song, J. E., & Park, K. (2007). Sliding Window Method for NTRU. In *ACNS (LNCS)*, *(vol. 4521*, pp. 432–442). New York, NY: Springer-Verlag.

Lee, M. K., Kim, J. W., Song, J. E., & Park, K. (2013). *Efficient Implementation of NTRU Cryptosystem Using Sliding Window Methods*. IEICE Trans. Fundamentals, E96-A(1), 206–213.

Lee, W., & Stolfo, S. J. (1998). Data Mining Approaches for Intrusion Detection. In *Proceedings of the 7th USENIX Security Symposium*. San Antonio, TX: USENIX.

Lee, Y., Kim, H., & Park, Y. (2009). A new data hiding scheme for binary image authentication with small image distortion. *Information Sciences*, *179*(22), 3866–3884. doi:10.1016/j.ins.2009.07.014

Lee, Z. J., & Chang, L. Y. (2014). Apply fuzzy decision tree to information security risk assessment. *International Journal of Fuzzy Systems, 16*(2), 265–269.

Leier, A., Richter, C., Banzhaf, W., & Rauhe, H. (2000). Cryptography with DNA binary strands. *Bio Systems, 57*(1), 13–22. doi:10.1016/S0303-2647(00)00083-6 PMID:10963862

Lewko, A., Okamoto, T., Sahai, A., Takashima, K., & Waters, B. (2010). Fully secure functional encryption: attribute-based encryption and (hierarchical) inner product encryption. In Advances in Cryptology—EUROCRYPT 2010 (pp. 62–91). Springer.

Li, J., Zhang, F., & Wang, Y. (2006). A new hierarchical ID-based cryptosystem and CCA-secure PKE. In *Embedded and Ubiquitous Computing, International Conference (EUC)* (LNCS), (pp. 362–371). Springer.

Lian, S. (2009). A block cipher based on chaotic neural networks. *Neurocomputing, 72*(4), 1296–1301. doi:10.1016/j.neucom.2008.11.005

Lian, S., Chen, G., Cheung, A., & Wang, Z. (2004). A chaotic-neural-network-based encryption algorithm for JPEG2000 encoded images. In *Advances in Neural Networks-ISNN 2004* (pp. 627–632). Springer Berlin Heidelberg. doi:10.1007/978-3-540-28648-6_100

Libgcrypt. (2011). *Libgcrypt.* Retrieved from www.gnu.org/software/libgcrypt

Lin, W., & Hauptmann, A. (2003). Meta-classification: Combining Multimodal Classifiers. In O. R. Zaïane, S. J. Simoff, & C. Djeraba (Eds.), Mining Multimedia and Complex Data (pp. 217–231). Berlin: Springer.

Lin, F., & Kao, C. (1995). A Genetic Algorithm for Ciphertext-Only Attack in Cryptanalysis. In *Proceedings of the 1995 IEEE International Conference on Systems, Man and Cybernetics.* Vancouver: IEEE.

Lin, S. D., & Chen, C. F. (2000). A robust DCT-based watermarking for copyright protection. *IEEE Transactions on Consumer Electronics, 46*(3), 415–421. doi:10.1109/30.883387

Li, T., Li, J., & Zhang, J. (2014). A Cryptanalysis Method based on Niche Genetic Algorithm. *Appl. Math. Inf. Sci., 8*(1), 279–285. doi:10.12785/amis/080134

Liu, C. Y., Woungang, I., Chao, H. C., Dhurandher, S. K., Chi, T. Y., & Obaidat, M. S. (2011, December). Message security in multi-path ad hoc networks using a neural network-based cipher. In *Proceedings of Global Telecommunications Conference* (GLOBECOM 2011). Academic Press.

Liu, J., & Yin, Z. (2013). Based on DNA Self-Assembled Computing to Solve MH Knapsack Public Key Cryptosystems of the Knapsack Problem. In *Proceedings of The Eighth International Conference on Bio-Inspired Computing: Theories and Applications (BIC-TA)* (pp. 975-983). Springer Berlin Heidelberg. doi:10.1007/978-3-642-37502-6_114

Liu, H., Wang, X., & Kadir, A. (2013). Color image encryption using Choquet fuzzy integral and hyper chaotic system. *Optik-International Journal for Light and Electron Optics, 124*(18), 3527–3533. doi:10.1016/j.ijleo.2012.10.068

Liu, L., Zhang, Q., & Wei, X. (2012). A RGB image encryption algorithm based on DNA encoding and chaos map. *Computers & Electrical Engineering, 38*(5), 1240–1248. doi:10.1016/j.compeleceng.2012.02.007

Li, X., & Wang, J. (2007). A steganographic method based upon JPEG and particle swarm optimization algorithm. *Information Sciences, 177*(15), 3099–3109. doi:10.1016/j.ins.2007.02.008

Li, Y., & Qian, Z. (2010). Mobile agents-based intrusion detection system for mobile ad hoc networks. In *Proceedings of the International Conference on Innovative Computing and Communication and 2010 Asia-Pacific Conference on Information Technology and Ocean Engineering* (pp. 145-148). Macao, China: IEEE. doi:10.1109/CICC-ITOE.2010.45

Li, Y., Yin, J., & Wu, G. (2011). An approach to evaluating the computer network security with intuitionistic fuzzy information. *AISS: Advances in Information Sciences and Service Sciences, 3*(7), 195–200. doi:10.4156/aiss.vol3.issue7.23

Lopez-Alt, A., Tromer, E., & Vaikuntanathan, V. (2012). On-the-fly Multiparty Computation on the Cloud via Multikey Fully Homomorphic Encryption. In *Proceedings of the 44th ACM Symposium on Theory of Computing* (pp.1219-1234). New York, NY: ACM. doi:10.1145/2213977.2214086

Lowe, G. (1998). Casper: A compiler for the analysis of security protocols, *Journal of Computer Security, 6*(1-2), 53-84.

Lu X, Feng D G. (2005). An arbitrated quantum message signature scheme. In *Computational and Information Science.* Springer Berlin Heidelberg.

Lu, X., & Feng, D. (2005). Quantum digital signature based on quantum one-way functions. In *Proceedings of Advanced Communication Technology.* IEEE.

Lu, M., Lai, X., Xiao, G., & Qin, L. (2007). Symmetric-key cryptosystem with DNA technology. *Science in China Series F: Information Sciences, 50*(3), 324–333. doi:10.1007/s11432-007-0025-6

Luo, L., Chen, Z., Chen, M., Zeng, X., & Xiong, Z. (2010). Reversible image watermarking using interpolation technique. *IEEE Trans. Inf. Forensics Secur., 5*(1), 187–193. doi:10.1109/TIFS.2009.2035975

Luo, M. X., Chen, X. B., Yun, D., & Yang, Y.-X. (2012). Quantum Signature Scheme with Weak Arbitrator. *International Journal of Theoretical Physics, 51*(7), 2135–2142. doi:10.1007/s10773-012-1093-y

Lyubashevsky, V., Peikert, C. and Regev, O., (2013). On Ideal Lattices and Learning with Errors over Rings. *Journal of the ACM, 60*(6), 43:1-43:35.

Lyubashevsky, V., Micciancio, D., Peikert, C., & Rosen, A. (2008). SWIFFT: A Modest Proposal for FFT Hashing. In *FSE (LNCS), (vol. 5086,* pp. 54–72). New York, NY: Springer-Verlag. doi:10.1007/978-3-540-71039-4_4

Ma, L., & Song, S. (2009).Improved image watermarking scheme using nonnegative matrix factorization and wavelet transform. In *Proc. International Conference on Wireless Communications & Signal Processing* (pp. 1–5). Academic Press. doi:10.1109/WCSP.2009.5371664

Maass, W. (1997). Networks of spiking neurons: The third generation of neural network models. *Neural Networks, 10*(9), 1659–1671. doi:10.1016/S0893-6080(97)00011-7

Macq, B. M., & Quisquater, J. J. (1995). Cryptology for digital TV broadcasting. *Proceedings of the IEEE, 83*(6), 944–957. doi:10.1109/5.387094

Malčík, D., & Drahanský, M. (2012). Microscopic Analysis of The Chips: Chips deprocessing. *Advanced Science and Technology Letters, (7)*, 80-85.

Maleki, F., Mohades, A., Hashemi, S. M., & Shiri, M. E. (2008). An image encryption system by cellular automata with memory. In *Third International Conference on Availability, Reliability and Security.* doi:10.1109/ARES.2008.121

MalwareBytes. (2013) Retrieved from https://blog.malwarebytes.org/intelligence/2013/02/digital-certificates-and-malware-a-dangerous-mix/

Manavski, A. S. (2007). CUDA Compatible GPU as an Efficient Hardware Accelerator for AES. In *Proceedings of IEEE International Conference on Signal Processing and Communications* (pp.65-68). Dubai, UAE: IEEE. doi:10.1109/ICSPC.2007.4728256

Manoharan, J. S., & Vijila, K. S. (2013). A Hybrid Transform for Robustness Enhancement of Watermarking of Medical Images. *Int. J. Imaging & Robotics, 9*(1), 73–83.

Mantha, A. (2012). *Improving Reliability in DNA based Computations with Applications to Cryptography.* (Doctoral dissertation). University of Cincinnati, Cincinnati, OH.

Mao, Y., & Chen, G. (2005). Chaos-based image encryption. In *Handbook of Geometric Computing* (pp. 231–265). Springer Berlin Heidelberg. doi:10.1007/3-540-28247-5_8

Marjuni, A., Logeswaran, R., & Ahmad Fauzi, M. F. (2010). *An image watermarking scheme based on FWHT-DCT. Proc. Networking and Information Technology.* Manila: ICNIT.

Massey, J. L. (1976). Shift register sequences and BCH decoding. *IEEE Transactions on Information Theory, 15*(1), 122–127. doi:10.1109/TIT.1969.1054260

Matsumoto, T., Matsumoto, H., Yamada, K., & Hoshino, S. (2005). Impact of Artificial "Gummy" Fingers on Fingerprint Systems, In *Proceedings of SPIE* (Vol. 4677, p. 11). SPIE.

Maza, M. M., & Pan, W. (2010). Fast Polynomial Multiplication on a GPU. In *High Performance Computing Symposium* (vol. 256, pp. 1-13). IOP Publishing.

Mazloom, S., & Eftekhari-Moghadam, A. M. (2009). Color image encryption based on coupled nonlinear chaotic map. *Chaos, Solitons, and Fractals, 42*(3), 1745–1754. doi:10.1016/j.chaos.2009.03.084

Mazloom, S., & Eftekhari-Moghadam, A. M. (2011). Color image cryptosystem using chaotic maps. In *IEEE Symposium on Computational Intelligence for Multimedia, Signal and Vision Processing (CIMSIVP).* IEEE.

McCarthy, J. (1979). *The implementation of Lisp, History of Lisp.* Stanford University.

Mechtri, L., Djemili, F. T., & Ghanemi, S. (2012). MASID: Multi-agent system for intrusion detection in MANET. in *Proceedings of the Ninth International Conference on Information Technology - New Generations (ITNG'12)* (pp. 65-70).Washington, DC: IEEE. doi:10.1109/ITNG.2012.18

Mehrotra, K., Mohan, C. K., & Ranka, S. (1997). *Elements of Artificial Neural Networks.* MIT Press.

Menezes, A. J., Van Oorschot, P. C., & Vanstone, S. A. (2010). *Handbook of applied cryptography.* CRC Press.

Merkle, R. C. (1989). A certified digital signature. In CRYPTO (pp. 218–238). Academic Press.

Micciancio, D. (2001). Improving Lattice Based Cryptosystems Using the Hermite Normal Form. *Lecture Notes in Computer Science, 2146*, 126–145. doi:10.1007/3-540-44670-2_11

Microsoft. (n.d.). Retrieved from http://www.microsoft.com/security/portal/mmpc/shared/glossary.aspx#rogue_security_software

MicrosoftTechnet. (2013). Retrieved from https://technet.microsoft.com/library/security/2798897

Mihara, T. (2002). Quantum identification schemes with entanglements. *Physical Review A., 65*(5), 052326. doi:10.1103/PhysRevA.65.052326

Millan, W., Clark, A., & Dawson, E. (1997). An effective genetic algorithm for finding highly nonlinear Boolean functions. In *The First International Conference on Information and Communications Security* (LNCS), (vol. 1334, pp. 149-158). Berlin: Springer.

Miller, B. L., & Goldberg, D. E. (1995). Genetic Algorithms. Tournament Selection and the Effects of Noise. *Complex Systems, 9*(3), 193–212.

Mills, A. P. Jr, Yurke, B., & Platzman, P. M. (1999). Article for analog vector algebra computation. *Bio Systems, 52*(1-3), 175–180. doi:10.1016/S0303-2647(99)00044-1 PMID:10636042

Mir, F. A., & Banday, M. T. (2012). Authentication of Electronic Records: Limitations of Indian Legal Approach. *Journal of International Commercial Law and Technology, 7*(3), 223–232.

Mislovaty, R., Klein, E., Kanter, I., & Kinzel, W. (2003). Public channel cryptography by synchronization of neural networks and chaotic maps. *Physical Review Letters, 91*(11), 118701. doi:10.1103/PhysRevLett.91.118701 PMID:14525461

Mitchell, M. (1996). *An Introduction to Genetic Algorithm*. Cambridge, MA: MIT Press.

Mohammad, M. N., Sulaiman, N., & Muhsin, O. A. (2011). A Novel Intrusion Detection System by using Intelligent Data Mining in Weka Environment. *Elsevier, Procedia Computer Science, 3*, 1237–1242.

Mohammed, R. G., & Awadelkarim, A. M. (2011). Design and Implementation of a Data Mining-Based Network Intrusion Detection Scheme. *Asian Journal of Information Technology, 10*(4), 136–141. doi:10.3923/ajit.2011.136.141

Mohanty, S. P., & Bhargava, B. K. (2008). Invisible watermarking based on creation and robust insertion-extraction of image adaptive watermarks. *ACM Trans. Multimedia Comput. Commun. Appl., 5*(2), 12:1–12:22.

Mohanty, S. P., Ramakrishnan, K. R., & Kankanhalli, M. S. (2000). A DCT domain visible watermarking technique for images. In *Proc. IEEE International Conference on Multimedia and Expo (ICME)* (Vol. 2, pp. 1029–1032). IEEE. doi:10.1109/ICME.2000.871535

Mordell, L. J. (Ed.). (1969). *Diophantine equations* (Vol. 30). Academic Press.

Mu, N., & Liao, X. (2013). An approach for designing neural cryptography. In Advances in Neural Networks (pp. 99–108). Springer Berlin Heidelberg. doi:10.1007/978-3-642-39065-4_13

Muda, Z., Yassin, W., Sulaiman, M. N., & Udzir, N. I. (2011). A K-Means and Naïve Bayes Learning Approach for Better Intrusion Detection. *Information Technology Journal, 10*(3), 648–655. doi:10.3923/itj.2011.648.655

Mukkamala, S., Sung, A. H., & Abraham, A. (2005). Intrusion detection using an ensemble of intelligent paradigms. *Journal of Network and Computer Applications, 28*(2), 167–182. doi:10.1016/j.jnca.2004.01.003

Munz, G., Li, S., & Carle, G. (2007). Traffic Anomaly Detection using K-Means Clustering. In *Proceedings of performance, reliability and dependability evaluation of communication networks and distributed systems.* 4 GI / ITG Workshop MMBnet.

Nadiammai, G. V., & Hemalatha, M. (2014). Effective approach toward Intrusion Detection System using data mining techniques. *Egyptian Informatics Journal, 15*(1), 37–50. doi:10.1016/j.eij.2013.10.003

NakedSecurity. (2013). Retrieved from http://nakedsecurity.sophos.com/2013/01/04/turkish-certificate-authority-screwup-leads-to-attempted-google-impersonation/

Nalini, N., & Raghavendra, R. G. (2007). Attacks of simple block ciphers via efficient heuristics. *Information Sciences, 177*(12), 2553–2569. doi:10.1016/j.ins.2007.01.007

National Institute of Standards and Technology. (2007). *Guide to Intrusion Detection and Prevention Systems (Special Publication 800-94)*. Gaithersburg, MD: US Department of Commerce.

Nauck, D., Klawonn, F., & Kruse, R. (1997). *Foundations of Neuro-Fuzzy Systems*. John Wiley & Sons, Inc.

Naur, P. (1963). Revised report on the algorithmic language ALGOL 60. *Communications of the ACM, 6*(1), 1–17. doi:10.1145/366193.366201

Naveen, J. K., Karthigaikumar, P., Sivamangai, N. M., Sandhya, R., & Asok, S. B. (2013). Hardware implementation of DNA based cryptography. In *Proceedings of IEEE Conference on Information & Communication Technologies (ICT)*. IEEE. doi:10.1109/CICT.2013.6558184

Nettle. (2015). *Nettle*. Retrieved from www.lysator.liu.se/~nisse/nettle

Neuman, B. C. & Ts'o, T. (2004). Kerberos: an authentication service for computer networks. *IEEE Communication Magazine, 32*(9).

Neves, S., & Araujo, F. (2011). *On the Performance of GPU Public Key Cryptography. In Proceedings of IEEE Application-Specific Systems, Architectures and Processors (ASAP)* (pp. 133–140). Santa Monica, CA: IEEE.

Niederreiter, H. (1986). Knapsack-type cryptosystems and algebraic coding theory. *Problems Control Inform. Theory/ Problemy Upravlen. Teor. Inform (Silver Spring, Md.), 15*(2), 159–166.

Nielsoen, R. (2005). Observations from the development of large scale PKI. In *Proceedings 4th Annual PKI R&D Workshop*. NIST.

Ning, K. (2009). *A pseudo DNA cryptography method*. Retrieved from http://arxiv.org/abs/0903.2693

NIST. (2012). *Third-Round Report of the SHA-3 Cryptographic Hash Algorithm Competition*. doi:10.6028/NIST.IR.7896

NIST. (2014). *FIPS SHA-3 Standard: Permutation-Based Hash and Extendable-Output Functions*. DRAFT FIPS PUB 202. Retrieved from http://csrc.nist.gov/publications/drafts/fips-202/fips_202_draft.pdf

Noraini, M. R., & John, G. (2011, July). Genetic algorithm performance with different selection strategies in solving TSP. In *Proceedings of the World Congress on Engineering*. Academic Press.

Noraini, M. R., & John, G. (2011). Genetic Algorithm Performance with Different Selection Strategies in Solving TSP. In *Proceedings of the World Congress on Engineering*. London, UK: Academic Press.

NSS. (2014). *Network Security Services*. Retrieved from https://developer.mozilla.org/en/docs/NSS

NVIDIA CUDA. (2014). *CUDA Toolkit Documentation*. Retrieved from http://docs.nvidia.com/cuda/eula/index.html

Nvidia Graphics. (2014). Retrieved from https://research.nvidia.com/

Obaidat, M. S., & Macchairolo, D. T. (1994). A multilayer neural network system for computer access security. *IEEE Transactions on Systems, Man, and Cybernetics, 24*(5), 806–813. doi:10.1109/21.293498

Ochoa, G., Harvey, I., & Buxton, H. (1999). On recombination and optimal mutation rates. In *Proceedings of the Genetic and Evolutionary Computation Conference* (vol. 1, pp. 488-495). San Francisco, CA: Academic Press.

Olariu, S., & Zomaya, A. Y. (Eds.). (2005). *Handbook of bioinspired algorithms and applications*. CRC Press. doi:10.1201/9781420035063

O'Neill, M., & Conor, R. (2003). *Grammatical Evolution: Evolutionary Automatic Programming in an Arbitrary Language*. Springer. doi:10.1007/978-1-4615-0447-4

Open, C. A. (2015). *OpenCA*. Retrieved from http://www.openca.org/

OpenSSL. (2014). *Open Source Secure Socket Layer Project*. Retrieved from https://www.openssl.org/

Oppliger, R. (2004). Certified Mail: The next challenge for secure messaging. *Communications of the ACM, 47*(8), 75–79. doi:10.1145/1012037.1012039

Oracle Corporation. (2014). *Java Card Classic Platform Specification 3.0.4*. Available at: http://www.oracle.com/technetwork/java/javame/javacard

Ott, E. (2002). *Chaos in dynamical systems*. Cambridge university press. doi:10.1017/CBO9780511803260

Paar, C., & Pelzl, J. (2010). *Understanding Cryptography*. Springer. doi:10.1007/978-3-642-04101-3

Panda, M., Abraham, A., & Patra, M. R. (2012). A Hybrid Intelligent Approach for Network Intrusion Detection. In *Proceedings of International Conference on Communication Technology and System Design*, (pp. 1-9). doi:10.1016/j.proeng.2012.01.827

Panda, M., & Patra, M. R. (2007). Network Intrusion Detection using Naïve Bayes. *International Journal of Computer Science and Network Security*, *7*(12), 258–263.

Panduranga, H. T., & Kumar, S. N. (2014). Image encryption based on permutation-substitution using chaotic map and Latin Square Image Cipher. *The European Physical Journal. Special Topics*, 1–15.

Papadimitriou, C. H., & Steiglitz, K. (1982). *Combinatorial Optimization—Algorithms and Complexity*. New York: Dover.

Papadimitriou, S., Bezerianos, A., & Bountis, T. (1999). Radial basis function networks as chaotic generators for secure communication systems. *International Journal of Bifurcation and Chaos in Applied Sciences and Engineering*, *9*(01), 221–232. doi:10.1142/S0218127499000109

Pareek, N. K., Patidar, V., & Sud, K. K. (2006). Image encryption using chaotic logistic map. *Image and Vision Computing*, *24*(9), 926–934. doi:10.1016/j.imavis.2006.02.021

Pareek, N. K., Patidar, V., & Sud, K. K. (2013). Diffusion–substitution based gray image encryption scheme. *Digital Signal Processing*, *23*(3), 894–901. doi:10.1016/j.dsp.2013.01.005

Parekh, S. P., Madan, B. S., & Tugnayat, R. M. (2012). Approach For Intrusion Detection System Using Data Mining. *Journal of Data Mining and Knowledge Discovery*, *3*(2), 83–87.

Parvin, Z., Seyedarabi, H., & Shamsi, M. (2014). A new secure and sensitive image encryption scheme based on new substitution with chaotic function. *Multimedia Tools and Applications*, 1–18.

Patel, K. D., & Belani, S. (2011). Image encryption using different techniques: A review. *International Journal of Emerging Technology and Advanced Engineering*, *1*(1), 30–34.

Paterson, N. R., & Livesey, M. (1996). Distinguishing Genotype and Phenotype in Genetic Programming. In *Proceedings of Genetic Programming Conference*. Stanford University.

Patidar, V., Pareek, N. K., Purohit, G., & Sud, K. K. (2011). A robust and secure chaotic standard map based pseudorandom permutation-substitution scheme for image encryption. *Optics Communications*, *284*(19), 4331–4339. doi:10.1016/j.optcom.2011.05.028

Pattanayak, B. K., & Rath, M. (2014). A Mobile Agent Based Intrusion Detection System Architecture for Mobile Ad Hoc Networks. *Journal of Computer Science*, *10*(6), 970–975. doi:10.3844/jcssp.2014.970.975

Paugam-Moisy, H., & Bohte, S. (2012). Computing with spiking neuron networks. In *Handbook of Natural Computing* (pp. 335–376). Springer Berlin Heidelberg. doi:10.1007/978-3-540-92910-9_10

PCWorld. (2013). Retrieved from http://www.pcworld.com/article/2080620/bogus-antivirus-program-uses-a-dozen-stolen-signing-certificates.html

Pecho, P. (2009). *Security of Tamper-Resistant Nodes in Wireless Sensor Networks*. (Dissertation Thesis). FIT BUT 2009.

Pecho, P., Nagy, J., & Hanáček, P. (2009). Power Consumption of Hardware Cryptography Platform for Wireless Sensor. In *Proceedings of 2009 International Conference on Parallel and Distributed Computing, Applications and Technologies* (pp. 318-323). Academic Press. doi:10.1109/PDCAT.2009.39

Pecho, P., Zbořil, F., Jr., Drahanský, M., & Hanáček, P. (2009). Agent Platform for Wireless Sensor Network with Support for Cryptographic Protocols. In *Proceedings of J. UCS* (pp. 992-1006). Academic Press.

Peddabachigari, S., Abraham, A., Grosanc, C., & Thomas, J. (2007). Modeling Intrusion Detection System using Hybrid Intellegent System. *Journal of Network and Computer Applications*, 30(1), 114–132. doi:10.1016/j.jnca.2005.06.003

Peng, J., Zhang, D., & Liao, X. (2011). A novel algorithm for block encryption of digital image based on chaos. *International Journal of Cognitive Informatics and Natural Intelligence*, 5(1), 59–74. doi:10.4018/jcini.2011010104

Perrig, A., Szewczyk, R., Tygar, J., Wen, V., & Culler, D. (2002). SPINS: Security Protocols for Sensor Networks. *Wireless Networks*, 8(5), 521–534. doi:10.1023/A:1016598314198

PGP. (2015). *Pretty Good privacy (PGP)*. Retrieved from http://www.pgp.com

Picek, S., & Golub, M. (2011). On evolutionary computation methods in cryptography. In *MIPRO, 2011 Proceedings of the 34th International Convention*. Academic Press.

Ping, Y., Futai, Z., Xinghao, J., & Jianhua, L. (2007). Multi-agent cooperative intrusion response in mobile adhoc networks. *Elsevier Journal of Systems Engineering and Electronics*, 18(4), 785–794. doi:10.1016/S1004-4132(08)60021-3

Podilchuk, C. I., & Zeng, W. (1998). Image-adaptive watermarking using visual models. *IEEE Journal on Selected Areas in Communications*, 16(4), 525–539. doi:10.1109/49.668975

Pollard, J. M. (1971). The Fast Fourier Transform in a Finite Field. *Mathematics of Computation*, 25(114), 365–374. doi:10.1090/S0025-5718-1971-0301966-0

Popovici, C. (2010). Aspects of DNA cryptography. *Annals of the University of Craiova-Mathematics and Computer Science Series*, 37(3), 147–151.

Pöppelmann, T., & Güneysu, T. (2012). Towards Efficient Arithmetic for Lattice-based Cryptography on Reconfigurable Hardware. In *LATINCRYPT (LNCS), (vol. 7533,* (=pp. 139–158). New York, NY: Springer-Verlag. doi:10.1007/978-3-642-33481-8_8

Potdar, V. M., Han, S., & Chang, E. (2005). A survey of digital image watermarking techniques. In *Proc. IEEE International Conference on Industrial Informatics (INDIN 2005)* (pp. 709–716). IEEE. doi:10.1109/INDIN.2005.1560462

Powell, M. J. (1987, January). Radial basis functions for multivariable interpolation: A review. In *Algorithms for Approximation* (pp. 143–167). Clarendon Press.

Pratt, W. K., Kane, J., & Andrews, H. C. (1969). Hadamard transform image coding. *Proceedings of the IEEE*, 57(1), 58–68. doi:10.1109/PROC.1969.6869

Qi, H. (2008). *Stream Ciphers and Linear Complexity*. (Thesis of Master degree in Science), Available from National University of Singapore NUS Dissertations and Theses database.

Qinghai, G. (2010). Recent Developments on Applying Biometrics in Cryptography. *Journal of Applied Security Research*, 5(1), 107–137. doi:10.1080/19361610903176328

Qureshi, S., Asar, A., Rehman, A., & Baseer, A. (2011). Swarm intelligence based detection of malicious beacon node for secure localization in wireless sensor networks. *Journal of Emerging Trends in Engineering and Applied Sciences*, 2(4), 664–672.

Rajendra, G. N., & Kaur, B. R. (2011). A New Approach for Data Encryption Using Genetic Algorithms and Brain Mu Waves. *International Journal of Scientific and Engineering Research, 5*(5), 1–4.

Rakesh, K., & Jyotishree. (2012). Blending Roulette Wheel Selection & Rank Selection in Genetic Algorithms. *International Journal of Machine Learning and Computing, 2*(4), 365–370.

Ramachandran, C., Misra, S., & Obaidat, M. S. (2008). A novel two-pronged strategy for an agent-based intrusion detection scheme in ad-hoc networks. *Elsevier Comput. Commun, 31*(16), 3855–3869. doi:10.1016/j.comcom.2008.04.012

Ramani, R. G., & Balasubramanian, L. (2011). Genetic algorithm solution for cryptanalysis of knapsack cipher with knapsack sequence of size 16. *International Journal of Computer Applications, 35*(11).

Ramesdell, B. (2004b). *Secure/Multipurpose Internet Mail Extensions (S/MIME) Version 3.1 Certificate Handling*. Internet Engineering Task Force (IETF), RFC 3850.

Rao, A. R., Braudaway, G. W., & Mintzer, F. C. (1998). *Automatic visible water- marking of images. In Proc. Photonics West'98 Electronic Imaging* (pp. 110–121). International Society for Optics and Photonics.

Rao, K. S., Krishna, M. R., & Babu, D. (2009). Cryptanalysis of a Feistel Type Block Cipher by Feed Forword Neural Network Using Right Sigmoidal Signals. *International Journal of Soft Computing, 4*(3), 131–135.

Ratan, R. (2014). Applications of Genetic Algorithms in Cryptology. In *Proceedings of the Third International Conference on Soft Computing for Problem Solving* (pp. 821-831). Springer India. doi:10.1007/978-81-322-1771-8_71

Raut, R. G., & Gawali, Z. (2012). Intrusion Detection System using Data Mining Approach. *International Journal of Computer Science and Information Technology Research Excellence, 2*(2).

Regev, O. (2005). On lattices, learning with errors, random linear codes, and cryptography. In *Proceedings of STOC* (pp. 84–93). STOC.

Rehman, Z., Rehman, S. S. A., & Khan, L. (2009). *Survey Reports on Four Selected Research Papers on Data Mining Based Intrusion Detection System* [PowerPoint slides]. Retrieved from http://web2.uwindsor.ca/courses/cs/aggarwal/cs60564/surveys/ZillurRahmanKhan.ppt

RF Control and RF Touch product pages . (2014). Retrieved from http://www.elkoep.cz/produkty/inels-rf-control/

Rhouma, R., & Belghith, S. (2011). Cryptanalysis of a chaos-based cryptosystem on DSP. *Communications in Nonlinear Science and Numerical Simulation, 16*(2), 876–884. doi:10.1016/j.cnsns.2010.05.017

RIPE. (1995). *Integrity Primitives for Secure Information Systems. Final Report of RACE Integrity Primitives Evaluation (RIPE-RACE 1040), LNCS, 1007*. Springer-Verlag.

Rivest, R. (1992). *The MD5 Message-Digest Algorithm*. IETF RFC 1321, Retrieved from http://www.ietf.org/rfc/rfc1321.txt

Rivest, R. L., Adleman, L., & Dertouzos, M. L. (1978). On data banks and privacy homomorphisms. In Foundations of Secure Computation.

Roberts, C. (2006). Biometric Attack – Vectors and Defences. Academic Press.

Ross, T. J. (2009). *Fuzzy Logic with Engineering Applications*. John Wiley & Sons.

Roy, B., Rakshit, G., Singha, P., Majumder, A., & Datta, D. (2011). An improved Symmetric key cryptography with DNA Based strong cipher. In *Proceedings of International Conference on Devices and Communications (ICDeCom)* (pp. 1-5). Academic Press. doi:10.1109/ICDECOM.2011.5738553

Roy, D. B., & Chaki, R. (2011). MABHIDS: A New Mobile Agent Based Black Hole Intrusion Detection System. In N. Chaki & A. Cortesi (Eds.), *CISIM 2011, CCIS 245* (pp. 85–94). Springer Verlag-Berlin. doi:10.1007/978-3-642-27245-5_12

RSA. (2002). *RSA Cryptography Standard*. RSA Security Inc. Retrieved from ftp://ftp.rsasecurity.com/pub/pkcs/pkcs-1/pkcs-1v2-1.pdf

Rueppel, R. A. (1986). *Aanalysis and design of stream ciphers*. Berlin: Springer-Verlag. doi:10.1007/978-3-642-82865-2

Ruttor, A., Kinzel, W., & Kanter, I. (2007). Dynamics of neural cryptography. *Physical Review E: Statistical, Nonlinear, and Soft Matter Physics*, 75(5), 056104. doi:10.1103/PhysRevE.75.056104 PMID:17677130

Ruttor, A., Kinzel, W., Naeh, R., & Kanter, I. (2006). Genetic attack on neural cryptography. *Physical Review E: Statistical, Nonlinear, and Soft Matter Physics*, 73(3), 036121. doi:10.1103/PhysRevE.73.036121 PMID:16605612

Ruttor, A., Kinzel, W., Shacham, L., & Kanter, I. (2004). Neural cryptography with feedback. *Physical Review E: Statistical, Nonlinear, and Soft Matter Physics*, 69(4), 046110. doi:10.1103/PhysRevE.69.046110 PMID:15169072

Ryan, C., Collins, J., & Neill, M. O. (1998). Grammatical evolution: Evolving programs for an arbitrary language. *LNCS*, *1391*, 83–96.

SaberiKamarposhti, M., AlBedawi, I., & Mohamad, D. (2012). A new hybrid method for image encryption using DNA sequence and chaotic logistic map. *Australian Journal of Basic and Applied Sciences*, 6(3), 371–380.

Sahai, A., & Waters, B. (2005). Fuzzy identity-based encryption. In Advances in Cryptology—EUROCRYPT 2005 (pp. 457–473). Springer. doi:10.1007/11426639_27

Santesson, S., Nystrom, M., & Polk, T. (2004). *Internet X.509 Public Key Infrastructure – Qualified Certificates Profile*. Microsoft & RSA Security & NIST.

Santhi, V., & Thangavelu, A. (2009). DWT-SVD combined full band robust watermarking technique for color images in YUV color space. *Int. J. Comput. Theory Eng.*, 1(4), 424–429. doi:10.7763/IJCTE.2009.V1.68

Sathya, S. S., Chithralekha, T., & Anandakumar, P. (2010). Nomadic genetic algorithm for cryptanalysis of DES 16. *International Journal of Computer Theory and Engineering*, 2(3), 1793–8201.

Schmidt, S., Steele, R., Dillon, T. S., & Chang, E. (2007). Fuzzy trust evaluation and credibility development in multi-agent systems. *Applied Soft Computing*, 7(2), 492–505. doi:10.1016/j.asoc.2006.11.002

Schneier, B. (1996). Applied Cryptography: Protocols, Algorithms, and Source Code in C (2nd ed.). John Wiley & Sons, Inc.

SEAL. (1998). *Digital Signature And Electronic Authentication Law*. Retrieved from http://thomas.loc.gov/cgi-bin/query/z?c105:H.R.3472.IH

Security Innovation the Application Security Company. (2014). Retrieved from https://www.securityinnovation.com/

SecurityWeek. (2013). Retrieved from http://www.securityweek.com/opera-software-hit-infrastructure-attack-malware-signed-stolen-cert

Sekar, R., Bendre, M., Dhurjati, D., & Bollineni, P. (2001). A Fast Automation-Based method for Detecting Anomalous Program Behaviors. In *Proceedings of the Symposium on Security and Privacy* (pp. 144-155). IEEE.

Sendhoff, B., Roberts, M., & Yao, X. (2006). Evolutionary computation benchmarking repository. *IEEE Computational Intelligence Magazine*, 50–60.

Sen, J. (2010). An Intrusion Detection Architecture for Clustered Wireless Ad Hoc Networks. In *Proceedings of the Second International Conference on Computational Intelligence, Communication Systems and Networks* (pp. 202-207). Liverpool, UK: IEEE. doi:10.1109/CICSyN.2010.51

Servin, A., & Kudenko, D. (2008). Multi-agent Reinforcement Learning for Intrusion Detection. In K. Tuyls et al. (Eds.), *Adaptive Agents and Multi Agent Systems III: Adaptation and Multi Agent Learning* (pp. 211–223). Springer-Verlag Berlin Heidelberg. doi:10.1007/978-3-540-77949-0_15

Seyedzadeh, S. M., & Mirzakuchaki, S. (2012). A fast color image encryption algorithm based on coupled two-dimensional piecewise chaotic map. *Signal Processing*, *92*(5), 1202–1215. doi:10.1016/j.sigpro.2011.11.004

SHA. (1995). *Federal Information Processing Standards Publication 180-1*. Retrieved from http://www.itl.nist.gov/fipspubs/fip180-1.htm

Shaheen, J., Ostry, D., Sivarman, V., & Jha, S. (2007). *Confidental and Secure Broadcasting in Wireless Sensor Networks, Personal, Indoor and Mobile Radio Communications, 2007*. IEEE.

Shahzad, W., Siddiqui, A. B., & Khan, F. A. (2009). Cryptanalysis of four-rounded DES using binary particle swarm optimization. In *Proceedings of the 11th Annual Conference Companion on Genetic and Evolutionary Computation Conference*. doi:10.1145/1570256.1570294

Shanon, C. (1949). Communication theory of secrecy systems. *The Bell System Technical Journal*, *28*(4), 656–715. doi:10.1002/j.1538-7305.1949.tb00928.x

Sharma, M., Kowar, M. K., & Sharma, M. (2008). An improved evolutionary algorithm for secured image using adaptive genetic algorithm. *Journal of Discrete Mathematical Sciences and Cryptography*, *11*(6), 673–683. doi:10.1080/09720529.2008.10698397

Shelby, I., & Bormann, C. (2009). *6LoPAN: The Wireless Embedded Internet*. Wiley.

Shi, Y., & Eberhart, R. C. (2001). Fuzzy adaptive particle swarm optimization. In *Proceedings of the 2001 Congress on Evolutionary Computation*, (Vol. 1, pp. 101-106). doi:10.1109/CEC.2001.934377

Shor, P. W. (1995). *Polynomial-Time Algorithms for Prime Factorization and Discrete Logarithms on a Quantum Computer*. arXiv:quant-ph/9508027, Retrieved from http://arxiv.org/abs/quant-ph/9508027

Siebel & Peter (2005). *Practical Common Lisp*. Author.

SIGNiX. (2014). Retrieved from http://www.signix.com/

Simpson, P. K. (1991). *Artificial neural systems: foundations, paradigms, applications, and implementations*. Windcrest/McGraw-Hill.

Singh, A. (2006). *Tree-augmented naive bayes* [PDF Document]. Retrieved from Lecture Notes Online Web site: http://courses.cms.caltech.edu/cs155/

Sivanandam, S. N., & Deepa, S. N. (2008). *Introduction to Genetic Algorithms*. New York: Springer.

SmartCardsBasis. (2011). Retrieved from http://www.smartcardbasics.com/smart-card-types.html

Sodium (2013). *Sodium*. Retrieved from http://labs.opendns.com/2013/03/06/announcing-sodium-a-new-cryptographic-library

Solak, E. (2011). Cryptanalysis of chaotic ciphers. In *Chaos-Based Cryptography* (pp. 227–256). Springer Berlin Heidelberg. doi:10.1007/978-3-642-20542-2_7

Solak, E., Rhouma, R., & Belghith, S. (2010). Cryptanalysis of a multi-chaotic systems based image cryptosystem. *Optics Communications*, *283*(2), 232–236. doi:10.1016/j.optcom.2009.09.070

Song, C., & Ma, K. (2009). Design of Intrusion Detection System Based on Data Mining Algorithm. In *Proceedings of International Conference on Signal Processing Systems* (pp. 370-373). IEEE. doi:10.1109/ICSPS.2009.202

Song, D. X., Wagner, D., & Perrig, A. (2000). Practical techniques for searches on encrypted data. In *Proceedings of the IEEE Symposium on Security and Privacy* (pp. 44–55). IEEE.

Song, J., Zhang, H., Meng, Q., & Wang, Z. (2007). Cryptanalysis of four-round DES based on genetic algorithm. In *International Conference on Wireless Communications, Networking and Mobile Computing, WiCom.* doi:10.1109/WICOM.2007.580

Soni, R., & Johar, A. (2012). An encryption algorithm for image based on DNA sequence addition operation. *World Journal of Science and Technology*, *2*(3), 67–69.

Souici, I., Seridi, H., & Akdag, H. (2011). Images encryption by the use of evolutionary algorithms. *Analog Integrated Circuits and Signal Processing*, *69*(1), 49–58. doi:10.1007/s10470-011-9627-4

Spears, W., & Jong, D. C. K. A. (1990). An analysis of multi-point crossover. Morgan Kaufmann Publishers.

Spears, W., & De Jong, K. A. (1990). *An Analysis of Multi-Point Crossover*. Morgan Kaufmann.

Specht, D. F. (1990). Probabilistic neural networks. *Neural Networks*, *3*(1), 109–118. doi:10.1016/0893-6080(90)90049-Q PMID:18282828

Spillman, R., Janssan, M., Nelson, B., & Kepner, M. (1993). Use of genetic algorithms in the cryptanalysis of simple substitution ciphers. *Cryptologia*, *17*(1), 31–44. doi:10.1080/0161-119391867746

Srinivas, M., & Patnaik, L. M. (1994). Adaptive probabilities of crossover and mutation in genetic algorithms. *IEEE Transactions on Systems, Man, and Cybernetics*, *24*(4), 656–667. doi:10.1109/21.286385

Srinoy, S. (2007, April). Intrusion detection model based on particle swarm optimization and support vector machine. In *Proceedings ofIEEE Symposium on Computational Intelligence in Security and Defense Applications, CISDA 2007* (pp. 186-192). IEEE. doi:10.1109/CISDA.2007.368152

Stafrace, S. K., & Antonopoulos, N. (2010). Military tactics in agent-based sinkhole attack detection for wireless ad hoc networks. *Elsevier Comput. Commun.*, *33*(5), 619–638. doi:10.1016/j.comcom.2009.11.006

Stalling, W. (2006). *Cryptography and network security: Principles and practices* (4th ed.). Prentice Hall.

Steinfeld, R. (2014). NTRU Cryptosystem: Recent Developments and Emerging Mathematical Problems in Finite Polynomial Rings. In H. Niederreiter, A. Ostafe, D. Panario, & A. Winterhof (Eds.), *Algebraic Curves and Finite Fields: Cryptography and Other Applications: 16* (pp. 1–33). De Gruyter. doi:10.1515/9783110317916.179

Straub, T. (2004). *Spezifikation von X.509-Zertifikatsprofilen unter dem Gesichtspunkt Benutzbarkeit*. Technical University Darmstadt.

Stützle, T., & Hoos, H. (1996). *Improving the Ant System: A detailed report on the max-min ant system. Technical Report*. Technical University of Darmstadt.

Stützle, T., & Hoos, H. H. (2000). Max–min ant system. *Future Generation Computer Systems*, *16*(8), 889–914. doi:10.1016/S0167-739X(00)00043-1

Syswerda, G. (1989). *Uniform crossover in genetic algorithms.* Paper presented at the 3rd International Conference on Genetic Algorithms, San Francisco, CA.

Syswerda, G. (1989). Uniform crossover in genetic algorithms. In *Proceedings of the 3rd International Conference on Genetic Algorithms.* San Francisco, CA: Academic Press.

Szaban, M., Seredynski, F., & Bouvry, P. (2006). Collective behavior of rules for cellular automata-based stream ciphers. In *Proceedings of IEEE Congress on Evolutionary Computation* (pp. 179-183). IEEE. doi:10.1109/CEC.2006.1688306

Szerwinski, R., & Güneysu, T. (2008). Exploiting the Power of GPUs for Asymmetric Cryptography. In *CHES 2008 (LNCS), (vol. 5154*, pp. 79–99). New York, NY: Springer-Verlag. doi:10.1007/978-3-540-85053-3_6

Taggu, A., & Taggu, A. (2011). TraceGray: An Application-layer Scheme for Intrusion Detection in MANET using Mobile Agents. In *Proceedings of the IEEE 3rd International Conference on Communication Systems and Networks (COMSNETS)* (pp. 1-4). Bangalore: IEEE. doi:10.1109/COMSNETS.2011.5716475

Tanaka, K., Okamoto, A., & Saito, I. (2005). Public-key system using DNA as a one-way function for key distribution. *Bio Systems, 81*(1), 25–29. doi:10.1016/j.biosystems.2005.01.004 PMID:15917125

Tan, S. Y., Yau, W. C., & Lim, B. H. (2014). An implementation of enhanced public key infrastructure. *Multimedia Tools and Applications.* doi:10.1007/s11042-014-2119-7

Tatiana, H., Mircea-Florin, V., Monica, B., & Cosmin, S. (2008). A java crypto implementation of DNAProvider featuring complexity in theory and practice. In *Proceedings of 30th International Conference on Information Technology Interfaces.* Dubrovnik, Croatia. doi:10.1109/ITI.2008.4588479

Tedmori, S., & Al-Najdawi, N. (2014). Image cryptographic algorithm based on the Haar wavelet transform. *Information Sciences, 269*, 21–34. doi:10.1016/j.ins.2014.02.004

ThreatPost. (2015). Retrieved from http://threatpost.com/final-report-diginotar-hack-shows-total-compromise-ca-servers-103112/77170

Tian, J. (2003). Reversible data embedding using a difference expansion. *IEEE Transactions on Circuits and Systems for Video Technology, 13*(8), 890–896. doi:10.1109/TCSVT.2003.815962

Tian, L., Zheng, N., Xue, J., Li, C., & Wang, X. (2011). An integrated visual saliency based watermarking approach for synchronous image authentication and copyright protection. *Signal Processing Image Communication, 26*(8), 427–437. doi:10.1016/j.image.2011.06.001

Tiresias. (2011). Retrieved from http://www.tiresias.org/research/guidelines/cards_and_smart_media.htm

Tkalcic, M., & Tasic, J. F. (2003). *Colour spaces: perceptual, historical and applicational background.* Eurocon.

Tobarra, L., Cazorla, D., Cuartero, F., Díaz, G., & Cambronero, E. (2009, April). Model checking wireless sensor network security protocols: TinySec + LEAP + TinyPK. *Telecommunication Systems, 40*(3-4), 91–99. doi:10.1007/s11235-008-9131-z

Tobias, B., & Lothar, T. (1995). *A comparison of selection schemes used in Genetics Algorithms.* TIK Report.

Toemeh, R., & Arumugam, S. (2008). Applying Genetic Algorithms for Searching Key-Space of Polyalphabetic Substitution Ciphers. *The International Arab Journal of Information Technology, 5*(1), 87–91.

Tomko, G. J., Soutar, C., & Schmidt, G. J. (1996). *Fingerprint controlled public key cryptographic system.* U.S. Patent 5541994, July 30, 1996 (Filing date: Sept. 7, 1994).

Tornea, O., & Borda, M. E. (2009). DNA cryptographic algorithms. In *Proceedings of International Conference on Advancements of Medicine and Health Care through Technology* (pp. 223-226). Springer Berlin Heidelberg. doi:10.1007/978-3-642-04292-8_49

TrendMicro. (2014). Retrieved from http://blog.trendmicro.com/fake-antivirus-solutions-increasingly-stolen-code-signing-certificates/

Tripathi, S. P. N., Jaiswal, M., & Singh, V. (2013). Securing DNA Information through Public Key Cryptography. *MIS Review*, *19*(1), 45–59.

Tsai, J. S., Huang, W. B., & Kuo, Y. H. (2011b). On the selection of optimal feature region set for robust digital image watermarking. *IEEE Transactions on Image Processing, 20*(3), 735–743. doi:10.1109/TIP.2010.2073475 PMID:20833602

Tsakonas, A., & Dounias, G. (2002, April). Hybrid computational intelligence schemes in complex domains: An extended review. In *Proceedings of the Second Hellenic Conference on AI: Methods and Applications of Artificial Intelligence* (pp. 494-512). Springer-Verlag.

Tsui, T. K., Zhang, X. P., & Androutsos, D. (2008). Color image watermarking using multidimensional Fourier transforms. *IEEE Trans. Inf. Forensics Secur., 3*(1), 16–28. doi:10.1109/TIFS.2007.916275

Tsutomu, M., Tadahiro, S., & Keisuke, I. (2007). *Time stamping system for electronic documents and program medium for the same*. US Patent No. 7266698, Retrieved from http://www.patentgenius.com/ patent/7266698.html

UCC. (2010). *The Uniform Commercial Code*. Retrieved from http://www.law.cornell.edu/ucc

UECA. (2003). *Uniform Electronic Commerce Act*. Retrieved from http://gcis.nat.gov.tw/eclaw/english/PDF/Uniform-ElectronicCommerceAct.pdf

UETA. (1999). *Uniform Electronic Transactions Act*. Retrieved from http://euro.ecom.cmu.edu/program/law/08-732/Transactions/ueta.pdf

UNCITRA. (2001). *UNCITRAL Model Law on Electronic Signatures with Guide to Enactment*. United Nations Publication, Sales No. E.02.V.8. Retrieved from http://www.uncitral.org/pdf/english/texts/electcom/ml-elecsig-e.pdf

USDA. (2000). *USDA EIA (Coggins) Testing*. Retrieved from http://207.57.99.197/legislation/paeia.htm

Van Schyndel, R. G., Tirkel, A. Z., & Osborne, C. F. (1994). A digital watermark. In *Proc. IEEE International Conference on Image Processing* (Vol. 2, pp. 86–90). IEEE. doi:10.1109/ICIP.1994.413536

Vasseur, J.P., Agarwal, N., Hui, J., et al. (2011). *RPL: The IP routing protocol designed for low power and lossy networks*. IPSO Alliance.

VeriSign. (2015). Retrieved from http://www.verisigninc.com

Verma, A. K., Dave, M., & Joshi, R. C. (2007). Genetic Algorithm and Tabu Search Attack on the Mono-Alphabetic Subsition Cipher in Adhoc Networks. *Journal of Computer Science, 3*(3), 134–137. doi:10.3844/jcssp.2007.134.137

Verma, O. P., Nizam, M., & Ahmad, M. (2013). Modified multi-chaotic systems that are based on pixel shuffle for image encryption. *Journal of Information Processing Systems, 9*(2), 271–286. doi:10.3745/JIPS.2013.9.2.271

Vijayakumar, P., Vijayalakshmi, V., & Zayaraz, G. (2011). DNA Computing based Elliptic Curve Cryptography. *International Journal of Computers and Applications*, 36.

Vohra, R., & Patel, B. (2012). An efficient chaos-based optimization algorithm approach for cryptography. *International Journal of Communication Network Security, 1*(4), 75–79.

Volná, E. (2000). Using Neural network in cryptography. In *The State of the Art in Computational Intelligence* (pp. 262–267). Physica-Verlag HD. doi:10.1007/978-3-7908-1844-4_42

Wang, K., Zou, L., Song, A., & He, Z. (2005). On the security of 3D Cat map based symmetric image encryption scheme. *Physics Letters. [Part A]*, *343*(6), 432–439. doi:10.1016/j.physleta.2005.05.040

Wang, S. (2009). *Intelligent Buildings and Building Automation*. London: Spon Press.

Wang, W., Wang, H., Wang, B., Wang, Y., & Wang, J. (2013). Energy-aware and self-adaptive anomaly detection scheme based on network tomography in mobile ad hoc networks. *Elsevier Information Sciences*, *220*(20), 580–602. doi:10.1016/j.ins.2012.07.036

Wang, X., & He, G. (2011). Cryptanalysis on a novel image encryption method based on total shuffling scheme. *Optics Communications*, *284*(24), 5804–5807. doi:10.1016/j.optcom.2011.08.053

Wang, X., & Luan, D. (2013). A novel image encryption algorithm using chaos and reversible cellular automata. *Communications in Nonlinear Science and Numerical Simulation*, *18*(11), 3075–3085. doi:10.1016/j.cnsns.2013.04.008

Wang, X., Luan, D., & Bao, X. (2014). Cryptanalysis of an image encryption algorithm using Chebyshev generator. *Digital Signal Processing*, *25*, 244–247. doi:10.1016/j.dsp.2013.10.020

Wang, X., & Wang, Q. (2014). A novel image encryption algorithm based on dynamic S-boxes constructed by chaos. *Nonlinear Dynamics*, *75*(3), 567–576. doi:10.1007/s11071-013-1086-2

Wang, Y., Wong, K. W., Liao, X., & Chen, G. (2011). A new chaos-based fast image encryption algorithm. *Applied Soft Computing*, *11*(1), 514–522. doi:10.1016/j.asoc.2009.12.011

Wang, Y., Wong, K. W., Li, C., & Li, Y. (2012). A novel method to design S-box based on chaotic map and genetic algorithm. *Physics Letters. [Part A]*, *376*(6), 827–833. doi:10.1016/j.physleta.2012.01.009

Wasiewicz, P., Mulawka, J. J., Rudnichi, W. R., & Lesyng, B. (2000). Adding numbers with DNA. In *Proceedings of 2000 IEEE International Conference on Systems, Man and Cybernetics*. Nashville, TN: IEEE. doi:10.1109/ICSMC.2000.885000

Waters, B. (2013). Functional encryption: origins and recent developments. In Public-Key Cryptography—PKC 2013 (pp. 51–54). Springer. doi:10.1007/978-3-642-36362-7_4

Whiten, A., & Tygar, J. (1999). Why Jonny can't Encrypt: A usability evaluation of PGP 5.0. In *Proceedings of 8th USENIX Security System*. Retrieved from http://www.ieee-security.org/Cipher/PastIssues/1999/issue9911/issue9911.txt

Wilt, N. (2013). *The CUDA Handbook: A Comprehensive Guide to GPU Programming*. Addison-Wesley.

Winkler, F. (1996). *Polynomial Algorithms in Computer Algebra*. New York, NY: Springer-Verlag. doi:10.1007/978-3-7091-6571-3

Wolf, C., & Preneel, B. (2005). *Taxonomy of public key schemes based on the problem of multivariate quadratic equations*. Retrieved from http://eprint.iacr.org/2005/077/

Woźniak, S., Almási, A. D., Cristea, V., Leblebici, Y., & Engbersen, T. (2015). Review of advances in neural networks: Neural design technology stack. In *Proceedings of ELM-2014* (vol. 1, pp. 367-376). Springer International Publishing. doi:10.1007/978-3-319-14063-6_31

Wu, H. (2010). *Implementation of Public Key Algorithms in CUDA*. (M.Sc. Thesis). Gjovik University, Norway.

Wu, S. X., & Banzhaf, W. (2013). The use of computational intelligence in intrusion detection systems: A review. *Applied Soft Computing*, *10*(1), 1–35. doi:10.1016/j.asoc.2009.06.019

Wu, Y., Yang, G., Jin, H., & Noonan, J. P. (2012). Image encryption using the two-dimensional logistic chaotic map. *Journal of Electronic Imaging*, *21*(1), 013014–1. doi:10.1117/1.JEI.21.1.013014

XCA. (2014). *X Certificate and Key Management*. Retrieved from http://xca.sourceforge.net/

Xiang, C., Yong, P. C., & Meng, L. S. (2008). Design of Multiple-Level Hybrid Classifier for Intrusion Detection System using Bayesian Clustering and Decision Trees. *Pattern Recognition Letters Elsevier*, *29*(7), 918–924. doi:10.1016/j.patrec.2008.01.008

Xianghong, T., Lianjie, Y., Hengli, Y., & Zhongke, Y. (2005). A watermarking algorithm based on the SVD and Hadamard transform. In *Proc. International Conference on Communications, Circuits and Systems* (*Vol. 2*, pp. 874–877). Academic Press. doi:10.1109/ICCCAS.2005.1495248

Xiang, T., Wong, K. W., & Liao, X. (2007). Selective image encryption using a spatiotemporal chaotic system. Chaos: An Interdisciplinary. *Journal of Nonlinear Science*, *17*(2), 023115.

Xiangyang, X. (2010). A New Genetic Algorithm and Tabu Search for S-Box Optimization. In *Proceedings of International Conference on Computer Design and Applications (ICCDA 2010)* (vol. 4, pp. 492-495). Academic Press.

Xiao, D., & Shih, F. Y. (2010). Using the self-synchronizing method to improve security of the multi chaotic systems-based image encryption. *Optics Communications*, *283*(15), 3030–3036. doi:10.1016/j.optcom.2010.03.063

Xiao, G., Lu, M., Qin, L., & Lai, X. (2006). New field of cryptography: DNA cryptography. *Chinese Science Bulletin*, *51*(12), 1413–1420. doi:10.1007/s11434-006-2012-5

Xin, Y., Liao, S., & Pawlak, M. (2004).Geometrically robust image watermarking via pseudo-Zernike moments. In *Proc. Canadian Conference on Electrical and Computer Engineering* (*Vol. 2*, pp. 939–942). Academic Press.

Xing-Yuan, W., & Guo-Xiang, H. (2012). Cryptanalysis on an image block encryption algorithm based on spatiotemporal chaos. *Chinese Physics B*, *21*(6), 060502. doi:10.1088/1674-1056/21/6/060502

Yang, H. Y., Wang, X. Y., & Wang, C. P. (2012). *A robust digital watermarking algorithm in undecimated discrete wavelet transform domain*. Comput.Electri.Eng.

Yang, J., Ma, J., Liu, S., & Zhang, C. (2014). A molecular cryptography model based on structures of DNA self-assembly. *Chinese Science Bulletin*, *59*(11), 1192–1198. doi:10.1007/s11434-014-0170-4

Yang, X. S. (2015). *Recent Advances in Swarm Intelligence and Evolutionary Computation*. Springer. doi:10.1007/978-3-319-13826-8

Yang, Y., Sun, X., Yang, H., Li, C. T., & Xiao, R. (2009). A contrast-sensitive reversible visible image watermarking technique. *IEEE Transactions on Circuits and Systems for Video Technology*, *19*(5), 656–667. doi:10.1109/TCSVT.2009.2017401

Yao, J. T., Zhao, S. L., & Saxton, L. V. (2005, March). A study on fuzzy intrusion detection. In *Defense and Security* (pp. 23–30). International Society for Optics and Photonics.

Yao, X. (1999). Evolving artificial neural networks. *Proceedings of the IEEE*, *87*(9), 1423–1447. doi:10.1109/5.784219

Yasir, M. A., & Azween, B. A. (2009). Biologically Inspired Model for Securing Hybrid Mobile Ad hoc Networks. In *Proceedings of the International Symposium on High Capacity Optical Networks and Enabling Technologies* (187-191). Penang: IEEE.

Yayik, A., & Kutlu, Y. (2013, April). Improving Pseudo random number generator using artificial neural networks. In *Proceedings of Signal Processing and Communications Applications Conference* (SIU). doi:10.1109/SIU.2013.6531494

Yee, L. P., & De Silva, L. C. (2002). Application of multilayer perceptron networks in symmetric block ciphers. In *Proceedings of the 2002 International Joint Conference on Neural Networks, IJCNN'02. (Vol. 2*, pp. 1455-1458). Academic Press.

Ye, G. (2010). Image scrambling encryption algorithm of pixel bit based on chaos map. *Pattern Recognition Letters, 31*(5), 347–354. doi:10.1016/j.patrec.2009.11.008

Yeung, M. M., Mintzer, F. C., Braudaway, G. W., & Rao, A. R. (1997).Digital watermarking for high-quality imaging. In *Proc. IEEE First Workshop on Multimedia Signal Processing* (pp. 357–362). IEEE. doi:10.1109/MMSP.1997.602661

Ye, X., & Li, J. (2010). A Security Architecture Based on Immune Agents for MANET. In *Proceedings of the International Conference on Wireless Communication and Sensor Computing* (pp. 1-5). Chennai: IEEE.

Yoon, J. W., & Kim, H. (2010). An image encryption scheme with a pseudorandom permutation based on chaotic maps. *Communications in Nonlinear Science and Numerical Simulation, 15*(12), 3998–4006. doi:10.1016/j.cnsns.2010.01.041

Younes, M. A. B., & Jantan, A. (2008). An image encryption approach using a combination of permutation technique followed by encryption. *International Journal of Computer Science and Network Security, 8*(4), 191–197.

Yuen, C. H., & Wong, K. W. (2011). A chaos-based joint image compression and encryption scheme using DCT and SHA-1. *Applied Soft Computing, 11*(8), 5092–5098. doi:10.1016/j.asoc.2011.05.050

Yu, W., & Cao, J. (2006). Cryptography based on delayed chaotic neural networks. *Physics Letters. [Part A], 356*(4), 333–338. doi:10.1016/j.physleta.2006.03.069

Zadeh, L. A. (1965). Fuzzy sets. *Information and Control, 8*(3), 338–353. doi:10.1016/S0019-9958(65)90241-X

Zadeh, L. A. (1975). The concept of a linguistic variable and its application to approximate reasoning—I, II, III. *Information Sciences, 8*(4), 301–357. doi:10.1016/0020-0255(75)90046-8

Zadeh, L. A. (1994). Fuzzy logic, neural networks, and soft computing. *Communications of the ACM, 37*(3), 77–84. doi:10.1145/175247.175255

Zadeh, L. A. (1998). Some reflections on soft computing, granular computing and their roles in the conception, design and utilization of information/intelligent systems. *Soft Computing, 2*(1), 23–25. doi:10.1007/s005000050030

Zalzala, A. M., & Fleming, P. J. (1997). *Genetic Algorithms in Engineering Systems*. IET. doi:10.1049/PBCE055E

Zeghid, M., Machhout, M., Khriji, L., Baganne, A., & Tourki, R. (2007). A modified AES based algorithm for image encryption. *International Journal on Computer Science and Engineering, 1*(1), 70–75.

Zelinka, I., Celikovsk`y, S., Richter, H., & Chen, G. (Eds.). (2010). *Evolutionary algorithms and chaotic systems* (Vol. 267). Springer. doi:10.1007/978-3-642-10707-8

Zelinka, I., & Jasek, R. (2010). Evolutionary decryption of chaotically encrypted information. In *Evolutionary Algorithms and Chaotic Systems* (pp. 329–343). Springer Berlin Heidelberg. doi:10.1007/978-3-642-10707-8_10

Zeng, G., & Keitel, C. H. (2002). Arbitrated quantum-signature scheme. *Physical Review A., 65*(4), 042312. doi:10.1103/PhysRevA.65.042312

Zeng, K., Yang, C., & Rao, T. R. N. (1991). Pseudorandom bit generator in stream cipher cryptography. *Computer, 24*(2), 8–17. doi:10.1109/2.67207

Zhang, Q., Guo, L., & Wei, X. (2010). Image encryption using DNA addition combining with chaotic maps. *Mathematical and Computer Modelling, 52*(11), 2028–2035. doi:10.1016/j.mcm.2010.06.005

Zhang, X., & Wang, X. (2013). Chaos-based partial encryption of SPIHT coded color images. *Signal Processing*, *93*(9), 2422–2431. doi:10.1016/j.sigpro.2013.03.017

Zhang, Y., & Fu, L. H. B. (2012). *Research on DNA Cryptography* (pp. 357–376). Rijeka, Croatia: Applied Cryptography and Network Security, InTech Press.

Zhang, Z., Zeng, G., Zhou, N., & Xiong, J. (2006). Quantum identity authentication based on ping-pong technique for photons. *Physics Letters. [Part A]*, *356*(3), 199–205. doi:10.1016/j.physleta.2006.03.048

Zhao, J., & Koch, E. (1995).Embedding robust labels into images for copyright protection. In *Proc. International Congress on Intellectual Property Rights for Specialised Information, Knowledge and New Technologies* (pp. 21-25). Academic Press.

Zheng, Y., Imai, H., & Imai, H. (Eds.). (2007). Public Key Cryptography. Springer.

Zhou, R. L. I. W., & Huan, T. (2014). Quantum Identity Authentication and Digital Signature through Quantum Digital Certificate. *Journal of Computer Information Systems*, *10*(10), 4425–4432.

About the Contributors

Wasan Shaker Awad is an associate professor of Computer Science, College of Information Technology, Ahlia University, Bahrain. Her research areas include information security, computational intelligence, and coding theory. She published a number of papers in computational intelligence, information security, and block codes in a number of international journals and conferences.

El-Sayed M. El-Alfy is currently working at King Fahd University of Petroleum and Minerals, Saudi Arabia as Associate Professor & Intelligent Systems Research Group Coordinator. He is on leave from the College of Engineering, Tanta University. His research interests are pattern recognition and machine learning, computational intelligence and soft computing, data mining with applications in the areas of computer networks, document analysis, information retrieval, multimedia content security and forensics. Dr. El-Alfy has published numerously in these areas, attended several international conferences and contributed in the organization of many world-class international conferences as program chair, track chair, tutorial committee member, program committee member, session chair, and reviewer. He is a senior member of IEEE, member of ACM, IEEE CIS, IEEE CS, IEEE SMC, APNNA, INSTICC, MRLAB, ACS; member of technical committees of ADPRL, CISTC, and Multimedia Computing. He is also an associate editor of the IEEE Transactions on Neural Networks and Learning Systems, associate editor, International Journal on Trust Management in Computing and Communications, associate editor of the International Journal of Network Protocols and Algorithms, editor of the Journal of Emerging Technologies in Web Intelligence (JETWI), editor of the International Journal of Advanced Science and Technology.

Yousif Al-Bastaki received a BSc. degree from University of Bahrain, Msc from University of Leeds, UK and a PhD degree from University of Nottingham, UK. Recently he has been appointed as an IT advisor at the Deputy Prime Minster at the Kingdom of Bahrain and previously worked as the Dean of College of IT at the University of Bahrain. Currently he is an associate professor and the Dean of Admission and Registration at the University of Bahrain. His research interests are Neural Networks, genetic algorithms E-Learning, Distance Education and e-government strategies and implementation.

* * *

D. P. Acharjya received his PhD in computer science from Berhampur University, India. He has been awarded with Gold Medal in M. Sc. from NIT, Rourkela. Currently he is working as a Professor in the School of Computing Science and Engineering, VIT University, Vellore, India. He has authored many national and international journal papers, and five books to his credit. In addition to this, he has also edited two books to his credit. Also, he has published many chapters in different books published by

International publishers. He is reviewer of many international journals such as Fuzzy Sets and Systems, Knowledge Based Systems, and Applied Journal of Soft Computing. Dr. Acharjya is actively associated with many professional bodies like CSI, ISTE, IMS, AMTI, ISIAM, OITS, IACSIT, CSTA, IEEE and IAENG. He was founder secretary of OITS Rourkela chapter. His current research interests include rough sets, formal concept analysis, knowledge representation, data mining, granular computing and business intelligence.

Sedat Akleylek received the B.Sc. degree in Mathematics majored in Computer Science from Ege University in 2004 in Izmir, Turkey. M.Sc. and Ph.D. degrees in Cryptography from Middle East Technical University in 2008 and 2010, in Ankara, Turkey, respectively. He is currently employed as an assistant professor at the Department of Computer Engineering, Ondokuz Mayis University, Samsun, Turkey. His research interests include in the areas of cryptography, algorithms and architectures for computations in finite fields.

M. Tariq Banday was born in Srinagar, India. He received his M. Sc., M. Phil. and Ph. D. degrees in Electronics (Network Security) from the department of Electronics and Instrumentation Technology, University of Kashmir, Srinagar, India in 1996, 2008, and 2010 respectively. At present, he is working as Senior Assistant Professor in the same department. He is member of IEEE, ACM, CSI, etc. He currently investigates a few government-sponsored projects in network security. He has to his credit over 80 research publications in reputed journals and conference proceedings. His teaching and research interests include microprocessors & micro-controllers: architecture, programming and Interfacing; programming and problem solving, computer organization, design & architecture, network, internet, e-mail & web security, internet of things, data structures and database management systems.

Mradul Dhakar has received M.Tech. degree in 2013 in computer science and engineering from Madhav Institute of Technology and Science, Gwalior, M.P. (India). He completed his graduation in 2011 in Computer Science and Engineering from Institute of Information Technology and Management, Gwalior, M.P. (India). He is currently working in ITM University Gwalior, M.P. India. His research interest includes Network Security and Data Mining.

Fatiha Djemili Tolba received a PhD degree in computer science from the University Franche Comte of Besançon, France in 2007. She is currently an assistant professor at the University of Annaba and is a member of the LRS research laboratory. Her research interests include: wireless networks, QoS support and energy control in ad hoc and sensor networks.

Martin Drahanský graduated in 2001 at the Brno University of Technology, Faculty of Electrotechnics and Computer Science in the Czech Republic. He achieved his Ph.D. grade in 2005 at the Brno University of Technology, Faculty of Information Technology. In 2010 he achieved his Associate professor grade at the Brno University of Technology, Faculty of Information Technology, Department of Intelligent Systems. His research topics include biometrics, security and cryptography, artificial intelligence and sensoric systems. For more information – see please http://www.fit.vutbr.cz/~drahan.

Salim Ghanemi earned a PhD from Loughborough University, England in 1987, Parallel and Distributed Processing, Master Of Science with thesis from Aston University in Birmingham, England, BSc in Computer Science from Constantine University, Algeria, Currently, working as an Associate Professor at Badji-Mokhtar University, Annaba, Algeria, Previously, he worked as an Associate Professor abroad in Philadelphia University in Amman, Jordan and King Saud University, Riyadh, Saudi Arabia Kingdom.

Petr Hanacek is an associate professor at the Faculty of Information Technology at Brno University of Technology. He concerns with information system security, risk analysis, applied cryptography, and electronic payment systems for more than ten years. He is an independent consultant in this area.

Martin Henzl received his M.Sc. from Masaryk University in 2009. He is currently a Ph.D. student at Faculty of Information Technology, Brno University of Technology. His research interests are in information technology security, especially in smart cards and applied cryptography.

Leila Mechtri is a Ph.D student at Networks and Systems Laboratory, Computer Science Dept., Badji Mokhtar University - Annaba, Algeria, meeting the security concerns of adhoc networks.

V. Santhi is working as Associate professor in VIT University, Vellore, India. She has more than 20 years of experience in both academic and Industry. She has pursued her B.E. in Computer Science and Engineering from Bharathidasan University. She did her M.Tech. in Computer Science and Engineering from Pondicherry University, Puducherry. She has received her Ph.D. Degrees in Computer Science and Engineering from VIT University, Vellore, India. She has carried out her research in the domain of Multimedia Security. She is senior member of IEEE and she is holding membership in many professional bodies. Her areas of research include Image Processing, Digital Signal Processing, Digital Watermarking, Data Compression and Computational Intelligence. She has published many papers in reputed journals and International conferences. She is a reviewer for many refereed Journals. Currently she is guiding research candidates.

Kyubark Shim received the M.S. and the Ph.D. degrees in Statistics from the Dongguk University at Seoul, Korea in 1986 and 1993, respectively. He is a Professor in the Department of Applied Statistics at Dongguk University at Gyeongju, Korea. His current research interests include Computational Statistics, Reliability Test, Analysis of Statistical Data, and Growth Curve theory and its applications. He has published more than 30 journal papers, 10 conference papers (mostly written in Korean Language), and several undergraduate textbooks.

Akhilesh Tiwari has received Ph.D. degree in Information Technology from Rajiv Gandhi Technological University, Bhopal, India. He is currently working as Associate Professor in the department of CSE & IT, Madhav Institute of Technology & Science, Gwalior, M.P. (India). His area of current research includes knowledge discovery in databases & data mining, and wireless Networks. He is also acting as a reviewer & member in editorial board of various international journals. He is having the memberships of various Academic/ Scientific societies including IETE, CSI, GAMS, IACSIT, and IAENG.

Zaliha Yuce Tok graduated in 2004 with a bachelor degree in Computer Engineering department followed by a M.Sc. degree in Cryptography in Middle East Technical University (METU). She is still Ph.D. student in the Institute of Applied Mathematics, METU. Tok's research focus is curve-based and lattice-based cryptography. She has involved on several projects on public key cryptography as a software engineer. From 2004, Tok also worked for in various positions in defense companies as an avionic software engineer in Turkey.

Frantisek Zboril (born 1974, Olomouc) is an associate professor at Brno University of Technology, Czech Republic since 2013. He obtained his Ph.D. In 2004 at Faculty of Information Technology, BUT in Information Technology. His major interests include artificial agents, their application in the area of distributed systems modelling and applications for wireless sensor networks.

František V. Zbořil is an Associate Professor at the Faculty of Information Technology of Brno University of Technology, Czech Republic. He received his M.Sc. in 1968 and PhD in 1978, both in Computer Science. He has started his research activities on analogue and hybrid computers with simulation of continuous systems, namely of systems described by partial differential equations. His next research was focused on classical artificial intelligence, robotics and neural networks. Now, the main objects of his professional interests are soft computing problems. He is the author of more than 100 papers and several lecture notes. He is a member of the board of the Czech and Slovak Simulation Society (CSSS) and a member of several other educational, research and academic boards or societies.

Index

Information Resources Management Association

Become an IRMA Member

Members of the **Information Resources Management Association (IRMA)** understand the importance of community within their field of study. The Information Resources Management Association is an ideal venue through which professionals, students, and academicians can convene and share the latest industry innovations and scholarly research that is changing the field of information science and technology. Become a member today and enjoy the benefits of membership as well as the opportunity to collaborate and network with fellow experts in the field.

IRMA Membership Benefits:

- **One FREE Journal Subscription**

- **30% Off Additional Journal Subscriptions**

- **20% Off Book Purchases**

- Updates on the latest events and research on Information Resources Management through the IRMA-L listserv.

- Updates on new open access and downloadable content added to Research IRM.

- A copy of the Information Technology Management Newsletter twice a year.

- A certificate of membership.

IRMA Membership $195

Scan code to visit irma-international.org and begin by selecting your free journal subscription.

Membership is good for one full year.

www.irma-international.org

Printed in the United States
By Bookmasters